Rules for a Flat World

This important book is at once an education and a manifesto. Drawing on economics, jurisprudence and legal history, Hadfield argues with authority that our legal institutions are out of step with advances in the digital world. She calls for greater investment, innovation, and competition in legal services and, crucially, challenges lawyers and policymakers to think very differently about the future role of law in society.

Richard Susskind, co-author, *The Future of the Professions*

Gillian Hadfield's *Rules for a Flat World* is a tour de force from an omnivorous intellect. Hadfield moves nimbly between history, sociology, law, and economics to explain how and why we built our modern legal system, and how complex changes in the global economy are forcing it to evolve. Hadfield makes clear that our increasingly wired world requires a new justice system, and opening the legal system to market-driven innovation is the best way to get there. *Rules for a Flat World* is an amazing accomplishment, and anyone who wants to clearly understand the trends driving change in law and society should put this book at the top of their reading list.

Colin Rule, Founder and COO, Modria.com, and former Director of Online Dispute Resolution, eBay and PayPal

The last few decades have witnessed extraordinary growth in complex, efficient and digitized supply chains. These activities create wealth while posing unprecedented challenges for legal institutions. Modes for enforcing contracts had to change, and governments and private actors continue to experiment with responses to piracy of intellectual property and trade secrets. Gillian Hadfield brings uncommon clarity, reach, and depth to her analysis of these trends and their causes. Her important book will open the reader's eyes to the legal challenges shaping all the major economies of the world.

Shane Greenstein, MBA Class of 1957 Professor of Business Administration, Harvard Business School and author, *How the Internet Became Commercial*

Gillian Hadfield brings together with remarkable clarity what I have seen and have struggled with for a long time in many countries, in many environments: not only do most justice systems not deliver the value they could and should, the design and production machine for getting them to deliver that value is also broken. For the sake of billions of our fellow global citizens and their aspirations we must open up to using markets more as "problem solving engines," in particular in the lower-income countries that are being told to mirror the models that have been used in the West. This is a must read for everybody who senses that good legal infrastructure is a prerequisite for almost everything else.

Sam Muller, CEO, HiiL Innovating Justice

Read *Rules for a Flat World* – it is your future. Hadfield is our Thomas Paine, illuminating the imbalances that have led to the emerging revolution in law. Brilliantly researched, sweeping in scope, *Rules for a Flat World* not only exposes the factors behind the "quiet crisis" but lays out a plan for correcting it.

Eddie Hartman, founder and Chief Product Officer, LegalZoom

This book is a must read for anyone who believes the legal system can be improved or who wants better results from legal services spending. From an insightful, engaging, and charming exploration of the history of how we came to have our current legal system, to careful analogies to the transformation other industries have experienced in the digital age, to a set of prescriptions for change in the legal system to grow the global economy, Gillian Hadfield never disappoints. I never expected that I would say about a book on the legal system, "I couldn't put it down."

Mark Chandler, Senior Vice President
and General Counsel, Cisco Systems

Here in Silicon Valley we pride ourselves on producing radical technological innovations paying but little attention to the messy but critical legal and social issues that require equally radical innovation in our legal systems. In this engrossing book, Hadfield takes us from Athens to modern times to help set the stage for dealing with the kinds of legal complexities we are now starting to encounter, such as autonomous vehicles governed by machine-learning algorithms or cloud computing that crosses so many international boundaries that governance issues become almost unfathomable. A fascinating book for fascinating times.

John Seely Brown, former Chief Scientist, Xerox, and Director,
Xerox PARC; co-author of *The Social Life of Information*
and *The Pragmatic Imagination*

A must read if you have ever wondered why law is like it is. Should be compulsory reading for every law student, legal academic, practicing lawyer and regulator. Read it and be entertained, educated, enlightened and inspired to reimagine law as the platform for justice and economic development that this book so skillfully describes.

Rosemary Martin, General Counsel, Vodafone Group Plc

Rules for a Flat World

Why Humans Invented Law and How to Reinvent It for a Complex Global Economy

GILLIAN K. HADFIELD

OXFORD
UNIVERSITY PRESS

OXFORD
UNIVERSITY PRESS

Oxford University Press is a department of the University of Oxford. It furthers
the University's objective of excellence in research, scholarship, and education
by publishing worldwide. Oxford is a registered trade mark of Oxford University
Press in the UK and certain other countries.

Published in the United States of America by Oxford University Press
198 Madison Avenue, New York, NY 10016, United States of America.

Library of Congress Cataloging-in-Publication Data
Names: Hadfield, Gillian K. (Gillian Kereldena) author.
Title: Rules for a flat world : why humans invented law and how to reinvent it for a complex global
economy / Gillian Hadfield.
Description: New York : Oxford University Press, 2017.
Identifiers: LCCN 2016022372 (print) | LCCN 2016023437 (ebook) |
ISBN 9780199916528 (hardback) | ISBN 9780199916535 (E-book) | ISBN 9780190613693 (E-book)
Subjects: LCSH: Law and economics. | Technology and law. |
Globalization—Economic aspects. | Law reform. | Law—Methodology. |
BISAC: POLITICAL SCIENCE / Globalization. | BUSINESS & ECONOMICS /
Economics / General. | LAW / Legal Profession.
Classification: LCC K487.E3 H335 2016 (print) | LCC K487.E3 (ebook) |
DDC 340/.115—dc23
LC record available at https://lccn.loc.gov/2016022372

1 3 5 7 9 8 6 4 2
Printed by Sheridan Books, Inc., United States of America

For my parents Audrey and Colin, who have carved out unconventional and inspiring lives by always knowing which rules to break

Contents

PART IV: *Global Legal Innovation*

Acknowledgments

THE IDEAS IN this book are the product of conversations too many to count, and I am grateful for every one: agreeable or contentious, each one taught me much. The book originally took shape when I was one of those happy campers at the magical Center for Advanced Study in the Behavioral Sciences at Stanford as a Fellow in 2006–2007. I am grateful to CASBS for funding my time there and particularly grateful to Roberta Katz for introducing me that year to a network of innovative legal thinkers in the Bay Area including Harvey Anderson, Ralph Baxter, Mark Chandler, Paul Lippe, Kent Walker, and Bruce Sewell. That network later grew to include Jonathan Anschell, Brian Cabrera, Laura Fennell, Mitch Gaynor, Ramsey Homsany, Rosemary Martin, Emily Porter, Chas Rampenthal, and Mark Roellig. Together these people have graced me with the generosity of their time and insights for the past decade; absent the confidence gained from discussions with them that I was getting more right than wrong, I'm not sure this book would have taken shape. Sam Muller and Maurits Barendrecht played a pivotal role in opening the scope of the book over time to reach beyond the challenges of an advanced legal system to the critical issues of how we build essential justice infrastructure in the poor and developing world. And with conversations that began in a field of buttercups at Stirling University in 2010, my dear friend and coauthor Barry Weingast helped to develop the ideas that ultimately took the book from being a critique of how law works to grounded theory about how to think about law better. Finally, I thank the members of the Dubai International Financial Centre Courts, including Chief Justice Michael Hwang, Chief Executive and Registrar Mark Beer, Case Progression Manager Ayesha Bin Kalban, and Registrar Linda Fitz-Alan of the Abu Dhabi Global Market Courts, for generously sharing their time and thoughts with me.

Being an academic is an enormously rewarding job, and I was reminded just how lucky I am to live in a rich academic community every time I asked someone to look at the manuscript as it developed. Don Lamm provided me with wonderful advice during the early stages as I was preparing a proposal and sorting out my plan for the book. For saving me from what would have been major missteps (and without implicating them in missteps that remain), I am especially grateful to Rob Boyd and Shane Greenstein. For reading the entire manuscript and providing sharp and tremendously helpful, detailed comments I thank Ben Barton and Maurits Barendrecht. Others who read all or parts of the manuscript and contributed to the final product and my morale in ways large and small include Erol Akçay, Pamhidzai Bamu, Federica Carugati, Neelam Chhiber, Bob Cooter and students in the Law and Economics Workshop at the University of California at Berkeley, Bry Danner, Mark Deuitch, Travis Giggy, Bob Gordon, Mitu Gulati, Colin Hadfield, Audrey Hadfield, Dylan Hadfield-Menell, Eddie Hartman, Matt Jennejohn, Robin Kar, Dan Klerman, Prasad Krishnamurthy, Timur Kuran, Paul Lippe, Sam Muller, Frank Nagle, Scott Page, Paul Romer, Dan Ryan, and Justin Simard. Bobby Allen provided very helpful editing assistance.

For funding and flexibility, in addition to CASBS, I am grateful for the ongoing support of my deans at the University of Southern California Gould School of Law. The Ewing Marion Kauffman Foundation funded, together with USC, a second sabbatical year on the hill at CASBS in 2010–2011; I am particularly grateful to Bob Litan and Dane Stangler for their support of my research over the years. I thank my editors Dave McBride and Katie Weaver for help navigating this book to completion. And for the intellectual and personal refueling without which my life would be much less and this book would never have found its way, I thank my sons, Dylan and Noah Hadfield-Menell, and, especially, my husband Dan Ryan, who, sixteen years after a U-turn in a coffee shop, still has the mind I admire the most.

Introduction

THE GROUND IS dancing beneath our feet. Technology and globalization—those twin drivers of so much change already—continue to uproot and reshape daily life and economics. Google's driverless cars are gliding silently along the streets of California and Texas, and Tesla's can take over at the flip of a switch. 3D printers stand ready to convert digital blueprints into replacement parts—machine or human. Workers in Kenya are sending money home to their villages on their mobile phones. Digital whiz-kids in Beijing are building e-commerce platforms that let small merchants across China ping nearby potential customers with deals. Companies and products that didn't exist a decade ago—Facebook, Twitter, Amazon Cloud, the iPhone—have rewritten how we communicate, generate, and store information, and network with friends, coworkers, and business partners. Companies that didn't exist just five years ago—Uber, Airbnb—are creating massive peer-to-peer platforms that convert Indonesian villagers and Londoners alike into microentrepreneurs—and continue the on-demand economy's disruption of traditional employment relationships and social insurance schemes. Digital currencies and payment systems put financial tools and transactions within the reach of whole new segments of the global economy and threaten to upend the capacity of global regulators to manage money supply and systemic risk. The oceans of data streaming across the internet are trawled for opportunity by innovators and cybercriminals alike. Vastly more efficient and digitally monitored production processes in nimble global supply chains squeeze down prices and put more goods within reach of more people—and simultaneously put the squeeze on the environment, human rights, and personal privacy. Today the peoples of the world are more connected than ever—through markets and networks, shared resources and shared threats.

The web-enabled platform for global collaboration that *New York Times* columnist Thomas Friedman called "the flat world" in his 2005 bestseller *The World is Flat* has moved far beyond the flattening of hierarchies and production processes into globally networked supply chains that Friedman highlighted. Today we are witnessing the flattening of just about everything, the tangible world squashed down into sequences of ones and zeros. Digitization on a global scale converts objects and actions and ideas into glimmers of magnetism or electricity—where they remain until brought to life in some place, some time, some context that possibly no one contemplated or could conceive.

Much of what we are witnessing is for the good, with expanding possibilities for generating more value for less. But some of it is for the bad, with yawning inequality within and between countries, growing opposition to integration from people burdened by change they don't understand or want, and threats to sustainability and the very role of humans on the planet.

Those at the heart of these transformations know that the pace of change is making it more urgent than ever to rethink the rules of our economic and social relationships. Over the last few years, as a member of the World Economic Forum, I've seen this at the Forum's annual agenda-setting meetings held in the United Arab Emirates as a lead-up to the January meeting of global leaders in Davos, Switzerland. In the sessions I attend, in darkened, cooled rooms away from the blazing sun and sand, the talk is all about how we need this law or that regulatory structure to manage the future of work, the challenge of artificial intelligence, and the pressing demands for inclusive, sustainable growth—demands that extend from the powerhouses of the advanced Western world to the still marginalized and impoverished corners of Africa, Asia, and Latin America. As the Forum's founder, Klaus Schwab, urged upon world leaders at Davos 2016 and in his book, *The Fourth Industrial Revolution*, there is a vital need for leaders to collaborate across academic, social, political, national, and industry boundaries to shape the transformations we are experiencing. Only then can we hope to ensure that these transformations promote human ends and not the end of humanity. Only then can the people struggling to manage lives outside those cooled rooms connect to the prosperity and security shimmering in the heat of the global economy.

As I listen to these discussions, I am energized by the communal focus on how to invent the future. But I also feel a growing unease, as though I am sitting on a big, dark secret that threatens to bring down our best ideas. All of the solutions being discussed involve, in one way or another, developing new or better legal rules. Regulations that promote sustainable production methods without squelching innovation. Treaties that preserve the flow of data around the globe without endangering privacy, integrity, or security. Legislation that ensures that the displacement of workers by robots and algorithms does not breed even greater inequality and social unrest. Agreements that channel collaborations across income and ethnic divides so as to promote development and not discord.

Leaders and policymakers assume that the hard part is figuring out what we want our rules to say and getting agreement across stakeholders on the right solutions. If only it were as easy as that.

What almost nobody is talking about is *how* we are going to build those rules. But here's the secret that troubles me: our mechanisms for creating and implementing law—or what I call more generally our *legal infrastructure*, the almost invisible platform of rules and practices on which we build everything else in our economy—are not up to the task. Our existing systems for developing the rules and legal practices we need to manage the galloping progress of the global digital economy are drowning in cost and complexity. As many of the general counsel at our most innovative companies told me in interviews, and as ordinary people around the world are angrily telling their politicians, the legal systems we have are failing ever more regularly to do what law is supposed to do: make it easier for people to work together and make life for all better, not worse. For the four billion who live in poor and developing regions of the world, even the most basic legal tools necessary to manage economic life in a reliable, predictable, and secure way are hard to find, much less the new tools needed to connect to the digital global economy. Half the planet lives outside of any formal legal framework. The other half operates inside frameworks that have stagnated in the twentieth century—well designed for the nation-based mass-manufacturing economy but badly out of step with the digitized, global environment we now inhabit.

This book brings the critical question of how we build and implement the legal infrastructure we need for a new complex and more inclusive global economy out of the shadows and onto center stage. It's crucial, I argue, that we figure out how to attract more research, money, and innovative energy to the task of developing rules and legal practices that are capable of managing the modern global economy. That means both developing rules and practices that can handle a fast-paced, digital, increasingly AI-infused, and enormously complex environment *and* figuring out how to help the four billion people living in the BoP—the base of the pyramid—produce effective legal infrastructure to support their efforts to grow and connect with the global economy. The second is as important as the first. For as anyone who knows anything about economic development will tell you, while there are lots of obstacles to growth in poor countries, the biggest is the failure of governance and what we have so far called "the rule of law." We've spent billions trying to help these countries build better legal systems, with little success. Meanwhile at home in the affluent West and on the international stage we continue to churn out reams of complicated and costly law—out of reach and alienating for ordinary citizens and small businesses and of waning usefulness to large companies and the pursuit of the public interest. The model is hardly one for the rest of the world to follow—although this is the law we continue to export. On all fronts we are falling far short of where we need to be.

To increase our capacity to invent and build the legal infrastructure we need throughout the complex global economy—in both rich and poor places—we have to think differently about how we produce rules and rule systems. Today, almost our entire legal infrastructure is produced in the public sector—by governments and bureaucracies—and by closed professions operating under government-granted monopolies—lawyers. I argue in this book that this approach no longer works. It is what we have to change. We need to bring to our legal infrastructure the kinds of responsive innovation and investment that competitive markets bring to the rest of the economy. We need more active markets for law and lawyers.

That doesn't mean doing away with governments—far from it. All competitive markets are regulated markets, and the lesson of democracy is that accountable governments are essential for markets that are effective, fair, and respectful of human dignity. And government performs essential functions, when it functions. I don't argue in this book for doing away with governments or their central role in protecting shared values and human well-being. I don't argue that we should abandon the goal of building better, more accountable, and less fragile governments around the world. I don't argue that governments should not be bound by the rule of law. What I do argue is that we should reposition the role of government in the production of the legal infrastructure on which our economy is built. We need to harness market incentives to invent more effective, less expensive, and easier-to-implement rules and regulatory systems, coupled with governments that ensure that those rules and systems achieve the goals set by an open political process. That's not happening today. Today the rules are designed almost exclusively in top-down fashion by elected officials and civil servants, often with the "help" of well-heeled lobbyists and the politically connected. Our legal systems are operated by lawyers and judges who make up a legal profession that faces only muted competition from innovators who might come up with better ways of getting law done.

It's really quite impossible to continue on this path in the complex global economy. The economic relationships that need regulating are increasingly digital and as difficult to nail down as jelly. Even physical goods and services hopscotch around the globe along flexible and increasingly fragmented global supply chains. The vaulting complexity and speed of economic life is something that the deliberate processes and soft incentives of governments and insulated monopoly professions can hardly keep up with. The result is what legal insiders and their clients know well: systems that are too expensive, too complex, and too misguided to do much good, at least not as much good as we need them to do. Our regulatory systems need to be as smart, connected, and rapidly adaptable as the economy they are regulating. The only way to get there, I think, is by getting more of the money and brains currently inventing the future of things involved also in inventing the future of law. By attracting some of the capital that is now directed to developing our leading-edge technologies to the problem of developing the regulatory technology we need. That means a bigger role for competitive markets in the production of our legal infrastructure.

It's not as crazy as it sounds. In fact, there's a story to be told that this is just the natural next step in the evolution of human systems for managing complexity. And that is the story I tell in this book.

The story goes like this. All human societies, in fact all animal societies, have to solve the problem of social order. That's the problem of managing conflicts, facilitating cooperation, and basically making life relatively predictable. Only if there is a reasonable degree of social order are people, even in the simplest societies, able to make reasonable decisions about how to invest their time and resources. (Should your hunter-gatherer self head off looking for better food, or do you need to stay back and guard your stuff?)

Social order is achieved with rules, about who can do what, when, and how. With good rules we waste less of our time fighting over things and pour less of our energies into things we can't keep or use, or activities that don't end up getting us more of what we want. (A rule against stealing people's stuff means that hunter-gatherer-you can feel more confident heading off to look for better food.) The rules that support social order are a platform: they provide the structure on which choices and interactions are built.

The platform of rules on which nonhuman animals build their choices and interactions is resident in their DNA. When lion and hyena both spy an appetizing carcass at the same time, the rule in lion DNA says, "Go for it!" and the rule in hyena DNA, seeing lion, says, "Come back later for the leftovers." Lion and hyena are both better off living by the rule "Lion eats first" and sparing a fight, and their life on the savannah is a little more productive and predictable as a result.

When humans came along, we of course had lots of rules written into our DNA as well. But humans effectively became humans because we wrote the rules for social interaction down not only—or even primarily—in DNA but instead in culture. Culture is a lot more adaptable than DNA, and as a result humans quickly outcompeted all other animals, making the most of our more agile cognition and language to solve problems and coordinate cooperative strategies for controlling resources. Culture provided the platform for a far more complex economic life, one that reaped the benefits, largely unavailable to other animals, of the division of labor, specialization, and trade.

Eventually the complexity of life that culture afforded tested the limits of culture. Cultural rules are slow to change, and even when they do change, change is organic and hard to channel. That's why humans took the next step and invented law: a deliberate means of choosing, and changing, the rules. That's what is special about law as a solution to the problem of social order: the capacity to go to sleep one day with one set of rules and wake up the next to a new set. Yesterday it was okay for people to bring their dogs along for a walk around the lake. Today there is a sign, posted by the park authorities, that says No Dogs Allowed. When law is working—and it doesn't always—people go along with the change in rules, and the goals the new rules were intended to achieve are (hopefully) the result.

We don't know exactly when humans invented law, meaning a deliberate systematic way of choosing rules. But by the time we invented writing, about four thousand years ago in Mesopotamia (modern-day Iraq, Syria, and Kuwait), law was right there: on the seven-foot stone pillars that displayed Hammurabi's code and in the contracts traders scratched into clay tablets. Over the thousands of years that followed, all kinds of groups and individuals built, destroyed, and rebuilt their platforms of legal rules. Some societies looked to religious groups for their rules. Others to local despots or family dynasties. Still others formed communes and co-ops and merchant guilds and wrote and enforced their own rules. In important ways, all these different systems competed with one another. Sometimes competition was direct in the sense of offering an individual a choice as to which rules to follow.

More often competition was indirect in the sense that societies with better rules did better.

On those legal platforms, human societies over the past millennia grew progressively more complex, with successful economies elaborating the division of labor further and further still. The legal infrastructure of Mesopotamia supported the development of writing and mathematics—tools of trade and taxation. The legal infrastructure of the Middle Ages underwrote the Commercial Revolution and the expansion of long-distance trade. The legal infrastructure of empire supported global colonial expansion and settlement. The legal infrastructure of the nation-state proved a platform for the Industrial Revolution, and the democratic nation-state supported the mass-manufacturing economy that powered fantastic growth in the twentieth century.

Along the path from the multiple rule systems that characterized the more fragmented worlds humans inhabited through the Middle Ages to the modern, sophisticated, highly choreographed and contained legal regimes of the nation-states that make up our international system, much was gained. Law became better, smarter, and more organized. It reached out to cover the great increases in the complexity of our interdependence in a world with continually advancing technology and extensive specialization, and so provided more confidence for people playing along with the uncertainties inherent in a market economy. At the beginning of the twentieth century there were great fears about the chaos of markets, and much pressure for governments to produce everything—nearly 40 percent of the world's population eventually lived in centrally planned economies. But by the end of the twentieth century, almost everyone around the globe was trusting even somewhat chaotic markets to do better than massive bureaucracies in deciding what houses to build, what food to put on the shelves, what technology to develop. The job of government, even in those formerly centrally planned societies, was repositioned to focus on regulating, rather than replacing, markets. Around the world, the sophistication of law and regulation to support ever more complex global markets soared.

But along that path from simple law to the comprehensive legal infrastructure coordinated by the nation-state something also was lost: the vibrancy of competing systems of rules. There are pockets of competition in our current systems. People and companies have some choice (subject to restrictions on immigration and foreign direct investment and export/import rules) about where to locate and so can exercise some choice about the rules under which they operate. Businesses in the United States can choose between Delaware and some other state's corporate law. Businesses around the globe can usually decide what body of contract law they want to govern their deals. There is some choice emerging over what securities regime to follow. But the pockets are small and the differences slight. More importantly, even where choices exist, the competition is almost exclusively between governments. But governments don't care too much about winning this competition—and they certainly don't respond to the kind of incentives that a business faces when it has competitors nipping at its heels. Most governments don't scramble to invent cheaper, simpler, and more effective ways of regulating so they can attract more users to their system. They don't develop new rule technologies.

Even when governments leave the production of legal rules and processes, strategies and solutions, up to private actors, here too competition is severely blunted. Some governments delegate some rule-making to nonprofit private organizations—international standard-setting bodies, for example, or self-regulatory bodies. Overwhelmed by pace and complexity many governments find themselves with little choice but to put the onus on the companies that need regulating to develop their own solutions—Google has been handed the task of developing a workable implementation of the European right to be forgotten on Google, for example. And almost all legal systems rely on private lawyers—who face the same kind of profit-making goals of any business, including other professionals like doctors and dentists—to operate the levers of our legal infrastructure. But bodies to which governments delegate rule-making and adjudication are almost always given a monopoly: those subject to the rules can't choose which regulator they want. And lawyers in almost all systems around the world (the UK and Australia are important exceptions) operate in markets that are heavily insulated from competition from providers who don't follow the rules lawyers choose for how law must be practiced. So while lawyers are in heavy competition with each other, lawyers as a profession are not at much risk of being displaced by, for example, software engineers.

And that's a bad thing. Without competition—in rule-making, in the design of regulatory and dispute resolution systems, in the technology of regulation, in the ways in which people and businesses access and use legal infrastructure—there's little incentive for anyone to build better legal infrastructure. More importantly, there's little incentive for anyone to invest either brains or money in the terrifically challenging task of figuring out *how* to build better legal infrastructure. That's the part that really worries me. In our most sophisticated legal markets we are churning out very smart lawyers from very fancy law schools, populated by very impressive law professors (my colleagues). But most of these lawyers and law professors are expert in doing what our legal systems do now. There's next to no research and education about how to design rule systems, institutions, and technologies that deliver what we need from legal infrastructure in a rapidly changing world. There's effectively no research money devoted to figuring out how to invent new kinds of legal systems—ones that don't cost as much and work better, in the great variety of settings in which we need law to work. There are essentially no private foundations devoted to innovating new ways of doing law. Globally, the only organization I know that does this is a small entity in the Netherlands known as HiiL Innovating Justice. (I'm on one of their advisory boards.) We need a thousand HiiLs.

We need as much energy and ingenuity and philanthropy devoted to solving the problem of law in the global digital age as we devote to figuring out how to develop clean energy, reduce poverty, and deliver safer disease-free communities.

More to the point: any solutions we think we are developing toward clean energy, reduced poverty, or safer disease-free communities *depend* on developing better legal infrastructure. Because any solutions we think we are developing to those and the other great challenges of the twenty-first century assume that there will be stable markets, organizations, and governments implementing the solution. This is even truer for the type of sustainable bottom-up solutions modern tech-savvy philanthropists hope to nurture. Those solutions will depend on developing new kinds of businesses, technology, social relations, and global arrangements. Businesses, technology, social relations, and global arrangements are built on platforms of rules. If we don't innovate legal infrastructure, we can't hope to innovate much else.

We need to do what we humans have done every time we've hit the max on what our existing rule systems can handle in terms of complexity: invent new ways of doing rules. I am quite sure that rules devised by humans and written down for us to argue about later will be with us through to the end of history. But I'm also quite sure we can't expect to manage a complex digital global economy without other rule technologies as well. Rules delivered through data. Rules generated by AI. Rules implemented by other rules. Rules not only created by governments and civil servants but also by the members of a virtual law club or a trading system or a profit-making enterprise. Rules that are produced in markets for rules that are kept competitive by other sets of rules.

So that's the story I tell in this book. It plays out like this. Part I asks, why did humans invent law? Chapter 1 sets the stage for this question. Most people start thinking about law from the usual assumptions—that law is something that, by definition, is produced by nation-state governments, courts, and lawyers. Chapter 1 proposes a different starting point: the more fundamental idea that law is just a system of rules. We learn a bit here about the California Gold Rush and how the miners (the 49ers) came up with rules to make life work pretty well when there were hundreds of thousands of people streaming in to pan for gold and yet no governments, police, courts, or jails. Chapter 2 then traces the invention of law from its origins in the order-producing systems in other animal societies, the emergence of culture and cognition, and the development of more complex human societies. Joining the California gold miners in this chapter are chimps, the Ju/'hoansi bushmen of the Kalahari, Hammurabi, the Vikings of medieval Iceland, the merchants of medieval Europe, and the traders of the Muslim Mediterranean. Chapter 3 relates the development of law to the basic problem humans have always faced: the problem of problem-solving. In this chapter I explore how DNA, culture, and law differ in how they help humans solve problems. And why we needed law to deal with the challenges for social order posed by the greater division of labor, economic specialization, and exchange that culture allowed us to develop. This chapter talks about complexity as a "dancing landscape"—a system in which many interdependent agents bounce off each other and where it can be difficult to predict where the system will go from moment to moment. Increasing complexity is the story of human evolution, and the story of how and why law emerged.

Part II of the book turns to the ways in which economic and legal complexity are intertwined. Chapter 4 tracks the birth of modern legal infrastructure and introduces a key idea: that there is an economic demand for law and that law is an economic input. If you are one of the (I'm sure very many) people who responds to my claim that we need legal infrastructure to build the solutions to global challenges by rolling your eyes, you might want to start with Chapter 4. Here I will convince you that you really don't want to live or try to do business in a world without good legal infrastructure. I define legal infrastructure in this chapter and explain why it is important to think of it as a shared platform for getting things done. With the concepts of legal infrastructure in place, we can trace the slow beginnings of our modern concepts of legal infrastructure in the sixteenth, seventeenth, and eighteenth centuries. Chapter 5 then looks at how legal infrastructure evolved over the course of the nineteenth and into the early twentieth century to support the shift from the simplicity of agriculture and local markets to the complexity of mass manufacturing on a national scale. For those who want to know why it's so hard to change the way we do law in America today, this chapter offers an answer: bar associations in the early twentieth century built a constitutional castle around the provision of legal work and established lawyers as the gatekeepers.

Chapters 6 and 7 lay out the growing chasm between what we need law to do and what our existing legal infrastructure can handle. We start in Chapter 6 with a careful look at how global collaboration, global supply chains, and mass digitization are producing a fundamental transformation in what the economy needs from legal infrastructure. Chapter 7 shows how our existing systems for producing legal infrastructure are failing to meet that economic demand. Put simply, our existing systems have hit the limits of the complexity they can handle. Focusing on examples and data from the American context, this chapter shows that we can see the failure of our existing legal infrastructure in three of its attributes: excess complexity, high cost, and dwindling quality—quality in the true economic sense of meeting the needs of a consumer. (This last one is the surprise I learned from talking to general counsel at some of the most important innovators of the new global economy such as Cisco, Google, and Apple.)

Why hasn't our legal infrastructure responded better to the needs of an innovation-driven, digitized, transformed global economy? The answers are in Part III: we rely too much on central planning and not enough on (properly regulated) competitive markets to solve the problem of how to create the rules and forms of regulation we need for a complex global economy. Chapter 8 traces the pervasive shift from planning to markets over the late twentieth century. This shift was brought about because we needed better ways of managing the information burdens of problem-solving in the face of complexity, and it happened in settings ranging from auto manufacturing to entire economies. That's what we need to do in legal production as well: move more of the production process out of closed and centrally planned systems and into markets to generate better data, better research, and better incentives to solve the complex problems of legal infrastructure. Chapter 9 looks specifically at why we need more competitive markets for lawyers than the ones we now have. The reason is that our closed professional systems deprive the innovation process of its essential ingredients: a diversity of ideas, feedback on how well things are working, and the human and financial capital that supports risk-taking. Chapter 9 sets out some simple changes (many of which the UK and Australia have already made) that could dramatically alter law's otherwise stagnant trajectory. Chapter 10 then takes up the more challenging question of how we can get more markets into the business of rule-making, starting with some easy cases (creating markets for business rules like the rules governing contracts) and moving on to the hardest cases—markets for regulation. I propose here an alternative that should be added to the mix of government-based regulatory tools we now consider: competition between approved private regulators.

Part IV shifts the focus from advanced market economies to the four billion people living with little or no legal infrastructure to speak of. These are the people of the BoP, living on less than the equivalent of $8 a day. Chapter 11 paints a picture of how development is undercut by the abysmal legal infrastructure of poor countries. Countries struggling in the BoP don't lack for law. Instead they are often drowning in a complex, incoherent, inaccessible, and corrupted mess of rules and regulations that are of little use to individuals trying to eke out a living or governments trying to help their citizens. Unfortunately, well-meaning international organizations trying to build "rule of law" often make matters worse. Chapter 12 explores an alternate path to building better legal infrastructure for the BoP, drawing on the basic lesson applicable to the advanced world facing an increasingly complex global economy: looking beyond the nation-state and monopolized legal professions as the sole source of legal innovation. In this chapter we look to, of all places, ancient Athens, and its heavily citizen-led institutions, for inspiration about how the countries of the BoP might build new rules and processes that ordinary people can use and support in their quest to raise themselves and their countries out of poverty. Chapter 13 then looks at how the international community could help build competitive global markets for legal infrastructure—giving poor countries an option to turn to third-party provision of some elements of what they need to build a better legal platform for their economies.

I wrote this book with a goal of reaching people who otherwise spend very little time thinking about law—indeed, who probably try their damnedest to avoid the topic—because, as one of the GCs I spoke to observed, law is too important to leave to lawyers. The quality of our legal infrastructure has played a tremendous role in moving us forward on our path from wandering peoples struggling to survive in the wild to the great wealth and complexity of the modern global economy. But there is much to be done: to generate and figure out how to share wealth within countries rich and poor in the face of the great changes of the last few decades. This book is not an ideological defense of markets. It's just that looking at the evolution of complexity, it seems pretty clear that there is no way to build the legal infrastructure we need to sustain our goals for the future without harnessing markets to drive greater innovation in how we make and implement the rules on which our shared economic life depends. That doesn't mean the end of governments or the nation-state or international cooperation to protect the vulnerable and secure shared goals—as I emphasize in the conclusion. But it does mean thinking very differently about what it means to do law.

PART I

Why Did Humans Invent Law?

I

Rethinking What We Mean by Law

FOR THE PAST thirty years, my extended family has owned a log cabin on Wolfe Island, the largest of the Thousand Islands in the great St. Lawrence River that divides Canada and the United States at the eastern end of Lake Ontario. Named after General James Wolfe—who led the British to victory over the French in Quebec in 1759—the island is where my family often spends holidays, holed up with food, music, books, and wood-burning stoves. Despite the occasionally smuggled in computer or game console, we usually find ourselves drawn to simple pleasures like playing cards: Cribbage, Gin Rummy, Hearts, Euchre.

Every year, the first few conversations around the massive oak table where we play are dominated by discussions about the rules: Can you count a four-card straight in Cribbage? What cards do you play with when there are five people in a game of Hearts? Are we playing "stick the dealer" in Euchre? As we play, subtle rule disputes, usually good-natured, emerge: Was that illegal table talk when someone hemmed and hawed before passing up hearts as trump? Is your Cribbage partner allowed to point out the pair you missed in counting up your hand? Should we count the hand if the ten-year-old who is just learning makes a clearly bad play? We play only for the pleasure of this form of cooperation, but that pleasure pivots on the strategy of conflict and competition. Rules are what make this cooperation mixed with strategy and competition possible. They create the framework of competing goals and contain it to produce the ultimate shared goal of talking and laughing and being together around the family table.

The enterprise of creating rules to organize our interactions to produce a collective good, often attended by competition and strategy, is as old as human society. We establish rules to create the collective goods of entertainment and sport—as when the Olmecs of Mexico in 1200 BCE invented rules for what may have been the first game played with teams and a rubber ball, prefiguring the invention of soccer. We establish rules to smooth the conflicts of daily existence—everyone is responsible for helping out with cooking or cleaning up after a meal each day at the family cabin. We establish rules to control the carnage of war—after General Wolfe defeated the French on the Plains of Abraham in 1759, representatives of the French and British crowns signed the Articles of Capitulation of Quebec, a set of rules that guaranteed the inhabitants of Quebec they would be safe from further attack and allowed free exercise of the Roman Catholic religion. And we establish rules to create the collective good of a market economy: is that idea yours to sell? Can you change your mind about doing that deal? Do you have to pay for the contribution your delivery trucks make to global warming?

Economists and policymakers sometimes treat markets as if they were elements of the natural world and rules something artificial imposed on them. The Western economists who focused their market-creating advice solely on the removal of government controls in formerly communist countries after the fall of the Berlin Wall were sometimes guilty of this view. But like the earliest forms of soccer in ancient Mexico, the card games we play at my family cabin, or the organized battle between the French and the English in eighteenth-century Canada, market economies exist only by virtue of the rules that define them. It may be natural to kick a ball or fight or trade, but we do not have games or battles or markets without rules. If there is no rule preventing you from taking back the goods you have just traded, there is no market. If there is no rule about paying tomorrow for goods delivered today, there is no market. If there is no rule for sharing the profits of a joint venture among investors, there is no market.

The rules that define things like games or battles or markets can come from anywhere. They can be invented by the group gathered around the card table or soccer pitch or by the generals sitting down after a rout on the battlefield. Sometimes rules simply emerge from repeated interactions: most of my family members, if pressed, can tell you about the rule that we all help out with a meal at the cabin, but nobody can say where the rule came from or when. Often when we cannot say where the rules came from we call them social norms—like the norms that seem to show up spontaneously when the snowfall in Boston makes a shoveled parking space a treasured object. Ignore the overturned shopping cart in the spot and you just may find your tires deflated the next morning, with no sympathy from your neighbors.

Fuller's Definition of Law

The best definition of "law" that I've come across understands that law is just another way in which people make rules. Harvard law professor Lon Fuller coined this definition in the 1960s. "Law," Fuller said, "is the enterprise of subjecting human conduct to the governance of rules."[1] There's a lot packed into that simple and elegant definition, including the very important ideas that help us to distinguish law from social norms and games, about which I will say more in a minute. But the first thing to notice about this definition is what it doesn't say. It doesn't say that law is what kings or congresses produce. It doesn't say that law is what judges and juries apply. It doesn't say that law is what police officers enforce. It doesn't say that law is what lawyers do.

The idea that law is, by definition, the set of rules made by state and federal legislatures, enforced by state and federal courts, and managed by lawyers is widespread. That's a natural presumption given that we live in a law-soaked environment in which almost all of our law comes in the form of statutes and regulations, jury verdicts and judicial opinions, and lawyer-drafted documents such as contracts and corporate bylaws. This presumption leads policymakers at institutions like the World Bank misguidedly to focus almost exclusively on building legal systems in law-poor environments—such as developing countries—by getting state legislatures to pass legislation and improve state-run courts. Even the economists who are most sophisticated about the differences among legal systems and the impact those differences have on economic growth make the understandable mistake of narrowing their vision to a choice between law made by legislatures and law made by judges.

But adopting a definition of law limited to the stuff produced by legislatures, courts, and lawyers introduces a major blind spot right from the get-go in our efforts to figure out how best to build legal systems to support global economic growth and prosperity. It's like assuming that finding information in an electronic database is necessarily the same thing as finding a book on a library shelf, something done with cataloging and subject matter indexes and managed by librarians. This is indeed what people thought in the early days of the internet. But then Larry Page and Sergey Brin of Google came along and showed us a whole new way of finding stuff on the net.

It's important to start out with a definition of law that is based on what law does, not what it currently looks like, if we hope to see the same kind of transformation in law that we've witnessed everywhere else, from the internet to the Berlin Wall. That's what Fuller's definition of law helps us to do. By defining law as "the enterprise of subjecting human conduct to the governance of rules," he helps us focus on what law does, not what it looks like. The project of law, Fuller's definition emphasizes, is how to get people to behave in particular, predictable ways without terrorizing or dominating them. The definition emphasizes that law is just another version of a familiar activity, one that we engage in all the time in our daily lives. A definition that emphasizes the simplicity and familiarity at the core of even complex legal systems is especially important for an argument I make in this book: that law needs to be something understood and designed by economists, policymakers, entrepreneurs, business leaders, and ordinary people, not just lawyers.

So we want to begin by thinking of law as something that conceivably can be done by people and organizations other than courts, legislatures, and lawyers. Ultimately we may want courts, legislatures, and lawyers to play a role even in a reinvented legal system, but only if we decide they help produce a better legal system, not because we can't have a legal system without them.

Making Law without Lawyers: The California Gold Rush

On a rainy afternoon in late January 1848, a soaking wet James Wilson Marshall walked into John Sutter's office at Sutter's Fort near present-day Sacramento, California. Swiss-born rancher and entrepreneur Sutter had hired Marshall, a native of New Jersey, to build a sawmill on the South Fork of the American River in the foothills of the Sierra Nevada. Marshall urged Sutter to lock the office door and took from his pocket a sodden rag in which were wrapped a few nuggets of yellow metal. Marshall had discovered gold in the streambed while constructing the sawmill. This was not the first discovery of gold in California; Mexicans had discovered gold just north of Los Angeles several years earlier. But the Mexican discoverers had managed to keep it a secret. Marshall's secret was out when a storekeeper and church leader at Sutter's Fort, Samuel Brannan—perhaps bent on generating business and a source of tithes from his Mormon followers—ran down the streets of San Francisco in May 1848 waving a bottle of gold dust in the air and yelling, "Gold! Gold! Gold from the American River!"[2]

Marshall's discovery came at a time when California was without any formal legal system or institutions: no police, no legislature, no courts, no legal profession. Marshall's visit to Sutter to share the news took place just a few days before the United States signed a peace treaty with Mexico and annexed the disputed territory of California. When Sutter had first built his fort in California in the early 1840s, he had secured permission to settle from the Mexican governor, but no land grant; after the US defeat of Mexico, all land became property of the US government. The US government had few resources to send in to police and adjudicate disputes over mining rights on federal land. So the miners were on their own in working out who was entitled to extract gold from the rocks and rivers of California.

The miners had little difficulty doing so. When few prospectors were in the area, most diggers were undisturbed in their efforts to extract gold from a hole they were working. But the infamous Gold Rush brought hordes of so-called 49ers to the state—causing the nonnative population to jump from around fifteen thousand in 1848 to over three hundred thousand by 1854—and the rush soon put pressure on simple norms. Disputes erupted and miners began holding meetings at their camps to choose some rules. There was no formal way of deciding who would call a meeting or who was entitled to participate. If you were at the camp when a meeting happened, you got a vote; if you weren't, you didn't. At these meetings, the miners decided how big a claim could be and how many a miner could possess, how a claim had to be marked, and whether and how long a miner could leave a claim unworked before losing his rights. (It was almost all "he's": California's population in 1850 was 92 percent male—98 percent in the mining counties.)

In what we will see is a key feature that made these rules "law," the miners' rules also set out a way of deciding how disputes about the rules would be handled. The miners at Jackass Gulch, for example, specified in their code that "as soon as there is sufficiency of water for working a claim, five days absence from said claim, except in case of sickness, accident or reasonable excuse, shall forfeit the property." But they didn't leave it at that: they also declared that any disputes—about what counted as a "sufficiency" of water or as a "reasonable" excuse, for example—would be decided by a jury of five persons. In some camps a jury would be selected on the spot by the disputants, perhaps by flipping a coin to decide who would choose a juryman first from among the assembled miners. In other mining codes, disputes were to be resolved by a designated arbitrator, perhaps the chairman elected to preside over miners' meetings or the "learned" man who had written down the rules. And neither jury nor arbitrator was likely to last long if they did not follow some basic rules giving the disputants a chance to argue their case and present their evidence.

There was no sheriff to enforce the rules; no militia to put out claim jump-
ers. But the rules worked remarkably well: the miners followed them, even
though they changed from camp to camp and could be changed one day to
the next. The rules weren't necessarily what everyone thought was fair, but
they were the rules that everyone knew everyone else was playing by. So why
did people comply? Because if they broke the rules enough of the other miners in the camp would object and find some way to show the scofflaw that the
rules were to be followed. Maybe the jumper would be thrown out from the
local saloon, discover his tools stolen in the night, or find himself unable to
rouse any help when the "owner" of the claim showed up with his six-shooter.
But this wasn't the mythically lawless Wild West, governed by might instead
of right. There were surprisingly few reports of violence; and the miner with
the faster hand on the trigger or a larger posse couldn't simply take claims as
he pleased. Everyone looked to the rules to decide if and when to help out in
ostracizing or punishing a miner who tried to take a claim.

How Rules Become Law: Rules for Making Rules

The miners in Gold Rush California were not so different from my family
around the card table or a spontaneous group of ball players around a field.
They were just choosing a set of rules and then living by them. So what makes
the rules at the 49ers' mining camps "law" but the rules of family card games
just rules? The simplest answer is that when we sit down to make rules for a
card game we all know it's just a game. The miners chose to make what they
were doing "law." They knew there were no police, courts, or governments
around, but they still marked their claims with signs that read, "This is my
claim, fifty feet on the gulch, cordin to Clear Creek District Law" and, more
colorfully, "Any person found trespassing on this claim will be persecuted to
the full extent of the law. This is no monkey tale butt I will assert by rites at
the pint of the sicks shirter if legally necessary so taik head and good warnin."
The miners at Jackass Gulch—probably with the assistance of one of the eastern lawyers who made his way to California with other migrants in search of
gold—referred to their rules as "articles" and the five people who could decide
a dispute as a "jury."

Engaging in the enterprise of law means more than simply labeling a particular set of rules "the law," of course. But the miners' labels reveal something
important. They reveal that the miners understood that their rules had this
special status. "Fifty feet on the gulch" was not a plot of land the Clear Creek
miner had staked out based only on his say-so; the dimensions were taken from

the "law." The miner who threatened to use his "sicks shirter" to defend his claim may have been a lousy speller, but he wasn't just waving his gun around to warn off intruders. He was asserting that he would enforce his "rites" if "legally necessary" to "persecute trespassers to the full extent of the law."

The law's special status comes from the fact that when we have governance by legal rules, the rules are in charge. This is what Fuller means when he says that law is the enterprise of subjecting human conduct to the governance of rules. That's different from subjecting human conduct to the governance of other humans. What counts as "lawful" is determined by the impersonal dictates of an inanimate object, a set of rules, and not by the judgment or caprice of any particular person. If the rules say that a miner's claim extends in a ten-foot square around the original digging site, then the way we decide what is in the claim is with a measuring stick. Nobody's opinion about whether that's a fair size or whether the owner is deserving of the claim matters.

In setting up a system of rules and calling it law, people are communicating with each other that they are creating a system of rules that they intend none of them to personally control. Since this will inevitably involve human beings making judgments about what the rules are and what they mean, they need a set of rules to control those human decisions: rules for making and using rules. This is how everyone can tell whether a decision is a decision according to the law, and not just some person's opinion. Once the miners had conducted their first meeting and adopted a first set of rules to govern claims, for example, the rules could only be changed by another meeting. They could only be interpreted and applied in the process required in the rules—after each had a chance to make his case to a jury or an arbitrator, for example. A meeting held secretly among a small group or the opinion of even an influential person who was not designated a proper decision-maker by the rules was not likely to be seen as valid. People no doubt sometimes tried to get around the rules governing the rules, but if they were too successful, then the enterprise of governing by rules would have broken down. The camp would have been returned to the "lawless" state it was in before the first meeting.

The deliberate structure of the enterprise of making and applying rules gives law one of its signature attributes: after all is said and done, there is just one final answer to the question of what the rules are and what they mean in a given situation. There may be lots of arguments about what that answer should be. But the deliberate structure of law includes a way of ending the argument, and everyone recognizes that this is the way arguments about law are ended in a particular legal system. Our modern systems have their supreme courts. In tenth-century Iceland the only government office the Viking settlers bothered to create was the position of the law speaker— about which, more in Chapter 2—whose sole job it was to have the final say in disputes about what the rules were. Many religious systems are legal in this sense: there is a human authority that is recognized as the ultimate interpreter of God's law. That's what makes the rules for card games, at least in my family, just rules: we may argue and we may end up at a consensus about the rules but there is no stable and recognized procedure or person capable of saying "that's it." At least, not for long.

The mutual recognition of an authoritative way of resolving tough calls in answering the question of whether someone has violated the rules is a key way in which law differs from social norms and conventions. Before the miners held a meeting and adopted a set of rules, social norms governed a small camp. It might be clear to everyone that according to these norms it was wrong to appropriate a miner's sluice box or to start digging in the same hole when the miner took a break for lunch. But law doesn't arise because of the easy cases. It arises because of the hard cases. How close to an existing hole can another miner dig? How long can a miner be away from his claim before losing it? What if he is sick or has had his shovel stolen? What if the miner is Mexican or Native American or Chinese? (These latter groups often were treated very differently, and unfairly, under the rules.)

It was when such difficult questions began to emerge that the system of norms broke down in the early mining camps. And it was when the miners' meeting produced a single method for authoritatively answering these questions that the miners embarked on the enterprise of subjecting their conduct to the governance of rules. Fuller's use of that word "enterprise" is not just a nice turn of phrase. An enterprise is a deliberate affair—an undertaking with a goal. Social norms are not the product of an enterprise. They are organic: they emerge and adapt in processes that may be hidden and hard to control. There may be social entrepreneurs who try to establish a social norm, by preaching from pulpit or billboard or blog, for example. But there is no single recognized process that everyone understands is *the* way that *a* norm becomes *the* norm. It is when norms become the subject of a deliberate project intended definitively to designate a particular set of rules, including the rules for making rules, as "law" that social norms can become law.

This publicly designated method of resolving ambiguity about what the rules are and what they mean is a vital feature that distinguishes legal rules from social norms. Once a jury of five at Jackass Gulch had told a miner who had been away for more than five days that a hangover does not count as "sickness," then everyone knew that everyone else knew that his site had become fair game. In the murkier world of social norms, which becomes murkier still as more people arrive and more factors weigh upon what people think (or at least will argue) is fair or right, it is hard for anyone to predict or rely upon what others will think. When there is a public and mutually recognized source for a single answer, everyone knows what everyone else knows about that answer.

Economists call the type of knowledge when everyone knows that everyone knows that everyone knows, ad infinitum, *common knowledge*. It's a very important type of knowledge because it allows anyone to think about how anyone else sees the world. Imagine the situation facing a miner who is contemplating leaving his claim unguarded while he travels to town for a day or two. If he has done everything the rules adopted by his mining camp require him to do to establish his claim—he has staked it out, limited it to the maximum size, and worked it continuously when there was enough water to do so—then he can travel feeling relatively confident that if someone jumped his claim in his absence, everyone at the camp would see the interloper as a claim jumper who has broken the rules. So the saloon owner might throw the claim jumper out and other miners might congregate threateningly to tell the jumper to get lost.

Here is where the importance of common knowledge really kicks in. When the saloon owner and the ad hoc mob take it upon themselves to punish someone, they risk their own reputation and safety: maybe some will think a claim left unattended for even a day or two counts as abandoned and the would-be enforcers will be perceived as behaving badly themselves. But when there is a commonly known interpretation of what the rules mean in any given situation—a claim is not abandoned until left for more than five days, for example—these community enforcers act with the knowledge that everyone else will also perceive what they are doing as within the bounds of the rules. Everyone recognizes that the saloon owner is not throwing out just any customer but throwing out a "claim jumper." Not only are the other patrons unlikely to interfere, they might help out; they might even patronize the saloon more for its support of their efforts to protect their claims. This is what common knowledge of the rules buys us. It allows us to feel fairly confident about how almost anyone will answer the question: was that okay or not under our rules? And that question applies not only to the initial transgression of claim jumping but also to all the ways in which members of the community respond to claim jumping.

From Redefining to Reinventing Law

So let's recap our definition of law. Law is the enterprise of subjecting human conduct to the governance of rules. People choose a set of rules to be law when they deliberately set out to create a system with the characteristics of law. These characteristics include rules about how the rules can be changed and how arguments about what the rules are and what they mean in any case will be definitively resolved. The rules are public in the special sense of common knowledge: everyone knows that everyone knows that everyone knows, and so on, that these are the rules we have designated as "law." The rules for making and applying these rules are also common knowledge. (It won't be necessary that everyone "know" the rules exactly, only that they can find out what the rules are—maybe by hiring expensive lawyers, although hopefully not. I'll have a lot more to say about this, including the problem of expensive lawyers, in Chapter 7.)

This definition makes it clear why it is overly narrow to limit our understanding of where law comes from to the legislatures and courts we know today. It just happens to be that we have constitutions and practices in place *now* that label the rules generated by legislatures and courts and the procedures they are required to follow as "law." What is essential to the idea of law, however, is not "legislature" or "court" but rather the fact that we all know that everyone else knows that this is what we recognize as law.

That's what we can change about how we do law. It's unlikely we would ever want to do away with legislatures and state-run courts. We probably won't even want to do away with lawyers. In the coming chapters I'm going to try to convince you, in fact, that people with special expertise in the enterprise of making and using rules to govern conduct are even more valuable in the new economy. But we might decide that legislatures, state-operated courts, and conventionally trained and licensed lawyers are not the only way that the enterprise of law can be conducted. I'm also going to try to convince you that some law could be made by private firms—competitive profit-making companies and nonprofit organizations—and "legal" services provided by a whole host of people in addition to conventionally licensed lawyers. A definition of law that focuses on what law does and not what law looks like today allows us to clear the decks for reinventing law in ways that make more sense for our new global web-based economy.

In Part III, I'll explain why I think there is great potential for reinventing law. Indeed, I think we could see in law the kind of transformation we have seen in most of the rest of the economy. Let's go back to gold. The

49ers found gold by accident and luck and eavesdropping. After that came 150 years of geology and drilling and data analysis. Then, in 2000 at the opening bell of the twenty-first century, Vancouver-based Goldcorp took an industry as old as humankind into the open-source heart of the new economy. Goldcorp's CEO, Rob McEwen, defied all conventional wisdom in the secretive world of gold mining when he put all of the company's data about its Red Lake, Ontario, property up on the web and invited people the world over to compete for $575,000 in prize money by finding gold his geologists had not. The experiment was a jaw-dropping success. Participants in the Goldcorp Challenge found eight million ounces of gold, half of it in locations that Goldcorp geologists had yet to identify. The experiment also proved what the new economy continues to prove on a regular basis: the best ideas come from a diversity of sources and problem-solving approaches. Participants in the Goldcorp Challenge came from fifty-one countries around the globe. They included lots of folks who were not professional geologists, and they used methods the industry had never seen before.[3]

Could we reinvent not just how we find gold but how we do the other thing the 49ers had to do get gold out of the ground: come up with a set of rules to govern our efforts? Modern legal systems, like the modern mining industry, have moved on from the simple tools used in the nineteenth century. Gone are the basic rules cooked up by the miners at camp, replaced by the complex rules and procedures governing land, mineral rights, water, intellectual property, employment, mine safety, finance, and so on, produced by courts, legislatures, regulators, and lawyers. But, like the simple, powerful question Rob McEwen dug out from beneath the complexity of modern mining—how can we find more gold?—there is a simple question to be dug out from beneath modern legal complexity: what rules work best to get what we want from this economic activity? What rules will protect incentives to expend time and money to find and extract gold, or any other type of wealth? What rules will share the wealth fairly? How will we resolve disputes about what the rules are and what they mean?

What if we put *those* questions up on a wiki and posted rewards, open to a global community of legal specialists and nonspecialists alike? Would we discover ideas and methods for creating a better set of rules? Nuggets of information and inspiration that the legal specialists have overlooked?

This is the ambition of a definition of law that does not begin with lawyers, judges, courts, and legislatures: to bring us back to what is simple and familiar about making rules to harness conflict and competition to produce collective goods. Without rules, we don't have the interconnectedness and trade that is generating such growth and change throughout the world. When that world changes as dramatically as it has over the past three decades, not only the rules need to change; the way we invent rules has to change. How and why to do that is what the rest of this book is about.

2

The Invention of Law

THE CALIFORNIA GOLD miners in 1849 were doing what people have been doing for millennia: creating sets of rules to reduce conflict and increase productive cooperation. Humans have been doing this long since before the nation-state—with its legislatures and courts and police officers—was born. Not all of our systems of rules, of course, are what we would want to call "law"—some are more informal systems of social norms; some are systems of commands imposed by a violent dictator. But at some point in human history, we invented law as something distinct from social norms and tyranny, and in this chapter we'll take a brief look at that history. This history will allow us to explore in greater depth what Fuller means when he defines law as "the enterprise of subjecting human conduct to the governance of rules." The history will also help us to understand why humans invented law. Our goal is to figure out what is fundamental about law. Getting back to first principles will prove essential to understanding later in the book how law has become a captive of a particular way of doing law and why we now need to reinvent how we do it to meet the needs of a rapidly transforming global economy.

The Law of the Jungle

The philosopher Thomas Hobbes warned us in 1651 about the state of nature. Without a powerful government to keep people in line, he said, life would be a war of all against all: solitary, poor, nasty, brutish, and short.

Hobbes was wrong. Humans, at least the ones who lasted long enough to get around to inventing law and government, have never lived in a Hobbesian state of nature. Social evolution takes time and persistence—multiple generations of sticking it out. And that requires a reasonable degree of social order. If everyone is killing everyone else all the time, there's little opportunity to mull over how much better things would be if we invented complex structures of law and government.

The need for some degree of social order to control conflict and support cooperation reaches back into the animal communities from which human societies eventually emerged. In the real state of nature, Hobbesian contests over resources—food, mates, safer places to sleep and shelter offspring—are ubiquitous, as is and the use of physical strength to decide these contests. But fights are costly, and many animal species develop ways of heading these off, deciding contests without expending too much time or energy on fights. Some manage the problem, when the environment allows or demands it, by forgoing the benefits of group defense against predators and living a mostly solitary existence. Others live in small groups with closely related kin, relying on the interest in having one's genes survive in relatives to blunt competition. Many rely to varying degrees on ranked dominance schemes to manage conflict and cooperation between individuals. To the extent that individuals know where they rank vis-à-vis others they encounter, dominance schemes can help to make life just a little more predictable.

But can we find in animal communities the seeds of the sophisticated rule-based systems of achieving social order we find among humans? Does the evolution of law begin before humans emerged?

Among evolutionary theorists this question has thus far been approached primarily as a question about the biological origins of morality. Researchers ask whether nonhuman animals have a sense of fairness, of what is right and what is wrong. Do animals show empathy and act out of concern for the well-being of others? Noted primatologist and best-selling author of *Our Inner Ape, The Age of Empathy,* and *The Bonobo and the Atheist* Frans de Waal is probably best known among those who believe that our closest relatives among the nonhuman primates share these traits. In one particularly famous experiment, de Waal and his coauthors presented evidence of a sense of fairness: capuchin monkeys who are quite happy to accept pieces of cucumber when snacking alone will reject these bland offerings when they see a monkey in a neighboring cage treated to sweet grapes. Over several decades, de Waal has presented example after example of what he argues is powerful evidence that monkeys and apes care about and act to help others, and punish those who renege on deals or treat them unfairly.

Other primatologists are not so sure. The picture that has emerged from the three decades of research on cognition, emotion, and social structure among nonhuman primates that de Waal's early work spurred is subtle and complex. Arizona State primatologist Joan Silk emphasizes, for example, that it is hard to rule out other explanations for the anecdotes that de Waal relies on to demonstrate chimp empathy. De Waal's story of a child who fell into the gorilla enclosure at a Chicago zoo and who was picked up by a female gorilla, cradled, and returned unharmed to the zoo staff may demonstrate empathy, sympathy, and compassion. But it may also demonstrate that the gorilla, who had been trained in infant care by zoo staff through the use of a doll that the gorilla was rewarded for holding correctly and returning to them, had learned her lessons well. A stump-tailed macaque might be consoling the victim of an attack with grooming and close contact because of empathy and sympathy, or because the apparent consoler was upset by the fight and is herself soothed or reassured by her actions. In her own experiments, Silk and her colleagues have shown, for example, that chimps do not consistently act to help others: chimps given a choice between pulling in a tray that delivers food to just their enclosure and one that delivers food to both their enclosure and another are no more likely to choose the option that delivers food to the other enclosure when it is occupied by another chimp than when it is empty—even when the other chimp begs for food. That shows indifference to helping out the other chimp. Other researchers (including de Waal) have obtained different results with chimps, and with different species: capuchins and marmosets choose the helpful option; tamarins don't. Further complicating the picture: chimpanzees in other experiments where they get nothing for themselves but can take an action to help another obtain food are more likely to help than not. What we don't know is why these choices are taken: maybe it is empathy; maybe it is in hope of later reciprocity; or maybe it is just random.[1]

I find all of this research on the biological origins of morality fascinating and important. But I'm not sure this research can tell us much about the roots of rule-based systems of social order and ultimately law. The definition of law we adopted from Fuller in Chapter 1 doesn't say anything about morality or empathy or compassion. It talks about rules. And I emphasized there that two critical features of rule systems are common knowledge of what the rules are in a given context and collective efforts to enforce them. A moral sense—of what is fair, of how others should be treated—might tell us something about why we pick the rules we do. But social order sustained through rules is more powerful than our moral inclinations. Indeed, we create rules enforced by punishment to get people to do things they are not inclined to do or to which they are indifferent. To understand the origins of law, we want to understand the origins of systems of rules characterized by common knowledge and collective enforcement. If we are interested in the biological origins of law, we want to know if there are hints of those features in the worlds inhabited by nonhuman primates.

If we want to find nonhuman elements of rule systems, the first thing to look for is an evaluative scheme that designates some behavior as acceptable and others as not. We know that nonhuman primates change their behavior based on how they expect a particular other to respond. That's what dominance and avoiding fights is all about: share your food with a higher-ranked animal or you'll pay for it. And there is some evidence, collected in a paper by Jessica Flack of the Santa Fe Institute and de Waal, that monkeys and apes behave as if they are responding to behavioral rules, particularly a rule of reciprocity: intervening in a fight to help out an individual who helped them in the past, seeking revenge against one who helped out their opponent.[2] But because these behaviors are responses to good or bad treatment of the individual who responds, it is very difficult to discern if those responses are the product of "rules" or simply biologically based reactions in the moment: good feelings toward those who have helped, aggression toward those who have harmed. What we really want to know is this: do these non-human primates evaluate choices—gobble up all the food or share with another—taking into account how third parties, not just the one who wants a share, will react? Do they act as if they are living in a world in which bystanders will punish them if they make the wrong choice?

There is broad consensus among primatologists that the answer to this question is no. Third-party punishment of rule violation is distinctively human.[3] Researchers Katrin Riedl, Michael Tomasello, and colleagues at the Max Planck Institute for Evolutionary Anthropology in Leipzig, Germany, have shown this with chimpanzees.[4] They ran an experiment in which chimpanzees were given an opportunity to punish a "thief" who pulled food away, either from the potential punisher or from a third chimpanzee. Punishment consisted of pulling a trapdoor that made the food disappear, preventing the thief from enjoying the fruits of his or her efforts. Chimpanzees who were dominant to the thief, sure enough, punished the thief, but only if the thief stole from them. They didn't punish the thief if the victim was someone else. (And subordinate chimpanzees who were victimized just took their lumps.) This is just one experiment, but there is little in the literature that suggests that researchers observe group-based third-party punishments. At most, there is evidence that among some nonhuman primates, dominant animals sometimes perform a policing role by intervening neutrally to break up a fight. This is dispute resolution and it contributes to social order, but it isn't punishment of rule violators.

The quest for the origins of law among nonhuman animals might end here. But a deeper understanding that law is a product of successfully coordinating third-party enforcement of rules, and not simply a more sophisticated expression of innate morality, suggests it's not yet time to abandon the search. Even if monkeys and apes are not engaged in systematic third-party enforcement of rules, are they nonetheless interested in coordinating with others on their understanding of what the rules of their group are? A complex story that de Waal told in his 1982 classic *Chimpanzee Politics*, the book that started all the fuss about nonhuman primate morality, hints that they might be. If so, that suggests a foothold for the kind of coordinated social understanding on which a system of third-party enforcement of rules—and ultimately law—depends.

The story takes us back to dominance schemes. Dominance schemes operate like rules do: providing a more reliable framework in which to make choices about how to spend time and energy and thereby making individuals better off. De Waal studied these schemes, and how they were made and changed, by observing a colony of chimpanzees that lived at the Arnhem Zoo in the Netherlands. He begins his story when a chimpanzee he refers to as the "crafty old fox," Yeroen, joined the colony and dethroned the existing leader, an adult female by the name of Mama. In de Waal's reading of the situation, Yeroen's status in the Arnhem hierarchy was not a simple case of superior strength. The Arnhem community at the time of Yeroen's accession had a number of other adult males, and two in particular of comparable or even greater strength—Luit and Nikkie—with whom Yeroen formed a close-knit group. Over the next six years, the position of alpha male changed hands four times among these three males.

De Waal argues that the story of how the top slot at Arnhem was determined shows that dominance within the colony was not simply a matter of physical strength. In his telling, dominance depends not only on who can win a fight between two individuals but also on what third parties in the colony think and do. In the struggles for dominance that he recounts, the outcomes take months to resolve. In one case, a decisive fight between Luit and Yeroen, proving Luit's superior strength, happened early in Luit's challenge for the position of alpha male. But, according to de Waal, because this fight took place in the night cages, separated from the females, it was a full seventy-two days from the time Luit first signaled his challenge to Yeroen before Luit's accession to the highest rank was secured. For much of that time, Luit's challenges were rebuffed with the help of at least eight adult females and a few smaller adult males. Until Yeroen finally acknowledged his lower status publicly—through what is known as a panting grunt, often delivered while the submissive animal literally grovels at the feet of the superior—the other apes in the colony continued to recognize and support Yeroen as the alpha male. In de Waal's portrayal, the dominance hierarchy was a complex living social phenomenon and not simply the tally of wins and losses in one-on-one power duels.

So what might this jockeying for position among chimps at the Arnhem Zoo tell us about the origins of systems of third-party punishment?

If we think of a stable dominance ranking as a set of rules—durable guidelines that predictably establish who takes precedence over whom in a contest—then we can see the seeds of a system of common knowledge in de Waal's emphasis on the social nature of the dominance ranking. By taking the position that dominance is not just a matter of winning fights—that it requires acknowledgment by third parties before it becomes stable and thus delivers its benefits to the community as a whole—de Waal is pointing to the idea that the rules are a matter of shared understanding. We don't know whether this is a matter of common knowledge—or even whether nonhuman primates are capable of common knowledge. So far, the emphasis among primatologists has just been on trying to determine whether other primates have a theory of mind, that is, the capacity to understand what others are thinking. (The evidence is mixed.)[5] Common knowledge goes a step further and asks whether an individual knows what another individual knows about what the first knows, and so on. Or, more simply, do we all know that we all know?

But even without common knowledge, de Waal's story is suggestive of something close: the idea that until individuals throughout the colony have acknowledged a shift in who holds the top spot, the top spot is not really held. The fact that dominance is at least in part a function of the willingness of other members of the group to help out in fights, and the willingness of some to accept their subordinate status and not to challenge in the first place, suggests that the fact of who tops whom can be subject to uncertainty. And the need for coordinated participation in fights—I would prefer to be helping out the same individual everyone else is helping out—means the uncertainty is about what others are going to do. Which depends on what they think I'm going to do. And so on. Even if the process among the chimpanzees isn't cognitively as sophisticated as common knowledge is in humans, it does have the coordination flavor of "Until we all know that we all know that Luit outranks Yeroen, it hasn't really happened."

This idea has been developed in careful and intriguing work that Jessica Flack has conducted with de Waal. This work considers the use of signals—in particular, what is known as a silent bared-teeth display (think of a smile) among monkeys known as pigtailed macaques. Macaques use this signal to say "uncle" in the context of an imminent contest. But they also send the signal during some peaceful interactions when there is no current contest or aggression. Flack and de Waal suggest that sending the signal in a peaceful interaction is a way of signaling something like agreement to submissive status. Since there is nothing to submit to at the time the signal is sent, that suggests an indication that the receiver of the signal can feel some confidence that the sender will follow the rule of "give in to the other guy" in future interactions. And this is what Flack and de Waal's study shows: peaceful signaling is associated with more stable relationships with lower conflict and greater cooperation. The dominant animal can effectively count on the submissive animal to follow the rule of "give in," so there's less to fight about.[6]

In further studies done with David Krakauer, also of the Santa Fe Institute, Flack has shown that the overall pattern of peaceful signals in a pig-tailed macaque group can be used to assess the power of an individual in the group to intervene in third-party conflicts. Individuals that receive more peaceful signals from more members of the group, they show, do not need to use as much aggression, and prompt less aggressive reactions, when they intervene. They also receive more requests for intervention support from others. Flack and Krakauer propose that this indicates that a monkey's power in a group is at least to some extent a function of consensus within the group.[7]

Together these studies suggest that while nonhuman primates may lack the ability to talk about what the rules are—even more so the ability to talk about what the rules should be—they may nonetheless possess at least an orientation to the question: what do others around here think the rules are? That is a question that is central to human social order and the origins of law. And quite independent of the question of the biological origins of morality.

Order without Law

Maybe monkeys and apes care about others, maybe they exchange signals about what the current rules of dominance are. Or maybe they don't. The studies in this area are still just too mixed and uncertain to say whether the origins of coordinated systems of third-party enforcement of shared rules lie with our nonhuman primate relatives. But it doesn't take much looking to find evidence of rule systems once we reach the human boundary. All known human societies are awash in normativity. Humans everywhere have lots and lots of rules about clothing, food, behavior toward family members, treatment of strangers, the use of space or time, and so on. These are rules that express the normative judgment that it's okay to do this, but not that. Most of these rules do not emerge from ingrained preferences, like the natural desire for food or comfort or sexual partners. They emerge instead from social processes: choice about what the group will deem okay and not okay. They gain their efficacy not from natural inclinations to abide by the rules but instead from a critically distinctive feature of human social structure: our reliance on third-party punishment of rule violations. Evolutionary anthropologists describe humans, relative to other animals, as "hypercooperative" and "ultrasocial." A thick blanket of rules laid on top of daily life and enforced by everyone around is why.

That the distinctive normativity and reliance on third-party enforcement we see in human societies today goes back to the earliest human societies is something we know from the few hunter-gatherer tribes that are still around to be studied by ethnographers like Polly Wiessner of the University of Utah. Wiessner, who has spent substantial time learning about the Ju/'hoansi Bushmen of the Kalahari, is one of the few ethnographers who has studied closely the mechanisms of norm enforcement in simple human societies.[8] Among the Ju/'hoansi, subsistence in a harsh environment is supported by strong norms of sharing and mutual aid. Living in bands of perhaps five or six families, the Ju/'hoansi expect food to be shared with anyone present in camp when it becomes available, and because the Ju/'hoansi engage in frequent, sometimes long-term, visits to neighboring bands, the camp population is constantly in flux. As with other !kung tribes, the Ju/'hoansi have rules governing hereditary land rights and claims over some personal possessions. Norms exist regarding behavior—excessive drunkenness or promiscuity, for example, is considered inappropriate. Most adults engage in individualized long-term, daisy-chain, gift-giving relationships with a network of partners in other bands; as Wiessner reports from her study of these *hxaro* partnerships, "All !kung agreed that one could visit a partner whenever one likes and expect to be welcomed and integrated into the local sharing system of the camp." But whereas *hxaro* partnerships entail reciprocal obligations—not an immediate return, but an expectation of assistance in the future if needed—food sharing is largely conditional only on being around at dinnertime.

The myriad rules of social life among the Ju/'hoansi are widely respected, resulting in largely stable and peaceful relationships both within and between bands. But respect for the rules is not a consequence of the exercise of higher authority. Rather, consistent with University of Southern California anthropologist Christopher Boehm's finding for a wide variety of such hunter-gatherer groups, the Ju/'hoansi have an overarching rule of equality among adults: no one individual can boss any other around. So how is this rule, along with all the other rules of life in this part of the Kalahari, enforced? Why do people follow the rules?

Wiessner spent two extended periods living with the Ju/'hoansi, first in the 1970s and then again in the 1990s, to find out. She sat under a tree, notebook in hand, and eavesdropped on group conversations. Turns out, group conversations—which she defined as more than three participants— are a principal way in which the rules are enforced. Wiessner identified four categories of this talk-based punishment. First, put-downs through jokes, mockery, or pantomime. Second, outright but mild criticism or complaint. Third, harsh criticism or complaint. And fourth, criticism with violent acts. In Wiessner's study of 171 cases of talk-based punishment, only 2 percent fell into the fourth category, where talk was coupled with violence. The bulk involved mild or harsh criticism or complaint, approximately equal amounts of each. Punishment often started at the lowest level with mocking put-downs, and escalated to criticism if ridicule was unsuccessful in solving the problem. Criticism was almost always delivered when the target of the complaint, or a close relative, was within earshot.

In about a quarter of the cases Wiessner documented, a complaint or criticism was leveled by only one person in the group. But in the great majority, criticism was expressed by a coalition of several individuals. Collective criticism shares the cost of enforcing the rules. Moreover, egalitarianism helps to ensure that the burden of enforcement is widely distributed: coalitions of complainers were drawn from all ages, both sexes, and included people perceived as weak as well as those perceived as strong.

Several of the differences between individual criticism and coalition criticism tell us a lot about the collective and shared nature of this type of punishment to enforce the rules. First, most mild criticism was delivered by individuals, but most harsh criticism was delivered by coalitions. Since one of the rules in Ju/'hoan society is a norm against excessive or overly harsh criticism of another, it is clear that delivering strong rebukes requires the safety of numbers. That means Ju/'hoansi have to be reasonably good at predicting what types of offenses will draw strong group criticism.

The collective nature of this talk-punishment to enforce the rules of Ju/'hoan life is also evident in another distinction Wiessner found between individual and coalition criticism. Individual criticism was much more likely to be used to create pressure to live up to kin obligations than was group criticism. The most frequent complaint made by individuals acting alone was a complaint about kinfolk. All other categories of bad behavior—acting like a big shot, failing to share, being greedy, engaging in inappropriate sexual activity, spreading malicious gossip, or being overly aggressive, for example—were handled almost exclusively with group complaints. That is, where rule-breaking caused problems experienced in roughly the same way by everyone in the group, the rule was by and large enforced by the group acting collectively.

A third difference between individual and group complaints is evident in Wiessner's observations about what happened after complaints were made. About two-thirds of the time, an individual complaint was heard but elicited no observable response. That happened only about one-third of the time with group complaints. Another 25 percent of the time an individual complainer earned either an argument from the target of the complaint or was told by others to pipe down. That happened less than 10 percent of the time with group complaints. All told, group complaints were much more effective in producing a result: a refusal by others to interact with or share with the accused, some corrective action by the accused, or a rallying of group opinion that put even more pressure on the rule-breaker to change his or her ways.

Wiessner's stories present a vivid picture of how collective punishment works. She tells the story, for example, of a village leader who was recognized for his skills in hunting, healing, music, and mediation. But when status appeared to be going to his head, and he became self-centered, he was repeatedly accused of acting like he was better than the rest and hence entitled—consuming extra tea and sugar on the side, for example. When these criticisms mounted, he would kill and distribute the meat from a large animal and entertain visitors with a musical performance, thereby quelling the uproar. In another two cases Wiessner describes, strong individuals were criticized widely for being reclusive—heading off to summer territories with kin and effectively sending the message that others were not welcome to visit (and hence share) with them. One leader, on hearing of the building public opinion critical of his departure, returned to invite others to join him. The other reclusive leader did not heed the criticism, prompting some village members to up the pressure by asserting land rights and horning in on the territory for a short while. Moreover, when the group was reunited in the following season, sharing with the rule-breakers declined.

In another example of group-based enforcement that goes beyond criticism, Wiessner tells of a collective refusal to share with a woman perceived as a promiscuous drunk with badly behaved children, forcing the woman and her husband and children to move to another area. As Wiessner emphasizes, ostracism is costly for the group because even the badly behaved contribute something to a hardscrabble existence. The price is especially high for the kin of the person or family that is excluded. This high cost is rarely borne because collective criticism is generally effective before things escalate to this level. But the willingness of the group to bear these ultimate costs if earlier milder forms of punishment are not effective is known throughout the group. And without the collective willingness to bear enforcement costs, large and small, there are no rules to speak of and no reliable social order.

Once you have heard about such careful studies of how people who lived as our earliest human ancestors did, it is hard not to recognize just how little things have changed in some parts of our modern life. Group criticism, ridicule, and ostracism are old hat to anyone who has ever spent time roaming the halls of a middle school, university department, or office tower. We are remarkably willing to follow the rules to avoid being clipped by disapproval from others; and remarkably willing to expend time and energy expressing disapproval when others transgress.

This is what Robert Ellickson also found when he talked to cattle ranchers and landowners in the study from which I borrowed the title of this section.[9] Ellickson, a professor of property law at Yale University, studied how ranchers in rural Shasta County in the early 1980s dealt with a problem that has troubled communities since the agricultural revolution displaced the hunter-gatherer life: When cattle go a-wandering, who pays for the damage to crops and fences? The law has long had complex rules about who pays, rules that can change ten times as you drive down a country highway.

Ellickson found that, for the most part, Shasta County ranchers and landowners pretty much ignore the law. In fact, few of them, even with legal training, know the law. Instead, they follow a couple of simple rules of neighborliness. Number 1, owners should try to prevent their cattle eating their neighbors' crops. Number 2, when crops do get eaten by roaming cattle, landowners should not press for compensation and should help return the vagabonds. These rules are enforced in much the same way that the Ju/'hoansi Bushmen enforce their rules: gossip and shared criticism of offenders. For those few offenders who are not brought into line by these methods, the community recognizes the legitimacy of more aggressive responses. In one of Ellickson's stories, a rancher who had suffered repeated problems with a trespassing bull—his early complaints unheeded—told the bull's owner that if it happened again he would castrate the offending animal. Although this would constitute a crime in the eyes of the law, there was a consensus in the community that even violent self-help in response to repeated violations could be justified. In fact, a local law enforcement official told the rancher who issued the threat that he would turn a blind eye if the threat was carried out, which apparently it was.

This is an important point to understand about what makes punishment collective. It isn't all about mob violence. There may be only one person who seems to be taking action against a wrongdoer—and often that person is the victim or a member of the victim's family. That looks like retaliation and not third-party punishment. But there is a critical role played by third parties even in systems that rely on retaliation by a victim. That role is the act of *not* turning against the victim who turns perpetrator. Not interfering with retaliation, and not retaliating for retaliation, is also a form of collective enforcement of the rules. This is what is going on when the Ju/'hoansi villagers criticize a failure to share in general, but not a failure to share with someone who has broken the rules by acting like a big shot. The community is collectively enforcing the rule that it is wrong not to share; it is also collectively enforcing the rules against big-shot behavior by not punishing someone who is punishing such behavior.

Collective social efforts to enforce rules that a community develops over time are thus a part of how human societies have been organized for millennia. They are central to groups large and small, from our foraging past to our complex modern economy. Human societies are literally blanketed with detailed rules of behavior.

So what role is there for law? Why, on the path from our hunter-gatherer past to our complex global present, did human societies invent law?

Why Law?

The Ju/'hoansi of the Kalahari clearly live under a set of rules that are effectively enforced without any centralized authority capable of dishing out punishment. And even though the ranchers and landowners of Shasta County could, if they wanted to, go to California courts to enforce one set of rules about roaming cattle and the damage they can do, they live instead under another set that is enforced only by the same type of social punishments relied on by the Ju/'hoansi Bushmen. Using the definition of law we explored in the last chapter, the social order we see in these settings doesn't count as law. Indeed, the very point of examples like these is to emphasize that human societies manage to generate lots of social order without law.

We can see what these settings lack from the point of view of law if we think back to Fuller's definition of law as the enterprise of subjecting human conduct to the governance of rules. This enterprise requires mutual recognition of an authoritative way of resolving disagreements about when a rule has been violated. We have law when we have rules about what counts as a rule. And in the settings in which we find order without law, that's what is missing. Among the Ju/'hoansi, as among middle-school kids or Shasta County ranchers, there is generally no mutually recognized entity that declares what is and is not a rule violation. There is of course lots of discussion and debate about whether some-one has violated the rules and should be punished—when a lone complainer among the Ju/'hoansi criticizes someone, as we saw, the complainer is often met with argument and dismissal by others. Much discussion in the school-yard, around the water cooler, and at the local diner in a close-knit community centers on working out what is and is not acceptable. Among the California miners, there would have been much discussion about whether a fellow miner had left his claim untended too long, making it fair game for others.

Such discussion can produce consensus about what the rules are and when punishment is warranted. We may even see in these settings the emergence of powerful voices—leaders who can move others by their forceful statements about what they believe to be right and wrong, acceptable and not. But in these cases of informal social order, even if there are well-established prac-tices and norms, there are no recognizable rules governing how the discussion is to be conducted or how disagreements are to be resolved; no rules about how the leaders are supposed to reach their judgments. And, most impor-tantly, there is no single person or body of people whom everyone recognizes is entitled to definitively state whether a rule has been violated or not. Today's discussion under the tree in the Kalahari Desert or around the table at the Shasta County diner may be reopened tomorrow or next week or next year by a shifting group of participants, who will feel no obligation to defer to the judgments of any other group or individual. It is when we start to see the emergence of established and authoritative rules and institutions for articu-lating the content of rules that we see the emergence of law.

Law in the Ancient World

We don't really know when law first emerged in human societies. It no doubt was a slow and uneven process and almost certainly happened before humans invented writing. By the time written history starts—in ancient Mesopotamia and Egypt in the fourth millennium BCE —we already have evidence of apparently well-understood legal regimes. Archaeologists of this period have found thousands of legal documents—writing inscribed on clay tablets or papyrus—memorializing contracts such as for the sale of land or animals or for the repayment of a loan. Other documents record the resolution of legal disputes by judges and oracles, or relate stories about law—such as the famous Tale of the Eloquent Peasant, from Egypt around 2000 BCE, who was tricked out of his goods and donkeys by a low-level official. The official had seized the peasant's goods when the donkeys, facing a blockage in the road engineered by the official, had no choice but to step onto the official's fields. As donkeys are wont to do, they ate a few stalks of his barley. This, the official said, authorized him to seize the donkeys and goods. A parable of legal corruption, the peasant presents nine petitions to a judge urging him to do right and uphold the law by ordering compensation.[10]

The most famous evidence of ancient law comes to us in the form of seven-foot-tall black stone pillars inscribed with cuneiform symbols and dating back to about 1800 BCE—relating what is called the code of the Babylonian king Hammurabi. Hammurabi was not the first king to erect a monument inscribed with rules—the earliest evidence of such monuments goes back at least another three hundred years to the Sumerian kingdom of Ur-Nammu. But Hammurabi's code was widely copied and distributed; tablets reciting its rules were still being composed a thousand years after he died. The pillars reciting the rules were erected throughout Hammurabi's kingdom. And although they were decorated with an impressive picture of Hammurabi communing with the Sun-God and in both prologue and epilogue Hammurabi is flattered for his greatness and his protection of the poor and weak, they mostly contain fairly mundane provisions like this:[11]

57. If a shepherd, without the permission of the owner of the field, and without the knowledge of the owner of the sheep, lets the sheep into a field to graze, then the owner of the field shall harvest his crop, and the shepherd, who had pastured his flock there without permission of the owner of the field, shall pay to the owner twenty gur [a quantity] of corn for every ten gan [an area of land].

77. If a man give silver to another man in a partnership arrangement they shall divide equally in the presence of the god any profit or loss which results.

233. If a builder has made a house for a man, and has not made his work solid enough and a wall has toppled, that builder shall strengthen that wall from his own resources.

Clearly the author of these code provisions is writing in the context of a world that already knows a lot of legal structure. Here we have basic examples of economic compensation for violations of property rights, rules governing profit-sharing in a partnership, and liability for breach of contract. Indeed, by my reckoning, nearly two-thirds of Hammurabi's code—generally famous for the lex talionis rules establishing "an eye for an eye, a tooth for a tooth"— deals with basic economic rules affecting property and commercial transactions. The provisions dealing with the much more exciting rules about what part of the body will be severed to compensate for what crime take up much less space—less than 10 percent. Important stuff, but hard not to see Hammurabi's code as being fundamentally a far more mundane exercise in the legal work necessary to improve economic cooperation.[12]

There is a lot of debate among historians of the ancient world about whether Hammurabi's code really was "law" or not, but most of the debate takes its cue from a narrower definition of law than the one we have borrowed from Fuller. The set of rules carved in the stone pillars doesn't cover every conceivable case, or even the full set of case decisions that are reported on in thousands of surviving clay tablets. To some historians' eyes, the rules are too particularistic to count as law. Many of the rules in the code appear to be very similar to rules found in other sources, suggesting that Hammurabi didn't make them up, as a modern-day legislature might. And of the 282 provisions in the code only one is addressed to a judicial official—judges who wrote down their decisions and were later proved wrong were fined and thrown permanently off the bench—so there is no prescription for how the rules are to be enforced.

But using Fuller's definition of law, none of these apparent shortcomings disqualifies Hammurabi's monument as evidence of a legal order categorically different from the rule-based social order we saw among the Ju/'hoansi. For neither the particular process by which rules are generated nor their method of enforcement really matters in deciding whether we can count Hammurabi's Babylon as an example of the deliberate enterprise of subjecting human conduct to the governance of rules. What distinguishes the social order achieved by the Ju/'hoansi from the legal order at least aspired to by Hammurabi and other ancient Near Eastern rulers is the presence of a set of institutions, people, and procedures recognized as being uniquely capable of making an authoritative announcement of what constitutes a violation of the community's rules. This is the same transition we saw in the California Gold Rush days: from a set of spontaneous social norms to manage claims to a deliberate effort to establish common-knowledge rules and procedures for deciding disputes about claim jumping. Somewhere between our hunter-gatherer past and the first recordings of written history, human beings found a way to definitively resolve disagreements about what the rules are and when they have been broken. That way was the way of law.

On the path from that unknown point where humans first began experimenting with law to today, the world has seen many variations on the enterprise of organizing human life with rules. Not all of them look like our modern legal systems with legislatures, police, permanent courts, and judges. But they all rely on some common-knowledge method of definitively putting an end to arguments about the rules, and for our purposes that makes them law.

Vikings and Outlaws in Medieval Iceland

No historical example of a legal regime makes this point about the central importance of a way of putting an end to arguments about rules more clearly than, surprisingly enough, tenth-century Iceland. Vikings from Norway settled in Iceland around 930. From the sagas that were first composed and recited orally and then recorded for posterity, we know that the Viking way of life was a brutal one—the sagas are replete with tales of axes being sunk in heads, eyes being gouged out, and hands being chopped off. But here's the surprise: the Vikings also loved the law and litigation. With so much hot-headedness to manage, they invented complex rules and procedures for deciding who could kill or maim whom when—and who had to pay and how much to avoid triggering blood revenge. As William Miller of the University of Michigan recounts in his book *Bloodtaking and Peacemaking*, the Icelanders had lots of detailed rules in place to govern vengeance. Miller recounts, for example, that "blows that left no bruises had to be avenged at the time and place they occurred, but a blow that left a bruise or caused bleeding could be avenged up until the next Althing." (The Althing was annual gathering at a place called Law Rock at which the freemen of Iceland—slaves and women not invited—chose their rules and litigated their bigger disputes.) Miller goes on:

> The right to avenge belonged to the injured party and to those who accompanied him; it was also lawful for anyone else to take vengeance legitimately on the wrongdoer within a day of the incident. Should vengeance not have been taken before the Althing, the right terminated; after that the claimant was relegated to an outlawry action. An explicit right to kill was . . . given for sexual assaults on a man's wife, daughter, mother, sister, foster-daughter and foster-mother, but it had to be carried out at the time and place of the assault. Likewise, a slave's

death could be avenged at the time and place of the killing. And only those persons who had incurred liability for the wrongdoing were legitimate targets of revenge.[13]

Miller notes that the sagas demonstrate that the rules were ignored enough to generate juicy tales to pass on to the grandchildren, but still the blood-lust must have been reasonably contained or else we would have few Viking descendants living in Iceland today.

Better evidence that law and litigation secured a workable legal order comes from the fact that the Icelanders took knowledge of the rules very seriously. Indeed, this was the only job they thought important enough to warrant the creation of a public office on the people's dime. This was the job of the lawspeaker. Elected for a three-year term at the annual Althing, the lawspeaker had the job of knowing the rules and reciting them at the annual meeting—particularly important in the era before the Icelanders started writing things down. The lawspeaker had three years to get through the full body of the law—but he was required to repeat the procedural rules every year. In his daily life, he was obliged to answer anyone's questions about the rules and, should the judges of one of the several courts established throughout the land be uncertain of the rules, it was the lawspeaker's unique responsibility to set them straight.

Carrying off the duties of the lawspeaker was no mean feat. The rules included not only those voted on at the annual assemblies but also the customary rules acquired through the ages and brought to Iceland's shores by its inhabitants from Norway and other Scandinavian or Celtic lands. They covered almost every detail of Icelandic life, not merely the problems of assault and murder. They regulated employment contracts and farm production levels—penalizing a failure to work a farm to its maximum, for example—marriage contracts, sales of goods, credit arrangements, and liability for property damage. Miller describes a "rococo complexity that suggests sheer pleasure in the formulation of law almost as if it were for law's sake alone." And some of their belabored provisions would make for a fine lawyer-skewering Monty Python skit:

> If a man wishes to move bones [to relocate a cemetery], the landowner
> is to call nine neighbors and their serving men to move the bones as
> if he were calling them for ship hauling. They are to have spades and
> shovels with them; he himself is to provide hides in which to carry the
> bones and draught animals to move them. He is to call the neighbors
> who live nearest the place where the bones are to be dug up and is to

have called them seven nights or more before they need to come. They are to be there at midmorning. A householder is to go with his serving men who are in good health, all except the shepherd. They are to begin digging in the outer part of the churchyard and search for bones as they would for money if that was what they expected to find there.[14]

And that's only the half of it. Failure to follow the bone-moving rules, the rules tell us, was grounds for a lawsuit at the local Thing—the annual spring assemblies held in the four Quarters of the country, at which issues and disputes not large enough for the all-country Althing held in midsummer were heard.

You would think that such a detailed legal system would entail the use of large numbers of public officers to carry out the duties of staffing courts, bringing defendants to trial, and carrying out the punishments meted out by judges. But you would be wrong. Iceland had no army, no police, no court officers, no permanent judges, no jails, and no wardens. Courts were called by the chieftains who presided over the Things established for each Quarter. Cases were heard by ad hoc panels of thirty-six thingmen—householders who had declared themselves "in Thing" with a particular chieftain—twelve selected by each of the three chieftains who oversaw the business of a particular Thing. Chieftains, however, had no formal power over their thingmen; they were not feudal lords. A householder could declare himself "in Thing" with any chieftain he liked, and he could be severed from the group by the chieftain with a simple announcement. None of these freemen—thingman or chieftain—saw himself as bound by the authority of anyone else. There was no king with soldiers, like Hammurabi, able to rain down on miscreants and make them pay heed. Icelandic courts issued decisions—and many of them—but once they did, it was up to the party declared in the right to secure compensation, collect a fine, or impose a punishment.

So why did anyone bother following the rules? More to the point, why did anyone who felt wronged hold off on his desire to exact retribution until after a court had ruled on his case?[15]

The answer is that waiting for a court decision was a less risky and less costly way of punishing a rule-breaker. If you wanted to punish someone whom you thought had stolen your goods or damaged your fields or violated your daughter, you were safer waiting for a judicial declaration that you had been wronged and were entitled to exact a particular punishment—a fine or revenge, for example. If you didn't wait for the declaration, you were at risk of being found at fault yourself—triggering further retaliation and strife and perhaps widening the scope of the dispute. Waiting lowered the risks of self-help. That's not necessary when the transgression is unambiguous—nobody will fault you for retaliating for brazen theft of your sheep—but it gets a bit wooly when the one you call thief can claim that the sheep had wandered onto his property and he was acting within his rights to corral them. Unjustified retaliation is grounds for justified retaliation. It may be better to find out first.

Another reason the Icelanders bothered to wait for a judicial declaration of who was in the wrong was that they could more easily secure the assistance of others in delivering authorized punishments. Not only was it less risky for the complainant to wait; it was much less risky for others to wait for a determination that retaliation was justified. A neighbor who helps you collect the compensation the court says you are owed is an upstanding member of the community who is probably not at risk of harm. One who helps you collect based only on your say-so risks being branded a thief and left to worry about when retaliation might strike.

The need for help from one's neighbors is especially clear in a particularly effective form of collective punishment for wrongdoing: outlawry. When a court declared someone an outlaw, it imposed on everyone in the country the obligation not to provide him any aid or support: don't trade with him, feed him, nurse him, or give him a bed for the night. His property was confiscated and he was banished from Iceland for three years. That was lesser outlawry. Full outlawry declared open season on the outlaw: he was banished permanently and anyone could kill him with impunity. In fact, the person who had prosecuted the case for outlawry was obligated to hunt the outlaw down. For those with a taste for killing or some other grudge, it was a freebie. For those who would kill only out of duty, it was (almost) a guarantee that the killing would not trigger retaliation.

The remarkable thing is that this system was as effective at securing order as it was. The Icelanders survived three hundred years without a king and without any centralized forces to impose law and order. The reasons that Iceland eventually came under the authority of the king of Norway are unclear. Miller suggests that it may be traceable to the power that accumulated in the hands of a few powerful chieftains, making the householders' capacity to change their attachment to a particular chieftain at will an illusory right and their vulnerability to plunder a concrete reality. Conflicts between powerful families stopped being orderly feuds and took on the character of all-out war, with plenty of collateral damage. But even a workable legal order may not be up to the destabilizing pressures of greed and inequality. Medieval Iceland is thus hardly a model for today, with our far greater complexity and inequality. But it is a sharp example of what it can mean to have legal order—with rules and courts and orderly judicial assessments of wrongdoing—without a centralized system of enforcement.

The Merchants of Venice, and Beyond

Iceland is not the only place where we can find examples of legal order without fully centralized enforcement systems during the Middle Ages.[16] Throughout the known world at this time, the Commercial Revolution was getting underway with the rapid expansion of long-distance trade. English wool, Italian textiles, German beer, French wine, Indian cotton, Chinese silk, Greek and North African wax, Baltic timber—all flowed widely throughout the European continent and the countries that ring the Mediterranean. But this was before the rise of the nation-state. Although we can speak today of "Italy," for example, as a single nation, in the Middle Ages it was a collection of independent towns and cities—Venice, Florence, Naples, Genoa, Milan, and so on—each with its own cobbled-together system of governance. Few had the luxury of a centralized force with a monopoly on the exercise of coercive power. Powerful aristocratic families wielded their own resources and made them available as mercenaries to fend off challenges and, no doubt, plunder as needed.

As exciting as the history of medieval political intrigue and power struggles might be, however, the explosion of economic growth in this era depended on the far more mundane development of reliable systems of ensuring that debts were paid, goods were delivered, property was safe, and profits and risks were shared as expected. Commercial law—known as *lex mercatoria*, or the law merchant—developed rapidly during this time. It grew not from a single source, but from the innovative efforts of a diverse collection of individuals and organizations: kings and nobles, religious communities, voluntary civic associations, royal courts, city governments, and, especially, merchants and their guilds. Indeed, these individuals and organizations in a significant sense competed with one another for the business of providing rules and courts to decide commercial disputes. The sponsors of international markets, such as the famous Champagne fairs of the twelfth and thirteenth centuries, provided rules and courts to adjudicate disputes among merchants at the fair—a feature that attracted a larger volume of trade. Merchants had some capacity to choose the sets of rules that would govern their transactions—by deciding what fairs and towns they would travel to and sometimes by deciding where they would settle. Many fairs and towns also ensured that juries deciding cases were composed of merchants and that the relevant law used to resolve disputes was the law reflected in the customs followed by local merchants. Merchants residing in a foreign town could also choose, as a group, whether to submit to foreign courts or try to reach a deal with the local authorities to let them be governed by their own law and judges. And even where merchants had no choice about the law they had to use, the towns and guilds and fair operators competed in the medieval ecosystem, growing wealthier and more powerful at least in part because their rules did a better job of supporting trade than their neighbors'.[17]

The merchant guilds in particular often struggled hard to ensure that their members' disputes were decided under their own rules, and not the rules of a local ruler or religious organization. Some guilds penalized their members for taking their cases into other courts and secured agreements from cities and towns in which they traded to ensure that the local courts would decline to decide guild cases. They ostracized merchants who sought to take their disputes into other courts. In some cases, the guilds succeeded in having all commercial disputes—whether involving their members or not—decided in their courts under their rules. This helped ensure not only that the rules were those that served merchant interests well—providing for swift resolution, for example—but also, perhaps more importantly, that everyone knew that everyone knew what rules were in play.[18]

Let's look at an example. Suppose there was a dispute between two medieval merchants—a wool merchant from England and a textile manufacturer from Italy—about whether or not they had finalized their agreement. This would have mattered to the wool merchant if he had found a subsequent buyer willing to pay more and to the textile manufacturer if he had found another seller willing to take less. In those circumstances, either one might have wanted to argue that there was no deal, no obligation to carry through. Under some rules applied by some courts at the time, there was no binding contract if there was no written document. Under others, there was no obligation on either party unless the buyer had paid a deposit known as earnest money. Some courts would say the seller was free to change his mind after the earnest money was paid, but the buyer got to keep the earnest money. Still others would say that the buyer was entitled to twice the earnest money if the seller backed out. Edward I of England declared in his Carta Mercatoria in 1303 that if a token amount—a "God's penny"—had been given over when the agreement was made, then this was enough to make the agreement fully enforceable. That meant that both buyer and seller were stuck with the deal they struck, no matter how tempting the alternatives.[19]

Provided they knew which rule would be applied if they ended up in a future quarrel, there were ways for both the buyer and the seller to accomplish what they needed. If the rule allowed the seller an easy out, then the buyer might require some additional security up front or purchase only stock on hand or pay a lower price. If the rule bound the seller tightly, then the seller might spend more time soliciting bids from other buyers before reaching an agreement, or demand a higher price. The most important thing to buyer and seller would have been to know just which rule they were dealing with so they could make the right adjustments. And that's what the guild efforts to bind their members and then anyone who dealt with their members to the rules they themselves controlled accomplished. They made it clear which rules were in play.

The medieval merchant guilds and other rule-making organizations not only provided rules; they also provided means for enforcing the rules. Powerful local rulers who sought to establish the rules for trade in their cities or regions did often make their officials available to help corral rule-breakers and enforce the judgments of their courts. But in this era before the consolidation of stable states, this kind of enforcement faced several shortcomings. First, it was probably spotty service, depending as it did on the inclination of the local potentate to send an official out to collect money owed or seize property or person—the restive state of medieval politics no doubt meant that the demand for such services would often outstrip supply, as men with weapons were called off to battle more serious threats. Second, local enforcement officials could do little to reach the merchant who had already left town or who had little wealth on his person or who stayed at home in a foreign land while his business was conducted by an agent whose imprisonment would cause the merchant little concern. Third, the local ruler had difficulty committing to playing the part of neutral in the management of trades between local and foreign merchants. Why not seize all the property of foreign merchants? Why not issue biased decisions in favor of those who live close enough to provide political and financial support? And yet such trade—between local and foreign merchants—was the very stuff on which medieval prosperity depended when a ruler's dominion might not extend beyond a set of city walls.

Several economists—including Avner Greif, Paul Milgrom, and Barry Weingast of Stanford University and the late Nobel laureate Douglass North—have studied this problem and demonstrated that enforcement of commercial rules in the Middle Ages rested significantly on community and commercial organizations such as the merchant guilds.[20] Harvard political scientist Robert Putnam makes a similar observation about the voluntary associations known as communes that emerged in medieval Italy.[21] Members of the commune swore an oath of mutual aid and economic cooperation. Guilds and communes had at their disposal the capacity to punish their members for failure to live up to the rules they articulated: they could kick people out of the group, depriving them of the benefits of trade or mutual protection. They could boycott them in commercial transactions. They could refuse to protect them if their goods were stolen or their agents were attacked or cheated. And, if one of their members was wronged by a merchant with whom they traded, they could collectively punish the transgressor by refusing further dealings with him.

In the twelfth century, the techniques of community enforcement took on the toughness ultimately exercised by many a beleaguered fourth-grade teacher. In what Avner Greif calls the "community responsibility system," the whole community was punished if one of its members broke the rules. So if a guild or other group member failed to pay up on a debt, for example, any other group member could have his goods seized to provide payment. This created a strong incentive in turn for the group to screen and discipline its own members to ensure they played by the rules.

In March 1240, for example, the Flemish cloth merchants agreed on and wrote up a set of rules governing their trade.[22] "This is the Ordinance of Those Men of Ypres and Douai Who Go to England," it said. First on the list: "If a merchant returns a cloth after he has bought it, giving no reason for the return . . . then henceforth no man of Ypres or Douai shall let him take any cloth away from any of our shops until he shall have paid the full price." That is: cheat one of our guys, and your credit rating goes to zero. Members of the alliance were forbidden to deal with craftsmen who "dealt falsely" with any merchant. Members who violated any of the rules "or do not hold faithfully to them" were barred from trading. "And no member of the alliance may house [the rule-breaker's] goods in England or keep company with the erring merchant." That's a form of collective enforcement: everyone in the guild refuses to deal with a wrongdoer. The Flemish merchants even went so far as to refuse admission to the alliance to any merchant who had sold cloth in a town where "wrongs were done to any merchant in the alliance" until the "aggrieved merchant" has been compensated. That's a form of community responsibility, enforced by another community: to be in the Flemish merchants' club, you had to stop doing business with everyone in the town where wrongs were done, not just the wrongdoer himself.

If these tactics for enforcement sound familiar, that is because they are effectively the same tactics employed by the medieval Icelanders: declare a rule-breaker an outlaw and banish him from the benefits and protections of the community. It's a set of techniques that puts the weight of enforcement on all the members of the guild—to refuse to deal with a rule-breaker. And when the value of being a member of the guild is high—as it was in the Middle Ages, when guilds operated as exclusive clubs that controlled trade in particular places and particular goods—the threat of ostracism can be very effective.

Boycotting and ostracism were also effective techniques, the medieval European merchant guilds found, for keeping local kings and princes in line. In this case, however, the members of the guild were required to refuse to deal with a local ruler who broke agreements to abide by a set of rules— particularly rules of protection—for guild members. Avner Greif has argued that the guilds played an essential role in securing protection from foreign rulers and thus an essential role in the explosive growth of long-distance trade in the Middle Ages. Merchants who traveled to distant places faced many risks: that their goods and money would be confiscated by rulers in foreign lands, that they would be robbed or beaten by local merchants jealous of their sales, that their agreements with foreign buyers and sellers would be breached without penalty. Greif recounts the story of a Flemish merchant and his compatriots in the English town of Boston in 1241. The Flemish merchant accused an English merchant of not repaying a commercial loan. His complaints triggered an all-out attack by the English merchants of the town on the Flemish merchants who sold cloth in the town. "The English . . . broke down the doors and windows and dragged out [the accuser] and five others, whom they foully beat and wounded and then set in the stocks. All the other Flemings they beat, ill-treated and robbed, and pierced their cloths with swords and knives."[23] Greif emphasizes that such attacks were commonplace throughout the medieval world. The Genoese traders in Constantinople, capital of the Byzantine Empire, were attacked in 1162 and again in 1171. Those that survived the first attack were forced to abandon their possessions and flee; the second attack destroyed the Genoese quarter of the city. In 1283 King Edward I of England was well aware that many foreign merchants were reluctant to travel to English towns and fairs because of the risk of undeterred theft and attack by local townspeople. Throughout Europe and the Near East, long-distance merchants faced the risk that local lords and rulers would confiscate goods or impose unexpected taxes and tolls.

The solution generally came in the form of contracts between the traders of distant cities and local potentates with the power to provide merchants security. Over time rulers who signed these contracts also promised not to use that power to excessively tax foreign goods or interfere with the guild's use of the services of their own guild courts and arbitrators. The enforcement of these contracts came down to the ability of the foreign merchants to organize embargoes of a ruler's town or fair if the ruler broke his promises about security or taxes or noninterference. As Greif has shown, figuring out how to make such embargoes effective was a prime mover of the development of guild institutions in medieval Europe. In the early twelfth century, for example, German merchants trading in a foreign city would form an organization known as a Kontor, and rulers who failed to live up to their agreements with the merchants of the Kontor would see their city boycotted. Members of the Kontor who cheated were faced with being drummed out of the group themselves.

But there was a gap in this strategy: other merchants who did not belong to the Kontor—from Germany or elsewhere—faced no threat if they ignored the embargo. And the embattled ruler faced every incentive to cut a special deal with those who did. This pressure ultimately led to the formation of a guild of guilds—or the Hanseatic League—which coordinated embargoes in which the merchants of the most significant German trading towns participated. Acting collectively, the Hansa was able to effectively cut off the supply of German goods to cities or entire countries when their rulers cheated on their promises. This is how the German merchants ultimately held the rulers of the city of Bruges, for example, to their promises to keep taxes to a specified level and to compensate German merchants who had their goods stolen or their bills left unpaid by Flemish citizens. According to historian Philippe Dollinger, by the end of the fourteenth century, acting together in this way, the German Hansa had secured an agreement from Count Philip the Bold of Flanders that the cities of Ghent, Bruges, and Ypres would compensate a Hanseatic trader if he was attacked within the count's territories by a Fleming who proved insolvent.[24] Even if the German merchants suffered an attack outside of the count's territories and by the resident of a foreign town—by pirates on the high seas, for example—these Flemish cities promised to arrest all the citizens of the attacker's hometown who were living within their borders if necessary to secure compensation. The power of the merchant guild to enforce such promises with foreign powers came down to the capacity of the guild to enforce the rules—including the rules prohibiting trade with an embargoed city—with its own members.

The competitive advantage of better rules to protect property and contractual agreements was not lost on market makers. The twelfth-century fairs of Champagne that established local fair courts to resolve conflicts about payments, debts, and quality did so to attract business. The organizers of English fairs in towns like Boston and St. Ives lured merchants from other English towns such as York by promising that these merchants could continue to use their own guild structures to adjudicate claims and disputes.[25] Edward I signed the Statute of Acton Burnell, passed in 1283 by one of the first English parliaments to include merchant representatives, creating a procedure for registering and quickly collecting upon debts among merchants. As the preamble to the statute tells us, the motivation was to draw to England foreign merchants who were staying away with their wares for fear they would never get paid.[26] His 1303 Carta Mercatoria which established a variety of rules for trade was largely a business transaction for the throne was plain: in exchange for providing the rules and agreeing to punish officials in fairs and market towns for failing to deliver honest adjudication of merchants' disputes, the merchants agreed to pay additional customs duties to the king when they brought goods in and out of England.

Free to Choose? Traders of the Middle East in the Middle Ages

The work of developing better rules and procedures, just like better techniques for dyeing wool and weaving cloth, will attract innovative thinkers if there is benefit to be had. Indeed, economist Timur Kuran of Duke University believes that the multiplicity of organizations—guilds, cities, churches—providing rules in medieval Europe helps explain why European traders in the later Middle Ages began to pull so far ahead of the merchants of the region we now call the Middle East—where the mighty ancient empires of Babylon and Egypt once reigned.[27] Muslim traders were bound to the rules and courts of Islam on all matters, personal and commercial. In contrast, provided their dealings didn't involve Muslims, Christian and Jewish traders living and journeying through the present-day territories of Iraq, Syria, Turkey and so on, were, in contrast, free to choose whatever commercial rules and courts they wanted. Those rules and courts were the subject of widespread jockeying and innovation throughout Europe. Jewish and Christian traders living in Muslim countries paid handsomely for the privilege of using the rules, courts, and other official services of foreigners—creating an economic incentive to provide better rules and systems to support trade. Islamic law, with a captive audience, was not under the same pressure to innovate.

According to Kuran, it was largely because Muslims lacked the menu of legal choices that foreigners and the Christians and Jews living in their midst enjoyed that Muslims lost economic ground, even in their homelands. By the time the nineteenth century had arrived, Christian and Jewish residents and European-owned companies dominated economic activity throughout the Middle East. In 1837 Alexandria had seventy-two merchant houses, of which only two belonged to Muslims. In 1848 Beirut's non-Muslims constituted 55 percent of the population as a whole, but almost 90 percent of importers and exporters. In 1912, non-Muslims constituted only 19 percent of the population of the Ottoman Empire but 85 percent of the major local traders.

In Kuran's analysis, the reason the Middle East struggled to keep up with European economic growth through to the twentieth century was not a result of inherent advantages of European culture or religion. At the start of the second millennium, European Judeo-Christian and Islamic law looked pretty similar from a commercial point of view. All disapproved of the payment of interest as sinful. All lacked any mechanism for separating personal identity from commercial identity. As a result, throughout the civilized world, commercial ventures were small scale, and any partnerships had only a few members who knew each other well. They generally lasted only so long as a particular venture lasted. None outlived their members, and none acquired a legal identity separate from their members.

The trouble for the Middle East was that these features, appropriate to small-scale commerce, persisted in the law of Islam much longer than they did in Europe, where competing law providers—churches, guilds, local rulers, civic associations—got busy changing them to accommodate broad-based, complex, and increasingly impersonal economic activity. European legal providers created the corporation and treated it as a separate legal person. The corporation could own and pledge assets, sue, and be sued in its own name. It survived the death or withdrawal of any of its founding members. These features allowed the corporation to grow in size, with large numbers of shareholders sharing and managing risk. They provided the basis for the growth of large-scale banking and investment. Islamic law, in contrast, did not separate the personal from the commercial until relatively recently. Into the twentieth century, an Islamic partnership did not survive the death or withdrawal of a member. No entities with a legal identity separate from their investors or owners came into existence. The Islamic version of a trust—which allowed a founder to dedicate assets such as a building to a specific purpose such as providing public services or schooling—required the founder to be a flesh-and-blood individual whose instructions had to be strictly followed in perpetuity. It also prohibited joint ventures among established trusts. These features of Islamic law slowed the emergence of large-scale economic ventures and complex organizations, including universities, to meet evolving needs.

Why did Islamic law not adapt sooner, the way European law did to generate better rules for commercial ventures? By tying the application of Islamic law to membership in the Islamic faith and community, early Middle Eastern rulers after Muhammad (himself of a successful sixth- and seventh-century commercial family) ensured that Muslim traders knew how things were to work when they did business with other Muslims, of whom there were plenty in the small-scale economies of the first millennium. That was a good thing. But the centrality of Islamic law to Islamic faith and community also insulated Islamic economic law from competition. And that deprived Muslim merchants of the essential changes in law needed to respond to a changing economy, one that extended beyond the local limits of Islamic communities. Muslim traders, as individuals, could not take their legal business elsewhere without risking a charge of apostasy, punishable by death. Christian and Jewish traders in the Middle East—and merchants throughout Europe—faced no such awful price for gravitating to better legal rules to manage their economic affairs. Competition for these mobile European merchants—between church, guild, ruler, and civic association—put pressure on rules to meet the needs of commercial innovation. Islamic law was not under similar competitive pressure. In Kuran's analysis, the poverty suffered in countries throughout the Middle East, even today, can be attributed in significant part to the impossible choice facing Muslim traders for centuries when Western legal systems were evolving rapidly. It was not until the mid-nineteenth century, by which time the economic gap between the Western and the Muslim worlds was yawning wide, that Muslim leadership saw the need to establish secular commercial courts and individual Muslims were freed to choose alternatives to Islamic law for their business dealings without risking death.

As we will see in the coming chapters, a less dire but nonetheless costly version of what happened to the once-thriving peoples of the Middle East—the cradle of civilization—is now happening throughout the affluent West. After the dust had settled on the Commercial and then the Industrial Revolutions in Europe, the nation-state had secured a lock on the business of developing and then enforcing legal rules. On the one hand, the provision of a unified and democratically controlled legal process has undoubtedly played a role in the enormous growth the West has experienced during the twentieth century. But like any good operating system, legal systems that are insulated from competition eventually grow stagnant and unresponsive, full of bugs and unnecessary protocols. The challenge for the twenty-first century is to figure out how to rejuvenate the process of choosing legal rules so as to meet the demands of a newly globalized and web-enabled world.

3

Law and the Dancing Landscape

WE LIVE IN a world increasingly challenged by complexity. In a study presented at the World Economic Forum in Davos in 2011, global accounting and consulting firm KPMG reported that of fourteen hundred CEOs and other senior executives at the world's largest companies, 70 percent saw increasing complexity as one of their biggest challenges. The accelerating pace of innovation and the exploding demand for information management in our globalizing technological world were critical sources of increasing complexity for many, particularly companies operating in emerging economies such as China and Brazil. But the number one source of complexity identified by executives worldwide? Law.[1]

Increasing complexity is the story of human evolution. Biologist Daniel McShea and philosopher Robert Brandon of Duke University call this biology's first law: the complexity (by which they mean diversity) of organisms will tend to increase over time, even in the absence of any forces such as natural selection, simply as a result of the randomness of variation within and between organisms. Variance increases indefinitely in the absence of limits or external forces. If children are a little different from their parents, and from each other, then grandchildren will be even more different, and great-grandchildren even more so. Simply by virtue of the random wiggles that happen at each stage in the transmission of genetic information.[2]

Increasing complexity is also the story of the evolution of law. I use the term complexity here in the way that complex adaptive systems theorists like Scott E. Page of the Santa Fe Institute and the University of Michigan use it: an environment is complex when it is dynamic and populated by multiple individuals who interact with each other.[3] These individuals pursue goals, follow rules, and make predictions about how others and the environment will behave. Making decisions—solving problems—in an environment that is complex is not just difficult; it requires nimble adaptation to what complex systems theorist Stuart Kauffman first described as a "dancing landscape."[4] A solution that works today may not work tomorrow because your solution today, together with a million other solutions, has unwittingly shifted the environment experienced by others distantly connected to you through a long and largely unpredictable causal chain. In response those others changed what they know, what they believe, and how they act. Networks upon networks of interaction frame the setting in which decisions are made. That's the source of great potential value in the globalizing world, but it's also the source of great complexity.

Law is not just something written on top of a complex world that makes it even harder to navigate. Law is not just another complication, another drag on the economy that we want to strip away. In fact, law is one of our critical institutions for the management of complexity. It undergirds what makes the evolution of value-creating complexity—expanding markets, innovative products, processes and organizations, new ways of doing more with less—possible. Although our current approaches to law are indeed making matters worse, the problem is not that we have too much law. The problem is that the way we have gone about producing law for the last few hundred years—exclusively through state-controlled political institutions such as legislatures, state-run courts, and lawyer-controlled legal professions—is starting to max out on its ability to manage the burgeoning economic and social complexity to which it has played midwife. We are at an inflection point in the evolution of legal systems, facing the need to reinvent how we do law.

In this chapter, I explore how law emerged in response to the very same dynamics of information and adaptation that have made human life progressively more complex. It is a natural consequence of the dynamics of that process that our current legal systems are reaching their limits; the solution they provided has run its course and it is time to adapt, yet again. The recurrent need to reinvent the very systems that support increasing complexity because complexity has pushed past the limits of those systems is a familiar theme in human evolution.

The Problem of Problem-Solving

Every organism is a little problem-solving machine. How to find food? Avoid being food? Reproduce? No organism—plant or animal—can survive as a species if it doesn't figure out solutions to these problems. And a solution is only a solution if it competes reasonably well with the solutions of other organisms. The glum-faced blobfish lives three thousand feet below sea level off the coasts of Australia and Tasmania. A gelatinous mass that lacks any muscle to move, it survives by just drifting a few feet above the ocean floor and eating whatever happens to float or crawl by. This solution to the food problem works for this sorry-looking fish but only because no other species with better food-collection strategies—like swimming or crawling toward food and grabbing it—can manage to survive in the extreme pressure at these ocean depths. Like all species, the blobfish has found its place in the world by securing a niche—a way of exploiting a particular environment that manages the extent of competition from other species. Fruit flies that live in wine cellars, for example, have greater tolerance for alcohol than those that live outside of wine cellars. These alcohol-friendly flies occupy the wine cellar niche, outcompeting their teetotaler relatives in this particular slice of the environment. The teetotalers occupy a different slice, apparently my kitchen.

All plants and almost all animals write their problem-solving strategies down in just one place: DNA. Following the recipe books in their DNA, they grow the physical features that serve them well—long beaks to dig seeds and insects out of the ground, for example, or large haunches to power a swift pounce on unsuspecting prey. DNA can also instruct the organism to behave in helpful ways in response to cues from the environment: Catch a glimpse of that cat-about-to-pounce? Run! Pick up the scent of that attractive member of the opposite sex? Saunter over. And stay away from that plant with the prickly leaves. These highly tailored relationships between the environment and an organism's physical structure and behavioral strategies serve them well, securing them a niche in the world where they can manage to reproduce at a rate somewhat higher than the rate at which their competitors in an adjacent niche are eating them. Which is great when they are in the physical and social neighborhood in which they evolved. Hand, meet glove.

Problem-solving strategies written in DNA, however, are not so great when the environment changes—new predators emerge or a favorite foodstuff is wiped out by disease or a competing species, for example. The poor blobfish is threatened with extinction because we humans have figured out a way to trawl the ocean floor at even these great depths in search of crab and lobster. We have changed our way of living in the environment, and this disrupts the blobfish's ways. The blobfish is defenseless against our trawlers and has nowhere else to go—shallower waters pose too many threats and too much competition for an animal that is basically a glob of jelly. The blobfish is thus suffering the cost of the trade-off for having genes that are highly adapted to a specific environment: genes are very slow to change. It can take generations for a new adaptation to arise. To you and me the rate of genetic change for fruit flies may be short—on the order of months—but to them it's several lifetimes. Humans experience genetic evolution at an even slower pace: human tooth size, for example, has been shrinking at a rate of 1 percent per thousand years since our ancestors ten thousand years ago developed methods of cooking that make large teeth less important for survival. Lactose tolerance—allowing humans to enjoy the nutritional benefits of nonhuman milk—has evolved over some seven or eight thousand years. Sickle-cell anemia—which provides a defense against malaria, albeit at the cost of inducing other painful and life-threatening disorders—has evolved over the last three to four thousand years. That's not nothing, but it's not fast.

How have human beings managed to speed up the rate of adaptation and broken the bounds of the narrowness of environment-specific survival? Why haven't we had to limit ourselves to small bits of the world like most of our animal relatives? The secret is in our breakthrough in problem-solving, and in particular, the fact that our problem-solving strategies are only partly written on our DNA. Instead of developing a fine digging tool around our mouths like the California thrasher bird did to dig for the seeds and insects underneath chaparral, we grew brains with the capacity to design and build digging tools. Then we supercharged that advantage by adding to it the capacity to transmit the designs from person to person and generation to generation via a more flexible medium than DNA: cognition and culture. That's a much better solution when the environment changes and digging for seeds and nuts is not our best food strategy. Or a wine cellar comes along. Then we can use our brain capacity to design and build tools adapted to the new environment: corkscrews, for example.

Evolutionary psychologists John Tooby and Irven deVore have dubbed humanity's place in the world the "cognitive niche."[5] Evolutionary anthropologists Robert Boyd, Peter Richerson, and Joseph Henrich have called ours the "cultural niche."[6] Whatever you call it, it is a very fine niche indeed, securing for us as it does practically the entire planet—heck, we can even compete with species living under three thousand feet of water at pressures that would flatten us like pancakes if we actually had to go there. The cognitive-cultural niche is a whole suite of strategies that allow our species to compete effectively against all comers and to do so in changing and novel environments, thus making practically the entire planet our home.

One of these strategies is the capacity for cause-and-effect thinking, which allows each of us to take what we observe happening in the world and develop mental models that make those observations useful in new situations.

Consider this experiment, conducted by David Buchanan and Professor David Sobel in Sobel's Causality and Mind Lab at Brown University. (Buchanan, then a PhD student, now works on the team that created the *Jeopardy!*-playing Watson at IBM.) Show a four-year-old a board on which you have put two small lights and a big one. One of the small lights should have a big black wire coming out of it, the other a big green one. The small lights light up when you press them. The big light lights up if you connect it with a wire to a small light. Start out by connecting the small light with a black wire to the big light and leaving the one with the green wire obviously disconnected. Now let the four-year-old press on the small lights and watch. What does she see? Pressing the small black-wired light lights up the big one. Pressing the small green-wired one does not. Now switch the wires while your wee experimental subject watches—connect the green wire to the big light and disconnect the black wire. Then ask the four-year-old to make some predictions: Which of these small lights should I press to turn on the big light? If I press on the "green" light, will the big light come on? What about if I press on the "black" light? Most four-year-olds get these predictions right. Three-year-olds, however, don't get it. They don't see any significance to where the wires coming out of the small lights go. They expect history to repeat itself: if the black-wired light lit up the big light before, it should do so again. That's what makes the four-year-old less like a rat than a three-year-old: the four-year-old has reaped the benefits of a more abstract form of causal reasoning. Score one for the cognitive niche. With a valid mental model of cause and effect, even a child can adapt to a change in the environment as quickly as you can make it.[7]

Causal reasoning is pretty powerful, all by itself. But it is even more powerful when packaged with another uniquely human strategy: language. Language allows us to share what we've learned about cause and effect. If you ask the four-year-olds in your experiment why the big light will come on when they press the small light, they can easily tell you: because it's connected, dummy. Well, that means that if another child interested in knowing which light to press comes along, the experienced child can tell him. No need to go through the experimental phase: the first kid already did that and with language the knowledge of cause and effect learned in that phase can be shared with others. Go straight to using the knowledge: making big lights come on in an environment that is not the same as it was when kid one was playing scientist.[8]

Language and abstract thinking also give humans the capacity for another critical mechanism for success: culture. We don't only use our causal thinking to try to solve a problem and sit down with our friends to talk about solutions. We also live in groups that take solutions and turn them into shared practices. Early humans didn't just wait for someone to explain how to do a better job of avoiding deadly plants or carving a useful tool; they didn't just rely on their own efforts at trial and error. They also watched and copied what others were doing—which gives rise to the cultural phenomenon: this is how "we" do things around here.

The social learning that is embedded in culture plays a key role in the human ability to adapt to widely varying and difficult environments—to truly exploit our capacities for abstract thought and language. Anthropologists Boyd, Richerson, and Henrich coined the term "cultural niche" to emphasize the inadequacy of cognitive skills alone to account for human adaptation. Imagine, they suggest, that you were plunked down in the Arctic and forced to survive as the Inuit have done for thousands of years. Just avoiding death by freezing when it's twenty-five below zero out, using only the clothing you can craft from the animals you have to figure out how to catch, is an extraordinarily difficult feat. It's unlikely you could do it even if you had massive cognitive ability. Survival for you, as for the Inuit, would depend critically on finding yourself lucky enough to have landed in a community with well-established practices for how to do all of these things. And when the price of making a mistake is death, even the ability to ask questions and understand explanations for how and why things are done is probably not enough to get by. You are likely to make mistakes with your cognition and your understanding of what you have seen and been told. You may have missed the subtle point that solution A works in situation A and not situation B, for example. Instead you will be well served by following a simple rule: follow the practices that this community treats as norms—at least unless and until you can reason your way to a very good reason to do otherwise. Unless you're good at such reasoning, don't question why people in this community use four different types of foot covering, alternating whether there is fur facing in or fur facing out on a layer, before putting on a boot: just do it.

If you are lucky, the community you land in will have gone beyond embedding lots of information about how to survive in a difficult environment in its cultural practices, there for you to follow or not as you choose. If you are lucky, they will also have *moralized* the strategy of conforming to their practices: they will punish you—with criticism, ridicule, and maybe even ostracism—if you don't. Like the Labrador Inuit girl who, according to legal anthropologist E. Adamson Hoebel, "was banished in the dead of winter because she persisted in eating caribou meat and seal together."[9]

Why is punishing nonconformity to cultural rules good for you? Because it reduces the likelihood you'll make mistakes, ignoring the practices and trying to figure it out for yourself. Certainly some embedded cultural practices may have little direct functional value for the individual. The taboo against eating seal and caribou meat together, for example, was critical in the Labrador cosmology—according to their beliefs, the animals would be angered by this failure to honor the separation of land and sea and so would shun the community, threatening starvation for many—but there was no obvious material (that is, nonsocial) risk to a hungry individual in combining these foods. But the strategy of following all of the culturally required rules is, in many settings, a better bet than relying exclusively on your brainpower. For all I—a person who has never tried to survive in the Labrador winter—know, avoiding eating seal and caribou meat together has some scientific basis. Perhaps there is a risk of contamination or illness. And that's the point: it's too hard for one individual to reason to all the information alone, even with substantial cognitive power. Hence the value of a community that makes it easy by punishing you for nonconformity. There's a good argument that these are the cultures that survive; those that require you to do too many useless or counterproductive things die out, as do those that lack a normative landscape in which what you do is entirely up to you and nobody cares if you follow the rules or not.

Abstract causal reasoning, the capacity to share reasoning with language, and the supporting structure of culture generate a quantum leap in the ability to adapt to changing and novel environments. This allows a quantum leap in the complexity of human life relative to other animals. These capacities allowed humans to migrate out of our environment of origin in Africa, eventually traversing practically the whole world in search of resources and reduced or improved competition with others for those resources. Variation in the environment both challenged the problem-solving abilities of human groups and nourished the process of progressive learning and problem-solving with myriad fresh materials. It also made sure that lots of different types of humans, with different problem-solving strategies, continued to survive and compete. Solutions were built on solutions, shared with others who saw different things, faced different challenges, and made different connections. As Scott E. Page puts it in his 2011 book *Diversity and Complexity*, diversity begets diversity.

Writing these solutions to concepts rather than genes also gave rise to critical new dynamics in the interaction of individuals because conceptual knowledge—information—is subject to two well-known features. First, unlike ordinary resources, information is, as economists say, nonrival in consumption: my use of an idea doesn't reduce the amount of the idea available for you to use. (Unlike, for example, an apple: once I've eaten it, you're out of luck.) Information can be expensive to produce for the first time and it may take effort to transmit it, but the marginal cost of increasing the number of people who use it is zero. And the more who use it, the more it is worth investing in producing it in the first place. "Information wants to be free," as the technology slogan goes. Or, as University of Toronto economist Joshua Gans usefully tweaks the phrase, information wants to be shared.[10]

Information is not only basically free once it's been produced, it is cumulative. That's well-known feature of information number two: it displays what economists call increasing returns. The more information you start with, the more valuable each new bit of information is—because you have more knowledge about how to deploy that new information to do useful things like prepare food or design houses or build computers. The information-rich get richer when you give them more information. But this is a good thing and it accounts for a characteristic of human organization that lies at the heart of our phenomenal success relative to other species, and the reason for the deep relationship between human complexity and law: specialization and the division of labor.

Specialization and Exchange: Problem-Solving Strategies of the Cognitive-Cultural Niche

Human beings face a powerful incentive to diversify and specialize precisely because abstract, cognitively stored, information—unlike genetic information—is cumulative and displays increasing returns. Demonstration of a new surgical technique to an experienced surgeon is of much greater value than demonstration of it to a surgical intern. The surgeon knows how best to deploy the technique to solve particular types of medical problems. But the intern is working with a smaller stock of knowledge about the types of things that can happen during surgery and what works when and what doesn't. This is why the intern is an intern: someone who is going to dedicate several years to specializing in surgical techniques, accumulating thousands of hours in the operating room and learning from those experienced surgeons. There is more value in a system like that than one in which all medical personnel do everything. All of us would rather have our problem solved by a specialist (so long as he or she is actually solving problems and not just implementing long-held routines) than by a jack of all trades.

This was Adam Smith's core insight in his 1776 masterpiece *The Wealth of Nations*: what distinguishes human from other animal societies is the phenomenon of specialization and the gains specialization brings. This is why the division of labor is so valuable. In his famous example of pinmaking, Smith waxes fine about how dividing the task of producing the humble steel pin into some eighteen tasks—drawing out the wire, straightening it, cutting it, sharpening one end to a point, grinding the other end to a head, and so on—allows a small factory of ten people, each of whom specializes in a few of the tasks, to produce more than forty-eight thousand pins a day. If each worked alone at pinmaking, having to execute each task separately and without the benefit of lessons learned from prior experts in each task, he speculates, "They certainly could not each of them have made twenty, perhaps not one pin in a day." Not only would they fumble as they sought to master the fine motor skills of each task, they would lack the deep knowledge of each task that a specialist accumulates. More to the point, so to speak, if they lived in a world where no one had ever specialized in these tasks, they would be faced with completing them without the benefit of proper machinery, which was the great leap in productivity that really impressed Adam Smith. "The invention of all those machines by which labor is so much facilitated and abridged," is itself, he conjectures, a result of the division of labor. "Men are much more likely to discover," Smith tells us, "easier and readier methods of attaining any object, when the whole attention of their minds is directed toward that single object, than when it is dissipated among a great variety of things." Although Smith did not speak the modern language of the economics of information, this is what he meant: specialization captures the benefits of increasing returns to information.[11]

The specialization that a division of labor makes possible only makes economic sense for an individual specialist, however, if that individual can coordinate his activities and engage in reciprocal and cooperative exchange with others. A lifetime spent straightening the wire for pins doesn't put bread on the table if the pin-straightener cannot pool his efforts with the ones who fashion the steel, create the point, package the pins, deliver them to market, and sell them. Specializing in pin-straightening is a really bad idea if you don't live in a world of exchange. This insight was the source of another of Smith's famous aphorisms: "The division of labor is limited by the extent of the market." This is why progress in transportation and communications have such enormous impact on economic development: the greater the reach of the market, the more refined the division of labor can be and thus the greater the returns to specialization that can be reaped. Although even a small village can support the specialization involved in having at least one of their number dedicating his or her efforts to medical care, a healthcare provider in a place with few connections to the outside world had better be a medical handyman, able to fix broken bones, deliver babies, and treat common infections. The doctor in a large metropolitan area, in contrast, who can treat patients who come from hundreds if not thousands of miles away, can afford to specialize in the treatment of an esoteric disease that afflicts only a tiny minority of the population. The more extensive our markets and systems of exchange, the more we all can benefit from increasing specialization and the cumulative returns to abstract causal reasoning.

The elaboration of the cognitive niche to a cultural niche and beyond is thus intimately connected to the development of human systems of exchange. Without exchange relationships, we cannot support specialization. And without specialization we cannot exploit the powerful increasing returns to abstract problem-solving that the human shift from genetic solutions to cognitive ones promises. Think back to Buchanan and Sobel's experiment with four-year-olds in the Causality and Mind Lab at Brown University. Now imagine that one four-year-old spends her morning learning that pressing on a small light connected to a big light turns on the big light, while her friend spends his morning in an experiment Sobel conducted with Alison Gopnik of the University of California, Berkeley, one that requires the child to figure out which of four wooden blocks is activating a machine (rather adorably called a "blicket detector") that plays *Für Elise*.[12] They can then enjoy the following deal: I'll handle the lights if you'll take care of the music. Both can enjoy lights and music with their peanut butter and jam sandwiches if they enter into this deal. Without exchange, they can have one or the other but not both.

Sustaining Exchange: Collective Enforcement of Social Norms

The deep puzzle of the human success story, then, is this: what sustains our systems of exchange? Adam Smith thought human beings had a natural propensity to "truck, barter and exchange one thing for another."[13] But whether the idea of trade is somehow naturally appealing to us is rather beside the point. Because even if we are inclined to enter into exchange relationships, we will not do so for long unless the central problem of exchange is solved in some reasonable way. We have to have sufficient confidence that our participation in exchange will not be a one-way street.

Smith envisioned the evolution of specialization and trade in simple human societies like this:

> In a tribe of hunters or shepherds a particular person makes bows and arrows, for example, with more readiness and dexterity than any other. He frequently exchanges them for cattle or for venison with his companions; and he finds at last that he can in this manner get more cattle and venison than if he himself went to the field to catch them. From a regard to his own interest, therefore, the making of bows and arrows grows to be his chief business, and he becomes a sort of armorer.[14]

For this story to ring true, the bow-and-arrow maker needs confidence that the exchanges he anticipates between himself and those who now specialize in hunting game will be forthcoming. He needs some assurance when he hands over bows and arrows to the hunters as they head out that they will reciprocate when they return with meat—which, given the uncertainties of the hunt, may not be for several days or longer. Both armorer and hunter would like to avoid the tensions and perhaps even physical risks generated by disagreements about just how much meat the armorer is entitled to and whether it depends on which arrow brought down the game or how well the bow was made, how true the arrow's course.

The armorer and the hunters need a system of rules—guidelines that reliably predict behavior about exchange. Smith projected an eighteenth-century system of "truck and barter" onto these simple societies, presuming that the bows and arrows the armorer produced were his private property and that exchange took place in the form of a contract: "I'll give you this many arrows if you'll promise to give me this much meat." But this is probably not how the earliest exchange systems worked. It is more likely that the exchange between the armorer and the hunters was grounded in social norms that said that every member of the community is entitled to a share of the meat brought back to camp—perhaps equal, perhaps differentiated by social status or particular contributions to the hunt—and that those who are lazy and unproductive, perhaps those who do not make the most of their special talents, are to be criticized and maybe even shunned or excluded from sharing. So the armorer can feel secure in his specialization: he will still be able to eat.

Even families of genetically related individuals—the most basic of human societies—are governed by deeply engrained cultural practices of exchange, with patterns of sharing and reciprocation that go beyond what can be explained by the impulses of the selfish gene. This is another sense in which humans occupy a cultural, not merely cognitive, niche. As Robert Boyd, working with anthropologist Sarah Mathew at Arizona State University and evolutionary game theorist Matthijs Van Veelen at the University of Amsterdam, has emphasized, cooperation in small-scale kinship groups has great payoffs in an evolutionary sense for many organisms, but only in human families do we see substantial cooperation and exchange.[15] If a baboon sees her sister fall from a tree and suffer an immobilizing injury, the baboon does not bring her injured sibling—who shares half of her DNA—food while she recovers. In humans, in contrast, caring for sick family members, and even for unrelated members of a group, is practically universal.

Boyd and his colleagues argue that even in small-scale kinship groups like human families, the cooperation and exchange that supports high payoff practices such as long-lived pair-bonding and long-term parental care for children depends on the enforcement of cultural norms by third parties. If caring for family members—a critical part of human success—were a problem-solving strategy encoded in our genes, we'd expect to see it routinely in other animals as well. But we don't. Boyd and his colleagues argue that it is the capacity for human groups to coordinate third-party punishment of those who violate norms that accounts for the distinctive features of even the smallest human groups such as the family. In a society with norms such as "A good uncle supports his nephews and nieces," "There's nothing wrong with a father who is absent after children are born," and "Good mothers live with their families of origin," the father who does not participate in child care suffers no punishment, but the uncle or mother who does the same is liable to criticism, ostracism, discipline, or worse—punishments carried out not by a centralized authority but by other members of the group. We know all about this, of course: Many mothers in the modern world worry about what others will think of them when they work long hours at the office. Uncles in our world are thought no less of if they never see their nieces and nephews, while we struggle with the social and legal consequences for "deadbeat dads" who disappear from their children's lives.

The basic structures of exchange in all human societies—even the most simple family group—thus rest on the same kind of fundamental enforcement dynamic we explored in the previous two chapters: the coordinated participation of third parties in efforts to ostracize or punish someone who breaks the rules. Indeed, the collectively enforced California Gold Rush rules we discussed in Chapter 1—staying away from a digging spot held by someone's tools or from a posted claim if it hasn't been left unworked for more than five days—are rules of a system of exchange. They support a miner's specialization in mining for gold in a riverbed, reasonably confident that the effort to find a good deposit, travel to town for needed supplies, and dig out the ore will pay off. Without those rules, the risk that others will descend on a successful find and grab the gold is too great to justify the risk of doing nothing else to feed oneself. Better to stay home and work the farm.

Relying on culture in the form of collectively enforced social norms to support exchange is highly effective. But culture contains the seeds of its own limitation. Precisely because culturally grounded norms of exchange are highly effective, they support ever-finer divisions of labor and ever-increasing specialization—reaping the exponential benefits of the zero marginal cost and increasing returns features of information. The result is true complexity: a dynamic environment populated by increasingly differentiated individuals who are engaged in problem-solving in their separate specialized domains and interacting with others whose behavior they have to predict. One of the primary behaviors these individuals have to predict is the extent to which people are going to comply with the norms. This means they also have to predict the extent to which people will participate in collective efforts to enforce the norms. But as the division of labor and specialization increase, people find themselves in circumstances unanticipated by the long-standing norms written into their culture. They find themselves dealing with people who are less and less like them. Those others spend their days working on problems different from the ones they do, and therefore may not see the world and hold the same beliefs that they do. This undermines common knowledge—and hence undermines the collective enforcement of the exchange-supporting cultural norms that spawned complexity in the first place.

We have already seen a version of this in the story of the California gold mines. Coordination of the social enforcement of the California gold miners' simple norms of exchange depended on common knowledge of the norms. Only then could each miner have thought that it made sense for him, personally, to go out of his way to help out when someone's claim was challenged: common knowledge gave him confidence that others would help out and would not see his own actions as wrongful. With stable expectations that the norms would be enforced, miners could get on with the business of mining.

The success of this system, however, was eventually its undoing. Because those early miners were successful in finding gold, people like Samuel Brannan began running down the streets of San Francisco shouting "Gold! Gold! Gold in the American River!" This caused miners of all different backgrounds and trying out all kinds of new methods of extracting gold to pour into the Sierra Nevada foothills. As a result, it became harder and harder for simple norms of exchange like "We don't dig in a spot where someone else has left his tools" to maintain that all-important characteristic of common knowledge. The miners who were there at the start may have known the norm and known that others who were there from the start knew that others who were there from the start knew, ad infinitum. But what about those new-comers? Not just the easterners from New York and Ohio, but the foreigners from Germany and Holland? What about those who aren't digging in one spot alone like the original miners but who work in groups of four with a newfangled twenty-foot-long contraption they call a "Long Tom"? What sig-nificance do they see in a set of tools apparently abandoned in the midst of a crowded and extensively dug-up riverbed? If they're not going to follow the norm—and help punish someone who doesn't—then why should the origi-nal miners waste effort trying to police on everyone else's behalf? Chances are, everyone started to doubt that anyone was on the same page about what counted as "fair" and what as "foul." The simple cultural norms succeeded in coordinating a stable system for exchange, and that success bred a level of complexity that undermined collective efforts to enforce the norms.

The story of the limits of the capacity of the original Gold Rush norms to stabilize exchange is a more general one. In a complex environment made up of different kinds of people with different backgrounds and beliefs, differ-ent experiences and ways of doing things, common knowledge of the rules—which is essential to coordinate everyone's needed participation in upholding the rules—breaks down. The rules become ambiguous: people think lots of different factors are relevant to deciding what is okay and what is not. And when the rules become ambiguous, the enforcement mechanism that stabi-lizes the exchange platform on which specialization is built begins to falter. Rules that are written down in culture can and do adapt to changing ideas and environments—indeed, we've already recognized that a critical reason that cul-ture outperforms DNA as a place to store behavioral rules is that culture can adapt more quickly than DNA to changing environments. But the California gold miners did not have time to wait around for culture to adapt, much less their genes. And this is where we, like the California gold miners, turn to law.

Law: Solving the Common-Knowledge Problem at the Limits of Culture

At the point at which the complexity of the gold-mining regions pushed past the capacity of organic culture to stabilize exchange, the miners turned to a deliberate method of creating norms: law. Holding a meeting, writing down a simple set of rules, and creating a method for resolving disputes allowed them to restore common knowledge of the rules and a reasonably stable system for third-party enforcement in the face of burgeoning differences among those in the camps. Note that they did not respond to the problem of complexity undermining their simple organic norms by adopting significantly more complex norms. The rules that came out of their meetings were still relatively simple: one man, one claim; claims must be marked; claims must be worked; a jury of five will resolve any disputes. The innovation to which they turned was not more complex rules. It was a system that did a better job of securing common knowledge of the rules in the face of an increasingly complex environment.

This is where we find the deep relationship between specialization, exchange, and complexity on the one hand and the evolution of systems of legal rules on the other. The economic growth generated by simple, stable, and culturally grounded exchange systems—the system that the early armorer and the hunter rely on—facilitates an expanded scope for exchange. The gains to trade between the armorer and the hunter may allow population to grow. As the armorer becomes even more expert at his craft—enjoying the cumulative nature of learning—he develops even more effective designs and methods. He teaches his methods to apprentices, who may specialize in either bows or arrows or even more refined steps in the production of bows and arrows, like Adam Smith's pinmakers. Through this greater specialization they may hit upon improvements, and maybe even truly novel methods for bringing down game. The hunters who now specialize in the hunt and anticipate that it will be more successful likewise can specialize more fully in developing their methods and techniques. More reliable meat production then frees up more of the nonhunters in the community—such as those who used to have to all spend as much time as possible gathering vegetal foods and capturing small prey—to specialize in new tasks, such as improved methods of cooking or treating wounds, or venture off to find better food and water sources.

As the extent of the market—the scope of exchange—grows, so too does a community's ability to reap the benefits of increased specialization. But as people become more specialized and the division of labor more extensive, they also become more different from one another—in their experiences, their needs, and their understandings of particular problems. They engage in new types of exchange and engage in novel activities, things that their ancestors knew nothing about. They migrate into new regions with different climates and vegetation, new challenges and opportunities. This diversity is a fundamental driver of value and growth in human societies. Not only does this differentiation reap the benefits of specialization in particular tasks, as Scott E. Page has shown in his book *The Difference*, but when people differ in how they frame, encode, and work with complex information, as a group they can outperform even the smartest individuals in problem-solving.[16]

But as differences and sources of novelty accumulate, they chip away at the base of embedded cultural norms on which they were built. The norms governing the sharing of meat with the armorer, for example, work well because since time out of mind they have told everyone what is a fair share. But what is fair when the armorer starts to use new materials that require more effort to secure? When the hunt becomes more productive? When the tribe migrates to a new environment with different types of game, where the armorer's bows and arrows don't work so well? Or when the armorer spends his time sitting under a shady tree while his apprentices toil away—which some see as being lazy but he sees as his new role as a coordinator and supervisor of workers?

The community that has written all of its exchange-supporting norms into culture is now in a situation not so different from the gloomy blobfish, which has written all of its strategies into DNA, confronting the invasion of the trawler. Culture can adapt to new information and new challenges at a faster pace than DNA, to be sure, but if survival depends on solving a problem within a few years, it doesn't matter whether your solution is late by a few generations or by several millennia. Your people won't be around to appreciate the difference.

Our capacities for abstract thinking and communication, fortunately, offer human communities a way out of this conundrum that is not available to the blobfish. We don't have to just wait until our norms (much less our genes) happen to adjust to change. Abstract causal reasoning allows us—particularly if we have enjoyed sufficiently stable and extensive systems of exchange to support the dedication of some of us to philosophizing—to confront the problem of how to adapt our norms to new problems and circumstances head-on. Can we see the causal relationship between our taken-for-granted norms about fairness and the escalating conflict and diminishing cooperation our increasingly diverse and changing community is experiencing? Can we invent a better understanding of fairness that resolves some of the conflict and restores cooperation? Can we figure out how to communicate this and shift our community from old ideas about fairness to new ones?

When we begin these deliberate and self-aware efforts to change our norms of exchange, we set off down the path to law. Lon Fuller, whose definition of law we adopted in Chapter 1, saw the emergence of diversity in human groups as the triggering condition for the turn to law—that purposeful "enterprise" of governing with rules. Fuller says he "can imagine a small group—transplanted, say, to some tropical island—living successfully together with only the guidance of certain shared standards of conduct, these standards having been shaped in various indirect and informal ways by experience and education." It is when commonality of views about the proper standards breaks down, he suggests, that the "legal experience might first come to such a society" in the form, perhaps, of a committee established "to draw up an authoritative statement of the accepted standards of conduct."[17]

Fuller's legal-philosophical debating partner in the 1960s, Oxford philosopher H. L. A. Hart—probably the most influential legal philosopher of the past century—also believed that the identifying mark of law is the capacity to provide legal norms with deliberate content to resolve differences about what the norms do and should say. "It is plain," wrote Hart, "that only a small community closely knit by ties of kinship, common sentiment and belief, and placed in a stable environment, could live successfully" on the basis of what he calls "unofficial rules" and we have been calling organic social norms. Put that community under the pressures created by diverse "sentiments and beliefs" and destabilize that environment with exploration, invasion, and invention, and this system, he says, will break down: the rules will be uncertain, they will be unresponsive to the needs of a new environment, and there will be time and resources wasted on "interminable" squabbling about what's a rule and what's a violation.[18] Hence, for Hart, the moment of law is the moment when, in addition to primary rules—which tell us what we are supposed to do—a society develops secondary rules—rules that tell us what counts as a valid primary rule. Rules that say that a primary rule (governing food sharing, for example) must, in order to be valid, be articulated by the elders speaking with one voice or passed by a majority of a democratically elected legislature are secondary rules. A system of secondary rules provides a systematic means of saying—and hence possibly changing—the content of our rules. The moment at which law emerges is the moment at which complexity has broken the limits of cultural adaptation alone. It is a moment akin to when biological complexity pushed past the limits of problem-solving through DNA to problem-solving through abstract thought and culture.

When we begin to write our exchange-supporting norms within a set of institutions and practices that, as a matter of common knowledge, take it as their self-conscious purpose to articulate exchange-supporting norms, we do more than simply shore up a system to stabilize social order and reduce conflict.

We create a deliberate and visible vehicle for change. With the invention of law, humans created for the first time the possibility of policy: of deliberately deploying our causal reasoning to design and adapt the form of our cooperative life. When the Babylonian king Hammurabi erected his seven-foot stone pillars inscribed with rules specifying, for example, that it is the shepherd and not the sheep-owner who owes the farmer when the sheep graze in the farmer's fields without permission, he was self-consciously seeking to provide a reliable and clear framework for the shepherds and farmers and sheep-owners within his domain. The rule may have reflected the custom that had emerged over many years and Hammurabi may only have had the distinction of writing it down and giving it his imprimatur, but it was surely part of an enterprise of seeking to achieve deliberate economic and social goals. Indeed, Hammurabi speaks to his welfare-enhancing aims in the opening inscription on his monument: "[The gods] Anu and Bel called by name me, Hammurabi, the exalted prince . . . to bring about the rule of righteousness in the land . . . to further the well-being of mankind." Hammurabi did this, remember, mostly by telling the populace how much corn the shepherd owed the farmer with the trampled fields and how much a man who stores corn in another man's house owes for the privilege; important but few are the rules tackling the deeper moral question of what one owes for the taking of an eye or a tooth. So was born the possibility of economic and social policy, the deliberate effort to shape human relationships: in response to change, in response to conflict, in response to ever-accumulating knowledge of how the world works.

Of course, the identity of the "ruler" who takes on the role of articulating— and potentially changing—the rules is a crucial part of the story. It probably didn't take rulers like Hammurabi long to realize that the capacity to articulate the rules and so coordinate the third-party enforcement efforts of a wide group of people presented tempting opportunities. Why not choose the rules that serve you and your cronies best?

In a world that depends on the participation of lots of individuals in a collective punishment effort—worlds like medieval Iceland and the gold-mining regions of California in 1849—the coordinators who articulate the law can't go too far in an effort to distort the rules to serve their own interests. My coauthor Barry Weingast of Stanford University and I have looked at this question, and what we see are strong reasons written into the coordinated and voluntary nature of collective punishment for anyone who hopes to be the provider of law to follow a lot of the principles of the rule of law: keeping law clear and stable, making sure it is public and openly responsive to the needs of the wide range of people needed for punishment to be effective, for example.[19]

If not, people will just ignore it: why help out enforcing a system of rules if the social order those rules produce treats you badly? Or if the rules that are announced are secret or so hard to understand or change so frequently that you have no basis for confidence that everyone else will be looking to them to decide when to help out with punishment? The rules the California gold miners came up with didn't just happen to be posted, simple, and changed only through the recognized procedure of a camp meeting. They were like this, we argue, because that was the only way they could effectively coordinate the only punishment mechanism available—the efforts of individual miners to criticize, shun, or gang up on a claim jumper or someone attempting to protect an invalid claim. In our view, this is why the rules included provisions that treated the early miners and the hordes of newcomers alike, for example, even though the early miners were the ones who set up the rules in the first place. The miners to first write down a set of rules for a camp could have written down a set of rules that said, "We were here first, we get it all; anyone who isn't here at this meeting now is a claim jumper and should be thrown off." But they didn't. Why not? Because the early miners depended on the efforts of all those newcomers to help enforce the rules. With so many of them around, they were the ones most likely to be digging next to a claim that came up for dispute and so in the best position to warn off the one violating the rules. And so the miners who were at that first rule-making meeting needed to make sure that newcomers saw the system as one that helped them out too and hence was worth upholding.

Hammurabi had more than the collective efforts of the community to help uphold his rules. He had some soldiers and officials—whom he could send out to punish people who broke his rules. But we suspect his power in this regard was quite limited. Babylon under Hammurabi grew to be the first city of more than two hundred thousand people. Most of the rules in his code are about mundane details such as how much is owed by someone who stores his corn in someone else's home or what the penalty is for a woman who runs a drinking house and who charges more in coin than corn for a drink. It's unlikely Hammurabi was sending out his soldiers every time a dispute like this arose. Soldiers are expensive, and probably best used to conquer new lands or protect the empire from invasion. So Hammurabi too probably depended extensively on the efforts of ordinary people to punish those who ignored his rules—in the same way that the Icelanders and Gold Rush miners depended on the enforcement efforts of the many. And this is why Hammurabi took obvious steps to reassure everyone that the rules he established would be lawlike: stable, open, public, and protective of the interests of a wide range of people. Not necessarily everyone; this wasn't an egalitarian society. Women and slaves fared much less well than free men under the rules. But that's consistent with the idea that women and slaves didn't play as great a role in enforcement and so they didn't need to be convinced that the rules were a good thing. Simply because it was lawlike doesn't mean it was fair or just for everyone. That's the ongoing struggle of even advanced legal systems.

Hammurabi's enduring genius—the reason we talk about him today and see his stone pillars as a representing a watershed in the evolution of law—may have been precisely in his intuitive grasp of the fact that his legal power depended on enforcement by ordinary people. He expressly invited "the oppressed, who have a case at law, [to] come and stand before this my image as king of righteousness; let him read the inscription, and understand my precious words: the inscription will explain his case to him; he will find out what is just." He carved his rules in monumental pieces of stone (not easily erased clay tablets, as his predecessors did) and erected them in multiple places throughout his kingdom, making it easy for everyone to find the rules and hard for anyone to change them. And he announced in those stone carvings that if any subsequent king should dare to "corrupt my words, change my monument," then a long parade of horribles would surely be visited upon him by the gods: drought, famine, death, ignorance, darkness, military defeat, you name it. Hammurabi secured the stability, and common knowledge of stability, of his code by publicly tying his own hands against the temptation to change the rules and scared off the efforts of his successors. It worked: his code survived a thousand years.

By now this should seem a familiar theme, this cycling from stability to complexity to adaptation and back to stability in problem-solving. Hammurabi responded to complexity by turning to a method of establishing rules that had the virtue of allowing him to deliberately choose the rules—and so better adapt them to the burgeoning complexity of Babylonian life and commerce. And then he made sure those rules were durable, unchanging, nonadapting. It is like the earlier stages in the evolution of complexity. The problem-solving strategies for organisms from single-celled plankton to apes are inscribed in a durable medium—DNA—and so remain stable over long periods of time, allowing the organisms that have landed on good solutions to flourish for as long as the environment remains stable. The complexity of the organisms that manage in this way evolves, until we hit the quantum leap of the human invention, inscribing our problem-solving solutions in cognition and stabilizing the systems of cooperation and exchange that supercharge our problem-solving capacities with strategies written into cultural norms—commonly held beliefs about what is right and wrong and collective efforts to sanction those who choose wrong. Securing the benefits of stability in culture, complexity accelerates in human communities through specialization and the division of labor. The flowering of heterogeneity among people and places and things puts pressure on faster-than-DNA-but-still-too-slow-to-adapt cultural practices. Eventually we add law to the mix—faster to adapt but still needing a quantum of stability in order to work its magic, creating a platform for even greater social and economic complexity.

Like DNA and culture before it, law also sows the seeds of its own limits, by generating ever-greater differentiation among us through specialization and the division of labor. Eventually systems that depended wholly on the coordinated efforts of widespread peoples for enforcement gave way to the modern regime: enforcement of law by the centralized and bureaucratized institutions of the nation-state—government-funded and -controlled police, courts, and prisons. These are the institutions we now take for granted as definitive of law itself. They responded well to the demands of the increasingly complex world of industrialization and mass production, where the extent of the market grew to encompass vast and diverse populations living within the territory of a single, hierarchically organized system of domestic law. Only trade between nations fell under law that lacked an overarching capacity for centralized enforcement: treaties and international institutions dependent on the ongoing willingness of their signatories and participants to uphold their rules.

The nation-state that secures what the towering social theorist Max Weber called in 1919 a monopoly over the legitimate use of force—able to bring all the mechanisms of rule-enforcement at work in its domain under the ultimate authority of its highest courts to judge and its police power to constrain—freed itself of the constraint under which Hammurabi operated. Once he had established the compensation the shepherd owed the farmer for trampled fields, Hammurabi had to promise to hold that rule fixed in order to secure the coordination and cooperation of many in its enforcement. Modern state legislatures ultimately emerged with the capacity to adapt the rules as much and as often as they wanted. With the resources and the authority to direct how courts and police will enforce their rules, they were constrained by politics, but not by the need (or so they thought) to induce the cooperation of wide swaths of the population in enforcement. In this way, our current systems achieved an extraordinary degree of flexibility to adapt to a complex environment. They were able to craft ever more detailed rules to manage ever more refined systems of exchange. That we find ourselves today at the brink of a whole new platform for social and economic complexity—the globalized, digitized, web-based world—is testament to how successful those legal solutions of the last few hundred years have been.

But we should not be surprised to realize that the circle is coming back around. Following the inevitable patterns of first biology and then economics, our diversity only continues its relentless march forward—we become more and more different from one another. Globalization brings those differences home; digitization streams them live. What worked well at the levels of complexity with which we started now struggles to keep up. Today, we are trying to manage the demands of vertiginous change with rules drawn up in remote, technocratic, and legalistic ways, far removed from the lives of the ordinary people who must live by them. But the rules that emerge from places like the cooled rooms I am lucky enough to enjoy at annual meetings at the World Economic Forum won't work as legal rules just because they look like the ones we have been calling law for the past century. This is one way of understanding the backlash against globalization and integration that played out in dramatic fashion in the British vote to leave the European Union in 2016 and the shocking success of politicians throughout the rich West promising to build walls to keep out immigrants and undo free trade agreements. A dancing landscape is a beautiful thing if you're a dancer; but it is just a terrifying shaking of the ground beneath your feet if you're not. And people who feel as though the rules don't care about them don't care about the rules. The nation state, with its awesome power to coordinate enforcement within its borders, allowed us to ignore that for a while.

In the next chapters, we'll turn to a take a closer look at the legal infrastructure we take for granted today—the legal solutions that took root in the Commercial Revolution, anchored the Industrial Revolution, and provided the seedbed for the Digital Revolution. These are the solutions that, like all our earlier complexity-managing solutions, have reached the limits of the increased complexity they facilitate and nurture. These are the solutions we, again, need to reinvent. Otherwise we end up at risk of being like the blobfish: hopelessly committed to strategies that worked well in the complex environment in which they were crafted but not the one to which they have delivered us.

PART II

Global Economic Complexity

What's Law Got to Do with It?

4

The Birth of Modern Legal Infrastructure

SO FAR WE have thought mostly about fairly quaint-sounding settings: bow-and-arrow makers trading with hunters, Babylonian residents consulting Hammurabi's code to decide who's in the right in a fight between shepherds and grain growers, Flemish cloth merchants traveling to medieval English fairs to sell their wares, Viking farmers trying to avoid killing one another off as they struggle over who owns the wheat blown into a neighboring field, dusty nineteenth-century miners digging by hand for gold. What relevance does this have for our modern, ultrafast, ultratechnological, ultraeverything global economy? Quite a lot really. Because although the complexity of our economy has skyrocketed, the basic economic role for law—the economic demand for law—has not changed. Only our means of producing and implementing it has changed. And that is where our problems lie today: in the failure to adapt a once-successful system for producing law to the greater complexity that system brought to life.

Try this thought experiment. Imagine you are one of our modern-day superheroes. Instead of a cape or retractable steel claws, you possess X-ray vision, into the future of the web-based global economy. You are an entrepreneur. You have a fantastic idea for a new web-based business. The future is golden. What do you need to make that happen?

You need some partners. You need some programmers. You need some money. You need space, computer equipment, and a high-speed internet connection. You need some more money.

You need some law.

Law? Isn't that the last thing you need? Isn't law likely to be the bane not the boon of your new venture? Isn't law what all those CEOs in global businesses are complaining about?

Nope. Just like the merchants in Europe in the Middle Ages and the gold miners in California, you really do need law. You will want law. You will be looking for law. You will be frustrated by the inadequacies of the law you have available to you. You just may not realize that what you are looking for is law. More precisely you will be looking for good *legal infrastructure*—the term I use to describe all the legal resources that will make a difference to your venture.

Think about those partners. Before you share your idea with them, you will be wondering: do I trust them? Will they steal the idea? Will they work on this project for a few months and then abandon me? Will they do good work? Will they put in their own money? Will we end up in constant fights about money and vision and dedication and go the way of that garage band I put together in high school?

True enough, you won't only be looking to law for reassuring answers to these questions. You will choose your partners in part because you trust them, law or no law, to keep a secret, ante up when necessary, and work hard. You will follow the advice of many a Silicon Valley entrepreneur and appreciate the fact that even if you get people to sign an NDA (nondisclosure agreement), your real protection comes from what in Silicon Valley is called a "frieNDA."[1] (That and a well-timed shrug as you appreciate the inevitable loss of your secrecy-based edge and the fact that your business better be built on more than that.)

But the deeper you get into your venture, the more you will find yourself, knowingly and unknowingly, drawing on legal resources to make your business a success. You'll be negotiating deals with your early investors to give all of you comfort about what share of the business each of you will own, how free you'll be to manage it without interference, and whether you can be ousted if and when you take the company public with an IPO. You'll be counting on rules of contract and employment law you probably don't know exist that allow you to lay off employees if you are overly optimistic about how fast your business will grow, or to stop them from moonlighting for your competitor. You'll be looking to immigration rules to make sure the amazing foreign-born computer science interns you want to hire permanently can get visas. Corporate law will allow you to form a company free of the risk that your partners' personal creditors can come after company assets. Trademark law will step in to make sure that a competitor doesn't confuse your customers by copying your impressive logo and maybe your URL. You'll be counting on the contracts with your landlord and local housing codes to ensure the lights stay on, the heat is working, and security is maintained as advertised at the front door. The rates you pay your internet provider? Regulated by state and local agencies, and by the antitrust and communications law that says your provider and its nearest competitor can't meet in a backroom and jack up your rates or slow down the speed enjoyed by your customers when they visit your server.

There's more: the police will respond when you call and say that your computers have been stolen—which helps make sure they're not stolen in the first place. You will find yourself with a persuasive legal threat if the unholy conditions at the sandwich shop next door make your employees sick or attract an army of nasty vermin that freak out your customers. Prospective employees will flock to your generous profit-sharing, healthcare, and pension plans in part because the law will give them confidence that they aren't part of a bait-and-switch scam you've cooked up. And if you do, sadly, end up in a major dispute with your partners—or your employees or your investors or the government—you will have an established set of rules about how that dispute will be resolved by neutral judges, should you discover that you can't resolve the matter effectively elsewhere.

Of course your venture will not be the center of the legal universe. There will be laws—you probably think first of these in fact—that get in your way and just cost you money. Those laws that allow you to fire your employees when you need to downsize will penalize you if you fire them because they're the wrong gender or ethnicity or just too old. They will put limits on how you manage the profit-sharing plans you put in place to attract the best and the brightest to your shop. The trademark laws that protect your commercial identity will also stop you from oh-so-innocently borrowing from others. You too will be prevented from fouling the neighborhood or blasting heavy metal at three in the morning even if it does help your programmers stay in the zone. You will enjoy that handcrafted tax credit delivered to you by your local politician, but you will also have to make sure you comply with all the other federal, state, and local tax laws that affect your business. The courts that are available to you if the going gets rough with your business partners are also available to them; and to the consumers, suppliers, employees, and competitors who can complain you have violated their rights. And so even for the parts of law that you wish would go away, you are going to want legal advice and expertise to help you navigate your business to profitable waters.

The central observation is this: in the modern advanced economy, law is ubiquitous. You can't turn around in launching or operating your business venture without both reaching for law and trying to reach around it. But much of it will be largely invisible to you; you are likely to operate largely oblivious to the role it is playing or could play. Until you reach for it and it is not there. Or it suddenly appears in your rear-view mirror, causing you to slam on the brakes.

I call that long list of legal resources that you are going to need to get your business venture off the ground *legal infrastructure*. Legal infrastructure includes not only the legal rules you can find in law books but also the quality—and cost—of the legal advice, planning, and solutions you can access. It includes not only the formal processes in regulatory agencies and courts but also the intangibles that affect outcomes: how lawyers and judges behave with one another, what and how they charge, what they believe is the right strategy or decision in a case, the advice they will, in practice, give. Because you don't really care about what it says in the law books. You care about how, in fact, all those aspects of the legal environment will impact your business. Great rules on paper that say investors may not interfere with management, for example, don't mean diddly-squat if you never find out about the rules because there are no lawyers you can afford to ask. Or if all the lawyers you find hold the belief, right or wrong, that the rules are useless. Or if the rules come embedded in legal documents so long and complex that everyone either misreads them or ignores them. I once had the unfortunate experience of being in family court in a dispute about child custody. I could look up all the legal rules I wanted. But what actually happened in family court was what the judges, clerks, mediators, social workers, and local attorneys did and said, whether that was consistent with "the law" or not. That complex mix of stuff is what determined the results in my case, not the rules on paper.

Legal infrastructure is a somewhat ponderous phrase for this amorphous collection of legal materials, organizations, norms, beliefs, and practices, but there are good reasons for using the term. One reason is that it helps to remind people that we are not just talking about formal legal rules and procedures— the language in statutes and court decisions that garner so much political attention. We are not just talking about "the law" or even "the legal system." Yes, formal legal rules and procedures matter. But formal rules are just so many inky squiggles on paper if the mechanisms for connecting people's actual behavior with the rules are missing or ineffective or too expensive. The function of the legal infrastructure we're talking about is to provide a reliable framework for interaction—which mere words on paper can't be without a lot of other features being in place.

I'm leveraging here off the concept of physical infrastructure: the roads and electrical grids and network cables that allow people and businesses in a vibrant economy to connect with relative ease. Think about roads, for example. We take for granted in our developed world that if we set up a meeting across town, we can hop in our car and drive there when the time comes. If there's a river to cross en route, we assume there is a bridge that crosses it. We spend no time figuring out whether there will be somewhere to buy gas or a coffee along the way. We are only likely to start thinking about the taken-for-granted transportation system when something goes wrong: the bridge collapses or the roadway is washed out by a flood.

Infra is Latin for below or under; *infrastructure* is the structure that lies beneath other structures. It is the platform on which we build. In our increasingly connected world, more and more of the resources we use to build our businesses, our organizations, and our relationships come from infrastructure. We don't only drive to meet with one another, we hop on planes and trains and Skype. We connect to the internet and search a million linked computers using IP addresses and search engines. We store our photos and business plans and tax records in the cloud. We assume that our employees and business partners—wherever they are located across the globe—will speak our language and know how to navigate our computer code and web interfaces. We take for granted that we can exchange money and goods and services with almost anyone almost anywhere in the world. We can know what is happening around the country, continent, and globe because millions of reporters, bloggers, tweeters, and friends on Facebook are sharing what they know over a vast interconnected array of wires and cables and allocated bands of radio communication frequencies.

Although we sometimes have to pay to use infrastructure—highway tolls or internet connection fees, for example—infrastructure is characterized by its widespread availability to all. It is a shared platform. You don't personally need to hire architects or engineers to design it for you. You don't need to oversee its construction and maintenance. You just need to plug in. Infrastructure is part of the environment; it was there before you got here.

Because infrastructure is a *shared* platform, it generally contains lots of things we wish worked differently. But to spend much time longing for infrastructure that is all good and no bad is to give in to magical thinking. Infrastructure is available to us as a preexisting platform precisely because it is *not* built to our personal specifications. Instead it is the product of crosscutting efforts by millions of people to satisfy an enormous and diverse array of needs. Parts of it are designed—like the system of root name servers on the internet—but many parts are the product of what all kinds of users created when they plugged stuff in. This means important characteristics of infrastructure are fundamentally emergent. They are not the product of a single omniscient engineer in the sky. Instead they are the on-the-ground, in-the-moment product of the interactions of millions of individuals, acting alone, acting collectively, acting at cross-purposes. The highway department might attempt to engineer traffic flow with exit ramps here and express lanes there, for example, but the thing that matters on the ground—how long it takes to get you to where you are going—is a function of all the different ways in which millions of users respond to the engineering: when they drive, with how many people in what kind of vehicles; where the sports arena gets built and how it is scheduled; how local city councils respond to their constituents' demands for zoning, parking, traffic signals, and one-way streets on the surface routes that feed on and off the highway. A picture of downtown Los Angeles's deserted highways and streets at three in the morning is a beautiful thing. The transportation infrastructure at 8:00 a.m. or 5:00 p.m. (and sometimes at 1:30 in the afternoon on a Saturday) is something else entirely.

Although we rail against the parts of infrastructure that make no sense and that get in our way, there is a reason to celebrate the fact that infrastructure claims to support not only our personal goals but also those of all the people, businesses, and organizations with which we interact. That's because infrastructure that does a better job of serving the needs of a wide set of people is more stable: more people, businesses, and organizations have an investment in seeing the package of services provided by infrastructure as a whole survive and thrive. And: the more people who find infrastructure valuable, the more widely the costs of infrastructure can be shared.

It is for all these reasons that I call the long list of legal stuff you rely on to launch your new venture *legal infrastructure*. Like the roadways, the airports, and the internet: it's all around you, you're plugging in all the time, you barely notice you're using it, but if it went away, you would find that the shared platform on which you were building your business had collapsed. It is partly designed but it is also an emergent structure produced by all the ways in which people react to it—the interpretations they give to the language of statutes and codes, the court decisions they generate by the way they pursue or defend or neglect their interests, the way they train their law students and what they tell their lawyers, the ways they fund their courthouses and government legal departments. It is a form of social capital on which your business depends. You want good legal infrastructure, just like you want well-maintained and well-managed highways, a well-educated workforce, and reliable wireless connectivity. But you could no more wish for legal infrastructure that did what you wanted it to do and nothing more than you could wish for a private highway that went only where you wanted it to go or a private internet that allowed you to access all the content you wanted at superfast speeds by keeping everyone else out.

Most people find the idea of ubiquitous law as a good thing hard to swallow. But it is critical, if we are to rethink how we do law in our new digital global economy, for us to get past any simplistic idea that the problems we face with law are ones that would be solved by just having less of it. Think about it. What's the alternative to ubiquitous law? It is not the absence of rules about how those millions of interactions you will have in running a new business will be managed. No, the alternative to law is just a different set of rules. No stable society based on interdependence gets away without a web of ubiquitous rules that govern what each of us can do, how, and when. Even the simple hunter-gatherer societies studied by anthropologist Polly Wiessner, which we read about in Chapter 2, display a thick web of rules: what can be said, worn, or eaten; with whom; when; and using what methods or tools or rituals. When Robert Boyd describes the cultural niche, as we emphasized in the last chapter, he is describing a world that is densely normative: everyone has an opinion about just about everything anyone does in just about every society. All those societies today that we think of as lacking in rule of law are a minefield of rules about what people can and cannot do. Even the problem of corruption, which so preoccupies those trying to build rule of law in poor and developing countries and which I discuss later in this book, is far from a simple pay-as-you-go system. There are lots of hidden rules about who can pay, who to pay, when, how and what to pay. There are strong norms and expectations about taking bribes—one study of bribe practices in Kenya, for example, found that families that had sacrificed to get their smartest child into a government position often did not take kindly to that child deciding to take some Western moral high road and turn down the money proffered by those who require government services.

Take away law from the world of your imaginary web-based venture and it's not as if there won't be opinions—lots of opinions—about whether it is okay for you to fire your employees or use a logo similar to your competitor's; for your partners to back out on their promises of financial contribution or to meddle in your control of the marketing side of the business; for the building manager to fail to keep trash out of the hallways or to demand additional payments to turn on the air conditioning; or for the property owner next door to dump chemicals into the groundwater or air. A world without law is not a world without rules. It is instead an even more complex environment in which people have lots of different ideas about what the rules should be, they act on their personal views of what's right and wrong, and there's a lot of unpredictability about how the whole process works.

Law emerges precisely at the point at which societies become complex enough to benefit from some authoritative coordination on what the rules are. In the modern world, law is ubiquitous because there are so many points of contact and potential conflict points between us. Take the law away from those points and you don't have freedom; you have the chaos of conflicting ideas about what is and is not an acceptable exercise of your freedom.

Maybe you don't believe me. Maybe you're still inclined to think that heaven is a place where legal never happens. If so, try another thought experiment. Imagine what it would be like to get your business venture off the ground in a world where your employees and other companies have no reliable identification or official addresses: you can't find out anything about potential employees or suppliers because you have no idea if any previous employers or customers they might have had are real or fictitious; you can't locate them. There are no reliable credit-rating agencies. There are no courts—at least no courts nearby or ones that are not easily bribed by those richer or better connected than you. So you have nowhere to turn if your customers fail to pay up or your suppliers say they won't deliver the goods you need unless you pay them twice their quoted price, in cash. Nobody answers the 911 call when your computers are stolen. You have no recourse when your investors show up one day and lock you out of the business. You can't find an internet provider because your competitors have entered into exclusive deals with all of them. Some government goon shows up and insists that you owe several thousands in back taxes you know you paid. Another one shuts you down because (he says) you didn't complete the forty-three-step process required to register a business with the state authorities. And there's no point trying to attract better programmers with promises of healthcare plans and profit-sharing deals because they're all smart enough to know they are not worth the paper they're written on.

You have just imagined yourself opening this new business in many parts of the developing world today. These are places with lousy legal infrastructure. You do not want to open a business there.

The Economic Demand for Law: Law as Economic Input

Our economic ancestors in the Western world found themselves in just these circumstances—trying to run a business venture in an environment with lousy legal infrastructure—about a thousand years ago. They were emerging from the collapse of the Roman Empire and beginning to imagine the possibilities of trading French wine for English wool, Arabian leather, Indian spices, and Chinese silk. The traders of the Middle Ages didn't have the luxury of taking legal infrastructure for granted, of just plugging in and taking off. They had to find or invent the legal resources they needed to make trade worthwhile. The Flemish merchants who traveled to the English fairs to buy wool and sell cloth needed a legal environment that protected them from theft and attack; they needed a set of rules governing payment for their wares; they needed mechanisms to ensure that those rules were reasonably effective. They had an *economic* demand for law. The story of the Commercial Revolution of the Middle Ages is in significant part a story about how that economic demand was met.

Thinking about law as something that is produced in response to economic demand is likely to be a little startling. After all, when most of us think about law, we think about the extraordinary accomplishments of the modern moral and political order. We think about constitutions and the fight for equality, liberty, and the pursuit of happiness. Our enlightened world is one in which law steps in to right wrongs and protect the vulnerable. The lawyers we see on TV get up in front of juries on a regular basis, making impassioned pleas about what is fair and just—convicting the guilty, acquitting the innocent. Our leading newspapers report regularly on the weighty constitutional issues of the day, issues that pit strong alternative visions of freedom and fairness against one another.

Law has come to do all of these things, and the pride many lawyers feel in being a part of the justice system is well placed. But as important as those values of right and justice are in the modern world, law is not only, or maybe even fundamentally, based on them. A large part of what has driven the development of the legal structures we take for granted is the economic demand for law. Even the basic interest in fairness in law is in significant measure an economic demand. We want to be fairly treated by the people with whom we share our time, ideas, energy, space, and resources not just because we like the idea of fairness but because if we aren't fairly treated we take our marbles and go home: everyone is worse off.

Once you've thought about what you yourself might take for granted in starting up your own business, the economic demand for law is not that complicated to understand. Economic activity is fundamentally cooperative activity: it rests on the willingness of each of us to put our time, money, or other assets at risk in order to produce value. The risk comes from our dependence on how others will behave: partners, investors, employees, customers, suppliers, neighbors, governments. People who are thinking about participating in cooperative economic activity have a demand for law because they get value from a reliable framework that governs how they and others conduct themselves. A reliable framework allows us to predict what will happen if we invest our time and money in a venture. Economic actors are willing to pay for such a framework.

We can break this economic demand for law into smaller component chunks. A key component is a demand for rules governing the *sharing* of the rewards generated by a cooperative venture. When you decide to quit your job to work on building your new entrepreneurial venture with your friends, you will be looking for a reasonably reliable prediction of how much of any profits the venture earns will be yours. You will want to assert ownership rights over ideas and assets and your time. Those rights help you ensure that you can bargain for payment if your ideas, assets, and time are useful: unless you are compensated, you can take what's yours and walk away.

You are also likely to want a reasonably reliable prediction about how much conflict you will run into when you undertake what you think are your tasks in the venture. Suppose you are the marketing brains of the partnership: how much grief will you suffer in trying to implement your vision of the best marketing strategy when your nonmarketing partners see things differently? If your programming skills are decidedly weak, how sure are you that your software engineering partner will assume responsibility for producing the code you need? You'll want to know what you're allowed to do with the assets you purchase or generate for the business. Are the tools you built exclusively yours? How about the ideas? Your evaluation of the potential for time and money to be burnt up in conflict and bad decisions will depend on rules determining who gets to decide what and your ability to *control* the resources of the venture to implement your decisions.

A third key component of the economic demand for law is the demand for rules that secure *commitment* so that a person who has to make his or her contribution first can be reasonably sure that a second mover will come through as expected. This is the core of basic contract law, the subject I've been teaching to first-year law students for the past twenty-five-plus years.

The structure of the quid pro quo is at the heart of just about any venture. I will deliver today the goods or perform the services you're asking for if you will promise to pay me in full next week; I won't bother you for payment for a full year if you promise to pay me with interest. I will invest in your company if you will agree to let me bring in a new chief financial officer. I'll tell you my ideas if you promise not to tell anyone else or to start your own business using my ideas. I will agree not to challenge your use of my technology if you agree not to challenge my use of yours.

We also have an economic demand for rules determining the *allocation of risk*. Who bears the loss if the warehouse where our goods are stored catches fire? A key employee quits? The government issues regulations requiring costly new investments? Our competitors bring out an awesome new product? Rules about who bears which risks allow us to plan and make decisions about minimizing risks and obtaining insurance. They also lower the likelihood and cost of the arguments that tend to trail in the wake of bad events.

Not all of the components of the economic demand for law concern the property and contract arrangements you can secure with the people and entities with whom you are engaged in your venture. Both you and the outside world will see a need for rules governing the relationship between your venture and third parties, including strangers you've never met and may hope never to meet. In the language of economics, these interactions often involve *externalities*: effects that our activities have on others who have no part in our venture and vice versa. A reliable environment is one in which we have reasonable confidence about the types of costs others can inflict on us, and on the limits they can impose on our impact on them. These are the rules that govern things like pollution or noise or security or access to shared resources like water or information. The ability to be confident that third parties will not interfere with your venture—by taking your tools or ideas, for example, or barging into your decision-making—is another aspect of the environment that you will be interested in. And, conversely, you will be interested in your ability to use the tools and ideas of third parties and to have a say when their decisions affect your business.

Last, there is an economic demand for procedures for figuring out what to do when any of these other rules are broken, or someone thinks they have been. That's a demand for people, processes, and tools for deciding what the rules mean, what the facts are, and what one person owes another, if anything, when they are broken. Rules for *resolving disputes* about rules help to secure the value of rules in the first place: avoiding the costs of what happens when people turn to self-help to get what they think they are owed.

The Vikings of medieval Iceland and the miners in the California Gold Rush understood this well. They didn't only write rules about when retaliation or claim jumping was authorized; they also said who would decide any arguments about the rules—a lawspeaker, an ad hoc jury, the learned man from the East. Rules like that made the rest of the rules worth the effort—and spared a lot of bloodshed.

Responding to the Economic Demand for Law: The Evolution of the Nation-State

The antagonistic relationship that many businesspeople today experience with law together with the invisibility of much of our legal infrastructure obscures the economic demand for law. Law is not just something we want less of; it is something we also want more of.

This was easier to see back in the Middle Ages when merchants across the civilized world were sparking the Commercial Revolution. With almost no legal infrastructure to speak of, traders could hardly take it for granted. Just as they could not take for granted that there would be a safe road between Byzantium and Flanders or a reliable means of keeping records. And so, just as they were willing to pay for a safe road or an expert record-keeper, they were also willing to pay for legal infrastructure. Their economic demand for legal infrastructure generated an incentive for enterprising types to supply the need.

As we saw in Chapter 2, a wide variety of institutions rose to meet the challenge of supplying rules and systems for deciding disputes between buyers and sellers, merchants and agents in medieval Europe. Merchants organized themselves into guilds and used the guild to establish the rules they needed. Towns and cities also got into the law-supplying game—offering an attractive set of rules and procedures to merchants who could choose where to conduct business. Feudal lords and church abbots put on fairs to attract merchants from across the known world and knew that an attractive regime for protecting the property and enforcing the contracts of merchants was an important competitive tool. European cities such as Venice sent consuls to establish legal rules and procedures to adjudicate disputes involving Italian merchants living or traveling in the far-off lands of the Byzantine and Ottoman empires. They attracted as well the business of local Christian and Jewish traders in the Muslim world. English courts began a practice in the thirteenth century of ensuring that the cases involving foreigners were heard by juries that were half foreigners—an important advantage over Ottoman courts that allowed only Muslims to serve as jurists, even in disputes that involved Christian or Jewish traders. English kings like Edward I were particularly active in trying to create an attractive legal environment for merchants.

It is somewhat difficult to imagine this robust competition between kings, nobles, guilds, church leaders, and town officials to supply the legal infrastructure needed to support the explosion of trade in the Middle Ages. No doubt the struggle was not only to produce the best legal product at the best price—powerful interests saw other benefits in imposing their own rules regardless of their economic attractiveness to traders. Edward I, after all, was in the end interested in collecting taxes to fund the royal coffers. And not everyone who needed legal rules was free to simply choose from the buffet. If you wanted to be a Flemish cloth merchant, you had to follow the guild on this. If you lived within the city walls of Florence, you could be hard pressed to avoid its civil courts—unless you were a member of a guild with its own statutes, courts, and draconian penalties for members who brought cases to the municipal rather than guild court. But in the broader sense, all of these different entities were competing either for legal customers or, in the more systemic sense of competition, for success vis-à-vis other entities—other courts in the same town; merchants from other cities; rulers and abbots seeking to establish fairs in other parts of the realm; cities from elsewhere in Europe. Guilds and towns struggled, sometimes paid, for an agreement that another potential rule-provider—local municipal authorities, foreign rulers—would not interfere with their efforts to use their own rules and courts

The key point is that the lively diversity of players lining up to meet a robust and mobile economic demand for law at the birth of the Commercial Revolution in medieval Europe serves as an illuminated backdrop for how we understand the legal world that greets the Digital Revolution.

It is important to remember that throughout the duration of the Commercial Revolution the world was not carved up into geographically bounded countries in the way we now think of them. The territorial nation-state with exclusive and comprehensive legal authority throughout a geographically defined region is a relatively recent phenomenon. It emerged in Europe only toward the end of the seventeenth century and extended across the globe only with the withering of colonial empires through the late nineteenth century and the first half of the twentieth century. Instead, during the time that the regions of Europe and the Muslim Mediterranean were emerging from the long period of political chaos that followed the collapse of the Western Roman Empire in the fifth century, the capacity to govern a people was hotly contested and constantly shifting. It fluctuated not only with the outcome of military campaigns but also with the shifting allegiances and voluntary cooperation of a dispersed group of landowners, merchants, religious leaders, military men, and ordinary folk. It did not necessarily track geographical boundaries on a map. The residents of a conquered land might only experience governance from a distant emperor in the sporadic collection of taxes, their daily life still governed in much the local ways it was before conquest. Authority might reside in the spiritual dimension, following not the contours on the map but those of faith—the pope could command the obedience of the Catholic faithful wherever they might be found throughout Christendom. Authority might be an attribute of culture and community, traveling as an unseen companion alongside the itinerant Jewish merchant. A citizen of an Italian commune might submit to his city's governing officials and principles even when resident in foreign lands. And, as we have seen, the members of a merchant guild might choose to follow one set of rules to govern their commercial life and another to govern their family, civic, and religious obligations. In many cases (although not all—territory still mattered), the rules in play were a function of membership—which groups you belonged to—not, as they are today, location—where a transaction takes place. To know what law someone followed in any setting, one needed to know a great deal: what faith, what allegiance, what city of origin, what recent upheavals in the balance of power between distant kings, nobles, and ecclesiastic officials, what the current mood of local landlords, barons, and burgesses.

That's a lot to keep track of. And it puts especially great pressure on a key ingredient of legal order: the achievement of common knowledge of the rules. As we saw in Chapters 1 and 2, in a world without a centralized and overwhelming police force—a world like medieval Iceland or the California Gold Rush territory—enforcement of a set of rules requires that everyone be reasonably confident that everyone is reasonably confident that everyone is reasonably confident . . . that the rules will be enforced by the efforts of ordinary people: a sinner or a cheater will be shunned and pay a price for his or her transgression. The riot of providers jostling to be the source of rules in the Middle Ages produced a cornucopia of legal ideas, but as trade expanded throughout Europe and the Muslim Mediterranean, it made it harder and harder for people to have confidence that they, and everyone else, knew what rules were in play.

One solution to this was for groups like the guilds to insist that all their members and all those who dealt with their members look only to their own rules and courts for dispute resolution. The Flemish merchants in the late thirteenth century read out their rules at the fairs where they traded, for all who traded with them to know and heed. The Italian guilds punished members who submitted to having disputes decided by municipal courts rather than their own guild court. The Maghribi traders studied by Stanford University economist Avner Greif—Jewish merchants who traveled throughout the Mediterranean in the eleventh century—limited their dealings as much as possible to members of their own tribe.

But this solution was inherently limited. It kept the scope of markets small—the very thing that Adam Smith told us we don't want to do if we want to exploit the economic benefits of specialization and the division of labor. What these merchant groups really wanted was to grow their membership, to bring more and more people into their group to uphold their rules. With more people in the group, the cost of abandoning the group and its rules is higher. With more people in the group, the chances that someone, somewhere, is around to punish a cheater are greater. With more people in the group, the more likely it is that the rules are remembered, talked about, and refined to respond better to different circumstances and experiences. But expansion is costly. Flemish merchants could not be sure at all about the rules in play if they traded outside of the established venues or sets of trading partners who knew their rules. As the volume of trade and the size of trading groups increased, monitoring guild members—to make sure they were using guild courts and not municipal courts—became very expensive. As for the Maghribi traders, there were only so many other Maghribis to trade with. This limited the effectiveness of the enforcement threat.

So there were these two forces, pulling in opposite directions. Small, close-knit groups that worked hard to control the rules used by their members could achieve the common knowledge necessary to make enforcement credible. But large, easily joined groups carried a bigger stick. Ideally you want a big group with common knowledge of the rules. But that was hard for the merchants' own organizations or city-based officials to achieve.

What were the alternatives? Great size and common knowledge could be achieved without regard for geographical boundaries by religious organizations. The pope, for example, with a terrific network of bishops, could ensure that the Catholic faithful wherever they might be knew the official view of the rules; the same could be said of Islam. But faith can be fickle, and as the Christian faith in particular splintered into different sects and authority structures during the later Middle Ages, knowing what someone believed and the rules he or she followed no doubt became trickier over time; predicting what others believed others believed about others became far trickier still.

Moreover, what makes the pope, or any religious leader, a good provider of the rules governing commercial dealings, as opposed to spiritual ones? We saw that Timur Kuran of Duke University has pointed to the ability of Christian and Jewish traders to follow commercial rules distinct from those articulated by religious leaders—unlike the followers of Islam—as a key factor explaining their domination of trade even in Muslim lands from the eighteenth century onward. This was the point at which the ability to form large-scale and perpetual organizations that went beyond the small partnerships of earlier days became crucial for economic growth. European commercial law had produced the means to create such entities, but Islamic law had not. Within Christianity itself, although it was initially clergy who rejected Catholicism and gave birth to the new Protestant religions that saw a role for purely secular law, it was the merchant class that took to Protestantism with enthusiasm. Italian cities like Florence, Pisa, and Milan worked hard to maintain their ability to govern themselves, free of the control of the pope in Rome, no doubt motivated in large measure by their desire to craft a set of commercially friendly rules. A more effective rule enforcement mechanism is great, if the rules are decent in the first place. But it's not worth much if the rules are the wrong ones.

The solution to the push-me-pull-you forces pressing for the achievement of uniformity in rules on the one hand—which argues in favor of small close-knit groups—and expanded adherence to the rules on the other—which argues in favor of large, loosely connected groups—was the territorially defined nation-state. It emerged not from the direct efforts of the merchant class to secure better legal infrastructure but rather as a byproduct of the political, religious, and military struggles of kings and nobles.[2]

This solution took shape in the face of the Protestant challenge mounted by the German monk Martin Luther and others in the early sixteenth century. In response to this challenge, the Catholic Church encouraged Catholic monarchs to attack kingdoms that had converted to Protestantism. Soon, much of Christendom was engaged in bloody struggles of this form. Ratcheting innovations in fortifications, weaponry, and the recruiting, training, and deployment of ever-larger armies fueled both the scale and the economic (not to mention human) cost of war. An early treaty—the Treaty of Augsburg signed in 1555—sought to call a truce by declaring that a monarch had the authority to determine the religion of his realm and his subjects. Peace was not secured in a lasting way, however, until the treaties of the Peace of Westphalia in 1648, signed between the Holy Roman emperor and the rulers of the kingdoms of Spain and France, the Swedish empire, the Dutch

Republic, and several free imperial cities in the Holy Roman Empire. These treaties affirmed what we understand today to be the basic principle of territorial sovereignty—the idea that other rulers recognize the power of a local ruler to determine the rules within a geographically delimited area and are bound not to interfere (by, for example, sending in forces to help out local groups who object to the exercise of power by the local ruler).

The Peace of Westphalia was fundamentally an agreement among powerful rulers to leave one another alone. It was not a resolution per se of the patchwork of rule-making institutions—guilds, churches, cities, nobles—that I have emphasized existed throughout the regions of Europe in the Middle Ages. But this external settling of scores and drawing of lines had the effect nonetheless of ultimately unifying a hierarchical system of exclusive jurisdiction exercised by the sovereign over legal matters. The merchant guilds that had successfully defended their right to adjudicate guild rules without interference from local civil courts, for example, gradually had their jurisdiction absorbed into a comprehensive scheme overseen by the state. A largely horizontal and fragmented system was pulled into a vertical and integrated one.

The kings, popes, emperors, and nobles who worked out the concept of the sovereign territorial state didn't come up with the idea to meet the economic demand for law—to enable the achievement of common knowledge of the rules across a larger group. They were just interested in putting an end to costly and seemingly unending warfare. But the effect of what they did was to provide a powerful means of coordinating decentralized enforcement of a set of rules over a wide territory, and making it relatively simple to achieve common knowledge of the answer to the question "What rules do we follow, and punish, around here?" The motivating factor may have been war and politics—as historians and political scientists have long argued—but a critical byproduct of the development of the nation-state was a new way of supplying the economic demand for law, of solving the complexity problem bred by the success of the ways in which medieval lords, guilds, cities, and church leaders had met demand in the previous centuries.

The other major effect of the emergence of the sovereign territorial state was the creation of a centralized and over time increasingly powerful enforcement authority. One of the consequences of building larger and larger groups under a single set of rules was a weakening of the incentives facing ordinary citizens to participate in the decentralized enforcement of those rules. Economists call this the free-rider effect: why should I bother helping to punish a rule-breaker if there are others around who can do it? In fact, there are lots of reasons, even in large communities. Often, those in a position to punish a rule-breaker are members of a small group—the people who observe the bad conduct, the small set of traders who deal with a cheating merchant. Incentives to help punish wrongdoers can persist within these small subsets of larger populations. Moreover, participation in punishment can be a way of signaling to one's friends and trading partners that one continues to support the rules. So long as the cost of punishment is not too high—and remember, as groups grow larger, they share the cost of punishment more widely so the costs to any individual go down—it can be worthwhile to send those signals. Nonetheless, as the state grew larger, more complex, and more anonymous, centralized enforcement gradually came to dominate. But the process took time.

And money: Louis XIV established the first police force, to patrol Paris in the late seventeenth century, but it was not until after the Industrial Revolution and the wealth it generated that governments more broadly could afford the cost of professional and bureaucratized policing. Similarly, although criminals were throughout much of history put into bondage or forced labor, it is only in the eighteenth century that the modern idea of imprisonment—separation from society—emerges. It is not until the nineteenth century that the modern bureaucratic prison carrying out sentences of time under confinement becomes the principal means of criminal punishment. What we think of today as the defining feature of law—the imposition of punishment by a centralized enforcement authority with a monopoly over the legitimate exercise of force—is in fact a relatively recent phenomenon, even more recent than the consolidation of the nation-state as territorial sovereign.[3]

Politics and the Production of Modern Legal Infrastructure

And so we find ourselves in the modern state. Gone is the jostle of overlapping and competing rule systems with ill-defined and shifting boundaries. Replacing it within the state is a marvelously coherent and singular system of jurisdiction with a definitive set of rules and institutions for resolving questions about what rules apply to what transactions and interactions. If the brakes on the car you bought in New York fail while you are driving through Oklahoma and you injure people on the highway, it will be easy to figure out that any personal injury claims you face will be resolved under the rules of Oklahoma's tort law. It will be somewhat harder to figure out what law applies to any product liability claims you want to bring against the manufacturer of the car you were driving. They may be governed by New York law because that's where you bought the car or by Oklahoma law because that's where the accident happened or by the law of the state where the manufacturer has its headquarters or factory. It may be complicated to resolve this choice-of-law question. But the difference between medieval Europe and modern states is that there is a single, clearly defined, and well-accepted process and set of rules about how to resolve it, organized under an umbrella of constitutional rules about when courts in different states can exercise jurisdiction. If the mess cannot be sorted out in the state courts, the buck stops with the US Supreme Court. That is the apex of the pyramid, the end of the line.

This orderly means of reaching a final answer to the question "What law do we follow around here?" is what it means to have a unified system of law, organized on the basis of the monopoly of legitimate authority in the nation-state. Even if there are multiple possible sets of legal rules that could be in play, in an established modern legal order there is a stable system for picking just one. In the United States, the Supreme Court is the final answer—either it takes jurisdiction to finally resolve a dispute itself or it definitively declares that the final decision rests with another court. The state courts or other state officials could decide to ignore the US Supreme Court—as happened, for example, in some states after the *Brown v. Board of Education* case in 1954 that ordered states to desegregate their schools. But that is when the monopoly of the legitimate use of force comes into play: the federal government sent federal police and military into the recalcitrant states after they resisted *Brown*. For these states to continue to fight federal forces and to resist the ultimate legal authority of the US Supreme Court would have been to challenge the continued vitality of the unified state in the first place—to threaten civil war. That is, to threaten the stability of the nation-state itself.

Two key things happened in this process of shifting from the cacophonous legal terrain of the Middle Ages to the orderly legal structures of the modern nation-state. One was this achievement of a singular system that is never at a loss for answering the question "Which rules govern around here?" The second was the placing of control over that system into political hands. These were probably not unrelated changes. The settling of boundaries between princes, popes, and nobles across Europe did not necessarily have to lead to the gradual absorption of the multiple legal rule systems that existed within the newly formed states—rules provided by guilds, towns, abbots, landlords and so on—into a single hierarchical regime for producing rules with its apex in a state institution.

One theory of why the establishment of the nation-state system led to internal rationalization of legal regimes into a singular legal system under political control is based on the idea that what matters is force. With resources freed up from defending the realm from external challenges, the state could focus on bringing internal challengers into line. No doubt much of this went on. And as we've seen, there are free-rider pressures on decentralized enforcement systems as economies develop and become larger and more complex, making the centralization of enforcement more attractive at the same time that government wealth is increasing as a result of economic development.

But my work with Barry Weingast of Stanford University suggests that there was something else at play as well. That something else is the economic demand for law—and for a solution to the problem of common knowledge to coordinate decentralized enforcement of rules. That demand gives the people who need law—particularly the economic actors seeking to build their ventures on the platform of a set of rules that is widely shared and accepted—no particular loyalty to a given set of rules. Rather, it gives them an incentive to go along with any institution that can convince them that it is providing a stable platform of rules—so long as the rules are reasonably good ones.

The medieval merchant guilds, for example, would no doubt have seen a trade-off between persisting in their efforts to impose their own rules on everyone who dealt with them and expanding the scope and reliability of the rules they followed by integrating into a broader legal platform rooted in the now recognizable state. But they would not have wanted to do this if it came at the expense of submitting to a system that ignored their interests. This is where politics—and in particular democracy—enters the picture. The merchant guild was a group with pretty closely aligned interests; they expected their rules to work well for people with their needs and goals. To switch their allegiance to a state-based rule provider, they would have wanted some capacity to shape the direction that provider took with the rules.

If the merchants were thinking very carefully, they would also have wanted to make sure that other people—who didn't share the merchants' interests—also had the capacity to prod the state to respond to their interests. Why? Because the merchants needed those other people—the merchants in other cities and towns or other guilds, the buyers of their wares whether merchants or not, the landlords, abbots, and local nobility who continued to hold sway in their communities—to be on board with supporting the rules in this broader system. That was the very reason a broader platform was valuable—it received wide support. But a reasonable person can't expect others to support a system of rules if it ignores their interests. This was the point about infrastructure that we saw earlier: infrastructure is more valuable if more diverse people use it and find it useful. That necessarily means it is not tailored to anyone's particular desires. So as enticing as it may have been for a merchant guild to plot a means to gain control of a state-based rule system to serve its own interests, ultimately the lesson of that effort would have been that a closed system that can be manipulated to serve exclusively the interests of the members of a particular guild ultimately lacks the support it needs from a broader community. This is the lesson that Weingast and I argued that the gold miners in nineteenth-century California understood: using the miner's meeting to craft a set of rules that benefited the miners who already had staked claims at the expense of newcomers would have given those newcomers no reason to support the rules. Without a police force around to serve the interests of the initial miners, a self-serving set of rules was not going to survive for long.

The need to get a broad group of individuals on board to support a system of rules helps explain why it was political, in particular democratic, bodies that came to be the providers of a neat, orderly, unified system of law within the state. These providers were designed to be open and responsive to the needs of a diverse population. Not everyone at first: it takes hundreds of years for these political bodies to even begin to be open and responsive to the needs of women, people without property, members of religious or ethnic minorities, immigrants. In the early phases of the developing state, these people were not seen as particularly important to upholding the stability of a legal order—they didn't have much capacity to act in ways either to punish those who transgressed or to resist the control of those wielding economic or political power. But even if the early flowerings were reedy and stunted, the seeds were planted: political bodies intended to be responsive to their constituents became the ultimate providers of legal rules. Law, it was now understood, flowed not from the divine right of kings or the tyranny of the conqueror, but from increasingly stable representative bodies like appointed councils and elected legislatures. Over time that basic idea bloomed, in the developed world, into a more securely inclusive democratic regime.

For the merchant guild contemplating a shift from insisting on a set of rules it controlled but which could be effective only over a small group of traders to a state-based regime that offered a broad-based platform controlled by a somewhat responsive political body, the state system also offered something else: organized enforcement resources. These no doubt helped overcome weaknesses in decentralized collective enforcement—the social and economic sanctions that individuals imposed on rule-breakers themselves. But it is important to remember—it will be critical to remember when we think about the challenges of building legal order in places in the developing world that are now struggling—that the creation of the nation-state did not do away with the need for a general willingness in the population to go along with and support the state's rules. It was a long time after the birth of the idea of the nation-state before the state reached today's level of internal police power. In the American colonies, for example, settled at the same time as the nation-state in Europe was forming, a lone elected sheriff depended on sometimes the assistance and almost always the acquiescence of local citizens when he went to seize goods or land or bodies to satisfy the judgments of local courts. Anyone who was the victim of a crime or other offense was normally responsible for pursuing the offender in court; there were no public prosecutors.

In this the colonies were not so different from medieval Iceland or later Gold Rush California. Even today, with our massive and professionalized police forces, still a great deal of our legal order comes from people complying with the law not just because they fear the siren's wail. No, in a well-established legal order, many people go along with the rules for the same reason they did in medieval Iceland or Europe: because everyone else is expecting them to and there are social and economic sanctions for breaking those rules. And the reason those social and economic sanctions exist is because all the ordinary people needed to help keep legal infrastructure stable and effective—by both resisting the temptations of transgression themselves and sanctioning those who don't—see a reason to do their part. The legal infrastructure they support is the legal infrastructure that makes them better off than the alternative. That's a lesson that's getting lost as we confront how to adjust our rulemaking systems to the modern world.

5

Building a Stable Platform
for Complexity

THE LEGAL INFRASTRUCTURE that emerged over the centuries that followed the seventeenth-century Westphalian truce between warring kings, princes, popes, and emperors in Europe served the economic demand for law well. Eventually a rich stable system of responsible rule of law helped Western countries leave behind the world of small-scale craft production and long-distance merchant trade and enter the industrialized world of factories and mass manufacturing. The result of that economic transition was skyrocketing levels of growth and prosperity. Real per capita income tripled in the eight hundred years between what economic historian Angus Maddison calls the "nadir" of Western European economic prosperity in the year 1000—when people were significantly worse off than they had been a millennium earlier during the Roman Empire—and the close of an eighteenth century that had delivered revolutions in scientific thinking, manufacturing, and government. Life expectancy increased 50 percent, rising from twenty-four to thirty-six years by the end of the first phase of the Industrial Revolution in 1820.[1]

Even this impressive growth, however, soon grew pale in comparison with what was to come. In the next two hundred years, between 1820 and 2000, the second phase of the Industrial Revolution delivered phenomenal economic growth in the Western world. Life expectancy doubled, reaching almost eighty years. In Western Europe real per capita income increased by almost 1,600 percent. In the Anglo-American countries of the United States, Canada, Australia, and New Zealand, growth over the nineteenth and twentieth centuries exceeded 2000 percent, pushing real per capita income from about $1,500 in 1820 to over $35,500 in 2000. That's ten times the growth in one-fourth the time as compared with the accomplishments of the Commercial Revolution of the Middle Ages and the first phase of the Industrial Revolution combined. Lots of things help to account for this phenomenal growth—and the stability, reach, and richness of legal infrastructure is surely one of them.

In this chapter I look at how the evolution of the economy and legal infrastructure followed similar paths in achieving the enormous levels of growth experienced over the nineteenth and twentieth centuries in what grew to become the largest economy on earth—the United States. Both the American economy and legal infrastructure became more complex and differentiated. And both became more rationalized and controlled.

Economic Transformation, 1800–2000

Let's look first at a picture taken from thirty thousand feet of what was going on in the economy in the West over the last two hundred years.[2] At the beginning of the 1800s, economies throughout Europe and North America, as throughout much of the world, were still based largely on agriculture and household production of goods such as clothing, candles, furniture, and soap. Specialized manufacturing—of shoes, cloth, iron tools, and so on—was carried out almost exclusively in small shops where an owner worked alone, perhaps with an apprentice or two, using a few simple tools or machines. Other goods made their way to market through small-scale cottage industry, with family members producing goods—spinning yarn, for example, or harvesting lumber, animal furs, or coal—that they either sold in local markets or on a piece-rate basis to merchants.

Things looked pretty much then as they did to Adam Smith half a century earlier when he marveled at the productive capacity of a newfangled ten-person pin manufactory, able to produce through specialization and the division of labor "upwards of 48,000 pins in day," far outstripping the tiny number those ten people could produce working alone. Until 1840 only a handful of enterprises employed more than fifty workers, and the largest of these rarely topped a few hundred. The slavery-based plantations growing cotton and tobacco in the American South were structured on a model that barely recognized workers as capable of legal or market relations; slaves were treated as the property of the plantation owner. Most plantation owners oversaw production themselves or with the help of one or two other workers recognized as employees. There were thus millions of independent producers who produced a relatively short list of products. Many primarily lived off their own production and participated in the market only minimally for purchases of goods they couldn't produce at home. In 1800 barely 5 percent of the American population lived in towns or cities; 90 percent of the labor force was made up of farmers.

By the end of the nineteenth century, however, all this had changed in the West, especially the United States and Britain. The economy was a booming industrial powerhouse. Networks of railways and telegraphs—together with the deployment of coal-fired furnaces and steam-powered machines, the internal combustion engine and electricity—fostered tremendous growth in the scale of manufacturing and the extent of the market. As Alfred Chandler documents in *The Visible Hand*, his 1977 Pulitzer Prize–winning chronicle of the evolution of American business, the industrial corporation that characterized the mid-twentieth century took shape over the latter decades of the nineteenth century. Leading the way were the railroads and companies such as Standard Oil, U.S. Steel, and General Electric and their famous founders and financiers: Vanderbilt, Rockefeller, Carnegie, Drexel, J. P. Morgan. These corporations grew rapidly through horizontal and vertical integration as their owners strove to bring as much of the economic process as possible, from raw materials to final sale, under the control of a single organization.

Integration generated huge economies of scale in these largely capital-intensive industries. The result was the mass production and distribution of standardized goods to a rapidly growing market, both domestic and international. Although farming remained a major activity, huge numbers of the population (with the exception of the newly freed African American population, who were still mostly bound by sharecropping and discrimination to plantations) shifted from sustaining themselves through farming with minimal participation in markets to a fully market-based existence. They earned wages and purchased everything they needed from the businesses that stocked store shelves with an exploding array of standardized consumer goods. By the turn of the twentieth century half of the American population lived in towns and cities.

Industrialization and mass production transformed the economy from one with millions of disparate producers to one dominated by massive corporations. By 1917, almost a quarter of all manufacturing output in the United States was produced by the one hundred largest firms. With the exception of firms devoted to mining and extraction of oil and gas, all of these industrial giants were vertically integrated firms, controlling not only production but also marketing and distribution or raw materials and their transportation, or both. This integration brought about a fundamental shift in how economic activity was coordinated. Adam Smith a century earlier famously described the English economy as one coordinated by an "invisible hand." Guided by prices, highly decentralized and relatively unfettered markets, he argued, promoted the public's interest in securing the benefits of lower-cost and higher-quality goods. By the end of the nineteenth century, however, massive amounts of economic activity in the United States were coordinated by what Chandler dubbed the "visible hand" of corporate managerial bureaucracies. Centralized management was a natural consequence of building massive integrated firms. But it was also achieved by agreements between ostensibly competitive firms. The great railroad cartels—which Chandler identifies as the first modern enterprises—pioneered this form of coordination in the late 1870s, subjecting the prices and operations of the nation's transportation system to what they saw as the centralized "intelligent control" of a single administrative office with the power to set and enforce rates. Other megacorporations soon followed the same model. In 1881, fully 90 percent of the country's petroleum-refining capacity was under the centralized control of an alliance, spearheaded by John D. Rockefeller's Standard Oil Company, that coordinated agreements on prices and production schedules.

What Chandler called the managerial revolution in American business mirrored the rationalization that took hold throughout the emerging modern Western states in the late nineteenth century. This was a time of great belief in the idea that scientific thinking could be deployed to engineer just about everything, from the assembly line to education. As one of the great theorists of this stage in history, Max Weber, wrote in 1919, the governing belief was that "one can, in principle, master all things by calculation."[3] The technocratic ideal of deliberately coordinating economic activity saw its most dramatic form in the centrally planned economy of Stalin's Soviet Union. In the democratic West, however, most of the economy's calculations were carried out in the elaborate system of hierarchical planning within the boundaries of the megacorporation.

Legal Transformation, 1800–2000

The legal infrastructure that underwrote the simple preindustrial economy of the eighteenth and early nineteenth centuries was itself relatively simple.[4] It consisted primarily of the basic rules of property and contract on which the medieval merchants had also relied. Merchants required basic instruments of finance and insurance, as they had in the medieval period, for long-distance transport. Legal structures such as partnerships and small corporations enabled merchants to pool capital and a few budding industrialists, like

Adam Smith's pinmaker, to establish small factories. Although there was much local effort to regulate economic activity—the American colonies, for example, were rife with local laws that required bread, leather, grain, tobacco, meat, and more to be branded, inspected, and sold only as approved, sometimes only at designated times, places, and prices—the economy was sufficiently undifferentiated that the rules were relatively simple. Indeed, with the notable distinction of the land tenure rules in England, which had grown up to structure the feudal relationships between king, land, lord, and serf in the medieval period and which were irrelevant for most of the population, the complexity of most legal rules was relatively low. As in the medieval period there was in the commercial sphere a strong bias toward using rules that were widely understood and rooted in custom. Documents were simple, serving primarily as evidence that a deal had been struck or a payment owed or made.

In England, few outside of the landed gentry squabbling over land required the services of trained lawyers to interpret the laws or conduct litigation. Merchants kept their dealings as much as possible within merchant courts where process was quick and formality low. Across the Atlantic, the role of lawyers in the American colonies initially tracked the English model. There were fifteen lawyers in Massachusetts in 1740, one for every ten thousand residents. That's one-fortieth the ratio in the United States today. But colonial efforts to restrict the number of lawyers who could be trained and allowed by the courts to practice were not successful in America as they continued to be in England. Any such efforts eventually crumbled in the United States during the early nineteenth century in the face of enormous demand for basic legal assistance from a swelling population with widely dispersed landownership. Fifty years after independence, the practice of law in America was almost completely unrestricted—anyone (well, any white male) could become a lawyer by apprenticing for a few years in a law office and being admitted to practice by some local court. Elite lawyers earned high salaries and continued to play an outsized role in the political life of the United States—twenty-five of the fifty-six signers of the Declaration of Independence were lawyers, as were thirty-one of the fifty-five delegates to the 1787 convention that drafted the US Constitution. But many lawyers were part-timers earning a small supplemental income for helping out in small cases, collecting unpaid accounts, drafting promissory notes, and overseeing land sales on the frontier. If trials were needed, they were short and sweet, often presided over by laypeople who had better things to do than listen to people argue. Courts were largely local and disorganized, with overlapping and ambiguous jurisdiction. There was little in the way of organized enforcement, even of criminal law. Anyone who had suffered an offense was largely responsible for pursuing the offender in court; with luck the sheriff would help out in the event of a successful outcome at trial.

This highly decentralized, relatively simple, and somewhat chaotic system was, like the economy, transformed over the nineteenth and early twentieth centuries into a rationalized hierarchical structure focused on planning and control. In this process, legal infrastructure ultimately approached what the seventeenth-century Westphalian peace hinted at: the singular coherence of a nation-state that governed exclusively within its borders.

In the first stages of this transformation, Western legal infrastructure grew substantially both more intricate and more standardized to manage an increasingly complex and differentiated economy. Soon basic rules of property and contract law and the ad hoc financial instruments and trading mechanisms invented by merchants, bankers, and the new industrialists were integrated into a legal world populated by statutes and uniform standards. Much of this filled out the commercial infrastructure that was necessary to manage increasingly complicated relationships, supplying standardized terms (many operating as defaults that parties could specialize through contract if needed). The business of incorporating a company shifted from the centuries-old process of seeking a special charter from the legislature— a process that began life as royal authorization to wield a monopoly in a particular line of trade or venture—to a routine administrative procedure under general incorporation statutes. Anyone could incorporate a business on standardized terms for any legal purpose and the corporation became an autonomous legal entity that didn't die when its founders did. This standardization-driven period sees the emergence of things such as partnership statutes, corporate law codes, secured lending rules, intellectual property laws, and uniform sales law.

In this late nineteenth- and early twentieth-century drive to uniformity and standardization, legal infrastructure mirrored the emerging mass production manufacturing economy, with "off-the shelf" legal products that anyone could use. Increasingly uniform rules of procedure and evidence and organized systems of jurisdiction in courts did away with the confusing array of courts that characterized the legal world up through the eighteenth and much of the nineteenth centuries. Uniformity and standardization also mitigated the risk of making mistakes with highly formal and technical requirements, mistakes that made legal process unpredictable and expensive. Standardized legal processes across courts allowed businesses to plan their legal relationships and disputes throughout a wider legal market.

Standardized legal education and bar exam requirements raised not only the quality but also the consistency of legal analysis and advice. Consistency across the legal profession helped promote coordination of the legal expectations held by the burgeoning numbers of those participating in producing, selling, and buying goods in an expanding and dynamic market.

Along with the push to standardization in existing legal structures came the emergence of something wholly new on a national scale: the modern regulatory state. Unlike the haphazard and intrusive local regulation that characterized the preindustrial economy, the new regulatory state was managed by increasingly sophisticated and technocratic bureaucracies, often with minimal legislative guidance. The 1887 Interstate Commerce Act, for example—the first major piece of federal legislation in the United States—set out in just a few short sentences the general rule that the rates charged by railroads could no longer be set by their private cartel. Congress did not prescribe the details of railroad transport pricing; it merely said that rates set by common carriers had to be "reasonable and just," nondiscriminatory as between customers, and published. The act, a grand total of seven pages long, also created the first federal regulatory agency, the Interstate Commerce Commission, with the power to investigate the carriers to ensure compliance. Both the agency and private individuals were granted the power to take the carriers to court for violations.

The Interstate Commerce Act was swiftly followed in 1890 by the Sherman Antitrust Act, which made it illegal for anyone in any industry to enter into agreements or arrangements that restrained competition. The Sherman Act, taking aim at the type of arrangements that Standard Oil had used to control prices and markets in the petroleum industry, was even more succinct than the Interstate Commerce Act. Less than two pages long, it simply declared that contracts in restraint of trade were illegal and that anyone entering into them or monopolizing "any part of trade or commerce" was guilty of a misdemeanor. The act declared that public prosecutors throughout the country could seek court orders to enforce it and that anyone harmed by an antitrust violation could sue for three times the amount of harm they had suffered.

This late nineteenth-century foray into broad-based industrial regulation in the United States was followed by an extended lull during which the courts seemed to join forces with the industrialists to resist any further incursions on their freedom to run their businesses as they saw fit. This was the height of the laissez-faire economy, known among American lawyers as the *Lochner* era. *Lochner* was a famous 1905 case in which the US Supreme court struck down as unconstitutional a New York law that said that bread-making factories could not make employees work more than sixty hours in a week. Even during this period, however, regulation was growing in its reach and detail, a more organized approach to the kind of local regulation the American states had known since colonial days. Although the Supreme Court struck down the section of the New York statute on bakeries that capped work hours, it left in place lots of other rules about how the business had to be run: where factory washrooms and sleeping quarters could be located, how high the ceilings had to be, where equipment and furniture could be placed, and how rooms were to be constructed, drained, ventilated, and painted.[5]

The *Lochner* era was relatively short-lived. The Great Depression of the 1930s changed both politics and judicial inclinations and ushered in the New Deal era of comprehensive economic regulation. In a hundred-day sprint in 1933, the administration of President Franklin Delano Roosevelt pushed through Congress over fifteen major pieces of legislation, including the federal Securities Act, which for the first time brought trade on the stock exchanges under public regulation; the Emergency Banking Act, which put banks under the supervision of the Treasury Department; the Glass-Steagall Act, which limited the ability of commercial banks to engage in speculative trading and established federal deposit insurance; and statutes governing farm credit, mortgages, and agricultural quotas to support prices. The next few years saw the enactment of comprehensive social security and national labor relations laws and the creation of a federal housing authority. Governments then turned to the tax code to direct behavior and investment after World War II. By the mid-1960s, the concept of the "tax expenditure" had been invented to highlight the fact that the increasingly common practice of using tax breaks to encourage businesses to do something cost government just as much as a subsidy did. Increasingly detailed tax provisions began to drive more and more economic decision-making.

The next major expansion of the regulatory state took place in the 1960s and 1970s. Economic regulation continued to expand in response to increasing specialization and differentiation. The mass consumer market, for example, spurred an explosion in a new form of retailing—franchised chains selling everything from hamburgers to hotel rooms—that would soon account for a third of all retail sales. Specialized legislation arose to regulate the sale and conditions of franchise contracts. This pattern was repeated throughout the economy: new products, services, business models, and investment vehicles spurred new product-/service-/model-/vehicle-specific regulations. The 1960s and 1970s also saw the expansion of legislation that took aim at a broader conception of social welfare, one that went beyond economic concerns with prices, wages, and the quality of goods. Statutes were put in to place to improve healthcare, education, civil rights, environmental protection, occupational health and safety, and more.

The remaining decades of the twentieth century saw some reversals on the regulatory front, with broad-based deregulation in airlines, trucking, communications, and eventually the financial sector. It is unlikely, however, that overall regulatory load was reduced, even if particular forms and theories of regulation were abandoned. For example, for fifty years, beginning in 1938, the US Civil Aeronautics Board exercised direct control over what routes airlines could fly, what prices they could charge, and when they could schedule flights. Then in 1978 the airlines were deregulated so that they could set their own routes, prices, and schedules.[6] But airlines still operated then as now within a complex regulatory regime that impacts decisions about aircraft production and maintenance, flight protocols, employment practices, merger activity, pricing, security, rewards programs, compensation for delays and lost baggage, and more. A deregulated market is still heavily shaped by legal infrastructure.

As the end of the twentieth century pulled into view, then, legal infrastructure in the United States, and eventually worldwide, mirrored the mass-manufacturing economy that it had helped to build. As the number of different types of goods on the mass-consumer market grew, so did the number of different types of legal "goods" produced by lawyers. As the methods of producing consumer goods grew in sophistication and standardization, so too did the methods of producing legal goods, with contractual boilerplate, uniform laws, and consistent court procedures. As corporations became more elaborately organized managerial entities, governments became more elaborately organized regulatory entities.

Lawyers Triumphant

The story of legal infrastructure in the United States over the past century is often told as a story about law and politics: all the new rules and regulations that issued from legislatures and regulatory agencies, all the bruising political battles that produced them. But there is another story to be told as well. This is the story of how an initially small and elite group of lawyers and law professors secured a pivotal role in shaping law, legal institutions, and legal practice. To this effort and the expansion in size and sophistication of the legal profession we owe much of the success of the legal infrastructure that served as a platform for the fantastic growth of the twentieth century. But as we'll see in chapters to come, one of the most substantial obstacles to our evolution to the next phase of legal infrastructure—achieving the changes necessary to support yet another transformation in our economic and social world— is found in the outsized control that this elite group ultimately secured for today's lawyers over how law gets done.

It begins with a meeting in 1878 in the resort town of Saratoga Springs in upstate New York.[7] At the time a hotbed for hot springs, horse racing, and then-still-legal gambling, this town had been the meeting ground a few years earlier for those organizing the early railroad cartels. But in 1878 it became the place where leading American lawyers created the American Bar Association. The impetus for the Association came from Simeon E. Baldwin, a descendant of a signatory of the Declaration of Independence and five Connecticut governors. In an illustrious career, Baldwin served as governor and chief justice of Connecticut, legal counsel to the New York and New England railway, and professor at the Yale Law School. He and the other ABA founders articulated from the outset a soaring mission to assume what they perceived as the American lawyer's singular obligation in a constitutional democracy to safeguard the constitutional order. This was a "prerogative as never before was conferred upon a body of advocates," according to ABA founder and third president, Edmund J. Phelps. Phelps was the son of a US senator, a one-time candidate for Vermont Governor, short-lister for Chief Justice of the United States, and served as the US ambassador to Britain. Known for his rhetorical flourish, Phelps quoted in his address to the second annual meeting of the Association a sneering description of the English bar as composed of lawyers who, unlike the American legal elite, "know no more of the principles that control the affairs of state than a titmouse knows of the gestation of an elephant."[8] The simile clearly struck a chord. A toast to "the knowledge of the titmouse as to the gestation of the elephant" was later proposed at dinner by one Anthony Q. Keasbey, descendent of colonists at Salem. [9] Keasbey apparently liked Phelps's turn of phrase so much that he raised a toast the following year as well, this time to "the elephant after gestation."[10] (Perhaps Keasbey was unaware that the man to whom he was tipping his rhetorical hat was virulently proslavery and had once called the president who appointed Keasbey to his position as US district attorney for New Jersey, Abraham Lincoln, a "wooden-head" and "twentieth-rate back-country attorney.")[11]

The ambition of the Association's founders was extraordinary. ABA annual meetings were for decades attended by only about a hundred lawyers, and as of 1910 membership was still less than 3 percent of the lawyers in the country. But the founding lawyers and law professors (among those invited by Simeon Baldwin to the inaugural meeting was James Bradley Thayer, who then held the chaired professorship that originally founded Harvard Law School) were elite, politically well connected, and ultimately carved out effective strategies to bring forth order from the legal chaos of the earlier nineteenth century. Over the next fifty years or so they developed the legal infrastructure Americans know today and that informs legal development throughout the world. Through their efforts, lawyers assumed a central role in the development of uniform laws, uniform court organization and jurisdictional rules, court-controlled rules of procedure and evidence, codes of ethics for lawyer and judges, and the eventual monopoly over legal practice held by those who were admitted by state courts and under the disciplinary control of state bar associations.

The initial focus of the Association was clearly in the spirit of the times, aiming at the kind of "intelligent control" that was inspiring the new industrialists and railwaymen and their megacorporations. The drive was toward uniformity, order, and scientific reform to drive out variance and increase quality. Within a year of its founding, the ABA had created committees to establish uniform standards for legal education and admissions to the bar, to review judicial administration and procedures, and to promote the harmonization and reform of laws and legislative drafting throughout the country—pretty much the whole ball of legal wax. The motives were not wholly pure: the effort was heavily tainted by the desire to protect the profession from what many of the founders perceived to be the "stain" of immigrants, Jews, blacks, and women.[12] But the spirit of the times folded those discriminatory motives also into scientific rationality.

As elite and mostly corporate lawyers, the ABA founders were particularly focused on the kind of uniformity in commercial law that would relieve them, and their clients, of the headaches of a jumble of rules that varied from locale to locale in an increasingly national market. The Association put the development of uniform standards for negotiable instruments like commercial paper on its agenda in the very first year of its existence and created standing committees on commercial law and international law—the only standing committees devoted to substantive areas of the law. It substantially drafted the first nationwide bankruptcy code, adopted in the United States just before the turn of the twentieth century.

Legal training also became both more sophisticated and more standardized over the twentieth century as a result of ABA leadership. One of the highest priorities for the newly formed ABA in 1878 was to create uniform educational requirements for those allowed to practice law. The new Association looked out at a legal world in which anyone with some learning and gumption could call himself a lawyer. Or, as one cynic of the times put it, the law was "that great noble profession, for which every jackass in the country conceives himself more than equal."[13] The great majority of lawyers trained by serving as an apprentice in a law office. Others simply followed Abraham Lincoln's advice for the "cheapest, quickest, and best way" into the practice: read a few legal books, "get a license, go to the practice, and still keep reading."[14] In 1891 only four in ten states required any formal training to practice law. None required legal education or a formal bar examination. Such law schools as there were—fifteen in the United States in 1850—were predominantly an outgrowth of private law offices, with senior lawyers giving daily lectures and weekly quizzes on the law. A small number of university-based law schools—Harvard Law School was the first, founded in 1817—used a variety of methods to train students. Some gave lectures on legal rules; others, like Harvard, used a method in which students were required to memorize and recite portions of legal textbooks. None of these programs required a college degree. Indeed, as of 1896, only seven of seventy-six law schools in the United States required a high school diploma to attend; as of 1904, only three required a college degree and another three required some college. Most law school programs were two years or less. The training a prospective lawyer obtained was therefore up to him or, rarely, her. (The first woman, Belle Mansfield, was not admitted to a state bar until 1869.)

The ABA proposed to change all this within the first few years of its existence as an organization, recommending in 1881 that states should establish law schools with a minimum number of regular professors and a three-year course of study. By 1890, the Association was recommending that only the highest court in a state should be allowed to grant admission to practice, that examinations should be administered by a commission appointed by the court, and that admission should require a minimum of two years of law school education in a school with an adequate library and standards of classroom instruction.

The ABA made little progress with this agenda until the 1930s. As of 1927 law school was still not required to practice law in any state and 80 percent of US lawyers had no formal legal education (unlike doctors and ministers, almost all of whom had attended medical school or seminary). But then came the Wall Street crash of 1929 and a 40 percent plunge in lawyers' incomes (a fate also suffered by doctors and other professionals). The ABA together with the Association of American Law Schools hired a full-time lobbyist and began a successful campaign to get every state to adopt its standards for the education and licensing of lawyers. By the late 1940s in the United States nearly every state required anyone who wanted to practice law to complete some college prior to going to law school and pass a comprehensive bar examination. Legal education became much more uniform in the process. By 1914 nearly all leading law schools had adopted the "scientific case method" and Socratic teaching style pioneered at Harvard Law School in the 1870s. The drive to uniformity in legal education continued over the twentieth century. Today the first-year curriculum of virtually every law school in the United States is in large measure identical to the late nineteenth-century curriculum established by Harvard.

The pressures of the Great Depression also breathed new life into ABA efforts to ensure that legal practice was the exclusive preserve of those who had earned a law degree in an ABA-approved law school, passed a bar examination, been admitted to practice by a state supreme court, and were subject to the disciplinary control of the bar. In 1931, the ABA began an investigation into what it called the "unauthorized practice of law." It had in its sights the mushrooming array of businesses and professions that provided legal services to a citizenry in need of help to navigate an increasingly law-thick environment: banks and trust companies, collection agencies, trade associations and clubs, title companies, mortgage loan companies, claims adjusters, real estate brokers, protective associations, and automobile clubs. Many of these organizations hired lawyers to serve the public. Others without formal legal training provided help with forms and documents related to their core business. But the ABA argued no one, other than a bar-licensed lawyer practicing in a law firm or as a solo practitioner, should be allowed to do anything that touched the practice of law. Not only must the training of anyone who practices law be standardized, so too must be the manner and setting in which legal assistance is delivered.

As documented by Northern Illinois University law professor Laurel Rigertas, bar associations under the leadership of the ABA had during the early twentieth century followed the strategy of lobbying state legislatures to drive out what they deemed to be the unauthorized practice of law.[15] There were some successes—as early as 1909, for example, the New York State Assembly had enacted a law prohibiting a corporation from practicing law. But a 1931 ABA survey of state bar associations revealed that few states had laws on the books penalizing the practice of law by a person other than a licensed lawyer or an entity other than a law firm. The reason likely lay in the fact that many of the organizations and professions that lawyers were attempting to displace did not lie down for the effort. They fought back and were often successful in defeating legislation or at least carving out exceptions for themselves. The legislative route—as doctors, who eventually had to share the medical field with a wide array of other licensed practitioners such as nurses, chiropractors, and pharmacists, discovered—was an arduous and not a particularly promising path to the achievement of exclusive control over the legal sector.

But the ABA had an ace up its sleeve. It had the courts. Not merely as a forum in which to air lawyers' grievances and claims like any other citizen or group but as a constitutive part of the profession itself. Courts were headed by judges who, up until their appointment to the bench, had been lawyers. Judges were among the founding fathers of the ABA. And they had just managed to add significant regulatory authority to their traditional role.[16] In the mid-1930s the ABA had successfully pivoted off a failed effort to convince state legislatures and Congress to reform court procedures. It had shifted instead to a successful effort to get Congress on board with the idea that the power to make rules about court procedures lay with judges themselves. Judges in the 1930s were newly empowered, and they were in the club.

The strategy of arguing that the judges were in charge of the way law was to be done was a powerful one. And it worked not only with court procedure but also with the regulation of the practice of law. Fresh off its judicial rule-making success in Congress, the ABA abandoned the effort to get state legislatures to give lawyers a monopoly and turned instead to the Association's brethren on the bench. Bar associations began litigating in state courts against the trade associations, realtors, claims adjusters, and anyone else who was providing legal services, charging them with practicing law without a license. Where there was no law on the books making the activities of these nonlawyer entities unlawful, bar associations argued that they didn't need one: state courts, they urged, had the inherent authority to decide what constituted the practice of law. These courts, they argued, had the power to prevent unauthorized practice just as they had always had the power to decide who could appear before them in court. In 1937 such lawsuits were filed in virtually every jurisdiction in the country.

This litigation campaign to locate the power to control the practice of law in courts rather than legislatures can be seen as a natural outgrowth of the changes in the nature of legal demand. Nineteenth-century legal practice was largely litigation-related, and courts could naturally play gatekeeper by deciding who could and who could not file legal papers and appear before them. But the expansion of the economy and the shift to a much more formalized and regulated state brought with it a new role for lawyers: planning transactions, advising on compliance, and completing the myriad forms that the newly bureaucratic state required. This was office practice, not court practice, and it was much harder to monitor and control those who offered these services than it was to monitor and control those appearing in court. The bruising experience of trying to eliminate corporations and other professionals from the legal sector through legislation was a product of the ballooning of non-litigation-oriented legal work in the new, more complicated regulatory state. A broad prohibition was essential because it was impossible to anticipate all the new types of legal work and new legal providers that were cropping up. It was also almost impossible to achieve as banks, real estate agents, and insurance companies successfully lobbied for carve-outs to protect their slice of the market.

State supreme court judges got the legal profession out of this political mess. They took to the claim that they, not the legislatures, were the exclusive overseers of legal practice like ducks to water. Quickly, the claim was cemented in the best foundation around: grand constitutional principle. The separation of powers and the independence of the judiciary, no less, mandated that the courts and the courts alone decide who could practice law and how. Judicial control over the legal profession was inherent in the majesty of the American legal order, and found in the constitutions of every state in the union. Lawyers in this legal order were not merely functionaries to the regimes devised by politicians. They were officers of the courts that served as an equal and independent branch of government, critical to the checks and balances that were the genius of American constitutions, state and federal. "Not we the titmice of England," one might imagine a Phelps or Keasbey intoning.

Woody Allen says that 80 percent of success is showing up. The ABA has proved the aphorism in spades. No one else in the late nineteenth century—or since—was much interested in thinking about such dry and arcane subjects as the uniformity of standards in commercial paper or the problems created by different standards for pleading a complaint. Nor did many care about the educational requirements for those who desire to earn a living from thinking about such things. No one other than lawyers, and elite lawyers at that, was eager to wade into these waters in the early twentieth century. The fact that the ABA, organized as a fully private and volunteer club, did, and produced a coherent and phenomenally effective legal platform, is a testament to the innovative fluidity of the American regime of the time.

But the ABA's efforts to raise and unify the standards for legal training and admission to the practice of law didn't only improve the quality and consistency of legal services. They also ultimately imposed a fundamental structural constraint on modern American legal infrastructure, one with tremendous implications for our potential now to adapt to a changing economic and social world. By vesting in lawyers and judges alone the power to regulate the legal sectors of the economy, and planting that power on constitutional grounds, the American legal profession achieved an unheard-of level of private regulatory control over an increasingly critical part of the economy. Legal self-governance is no ordinary form of professional self-governance. Unlike the prerogatives enjoyed by, say, doctors and dentists, under the ABA's leadership, the legal profession managed to secure the idea that its power to control the legal sector is beyond the reach of legislatures and is constitutionally protected.

The influence payoff for the ABA and state bar associations was enormous. Although formally the state supreme courts are in charge, the judiciary is poorly designed to formulate policy. Courts have few policy staff and they have an already overwhelming workload deciding cases. Courts picking up the mantle of control in the late 1930s thus became heavily dependent on the volunteer efforts of lawyers, and in particular the ABA, to develop the rules. With this shift, the ABA went from an advisory group issuing guidelines to a powerful lawyer-only organization with the ability to effectively convert its proposals into binding rules of legal practice.

Controlling Lawyers, Controlling Law

At the same time as the ABA was discovering that it could avoid legislative battles with banks, claims adjusters, and consumer organizations by shifting to the courts, it was also realizing that it wielded a powerful tool to cut these competitors off at the pass: lawyers. The 1931 committee that reported on the gamut of legal providers that were popping up throughout the country also made a critical observation. In the words of one ABA historian, "It was the unanimous opinion of the committee that these unauthorized practices would largely cease if it were not for the participation therein of members of the Bar."[17] This meant that the legal profession didn't have to rely on ferreting out and suing the offending organizations; it could simply impose on lawyers an ethical obligation to refuse to work with the offenders. And this it did. The Association had adopted in 1908 a Canon of Professional Ethics, focused primarily on what constituted ethical conduct in the advocate's role as an officer of the court with a duty to uphold the law. Between 1928 and 1937, however, the ABA extended the concept of ethics beyond conduct in court and fundamental matters of maintaining dignity and fidelity to law to encompass the business format of legal practice. Over this period it introduced several new provisions that made it unethical—and thus grounds for being deprived of the right to practice law—for a lawyer: to enter into a partnership or divide fees (that is, share revenues) with anyone other than a lawyer; to work either under contract or as an employee for any non-lawyer owned organization or business that sought to supply legal services to its members or customers; to accept referral fees from anyone; to allow his or her name to be included in an "unapproved" list of available lawyers; to advertise in any manner that claimed specialization; or "to permit his professional services, or his name, to be used in aid of, or to make possible, the unauthorized practice of law by any lay agency, personal or corporate."[18]

The shift was a brilliant and durable one. The rules, largely unchanged today but elaborated in thousands of detailed ethical opinions from state bar associations and the ABA itself, effectively forced out of the legal sector anyone who wasn't a lawyer and any entity that wasn't a law firm. The exceptions that remained were minor: real estate agents could give their clients standardized lawyer-drafted form contracts to fill out, tax attorneys could still talk about what the tax code did or did not allow, charitable organizations could provide some legal aid services, nonlawyer advocates could help people in some administrative hearings. Today the legal services landscape in the United States consists of effectively only one type of legal practitioner: people who have received a graduate law degree (JD) from an ABA-approved law school, passed a state bar examination, obtained a valid license issued by the state supreme court, and who do legal work exclusively for their corporate or government employer or operate in a law firm that is exclusively owned, managed, and financed by lawyers.

The loop was now complete. Only licensed lawyers could participate in providing legal services. The requirements to obtain and keep those licenses were under the control of the state supreme court, in theory. In practice they were governed by rules adopted by lawyer-only state bar associations, virtually all of which followed the rules developed by the ABA. Lawyers had obtained a state constitutional privilege to control the legal sector within their state. As we will see in Chapter 7, lawyerly control over this important platform for economic activity today plays a substantial role in choking off the capacity for handling the problems we now face in adapting our legal environment to a rapidly changing globalized, digitized, and web-based world.

Big Law

Little has changed in the organization of legal practice except for its scale since these early twentieth-century developments secured the organizing framework for modern legal infrastructure. In the United States, between 1900 and 1930, the legal profession grew more slowly than the population, and the number of lawyers per 100,000 people fell from 150 to 115. When the first phase of the expansion of New Deal era regulation was over and the legal profession's position as exclusive provider of legal services had been secured, however, the lawyer population had ballooned by 30 percent, outpacing the slowed growth in the overall population; lawyers per 100,000 people shot back up to 140 between 1930 and 1940.[19]

Lawyer growth exceeded overall population growth for the remainder of the twentieth century, but lawyers per capita increased only steadily until we reached the second phase of legal and regulatory expansion in the 1970s. Over that decade, the number of lawyers grew by 75 percent and lawyers per 100,000 people jumped over 250, a 60 percent increase in just ten years. The 1980s were also a decade of substantial growth, although nothing as dramatic as the 1970s: total lawyer head count grew 30 percent and the number of lawyers per 100,000 people pushed up another 20 percent over 300. By the end of the century there were almost 400 lawyers per 100,000 Americans. Other Anglo-American jurisdictions saw similar growth, although the number of lawyers in Canada, the UK, and Australia topped out below the US high, at 250 to 300 per 100,000 people in the first decade of the twenty-first century.[20]

There is no mystery as to where all those lawyers came from in the 1970s. More law schools opened. The number in the United States went from 146 to 171 in ten years. Law schools expanded the number of students they admitted just before the decade hit. In 1968, 23,600 students enrolled in American law schools. That number had jumped over 50 percent, to 36,000, just three years later in 1971. At the same time, more students who started law school actually graduated. At the start of the decade, less than half of law students finished their degrees; five years later and for the rest of the decade, completion rates bounced between 80 percent and 90 percent.[21]

It wasn't only the scale of the profession that grew dramatically over the course of the twentieth century. The scale of legal business itself also swelled. In a sense the cottage industry of law itself became more factory-like. At the beginning of the twentieth century almost all lawyers practiced solo or in two-, three-, or four-person partnerships; most were general practitioners. This is still true for lawyers that serve individuals and small businesses today. Law firms serving corporate clients, large organizations, and governments, however, ramped up in size throughout the twentieth century. The rate of growth was modest at first. In 1950, the largest law firm in Chicago had 43 lawyers, 81 in 1965. As late as 1968, there were only twenty law firms in the country that had more than 100 lawyers; the largest had 169. But just as the profession exploded in the 1970s, so too did the large law firm. By 1979 the largest law firm in Chicago was over ten times larger than the largest Chicago law firm in 1950, with 500 lawyers, 700 by 1984. By 2008, twenty-three American law firms employed over 1,000 lawyers each. In 1980 the ABA counted so few firms over 100 lawyers that they didn't bother to report the share of attorneys working in firms of that size. By 2005, 16 percent of all attorneys worked in firms over 100. In 2015 nearly 10 percent of all lawyers worked in the 200 most-profitable firms, with an average lawyer headcount of almost 600.[22]

The main reason corporate law firms grew so large in this period is that as the legal and regulatory environment became more elaborate and differentiated, legal work became increasingly specialized. The development of a more complex regulated economy had generated a thriving new line of legal work to add to litigation and simple transactions: helping to negotiate and structure complex deals and to design organizations, products, and practices that complied with regulations and maximized tax and jurisdictional advantages. At the beginning of the twentieth century, this new line of work was dominated by elite lawyers who served as general business advisers to large corporations, few of which had any lawyers on staff. By the 1970s, however, it was simply not possible for any one lawyer to hold out expertise across the broad swath of the law. Understanding corporate tax law or securities regulation, managing labor relations, or overseeing compliance with detailed industry regulations, executing increasingly sophisticated litigation strategies: all required a lawyer to devote him- or (increasingly) herself to a relatively narrow specialty. The general service lawyer thus became the general service law firm, with more and more lawyers necessary to cover the waterfront of an expanding landscape of legal and regulatory affairs. At the same time, corporations also began to grow their in-house legal staffs, lawyers who could specialize in the particular legal issues of the corporation.

As corporate law firms grew, so too did the share of legal work that was done for corporate clients as opposed to individuals or small businesses. The growth of the American legal profession and the disappearance in the nineteenth century of regulatory limits on who could practice law was driven by broad-based legal demand. Most law involved land and most households in the United States were landowners. There were signs that legal demand would continue to be shaped by broad-based legal demand into the 1930s. When the American Bar Association began to investigate the "unauthorized practice of law" in 1931, the wide array of providers it identified—banks, claims adjusters, automobile clubs, and so on—were primarily serving the legal needs of the general population and small-business owners. But within a decade all of these providers were squeezed out of the law market by ABA regulations that prohibited lawyers from working for or with any entities other than law firms.

Over the rest of the twentieth century there was a continuing shift of legal work away from the needs of individuals and small businesses to the needs of large corporations, organizations, and governments. As of 1980, more than 35 percent of all active lawyers in the United States were working inside corporations and governments or for law firms with more than ten lawyers—firms that serve individual clients rarely and small business clients infrequently. That number grew to 42 percent by 2005. In a landmark study conducted in 1975 and published in 1982 as *Chicago Lawyers*, researchers John Heinz of Northwestern University and Edward Laumann of the University of Chicago found that 40 percent of legal work was done for individuals and small businesses. Only 21 percent of this work was devoted to what Heinz and Laumann called "personal plight": civil rights, family, immigration, employment, plaintiff-side personal injury, criminal defense, and so on. Over the next two decades, both numbers shrank. In 1995, only 29 percent of legal work was for individuals and small businesses; the "personal plight" segment of this work now accounted for a mere 16 percent of total legal effort.[23]

Although the numbers here reflect the fact that Chicago is a major financial center and so is likely to have proportionately more business lawyers than smaller cities and towns, the national figures are probably just a bit higher than these. A study of the Ontario legal profession that I conducted with sociologist Ronit Dinovitzer estimated that across the province the share of legal work done for individuals in 1998 was about 42 percent; the figure for Toronto—a financial center comparable to Chicago—was 31 percent. These estimates are also consistent with US economic census data that show that in 1975 about half of the money earned by law firms came from individuals; that number had dropped to 35 percent by 2010. Taking into account that about 20 percent of lawyers work not in law firms but for corporations and governments, that puts the share of legal work done for individuals (which includes people running a small business as a sole proprietorship) at about 28 percent.

Heinz and Laumann described the legal profession in 1975 as consisting of two hemispheres, one serving corporate clients and one serving individuals and small businesses. "Hemi" is no longer even close to accurate. But their deeper finding still holds: if you want to know just about everything about a lawyer, just ask him or her whether his or her clients are individuals and small businesses or corporations and other large organizations. If you get the first answer—and you're not talking to the tiny number of highly successful plaintiffs' lawyers who collect millions in contingency fees in personal injury cases against tobacco companies or asbestos manufacturers—you can then make a safe bet that this lawyer probably graduated from a lower-tier law school or in the bottom half of even a more highly ranked law school, does not earn a lot of money, and does not enjoy much prestige or influence in the profession. Over the past several decades, this group has not seen much growth in income. If you get the second answer you know that you've found someone who probably graduated well ranked from a top law school, who enjoys prestige and influence, and who makes buckets of cash.

For lawyers in the latter category, the last decades of the twentieth century were heady times. During the 1980s, the real-dollar value of the services provided by US law firms grew at an annual rate that rarely dipped below 5 percent and hit as high as 15 percent. This growth significantly outpaced the growth of the economy generally, which saw growth rates of about 3 percent. Fortunes for lawyers then flattened out for the remainder of the century but still grew at or just below the growth of GDP.[24]

The growth of the corporate law market, and in particular the fact that it became increasingly lucrative, also drove growth in legal education in the decades on either side of the turn of the twenty-first century. After the great spurt in the number of American law schools and enrollment in the 1970s, things settled down during the 1980s. But growth took off again in the 1990s. By 2010, there were over two hundred law schools in the United States, and enrollment hit an all-time high, with over 20 percent more law graduates than there had been twenty years earlier.

This is the legal infrastructure we now take for granted as definitive of what a mature regulatory state looks like. It has extensive regulation developed by legislatures and implemented by government agencies. Sophisticated and numerous courts adjudicate legal claims in elaborate trial procedures. It operates at a fairly integrated level on a national scale. The law is honeycombed by specialized statutes and practice areas. Lawyers are highly trained specialists who have completed a graduate law degree and are regulated state by state by bar associations and courts. The only way to buy legal help is from a law firm or by employing in-house attorneys.

For the economic world that drove the development of this legal infrastructure, things worked remarkably well. The national mass-manufacturing economy grew like gangbusters on this platform. But of course the mass-manufacturing economy that was at its zenith in the middle of the twentieth century did not stand still. Economic transformation was upon us by the closing decades of that century. But as we'll see in the next chapter, as the economy has transitioned to a globally integrated, digital, fast-paced, and innovation-driven knowledge basis, what we need from legal infrastructure has been fundamentally transformed as well.

6

The Flat World

IN 2005 *NEW YORK TIMES* columnist Thomas Friedman told the world it was flat. *The World Is Flat: A Brief History of the Twenty-First Century* spent two years on bestseller lists, was updated twice (in 2006 and 2007), and, according to Friedman's web page, has sold over four million copies in thirty-seven languages.

Friedman's book, or at least its title, rubbed many academics the wrong way. The metaphor of the flat world was intensely confusing, even disorienting. What does it mean? That you will sail off the edge? That modern science has got it all wrong? Is this just a fancy way of saying that the world is getting smaller because transportation and communication costs are falling? UCLA economist Ed Leamer, reviewing the book for the *Journal of Economic Literature,* suggested the term was used by Friedman to capture so many different phenomena about postindustrial economies that Humpty Dumpty would have been proud. (As Humpty Dumpty tells Alice in *Through the Looking Glass*, "When *I* use a word, it means just what I choose it to mean—neither more nor less.") Leamer noted that there were several (he thought much weightier) books on globalization published around the same time as Friedman's book, written by card-carrying PhD economists who had devoted their careers to understanding globalization and trade. But, as he also noted, these luminaries, professors all at Columbia University—Jagdish Bhagwati, Jeffrey Sachs, and Nobel Prize winner Joseph Stiglitz—never got within spitting distance of number one on Amazon, the spot easily reached and held by Friedman.

The World Is Flat sold big because it captured in a thumbnail the revolution that was taking place in the global economy at the dawn of the new millennium. Even if the metaphor fell awkwardly on academic ears when Friedman coined it, it has come to mean, yes, just what Friedman chose for it to mean. And even if it mashed together a multitude of things that were changing—some in gradual ways, some in revolutionary ways—it nonetheless captured something true about what was going on in the global economy. *The World Is Different*, Leamer drily observed, would have been a more accurate title, but the book wouldn't have sold as well.

Friedman's six-hundred-page ramble through a thousand and one stories of cool stuff going on around the globe ultimately served up a compelling picture of the ways in which communications technology had created, in the wake of the fall of the Berlin Wall, a truly global platform for doing work. This global collaboration platform, he marveled, allowed American product designers, Indian software engineers, and Asian manufacturers to collaborate over a massive video screen in a conference room at Infosys in Bangalore; US hospitals to have CAT scans read overnight by doctors in Australia or India; and Japanese homebuilders to have hand-drawn plans converted into digital designs by Chinese homeworkers. This world of web browsers, workflow software, uploading, outsourcing, offshoring, and deeply data-intensive logistical coordination, Friedman said, had leveled the playing field around the planet. It had flattened hierarchies, as companies and organizations reached out beyond their walls to collaborate and innovate. With the collapse of the barriers to global trade erected by the Soviet Union, India, and China, the number of potential players on the field had more than doubled. Anyone who could connect could come to the party.

Of course, as many critics pointed out (and Friedman himself confessed he was well aware near the end of the book), the world is not really flat. Far from it. It may be getting flatter in places, but there's a great deal that still tilts the odds in favor of some locations over others. After all, if all it takes is connection to the web to become an integral player in the global economy, Africa would be rich by now—or at least not as desperately poor as it has been for centuries. The playing field is still clearly slanted.

Some of the forces that make the world spiky (in sociologist Richard Florida's image) and uneven are based on the nature of the very technology and communication infrastructure Friedman lauds: increasing returns to knowledge make the knowledge-rich even richer; companies that live in innovation ecosystems, such as the vibrant Silicon Valley, outperform those toiling in more isolated outposts, even if the outliers can Skype into the meeting. Other forces tilting the playing field are related to the revolution in transportation infrastructure that, puzzlingly, Friedman never mentioned. The advent of cheap container-based shipping in the 1980s opened the world up for many countries but also widened the disadvantage for those landlocked in central Africa or Asia. Moreover, huge economies of scale in transportation and distribution favored even more so those capable of capturing massive markets. Some of the obstacles to flattening are ones that Friedman himself pointed out are prevalent in poor countries: disease, lack of education, poor transportation infrastructure, corruption, and exploitation of the poor by elites.

The most glaring hole in Friedman's flat-world story, however, is the absence of any mention of legal infrastructure. Cheap communications and transportation have given us the global supply chain. But flattening production processes with global supply chains requires more than technology and container ships. It requires resolution of that basic problem of how to coordinate and support collaboration and exchange. It requires ways of resolving the externalities and conflicts that upheaval in economic life creates. It requires a means of responding to the very unevenness—the nonflatness—that Friedman's critics pointed out have persisted, even been exacerbated, in the wake of the ways in which the global platform has rearranged work and resources.

These are the types of problems that, as we've seen, culture solved in simple human societies and that the many rule-making groups of medieval Europe—the guilds, town councils, churches, princes, and lords—helped to solve as economies grew more differentiated and complex. They are the problems that the emergence of the nation-state and centralized, democratically controlled legal systems responded to as the bounds of the Commercial Revolution of the Middle Ages gave way to the industrial revolutions of the eighteenth and nineteenth centuries. Those earlier solutions, however, are no longer working well, as we'll see in Chapter 7. And as we'll explore in more detail in the last chapters in the book, more than half of the world's population lives in poor places that are still waiting for the arrival of last century's legal solutions, in informal economies that operate outside any formal legal framework. Friedman made a nod to how the flat world challenged the norms and boundaries of the traditional nation-state—calling for a "great sorting out" of such problems—but he mostly emphasized how the transformation of the global economy would require new rules. That's the standard view, too, of most economists. What that view misses is the critical role of legal infrastructure in leveling playing fields and flattening production processes. Rules don't just happen, they have to be made. And our technology of making them has to keep up with the complexity of what the rules are trying to regulate.

In the decade since Friedman's book first appeared, the pace at which the world is being flattened has only accelerated. When Friedman was writing in

2005, Facebook was still an online directory for college students. YouTube had not yet launched. Twitter was a year away. Netflix streaming and the iPhone were two years out, the App Store three. Global online freelance platforms like o-Desk and Mechanical Turk were just gearing up. Amazon Web Services—the first significant cloud-computing platform—wouldn't be around for a year; Google and Microsoft's entry into cloud-based IT infrastructure and browser-based services for businesses wouldn't show up until 2008 and 2009 respectively. Bitcoin was four years away. The US Securities and Exchange Commission had only just introduced new rules for competition between stock exchanges that would fuel the race among high-frequency traders to shave transaction times down to microseconds; the general public wouldn't notice until the first stories started appearing in the *New York Times* and the *Wall Street Journal* in 2009. The global platform was getting ready to do much more than just reduce communication costs and expand labor markets to enable the global supply chains and opportunities for horizontal collaboration that dominate the story in *The World Is Flat*.

Mass digitization—the conversion of everything from phone calls, stock trades, movies, and documents to identities, social networks, geographic locations, and genetic information into flat sequences of zeros and ones that can race along fiber optic cables and over wireless networks—has made it possible to convert a vast array of our economic interactions from ones embedded in physical objects and fixed locations to disembodied ones that exist both nowhere and everywhere at the same time. Powerful computers that can analyze the information contained in those globally available ones and zeros in vastly greater quantity at vastly greater speeds than the human brain have dramatically reduced the time it takes to develop a new product or spread an idea or complete a transaction. Virtual reality devices allow us to immerse ourselves in places thousands of miles away, and robots allow us to do things there. 3D printers allow even physical objects—machine parts, clothing, food, human tissue—to exist only in digital form in the cloud until a user hits "print." The Internet of Things connects our homes, workplaces, devices, bodies to the world, beyond our awareness. Cars talk to weather and traffic sensors, regulators, and each other—and don't need humans in the driver seat. Your printer can order the ink it needs, all by itself.

The impact on the economic demand for law of all of these changes—from the global supply chains and horizontal collaboration that Friedman emphasized to the mass digitization of economic life that came after—is enormous. With yet another massive leap in the complexity of the economy, our legal infrastructure has yet to catch up.

Flattening Production

In the economy Friedman was writing about in 2005, the major impact of the global web-enabled platform was on the way work was done and in particular the emergence of global supply chains and global collaboration. So let's start our thinking about how the global platform transformed the economic demand for legal infrastructure there.

From Boxes to Networks

If you want a quick schematic of the economy that produced enormous growth in the twentieth century, picture a box. The box is Chandler's massive midcentury, vertically integrated, managerial corporation. Although it might have had outposts in scattered foreign lands, the control structure of the box sat squarely within the borders of the country in which its owners and managers resided. Into the box came investment dollars, raw materials, and workers. Inside the box, corporate managers organized in elaborate hierarchies, ordered dollars, raw materials, ideas, machines, and labor around to transform them into final products. Those final products were then shipped out of the box to buyers, and some of the dollars those sales produced made their way back to investors and lenders. Most of the resources that came into the box were from the same country in which the box sat. Most of the buyers of the goods that came out of a box lived in the same country as the box. The box got buffeted around by the economic winds that howled around it, but provided it was large enough, the box remained relatively stable as the managers inside the box redirected resources to adapt to change—unless and until the relatively rare event in which the whole thing collapsed in the face of bad management, competition, or obsolescence. You can label this box. Call it General Motors, General Electric, U.S. Steel, AT&T, IBM. Boxes like this could be found all over the Western world.

There were different kinds of boxes elsewhere. In regions where people lived under communist or socialist economic systems, there was only one massive box, and the hierarchy of managers ordering resources around was composed of government officials; that box was labeled the Soviet Union, China, India. Little made its way across the boundary of that box. In the poorest regions of the world, there may have been boxes with some government officials in them, but very little was happening inside because there were few resources to order around; you can label those boxes Sudan, Afghanistan, Haiti, Cambodia, Yemen, Bangladesh.

To get a quick schematic of the economy taking shape in the twenty-first century, blow up the boxes. Reassemble the pieces into a network. The network is global. It bounces around the planet, seemingly oblivious to the boundaries of politics or economic development. Every time the network touches down, a bundle of investment dollars, an idea, some raw materials, a few components, or a few workers are woven into the final production of goods and services. Now when the economic winds blow, connections in the network dissolve and are reformed to adapt to new opportunities and pressures. Large fractions of the work, materials, and components that go into production, not to mention the investment dollars, are intangible, digital, carried along fiber optic cables threaded under the seas and through the mountains. The physical products moving within the network are often components not yet assembled into final goods. We can still make out the boxlike outlines of corporations in the network, but now it is more difficult to judge what is inside and what is outside. The network flashes and changes with great velocity; the boxes are porous. Whole regions of the world that were once dark are occasionally sparking.

The emergence of a global web-enabled platform for economic activity reversed the drive to vertical integration that powered the twentieth-century economy. Manufacturers have reconfigured the patterns of what is produced in-house and what is outsourced to where. Steps all along the production and distribution process have been refined and spun out or spun in, depending on where they are best accomplished. Research and development—long the internal preserve of megafirms like IBM—are now supplemented by open innovation and methods of procuring ideas, both in the raw and as embodied in products and patents and business methods, from wherever they arise. Pharmaceutical companies still run massive internal R & D departments in industrial complexes, but they also post scientific challenges and offer rewards to scientists the world over on open innovation platforms like Innocentive and NineSigma; they partner with, license from, or acquire biotech start-ups operating with twenty people out of a converted warehouse in downtown Oakland, California. Clothing retailers gobble up designs from employees and independent contractors and put in orders for fabrics from India, buttons or zippers from Japan, silk-screening in China, and sewing in Bangladesh. Computer manufacturers like Dell take orders for new products designed in the United States and send orders for millions of different components to thousands of suppliers located in North America, China, Brazil, Europe, and Malaysia.

The shift from Chandler's boxes to Friedman's networks flattens the production process. There is still a lot of vertical integration, of course, but to a greater extent than was true in the middle of the twentieth century, economic activity is being organized on a horizontal firm-to-firm basis rather than vertically under the unified management of a firm or corporate group. Boeing, for example, outsourced 35–50 percent of the development and production of the 737, first built in the 1960s. It outsourced 70 percent of its new 787 Dreamliner introduced in 2011.[1] Boeing's experience tracks what is happening across all sectors in the economy. According to calculations done by economists Richard Baldwin and Javier Lopez-Gonzalez, the share of total manufacturing production that is made up of final goods as opposed to intermediate inputs (parts and components used to make final goods) fell between 1995 and 2009 from around 68 percent to 63 percent; in machinery the drop was from about 60 percent to 50 percent and in electronics from about 40 percent to 30 percent. The drop in services was from about 68 percent to 60 percent. Although the great majority of international trade (over 80 percent of manufacturing and over 90 percent of services) is still of final products, as it was in the box economy, the share of intermediate inputs—the parts and components that are shipped from country to country in global supply chains—has doubled worldwide from the 1970s, increasing several fold in Asia and high-tech industries, particularly communication equipment. And services that are inputs into final products—the work done by the software engineers in Bangalore or Chinese homeworkers converting building sketches to digital blueprints that Friedman focused on—make up an increasing share of all international trade in intermediate products, close to one-third.[2]

The world is not flat but it is getting flatter, in Friedman's sense, and that is transforming what the world needs from legal infrastructure.

Crossing the Boundary of the Firm

The most immediate impact of the flattening of the production process is an increase in the frequency with which economic activity crosses the boundary of the firm. In the box economy, most of the coordination of the process of first deciding what to produce and how, then converting raw materials, money, and people's effort into finished goods and finally delivering those goods to buyers takes place inside the box. And the main feature of legal infrastructure over the last century in advanced economies has been a largely hands-off approach to what happens inside the box. In its heyday, if senior managers at GM wanted to speed up or slow down production, abandon a model, pull resources from the Buick division to Oldsmobile, or use parts designed by Pontiac engineers for Chevrolets, the law had nothing to say about it. They just went ahead and did it. Regulation and collective bargaining agreements with unions may have limited how long a shift could be without paying overtime or the reasons for which a worker could be fired, but the very definition of an employee from a legal perspective is a person whose work activities are subject to the control of the employer. As Nobel Prize–winning economist Oliver Williamson observed, the process of adapting production within a firm is a matter of fiat, and the law intrudes very little.[3] It is only when the process of production crosses the boundary of the firm that law gets in on the action. In the vertically integrated firm, boundary crossing is kept to a minimum. At the extreme, nothing is brought in except money, capital equipment, workers, and raw materials, and nothing is sent out except final goods and payments to suppliers, workers, and financiers.

In the network economy, however, things are constantly crossing the boundary of the firm. When Toyota pioneered the revolution in manufacturing known as lean production that eventually came to define modern flexible supply chains, it fundamentally shifted the relationship between the inside and the outside of the box. It didn't just bring raw materials across the boundary; it exchanged ideas, data, components, and workers with its suppliers, distributors, and customers all along the process of converting raw materials into automobiles.[4]

Rather than handing suppliers detailed blueprints and specifications for how to manufacture components such as brakes or seats, as GM did, Toyota supplied its manufacturers with exterior dimensions (so the parts would fit with other parts) and performance criteria, such as how quickly the brakes have to stop a car of a certain weight traveling at sixty miles an hour. Toyota left up to suppliers the task of designing the detailed way in which the part would be constructed to achieve those targets. Toyota focused its whole system on constantly uncovering problems and improving processes, and on having those closest to the problem play the biggest role in problem-solving. Even the famous just-in-time inventory system that Toyota introduced to the world—manufacturing just enough parts to feed the production process as needed—was part of an overall goal of finding and fixing problems as fast as possible. Small inventories meant problems with a part or process could be detected and fixed quickly. Close collaboration with suppliers meant a constant exchange of information about difficulties in assembly and component-level expertise about how to fix it.

Toyota crushed GM, and Ford, and Chrysler, because it could make use of vast amounts of information and expertise all along the value chain from raw materials to a final product in use by a consumer to continuously improve the quality of its cars and reduce the cost of producing them. But to do this Toyota had to count on the cooperation of people and organizations that it did not control. If Toyota wanted to use ideas or change resources or shift from one supplier to another, it couldn't just order people and resources in the production process around the way GM could. Toyota depended on a legal infrastructure that would support cooperation across the boundary of the firm to an extent that GM did not.

Some of the difference between what Toyota (or any business patterned on the Toyota model, including the reinvented GM that survived bank-ruptcy to live another day) needs from legal infrastructure compared to companies in the box economy like (the old) GM is simply a matter of scale. When firms are no longer as vertically integrated as they were in the twenti-eth century, there are many more steps in the process of finance, production, and distribution that require coordination and cooperation between inde-pendent businesses and individuals. That means, at a minimum, many more contracts and rules governing relationships. With more products changing hands, there are more opportunities for accidents and injuries, damages and loss. There are more opportunities for fights about who added how much value where and how big a share each should get when there are profits to go round. With more entities along the path from finance to design to produc-tion to distribution involved in sharing risk, there are more entities looking for insurance and to offload losses. There are more opportunities for fraud and anticompetitive behavior. There are more decision points at which strat-egies and interests can diverge.

But an increase in the sheer number of contracts and rules needed to connect firms into horizontal networks is only a small part of the transfor-mation in the demand for legal infrastructure wrought by a flattened pro-duction process. A much more challenging transformation in demand, one our existing legal infrastructure is struggling to meet, comes from the deeply integrated and information-rich nature of the connections in the network. That changes the very nature of the contracts and rules the economy needs, not just their number.

Let's go back to Boeing.[5] When Boeing set out in 2003 to build its revo-lutionary 787 Dreamliner—using innovative materials, systems, and designs to increase fuel efficiency, capacity, range, and cabin comfort, and decrease assembly times and maintenance costs—it shifted from a traditional sup-ply process to one patterned on the Toyota model. In the traditional model, Boeing entered into "build-to-print" contracts with thousands of parts suppliers. These standard supply contracts required suppliers to meet hundreds of pages of Boeing-supplied specifications exactly. The terms of the contract were based on fixed prices with penalties for delay. Boeing took delivery of all those parts and assembled the aircraft in its factories. For the Dreamliner, however, Boeing shifted to an approach that involved contracts with just fifty strategic partners, responsible for coordinating and assembling entire sections and systems for the plane. Those tier-1 partners contracted with tier-2 suppliers (some of which then contracted with tier-3 suppliers). At some point in the chain, the contracts being used could well have been standardized build-to-print contracts with fixed prices and penalties. But the contracts Boeing wrote with its strategic tier-1 partners were anything but standard. These were what are known as build-to-performance contracts— Boeing developed performance targets for the section or system the partner was responsible for. The tier-1 partner was then deeply involved in the innovation and development of the parts and systems it would take to meet those targets.

The types of contracts Boeing entered into with its strategic partners are enormously challenging to develop and manage. They involve risk-sharing, complex incentives, and a host of issues related to who owns what in the innovation. Proof of how complex those contracts were soon arrived. The Dreamliner project encountered huge budget overruns, multiyear delays, malfunctions in landing gear, engines, fuel lines, and hydraulics, and a battery fire that led regulators to ground the entire fleet. A joint study into the whole mess by Boeing and the Federal Aviation Administration pointed to the challenges of Boeing's innovative supply contracts as a culprit.

What Boeing needed from its contracts to support a more networked approach to innovation and production was far more complex than what it needed when it operated under the model of the box economy. Boeing could find most of what it needed in the legal infrastructure built up over the twentieth century, but only so long as it stuck to twentieth-century approaches to production. Sales transactions—the transfer of ownership over raw materials or final goods—have been with us for thousands of years. The legal systems of most advanced economies have since the late nineteenth century included a comprehensive and stable set of rules to structure agreements about how many widgets will be delivered by what date, at what price, with what payment terms, by what mode of transport. There are clear rules about who is responsible for paying for freight costs and who bears the loss (and thus is responsible for insurance) in the event goods are burned up in a warehouse or lost at sea or stolen from the railyard. Transactions like this are now fairly standardized, and the contracting parties just have to set out the basics: price, quantity, specifications, and delivery dates. There are hiccups—things that no one expected or planned for, such as the buyer's buyer canceling or shortages in raw materials or labor strikes or bankruptcy. But even these things are common enough that most industries have long-established rules for how to handle them. In fact, in a famous study of contracting conducted in the 1960s—in Chandler's box economy—University of Wisconsin law professor Stewart Macaulay found that business people didn't have much use for detailed written contracts.[6] Even when their legal departments required formal contracts, managers stuck them in a drawer and pretty much ignored them in practice. (Yale law professor Grant Gilmore in his 1974 book, *The Death of Contract*, deemed Macaulay the Lord High Executioner.) Macaulay found that business people didn't need formal contracts to manage problems as they came up because for the vast majority of transactions, it was pretty clear what the rules were. That's what standardization and stability buy you in the mass-manufacturing world of the twentieth century—standardized and stable legal infrastructure gets the job done.

Information-rich relationships across the boundary of the firm, however, pose great challenges that far outstrip what standardized sales law and stable industry practices from the nineteenth and twentieth centuries can handle. But information-rich relationships that cross the boundary of the firm are precisely what efforts to innovate better, cheaper, and faster ways of doing things in the flat world are made of. As economist Richard Baldwin of the Graduate Institute of International and Development Studies in Geneva has emphasized, globalization's "second unbundling," which allows the stages of production to be disaggregated across different companies and places, is fundamentally a consequence of the ways in which improved information and communications technology has allowed managerial and manufacturing know-how to move more easily around the world.[7] (The first unbundling, a consequence of the railways of the Industrial Revolution, decoupled the place of production and the place of consumption.) That's what enables a Japanese or German car manufacturer to take advantage of lower production costs in Thailand or China while still ensuring that the parts merge easily into the overall process of developing and assembling an innovative vehicle. Such tacit knowledge is critical to the way production is organized, a point originally emphasized by Nobel Prize winner Oliver Williamson, the father of transaction cost economics.[8] Williamson appealed to an anecdote from philosopher Michael Polanyi who, in his 1958 classic *Personal Knowledge*, wrote of having "watched in Hungary a new, imported machine for blowing electric lamp bulbs, the exact counterpart of which was operating successfully in Germany, failing for a whole year to produce a single flawless bulb." The machine could be purchased and shipped using standard contracts. But figuring out how to get tacit knowledge from one place to another was a challenge in the twentieth-century world Polanyi inhabited. Today there is a bevy of low-cost communication and analysis tools to help with problem-solving, all cheaper than sending a German engineer to sit in a Hungarian plant for weeks on end: digital cameras and video, low-cost international voice-over-internet phone calls, digital capture of machine behavior and product characteristics, big-data analysis, remote control of computers, and automated equipment. Transferring information is much easier and cheaper from a technological point of view.

But when information transfer happens across the boundary of the firm, from an economic point of view it is everything but easy. For one thing, there's what Nobel Prize–winning economist (and my former PhD adviser) Kenneth Arrow called the paradox of information. It goes like this. How much should you pay someone to tell you something when you don't know what it is they will tell you? Suppose I am your supplier and I tell you that I will come up with a great idea for how you can decrease costs and increase profits in your business. I want you to pay me to come up with this idea. How much are you willing to offer? Obviously if I come up with an idea that saves you a million dollars, you'd be willing to pay me a lot. But maybe I won't come up with anything nearly as valuable as that. Maybe all the ideas I think I can try out with your company won't work well for you. The problem is neither you nor I know right now the value of what I'll come up with. If we knew, well then you wouldn't need to pay me to come up with it. Or suppose I already have this idea and I want to tell it to you, for a price. Again, you don't know how much you want to pay until you see the idea, but once you've seen it, you don't need to pay me to tell you. Or if we've decided that I'll trust you to pay me after you've seen it and decided how valuable it is to you, how do I know you're telling me the truth when you say, "Oh, we already knew that. We're not paying you anything"? That's the paradox—information is valuable but really hard to contract over.

The paradox of information is related to the fundamental problem of what economists call asymmetric information. Another Nobel Prize–winning economist, George Akerlof, called one version of this the lemons problem. Suppose I do know how valuable my bright idea for a better component is for you. Maybe we managed to get past the paradox of information and you agreed to let me get started. Now I've discovered that the component works pretty well at first but it wears out more quickly than I expected—frankly, it's a lemon. But you won't know that until you've started using the components and running with them for a while. You're smart enough to know that there is always a risk that you're buying a lemon, so you're not willing to pay me as much as you would if the component worked the way it should. So that means I have little incentive to figure out how to fix the problem. Unless I can prove my components are not lemons—get rid of the asymmetry in information between us—you won't pay me what the good ones are really worth. But getting us both onto the same page information-wise may be very expensive. After all, I specialize in components and you don't—you don't have the expertise to judge what I'm showing you, perhaps. Or maybe I don't want to show you too much because I'm worried you'll pass on my secrets to a competitor or start using them yourself—you won't need me anymore.

Then there's the challenge of what economists call moral hazard. You want to encourage me to work hard and cut costs without cutting corners, and you'd like to give me great incentives by paying me on the basis of how good a job I do. But there's a problem: I know more about how good a job I'm doing than you do, more than you could ever know at reasonable cost. So I may take advantage of my information edge to get you to pay me for work I'm not doing or not doing as well or as cost-effectively as I know you want me to. Cheating like this is why this hazard is called moral. This is true even in traditional supply relationships. The GM of the twentieth century tried to manage this problem by rigidly defining specifications for supplier parts, soliciting bids, engaging in costly inspections looking for defects, and only granting short-term contracts, which allowed managers to dump a supplier they weren't happy with. They still had the problem, however, of not being able to perfectly monitor defect rates, and they could-n't monitor well at all the costs incurred in doing the job—costs that the supplier would try to use as leverage for price increases—unless they had a parallel in-house division capable of producing the same parts. The problem is exponentially more difficult, however, in the Toyota-type process, where suppliers are specialists and are asked to use their special knowledge and expertise to collaborate in meeting performance criteria to increase value and reduce costs.

Finally there's the problem that the very reason relationships across the network, as opposed to within the box, are valuable is that everyone is trying to come up with something new—to find a solution that we don't yet know about to a problem that we also may not yet know about. How do we even talk to each other about what we think our deal is? How and when we will be willing to pay for it? How will we know if we are both living up to the plan? How will we decide if what one of us thinks is cheating—talking to a competitor about solving a related problem, for example—is fair game or not? And who owns the new ideas we come up with—can I use the cost-cutting we devised to solve your problem in my next contract with your competitor? Can you share the details of the solution with my competitor or your in-house team?

For all these reasons, the problem of contracting across the boundary of the firm is orders of magnitude more complex in the network economy than it was in the box economy. Boeing's management of complex long-term relationships with suppliers who are expected to collaborate with each other and with Boeing in deep ways to continuously improve quality and reduce costs is not at all like contracting for the delivery of a thousand widgets built to spec for an agreed price per unit.

Law-and-economics researchers call these potentially long-lived and amorphous contracts relational contracts. They require continuous and complex adaptation to everything that is learned, by someone somewhere in the value chain, in the face of all the problems that come when you try to create incentives and share risk and value information is evolving and asymmetric.

It is conventional to see these complex feats of relational contracting as ones that rest on inherent trust and loyalty rather than law. During the 1980s, for example, when Toyota was beating the pants off GM, Ford, and Chrysler, American commentators often attributed Toyota's success to special features of Japanese culture. In his 1994 book *Trust*, Stanford political scientist Francis Fukuyama argued that a central explanation for the ascent of Japanese lean manufacturing, and the decline of the American manufacturing sector, was found in the deeply embedded culture of trust among strangers that was still vibrant in Japan and eroded in America. Economists studying relational contracts also tended to see relational contracts as having nothing to do with law. After all, the Japanese almost never litigated and had few lawyers.

The platform that supports complex relational contracting, however, has more legal structure than the trust, culture, and reputational sanctions explanations let on. Japanese lean manufacturing itself wouldn't have arisen without a heavily structured legal environment, driven by the Ministry of Commerce and Industry during World War II.[9]

Prior to the war, Japanese vehicle manufacturing largely consisted of Japanese assembly using imported parts from American and German suppliers. The war, however, cut off the supply of parts, and there was at the time almost no expertise in part design or manufacturing in Japanese firms or the Japanese labor force. To meet the need for military vehicles (Toyota was ordered by the government to stop producing passenger cars and specialize in military trucks in 1938), Japanese bureaucrats created the system of what they called "collaborative cooperation factories" and "dedicated cooperation factories," and the multitier system that eventually conquered worldwide auto manufacturing. Subcontractors were organized into associations to promote horizontal and vertical communications and were guaranteed minimum orders, technical instruction, and machinery on loan. Prime contractors were made responsible for the affiliated groups of their subcontractors. (Nobusuke Kishi, the minister of commerce and industry, described the plan in July 1943 like this: "MCI plans to make child factories dedicated to parent firms, and grandchild factories to child firms. Child and grandchild factories must stop manufacturing finished products and must manufacture components principally for their parent factories. Parents and children must share labor, management, materials, and capital.")[10]

The famous Japanese supply chain *keiretsu*—informal groups of businesses in long-standing relationships—emerged from this government-created industrial solution to a crisis in wartime manufacturing. Even if these relationships eventually bred a culture of commercial trust and loyalty, it's clear that they did not grow organically out of ancient Japanese traditions of hospitality and family. They grew on a dense platform of legal rules and practices. Japanese laws for decades regulated details such as how soon subcontractors were to be paid and facilitated the organization of subcontractors into small business cooperatives, able to share technology, machinery, and access to finance, by exempting them from antitrust law and prohibiting the participation of large enterprises.

Even the practice of lifetime employment in Japanese companies, another indicator to observers such as Fukuyama of the importance of the culture of loyalty and trust, grew up on the scaffolding of legal infrastructure. As auto researchers Womack, Jones, and Roos documented in *The Machine That Changed the World*, during the first few years of the American occupation of Japan following the end of the war, American-imposed credit restrictions triggered an economic depression. The founding president of Toyota, Kiichiro Toyoda, proposed to reduce the company's workforce by one-quarter in response. The company's union, however, newly strengthened by

Japanese legal reforms required by the occupying Americans, was able to broker a deal changing the rules of the workplace. In exchange for reducing the workforce by one-quarter the unions secured for the remaining employees a guarantee of lifetime employment, seniority-based rather than task-based pay, and bonuses tied to profits.

It doesn't matter whether these deals, bouncing back and forth across firm boundaries, were litigated or not; that is not what made them law. They clearly were built with legal tools and resources. This legal infrastructure served as the seedbed for the dramatic transformations that were to come. The lifetime employment guarantee enshrined in the contract with the unions now meant that Toyota needed to get the most it possibly could out of a labor force it could not get rid of. And so it focused on continuously enhancing workers' skills. There's a lot more going on here than long-standing cultural traits. The relationships that became the essence of the Toyota way were figured in terms provided by Japanese legal infrastructure.

Legal infrastructure is still playing a central role in scaffolding the complex information-rich relationships in our most innovative companies. I learned this in research I conducted with Iva Bozovic, a former PhD student of mine and now lecturer at the University of Southern California.[11] We wanted to know if contracting was still "dead" in the way Stewart Macaulay had suggested it was in the 1960s. How were companies managing their most innovation-critical relationships—the strategic alliances and codevelopment arrangements they needed to compete aggressively in a fast-paced global environment? What we heard from some of the leaders in Silicon Valley was: we use a lot of law. But not for the purposes of litigating and threatening big damages. We use a lot of lawyers and contracts to design our strategic alliances because it is critical that we have as much structure as we can put down to steer the informal development of our relationships in constantly churning waters.

That's what a 2012 study of corporate development professionals by consulting firm Deloitte found as well: upfront planning and a solid governance structure are critical to manage the tremendous challenges posed by strategic alliances such as joint ventures, equity alliances, and licensing arrangements.[12] These complex types of deals, the survey found, are increasingly critical tools for sourcing innovation, breaking into new markets, and managing both risk and capital. These strategic alliances are still very much relational contracts—largely enforced by the risk of losing a valuable relationship or doing damage to reputation—and trust and personal relationships play an important role. But they also depend significantly on law, lawyers, and legal advice to help define what actions will sink the relationship or reputation and what will keep everyone confident they are still on the same team.

What the innovators Bozovic and I interviewed told us they need from their contracts is very different from what companies need in the box economy. In the relatively stable world of vertically integrated mass manufacturing, discrete and standardized contracts can do the job. But in the flat world, infused with the complexities of contracting over information, off-the-shelf contracts and standardized legal reasoning and approaches don't cut it. What's needed are creative ways to manage enormously challenging and dynamic strategic relationships. As we'll see in the next chapter, lots of our most innovative companies are struggling to find this kind of legal infrastructure.

Crossing the Boundary of the State

The networked economy doesn't just cross the boundary of the firm on a regular basis. It also regularly crosses the boundary of the state. Friedman's flat world is fundamentally a globally networked platform. The global nature of the platform makes the answer to that critical question—what rules do we all follow around here?—ever more mind-boggling. It is small wonder that the number one complexity worry of CEOs in our largest companies is law: when you're constantly hopping national boundaries, you have to juggle not one but perhaps hundreds of legal systems.

Friedman's documentation of the chain that built the Dell computer on which he originally composed *The World Is Flat* is almost certainly out of date, but it still paints a nice picture of the boundary-hopping involved. The basic designs of Dell computers at the time were developed by Dell engineers in Austin, Texas, and specifications for these designs were developed by a Taiwanese company. As explained by a global production manager Friedman interviewed, "We put our engineers in their facilities and they come to Austin and we actually co-design these systems." The thirty key components then used to manufacture the computer came from a constellation of American-owned factories in the Philippines, Costa Rica, Malaysia, or China; Korean-owned factories in Korea or China; Taiwanese-owned factories in Taiwan or China; German-owned factories in Germany; Japanese-owned factories in Japan, Malaysia, China, Thailand, the Philippines, or Mexico; Chinese-owned factories in China; Irish factories in China; British-owned factories in China, Malaysia, or India; and an Israeli-owned factory in Israel. Connecting all these links in the chain were credit card services provided by an American credit card company, website services supported by American firms, broadband connections delivered by local telecommunications companies in every country in which Dell products were sold, airlines and shipping companies transporting components to service the Dell supplier logistics centers located near the Dell assembly plants in Malaysia, Ireland, China, Brazil, and the United States, and parcel delivery services such as UPS and FedEx coordinating logistics and delivery to customers in every country where Dell customers were found. That's a lot of borders crossed.

For megacompanies, operations that cross state borders are commonplace. General Electric operates in more than 170 countries. Cisco Systems has offices in 94 countries; Google in more than 40. IKEA has stores in 37 countries, Walmart in 28. There are brick-and-mortar Apple stores in 19 countries and online stores in 33; its supply and assembly chain spans about 30. If you go to the Intel website and search for job openings, you could be presented with a map showing openings in as many as 64 countries. These megacompanies (at least the ones that existed) were of course multinational throughout much of the twentieth century. Now they are even more so.

But it's not just megacompanies that are multinational anymore. The global web-based platform means that small and medium-sized businesses are, and increasingly must be, regularly crossing national boundaries as well. Smaller companies engaged in manufacturing in advanced economies, for example, are bringing in components and sending out their products worldwide—sometimes to foreign assemblers for the megacompanies that will ultimately import final products back into those advanced economies. Smaller companies in developing economies with lower wages and costs are precisely the companies that megamanufacturers are seeking to integrate into their global supply chains. E-commerce businesses, perhaps tiny to begin with, open their doors (and servers) to a global market. Particularly in technology industries, new businesses are frequently "global from day 1," as the GC of a network equipment manufacturer headquartered in Silicon Valley once told me: the day they started up, they had engineers on the team scattered in countries around the world. O-desk, the online freelance employment marketplace, connects even the smallest start-up needing services such as web design, software development, administrative support, or customer relations with freelancers from Asia, Eastern Europe, Latin America, North America, Western Europe, Africa, and the Middle East. Amazon's Mechanical Turk makes it possible for any company of any size anywhere to access anyone anywhere willing to do a small discrete task—draft, transcribe, translate, or proofread copy, for example, or test weblinks, check pricing accuracy, or identify images—for micropayments of a few pennies per task.

Nor is it just products, parts, and services that cross those borders in the globally networked economy. Money is transferring across electronic banking, payment, and trading systems. Global financial markets, as the world learned in stunningly painful fashion in the financial collapse of 2008, create tremendous demands for legal infrastructure that is coordinated globally. Financial instruments like the ones based on US subprime mortgages are traded in worldwide markets that are then linked to what American investor Warren Buffet called a "daisy chain of risk," at a level of complexity that even Buffet and his lawyer-partner Charlie Munger found impossible to evaluate.[13] Regulatory decisions in Iceland and Ireland and Greece and Spain, not to mention the United States, Britain, Germany, and France, are deeply interconnected. Money doesn't respect the nation-state.

And sometimes money seeks to deliberately eliminate the nation-state. Bitcoin is a global open-source and entirely digital means of payment that presents completely new demands for legal infrastructure. Some of this demand comes from Bitcoin boosters—who see it as a way to get out of the grips of big banks charging fees and government regulators controlling currency flows. Some of this demand comes from Bitcoin foes—who want to protect the capacity for government regulators to manage the money supply and control financial speculation and for law enforcement and national security analysts to track money flowing to terrorists, arms dealers, drug cartels, and tax evaders.

Information is also constantly zipping over the internet and dedicated networks between customers, banks, logistics companies, assemblers, manufacturers, and shipping companies. And because the goal is for continuous reduction in costs and improvements in quality, the information that is exchanged across these global networks, indifferent to state borders, is often of significant commercial value, feeding into innovation and competitive advantage and not merely coordinating purchase orders and delivery dates. That makes it the kind of information over which there is tremendous economic interest in the questions of who can do what with the information they access and how information is protected from unauthorized access and use.

And then there are those externalities. These include the things that cross borders that nobody wants, like crime, terrorism, and greenhouse gases, and the things that some people don't want, like Western culture and values, economic dislocation, and the upheaval of traditional ways of life.

The globalization of the production platform was in part brought on by changes in legal rules. As the twentieth century was drawing to a close, the former Soviet Union collapsed and the legal rules for moving goods and people across the borders of former Soviet states changed. Countries of the global South—and especially India and China—slashed tariffs, scrambled to make the legal changes needed to join the World Trade Organization, entered into bilateral investment treaties with rich countries, and signed regional trade agreements. These changes in the rules governing the movement of goods, services, and investment across state borders is what brought close to 40 percent of the world's population into global markets (at least theoretically; we'll see in Chapter 11 that many are still boxed out in practice). As a result, the G7 (Canada, France, Germany, Italy, Japan, the United Kingdom, and the United States) share of global manufacturing dropped from 71 percent in 1970 to 46 percent in 2010—with eighteen percentage points of the gain going to China and the remainder to Korea, India, Indonesia, Thailand, Turkey, and Poland.[14]

Global trade, however, isn't only affected by the rules governing when and how goods, services, and investments are allowed to cross borders. The great increase in the amount of economic activity across state borders also works a fundamental transformation in what the world needs from legal infrastructure. The shift from North-North trade to North-South trade, for example, has meant a substantial shift from trade between countries with comparable and advanced legal systems to trade between countries with very different, sometimes highly inadequate, legal infrastructure. Moreover, as Melissa Thomas documents in her book *Govern Like Us: Expectations of Poor Countries*, many of the "states" that were created when colonial powers departed were states on paper only, with little capacity to govern across the territories sketched on world maps. has generated fundamental challenges for a legal infrastructure organized around the nation-state.

One of the ways in which globalization affects legal demand is pretty obvious. Trying to do business across multiple legal systems all at once creates a demand for information about how those legal systems work, what their rules are. Companies need to know about how each individual state manages basic contract and property laws. How the state regulates employment, investment, product safety, and database security. How individual industries are regulated. What and when taxes are assessed. What commercial choices will bring the antitrust or anticorruption authorities, from which country, sniffing about.

But the transformation worked by the globally networked platform goes far beyond a simple increase in the volume of legal knowledge needed. When the business is boundary hopping to build the highest-quality, lowest-cost, most reliable product or service that legal infrastructure will support, the need is for smart big-picture views of how all these different locations conflict, cohere, and work together. Plopping down a pile of ponderous legal research memos in front of a senior manager responsible for figuring out how to squeeze out better logistics across a global supply chain or anticipate when and where the next important iteration in product design will be coming from is about as helpful as sending the modern urban dweller into the Arctic alone with instructions to figure it out. Much of what people need from law, particularly in a world where law is complicated, coming from thousands of sources at once and constantly in flux, is expert navigational judgment.

The terrain is spongy in places, and in some cases what looks like solid ground is just a deep dark hole. That's because legal infrastructure is not just a matter of laws on the books. It's a matter of the nature of legal expertise and advice available on the ground. It's a question of how rules and regulations are managed and implemented in practice, how responsive they are to the interests of a local trade group or company, to this political agenda or those cultural pressures. Court and regulatory systems that promise splendid-sounding procedures and protections can in practice be riddled with interminable delays, incompetent judges, opaque processes, or rampant bias and corruption. Consider the situation of a responsible company trying to ensure that the contractors it works with in developing countries are providing safe workplaces for their employees, not employing children, and ensuring that their products are not adulterated with unapproved ingredients or worse. It is hugely risky to rely just on either the local government's regulations or the workplace standards that teams of lawyers have written into the supply contracts. As the GC of a global communications company based in Europe once told me, it's enormously complex to figure out, for example, just why it is that workers are still falling to their deaths from cell towers in India, long after all kinds of rules have been put in place about what workers can and cannot be asked, or allowed, to do on the job. Assessing and solving that problem requires deeply knowledgeable cross-border understanding of the legal environment in the context of all the things that affect how rules on paper do, or do not, add up to changes in behavior.

Local norms, practices, culture, politics, economics: these all conspire to produce the hidden features of legal infrastructure. They too vary from country to country, sometimes from city to city. Traveling around the globe with only a map that shows engineering plans for glorious roads and bridges is not much good. What you need is a map like the one the Outward Bound guide had with her on a ten-day canoe trip I took through northern Ontario many years ago: one that has penciled in the information that the portage is "long and swampy."

Multiple legal environments that cross and conflict map out a terrain of risk, but they also chart the contours of opportunity. The KPMG study that found that 70 percent of senior executives at large global companies named regulation as the number one cause of complexity for their businesses also found that 75 percent saw complexity as a potential source of opportunity. Sometimes the challenge of responding to a complex patchwork of regulatory relationships or legal difficulties leads to creative restructuring of entire supply chains or the information management systems used to coordinate work and achieve compliance. Companies that excel at being proactive in anticipating the direction of legal change and in implementing effective responses earn a competitive advantage. Finding, or helping to shape, a legal environment that does a better job of meeting the fundamental economic demands of business—helping to manage complex contractual relationships, for example, or reduce labor disputes, or protect against fraud and corruption—helps a company to secure those economic benefits. There are at least as many gains to be had from expert management of global legal logistics as those to be found in global shipping, global information systems, or global strategic alliances. That too is part of the economic demand for legal infrastructure, and it is something that businesses need more and more of in a complex, globally connected economy.

Faster Problem-Solving: Novelty, Speed, and Complexity

One of the first principles of the Toyota system that laid the groundwork for the reconfiguration of global supply chains was the idea that nobody should rest on his or her laurels. Companies should be constantly striving to find and resolve the problems that add to cost, reduce quality, and breed other problems. Toyota opened a huge competitive advantage over GM and other traditional mass-manufacturing car companies by doing things like giving employees on the assembly line a cord that they were encouraged to pull to halt the entire line so problems could be fixed as soon as they appeared. Moreover, Kiichiro Toyoda, Toyota's founder, instilled companywide the idea that it wasn't enough just to find the first cause of a problem—such as a badly calibrated part. It was critical to keep asking why—why was the part badly calibrated? Perhaps it was because there was a rush order placed for these parts and the supplier had to turn to temporary workers with less training. Then why was a rush order needed, and why was the supplier not able to accommodate the order with its regular workforce? Maybe the rush order was a result of problems in the tracking of inventory or the integration of the IT systems between the assembly plant and the supplier. The solution might be a redesigned IT structure or a switch to a different communications service provider. Or maybe the problem was high absenteeism at the supplier factory and the solution was to resolve long-standing worker complaints that demoralized the workforce. A focus on fundamental problem-solving is at the heart of the new global economy.

Intense focus on problem-solving, and an appreciation of the systemic nature of problems—the central teaching of American statistician and management expert William Edwards Deming, who was brought to Japan by General Douglas MacArthur after the war to help with reconstruction of the Japanese economy and who played a major role in the development of lean manufacturing processes—breeds increased novelty, complexity, and speed. We study problems to find new ways of doing things. That generates new structures, new products, new services, new sets of relationships. We begin to see things we've never seen before. The capacity to talk for free over a video connection with someone in Wuhan or Waziristan. Smartphones with apps that allow ordinary people to share with anyone else on the planet with a smartphone or laptop or tablet the news about what they're making for dinner, the latest gossip about celebrities, or what caused that explosion that just rocked through Tahrir Square. A 3D printer you can assemble at home and use to print out cute little plastic objects, tools, pizza, or guns. Workers in Nairobi using mobile phones to transmit money back to their relatives in a tiny village in Kenya. A car that drives itself, and unmanned drones that deliver packages and payloads.

Of course, new things, and new ways of doing things, have been appearing on the scene for as long as humans have been around. The difference is the accelerating pace at which they appear and the exponential growth in their variety. Toyota enjoyed a tremendous competitive advantage in time to market with a new model once it had refined its new manufacturing systems. In *The Machine That Changed the World*, Womack, Jones, and Roos compared GM's new model development process with Toyota's. In the 1980s, the GM-10, the chassis and engine design that would ride inside the Buick Regal, the Olds Cutlass Supreme, and the Pontiac Grand Prix, took nine years to go from initial idea fully to market, practically the entire decade. Toyota developed its 1990 Accord in under half that time. Even Toyota's time to market seems now painfully slow. In the world of technology, building on Moore's law that the capacity of a silicon chip will double every eighteen months, we have grown completely accustomed to the idea that our computers, software, and devices will need upgrading every few years or faster. Phenomena like YouTube, Twitter, and Instagram appear on the scene one year and are ubiquitous the next. And quite possibly gone the one after that. New products, indeed whole new markets, emerge with great speed, knocking down the half-life of existing products. Commercial relationships form and fall apart quickly when flexible systems respond to increasing wages or changing political fortunes. The very ease of sharing data and communicating across a global web-based network that knows few bounds—Friedman's level playing field—makes changing partners far easier than in the days of custom-built information-sharing solutions. If you ask anyone in these industries about the pace of innovation, they will tell you that, like the great white shark, if you stop swimming, you die.

Constant innovation and problem-solving in the globally networked economy also makes business environments, products, and processes far more complex. I mean here complex in that complex adaptive systems sense. Lots of actors, lots of decisions, lots of variation—all in systems that are woven intricately together. A ripple here produces a tidal wave there. It may not be the butterfly flapping its wings in Thailand that causes a hurricane in Texas, but it may be the judge who is effectively bribed by a local magnate to rule that the local supplier can pour the concrete that brings down the tower that crashes the communications system that causes the computer manufacturer to cancel the Chinese contract and switch component purchases to Mexico. Risks are propagated, canceled, and amplified throughout millions of network connections. Weaknesses in one spot can damage even the strongest links elsewhere. An obscure development in how one of the thousands of components and services that ultimately go into a phone or a vacuum cleaner or access to a social network can trigger a fundamental restructuring. And as we know from the financial collapse, triggered domino-like by defaults in the subprime mortgage market in the United States in 2008, networked risks can sometimes bring the whole system down. Predicting where the system will move next and how robust it will be is next to impossible.

Novelty, speed, and complexity serve up a triple whammy in the economic demand for law. Now we need legal solutions and expertise, including regulatory expertise, that understand products and services and relationships and systems that didn't even exist a year ago, ones that we didn't even contemplate. Rapidly changing product, market, and network configurations reduce the half-life of legal solutions, such as how to ensure compliance with legal regulations or manage employee and supplier relations. That means we need legal solutions that don't take forever to develop and don't break the bank—because new solutions are likely to be needed in short order. We need legal solutions and strategies that both operate closer to the ground and yet are global and systemic in their design.

Novelty, speed, and complexity also mean that legal strategy has to be integrated with business and policy strategy. From the point of view of business, which regulations can you run the risk of violating while you figure out a compliance strategy? Which ones should you attempt to shape up-front rather than waiting to challenge them on the back end? How will moving operations from region A to region B, or from business type A to business type B, to maximize tax advantages impact overall logistics, costs, regulatory risk, and product quality? From the perspective of the policymakers, how do you intervene in a system that is in important respects fundamentally unpredictable? Should you wait for industry efforts to develop self-regulation to emerge, domestically or globally, preempt such efforts, or try to shape them? Should you design regulations for the way the system is now or the way you predict it is going to look a year from now? All of these questions are ones of how the global constellation of tax, trade, employment, industry, competition, anticorruption, and other areas of law all come together and the implications not just in one location but across the entire chain. They are questions of how all the legal variables interact with the complex structures in place to manage information technology, market conditions, and the political winds. Legal analysis can't exist off in a specialized corner by itself. It needs to be deeply integrated with business and policy thinking. As we'll see in the next chapter, our legal infrastructure is failing, badly, on that front. For reasons that would be pretty easy to fix.

Flattening Information

Much of the networking of the global platform is, of course, a result of digitization. Outsourcing call centers to the Philippines or software programming to India only started to make sense when it became possible to send voices and code in high volume in digital form over fiber optic cables. The offshoring of back-office functions began in the 1970s with batches of paperwork sent to the Caribbean by ship; by the mid-1990s thousands of low-cost workers in the Caribbean, Asia, and Ireland were being sent physical documents by cargo plane to keypunch and beam back by satellite or on magnetic tape. The capacity to digitize the original paper documents and send everything over fiber optic cables drastically changed the cost equation. The capacity of fiber optic cable to India alone increased sevenfold in just one year, between 2001 and 2002.[15]

Friedman's focus in *The World Is Flat* was largely on how digitization contributed to the flattening of production processes. As he put it, digitization puts the flattening process on "steroids." Together with ubiquitous wireless networks accessible from personal devices like mobile phones, digitization opens wide the channels for global collaboration. Faster, more extensive collaboration magnifies the impacts of the flat world on law that we've already considered. Wireless connectivity lowers the cost of bringing the billions of people not reached by phone lines onto the global platform and increases the volume of economic activity that leaps over firm boundaries and state borders. The analysis of big data puts problem-solving into hyperdrive, generating more new products and processes that come along at even faster rates with higher degrees of complexity. Legal infrastructure needs more, faster, better to keep up.

But digitization doesn't just contribute to the flattening of production processes. Digitization flattens *things*. It takes objects and actions, voices and images, and converts them all into single-dimensional strings of ones and zeros. It converts a concrete world that exists in time and space and reduces it to one that exists only as energy. All this stuff-as-energy is flying around the globe, hopscotching from server to server, in the seconds between hitting "send" and the "ding" of an email or text or update arriving. Moving it around and storing it is essentially free. The information contained in those ones and zeros: is it "in" Pakistan or Colombia or New Zealand or France when it flashes in a server there? In one sense, it is in all these places at once. In another, not any of them. Moreover, the information is both ephemeral, existing only for an instant, and yet also permanent, available forever.

Flattening information into digital form not only flattens time and place; it also flattens action, shrinking the role of humans. A truck that accelerates or brakes or steers into a wall because software—either loaded onto the truck's computer or beaming in over the internet—tells it to, for example. If the algorithms running the truck use machine learning—meaning the software running the computer learns and updates itself as it processes information—it may have been a long time since a human was involved. Self-driving vehicles are talking to servers, not humans. High-frequency trading algorithms are doing deals with other computers. My robo-caller may be scheduling meetings or confirming deliveries with your digital assistant. The malware that executes on a cyberattack is a full-on machine-only endeavor. Human agency begins to disappear from the picture.

The impact of digital flattening on the economic demand for legal infrastructure is profound.

Rules for Zero

Physicality, time, and agency are expensive. Physical things are made up of resources, and physical places have to be traveled to. Time is money and opportunity cost. Inducing people to do one thing rather than another often requires paying them, or punishing them, in some way. That's why the flattening of information into digital arrays has had such an enormous impact on economics: the cost of information starts screaming toward zero. And zero changes a lot.

Start with the zero that keeps innovators up at night: the cost of copying digital information. When all you have are zeros and ones, copying is perfect, and perfectly costless. Think of what it took to copy music just a few decades ago. A copier had to get access to a physical object, such as a vinyl record or CD, play it in real time, and capture the sound onto another physical object like a cassette tape. The time and resources and loss of fidelity involved in that process kept copying somewhat in check. Copying digital music, in contrast, gets you, practically instantaneously, a version that is identical to the original and stored for free on a device that can accommodate gigabytes (or more) of data. Moreover, anyone in the world can do this, at any time. The same is true of books, movies, software, and designs. As 3D printing develops, it becomes true of potentially anything.

Perfect, and perfectly free, copying exacerbates a risk that innovators have always faced, risks addressed for hundreds of years by patent, copyright, and trade secret laws. That heightened risk places new demands on our intellectual property laws. But it doesn't fundamentally change what we need law to do. Cheap and easy copying does, however, change what we need from law for a different reason: free copying turns everyone into a potential competitor. Our existing approaches focus on regulating commercial activity—the sale of copied and infringing goods. They are designed to protect a stream of profit from the sale of inventions and creations so that people and businesses can make a living from invention and creation. The owners of intellectual property secure the protection of intellectual property by identifying the one or five or ten businesses that are competing with them in the marketplace and going after those sellers for injunctions, disgorgement of their profits, and royalties on their sales. But when users can produce these goods at home for their own use, the scale and invisibility of copying is off the charts—practically impossible to reach with our existing intellectual property rules and tools. That's why in 2011 and 2012, as documented by economists Susan Athey of Stanford University and Scott Stern of MIT, piracy accounted for 25 percent of all installations of Windows 7 worldwide. Users stole encryption keys (over 90 percent of all pirated copies were attributable to just twelve keys) and posted them with copies of the Windows software to peer-to-peer sharing websites like Pirate Bay.[16]

Moreover, when copying is done by users and not competing businesses, it's not just about money anymore. Telling people what they can do in their own homes or on their personal devices, and tracking their behavior at home or on those devices, raises questions about individual autonomy and privacy. Users who don't just copy digital content to avoid purchasing it but also to use it to generate their own music, videos, writings, software, and objects are engaged in self-expression. And it turns out that when copying is free, there are lots of creators out there who are quite happy to create for free too—filling the world with free open-source software, books, music, and ideas. But autonomy, privacy, and self-expression, not to mention the willingness to create things for free, are values that are simply not in play in most of the existing legal infrastructure in place to protect commercial intellectual property and incentivize commercial innovation. It's not that we don't need to protect commercial innovation—we need new ways of addressing the risks of mass digital piracy taking place on a global scale—but the simple economic models we've used to construct those incentives are faltering as the Economics 101 boundary between who is a supplier and who is a consumer dissolves.

The ease of copying digital information once you get it puts greater pressure on controlling access to information in the first place. But there too the costs in the digital domain are much closer to zero than in the physical world. With data zooming around the globe on an open internet—deliberately designed to be accessible to anyone, anywhere—access means simply dipping into the river as it rushes by. Well, maybe not so simply. Protecting data has also been digitized, through the use of encryption—which is not costless. That sets up the contest between the hackers and the owners—also not costless. But data theft is much, much less expensive than when thieves had to break into a warehouse and truck out loads of documents or computer disks.

The still-not-zero-but-getting-closer costs of accessing data have given rise to legal demands we've really not seen before. Cybersecurity is a high-priority demand for businesses and governments alike and not just to protect the intellectual property value of information by warding off copycats in the market for goods and services. Hackers access data to steal it and sell it. To corrupt it. To compromise identities. To shut down local and global systems—emergency response, utilities, financial services—and wreak havoc with the Internet of Things. We are already facing the risk that a hobbyist's drone could be cyber-seized and crashed into a crowd. That the camera on your computer or nanny cam is not just showing you images, but also beaming your image who knows where to who knows who for who knows what purpose. That someone half a world away could become you online and drain your bank account, your credit rating, and your reputation. We've long faced the risks of eavesdropping, wiretapping, impersonation, and financial fraud. But in the almost-zero world of easy access to digital information, the scale, scope, and global reach of these risks is unlike anything our legal infrastructure has had to deal with before. Conventional solutions are outdated and inadequate before the ink has dried on the paper—as if ink on paper could keep up with the electrical, optical, and magnetic pulses that make up both the information we're trying to protect and the efforts of those who are trying to hack it.

There's another set of zeros that is upending our legal infrastructure as a result of digitization, one that is also upending conventional economic models of competitive markets. These are the zeros associated with platforms and scale in digital environments.

The first zero involves the cost of providing goods or services to an additional consumer. In conventional economic models, this is costly. For ordinary goods, selling to more people means producing more goods, and goods cost money to make, store, and distribute. Ordinary markets, however, sustain lots of competing sellers to meet growing demand because beyond some point (which may still be quite big) bigger is not better. Once a factory has reached optimal scale, expanding production to sell to more consumers requires building another factory, and some other company can do that just as well, and for the same marginal cost, as the first. In fact, expanding too big might cause marginal costs to increase. Those are the ordinary cases in economic models of eventually constant or diminishing returns to scale.

But for some digital products—think digital movies, music, books, software—the marginal cost of expanding the number of consumers is zero. In an era when people can carry terabytes of information in their pockets and bandwidth is almost unlimited, digital products are stored for free and distributed for free. This means digital products are subject to increasing returns to scale indefinitely: bigger is always better.

The value generated by zero costs of increasing scale in the digital economy poses a major challenge to our conventional approaches to regulating competition. That approach is grounded in an economics of static technology and an expectation that most markets reach efficiency with lots of relatively small-scale competitors. But increasing returns to scale can make monopolies valuable in some cases. Monopoly profits fund innovation and longer-term goals that go beyond maximizing quarterly sales. That's why venture capitalist and PayPal cofounder Peter Thiel wasn't apologetic about advising wannabe entrepreneurs in his 2014 bestseller, *Zero to One*, to focus on building monopolies: find the thing that no one is building, not the next-best iteration on an existing product. Monopolies built on big innovative leaps produce value for their builders and society.

The fact that monopolies can bring benefits in the digital environment, however, doesn't mean they don't also bring costs. The problem for legal infrastructure is that no one really knows how to think about, and regulate, monopolies in this far more complex environment. Digital monopolies may make consumers pay too much today—for what they're getting today. They may give corporations too much power to dictate what we can buy today. But they may produce something even better for tomorrow. Especially if (as may, or may not, be true in digital markets) the barriers to entry for new businesses to challenge a current monopoly are lower than in the world of factories and railways. Or if gobbling up potential competitors is an effective way of managing the complexities of protecting intellectual property. That's a key reason that large companies acquire small start-ups: to grab their patents, trade secrets, and engineers. Trade-offs like these are a bit mind-boggling for competition law.

These are challenges that our legal infrastructure has been struggling with for a few decades now. Antitrust authorities in the United States successfully sued Microsoft in 1998 for bundling the Internet Explorer web browser with the Windows operating system on the theory that Microsoft was exploiting its massive market share in operating systems for personal computers and hampering the development of Netscape as a competitor. Today that seems a little ridiculous given the growth of the Apple operating system and the development of competition from mobile devices and cloud-based computing. Unless, in ways that we just can't assess very well, the antitrust limits placed on Microsoft helped those competitors grow.[17] The 2015 European complaints against Google—alleging distortion of search results to benefit Google's shopping services—may look just as ridiculous when all is said and done.[18] Or they may play some role we can't yet see in sustaining a competitive internet. That will be a matter for economists to debate for a long time yet. But what is not up for debate is just how difficult it is to figure out how to protect competition without squelching innovation in digital markets.

The zero associated with expanding the number of consumers of digital products, however, is just the beginning. There are also major challenges arising from a basic organizing feature of the digital economy: the platform. Platforms employ standards to reduce the transaction costs of digital interactions—reducing them to near zero in many cases. The internet is a platform—created by a standardized protocol for routing packets of information between computers and other devices. Facebook and YouTube are platforms connecting people, companies, and advertisers. Amazon and eBay are platforms connecting buyers and sellers. Uber and Airbnb are platforms connecting riders and drivers, travelers, and people with extra space.

Zero transaction costs—for people on the same platform—generate what economists call network effects: a platform is more valuable the more people and businesses there are on it. The more people who are using a particular operating system, the more apps developers will make available on that system. The more people on a social network, the more connections a user can make. The more people using a particular search engine, the more data the engine's algorithms have available to figure out what people really want to find and the better the search results.

Platforms are rewriting conventional economic logic. In the standard economic model there is a firm that supplies goods to consumers. Producing goods is costly to the firm and generates value to consumers at differing amounts—higher value to some, lower value to others—as reflected in a demand curve. Markets work by facilitating competition between profit-seeking suppliers to better meet consumer demand at lower cost. Platforms, however, don't fit this conventional picture. Most importantly, they are multisided: they provide services to multiple groups of "consumers" at the same time. Apple and Android operating systems are simultaneously serving the demand for apps people can use on their devices and demand from businesses developing and selling apps. If the Apple or Android standards don't succeed with developers, then they don't succeed with users. And if users aren't interested, developers won't be either. Moreover, Apple and Android are also "consuming" a product generated by the platform—the data they get about users and developers, which can be used to build the next generation of platforms. They might "sell" that data to others to use to build other things, or to improve the capacity for targeted advertising. That's yet another source of demand.

I put scare quotes around "consume" and "sell" here because some of the transactions on a platform are not priced at all—more zeros. Developers might get access to the application programming interfaces (APIs) they need for free. Users might get access to the platform for free. Strategic partners might get access to the data for free. All because there is no value to the product unless there is sufficient scale on all sides of the platform. Figuring out how to get everybody on the same digital page, and keep them there, is almost the definition of complexity: lots of decision-makers, lots of interaction, lots of uncertainty. That's why a major challenge for new digital start-ups is figuring out what business they're really in.

Platforms are rewriting economic logic, and regulatory logic in the process. There's the initial question of competition law and monopoly. The monopoly in the Microsoft case from the 1990s involved a platform. The challenge to Microsoft's PC operating system monopoly didn't come from competing producers of PC operating systems as in conventional markets. It primarily came from competing platforms, in mobile devices and cloud computing. Those platforms took off not just (or even primarily) because they were more successful at offering users a better, cheaper product but also because they offered application providers and advertisers a better product. So the question of how to respond to Microsoft's monopoly was even more mind-boggling than economists at the time realized. Regulating competition sensibly requires some ability to predict what will happen in markets if a monopoly goes unchecked: will consumers be better or worse off? What would have happened if the antitrust authorities in the United States had done nothing? Or if, as some economists urged at the time, the courts had broken up Microsoft as they had AT&T in the 1980s? As Harvard Business School professor Shane Greenstein tells it in his fascinating account of *How the Internet Became Commercial*, breaking up AT&T played a critical role in the birth of the decentralized and open internet we now know. But even the best antitrust economists of the time could not have predicted the ways in which this transpired. (Some of the explanation, Greenstein emphasizes, was rooted in the "almost visceral dislike for centralization at Ma Bell" among computer scientists.) Conducting antitrust analysis and enforcement in the context of platforms is even more difficult now than in the good old days of factories, or when platforms like AT&T were stable, durable, and largely unchallengeable.

With the growing ubiquity and importance of platforms we also face sprawling problems with questions about access to platforms. Who sets the terms of use for a platform? What limits are there on the price of access— including the hidden price of, for example, being obligated to share data with a private company in exchange for access? As we'll see in the next chapter, the terms of use are currently being set largely by the providers, using the tools of standard contract law—stretching to its far outermost limit the concept that it's okay to hold people to a deal they knowingly and freely made. (When was the last time you read before you clicked "Agree"?) In the twentieth-century economy, essential platforms included services like phone, water, and electricity. These were either publicly owned or operated as regulated monopoly utilities, with a public body setting the rules of access. Digital platforms, however, are almost all privately owned and developed—and we wouldn't have many of them if they weren't. But what does that imply about how the rules of access are made when platforms become essential? What if almost no one has a phone line at home anymore and access to text messaging is the only, or most reliable, way to contact emergency services? It is increasingly the case that access to the internet is essential for a decent life. What of the "digital divide" between rich and poor? Urban and rural? Educated and not? The problem extends far beyond resolving political debates about redistribution and equality. When the platforms are the product of innovation and private investment, they move fast and break things, repeatedly. Including last year's solution. How do we regulate in that context?

The more radical rewriting of regulatory logic, however, comes from the way in which digitization disrupts basic categories of conventional economic analysis. When people and businesses are connecting on a digital platform, consumers can also be producers, assembling news and web content in a blog or creating videos on YouTube and selling clicks to advertisers or gated content to subscribers, for example. Widespread and cheap 3D printing will blur the line between producer and consumer still further, as well as the line between retailer and manufacturer. When platforms facilitate contracts between service providers and users, who is providing the service: the platform or the providers or both? Are Uber drivers employees? Or are they independent contractors running their own little microdriving business? And when platforms are layered and interconnected, creating what some call value webs with a multitude of services mixed and matched to produce what is ultimately consumed by a user, the boundaries between markets and services are very hard to find. Not to mention the challenge of identifying just where in this hairball a transaction is occurring—particularly when so many of them, at one time or another, might be given away for free.

Categories matter a lot for our existing legal infrastructure. Written with taken-for-granted stability in mind, many of our laws and regulations are anchored on existing categories. Labor laws that establish rights regarding wages, working conditions, and unionization, for example, can only be applied once we've decided who is an employee and who is an employer, who is worker and who is management. Is a service given away for free "sold" and so subject to consumer law governing sales? Does the platform that brands and facilitates the provision of a service need to be licensed as a provider? We face the kind of challenge on a massive scale that German courts faced in the late nineteenth century when people began tapping into electrical wires to siphon off electricity without paying for it and companies sought to have them charged with theft. The problem was that theft was defined in the German law as the taking of an asset, and electricity, the courts decided, wasn't an "asset." American courts similarly, as late as 1937, were being asked to decide whether electricity was "personal property" and therefore covered by larceny statutes. (They decided it was.)[19]

And then there is the massive disruption to the very concept of "work" that may lie in a future defined by digital automation, artificial intelligence, and robotics. Throughout human history, people have claimed their share of resources through their efforts. Prior to mass industrialization, the vast majority of people produced their own food and shelter, and traded for what else they needed by selling what surplus they had. In advanced countries, the industrial wage economy had, by the mid-twentieth century, displaced work on the family farm for all but a tiny percentage of the population, but it was still the case that what someone consumed was tied to what he or she produced and how the market compensated that production. Even the social safety net systems that grew up over the twentieth century—unemployment insurance, social security, welfare—were tied to worker productivity with access earned by past earnings or job-search efforts. When people's efforts need to be incentivized to produce what we need, there are rationales (and limits) to all of this. But if the future is one in which few need to work for our economies to produce everything we need, and our long-acquired equating of work with what one deserves comes under terrific pressure, how will we manage the sharing of resources and wealth?

There's nothing inherently new in these challenges. The economic demand for new rules to address new types of products and processes has been a constant in the history of economic development. What's important about the changes that digitization is wreaking in the economy today is the size of the challenge. Few things are staying still over there while we work on this piece over here. Speed and complexity are the state of play. The stage is global.

The Featureless Plains of the Digitized World

Digitization is not only disrupting what we need legal infrastructure to do. It is also fundamentally altering the materials with which to do it. This is because law, since it first emerged in human societies, has been constructed using the physicality of things in the world, the timing of events, and the agency of human actors. These are the handles that law grabs onto, the natural contours that law fits itself into and around. But in the featureless plains of the digital world, these handles and contours, like conventional economic categories, are dissolving.

For example, when information is embedded in a physical object—a floppy disk, a paper document, a machine—access to the information can be controlled by rules about access to the object—property law. Since the object exists in some place at some time, the rules of property are based on where the thing is when. If the disk, document, or machine is within the walls of my office or factory, I can control who can see, use, or potentially monkey with it by controlling who gets into my building. If an object in which the information is embedded travels out of my control—shipped to a customer or mailed to a business partner or licensed to a contractor—I can track where the object went, to whom, and when. I can write agreements and count on laws like copyright or patent that address how, when, and where the people who have the object can use the information it contains. Even if the information in the object makes its way out of my building without my permission, and maybe out of the object in which it was embedded—in the brains of my employees or a visitor—I can look to rules that are grounded in the concrete circumstances in which the building was accessed, the object seen or used, and the information distributed. If you broke into the building and stole the disks or the documents or the machine, you are guilty of theft in the jurisdiction where my building sits. If you are my employee—or you are a business partner who met with me to discuss a potential deal and I had stamped the information CONFIDENTIAL before our meeting—I can look to the law of trade secrets or the contract we entered into to complain that your use of the information to compete with me is unauthorized.

But when information exists only in digital form and bounces momentarily through servers that can be located anywhere on the planet, the natural constraints that the law depends on to control and identify access are gone. I can keep people out of the building or lock them out of my computers. But that has no impact on access to the flat arrays of ones and zeros that the work we're doing is constantly sending in and out of the cloud. I can't just keep track of who has been in the building or talked with my staff to sniff out the source of a leak. Any number of people I've never heard of or met can interact with my data in any number of places. In fact, my data might be accessed and used by systems and software without any human being involved.

This lack of physicality and agency is also what makes questions like who is responsible for the behavior of a self-driving car that causes injury so mind-boggling. It's not that there are no ways of carving up the problem. We can say that the manufacturer of the car is responsible. But that is no longer a natural solution, in the way that making one of the drivers involved in an accident responsible is natural. Any way we carve up the question of responsibility will be in some ways deeply arbitrary. Why the manufacturer and not the passenger who yanked the steering wheel thinking that the car was malfunctioning? The regulator who required a steering wheel to be installed in the first place? The programmer of the weather sensors that sent faulty information or the operator of the wireless network that crashed momentarily and delayed information reaching the vehicle? The stream of data that this vehicle, or this model of vehicle, happened to acquire as its algorithms were learning how best to evaluate and choose actions in complex settings?

Can a string of ones and zeros—the data that an artificially intelligent machine used to learn about its environment—be responsible for anything?

Drawing arbitrary lines is nothing new for law. We do it all the time. In fact, there is a famous theorem named for the late Nobel Prize winner and University of Chicago economist Ronald Coase that says that, provided transaction costs are zero, deciding who has a right to do something is essentially arbitrary from an economic efficiency point of view. The Shasta County ranchers that Yale professor Robert Ellickson studied and we heard about in Chapter 2 had two different rules they followed: some said ranchers had a right to let their cattle roam; others said farmers had a right not to have their crops trampled by roaming cattle. The Coase theorem says it doesn't matter which rule you choose, if all you're worried about is making sure that ranchers raise cattle and farmers plant crops in an efficient way. If the damage cattle do to fields exceeds the value of roaming, cattle will be corralled, even if ranchers have the right to roam: farmers will pay ranchers to keep their cattle at home. If ranchers have no right to let their cattle roam, they'll choose to keep them at home to avoid having to pay more in damages than they gained from roaming. (Although there's no impact on what happens in terms of economic activity, you'd always rather be the person with the right, because then you don't have to pay if it's efficient for you to exercise the right and you get bought off if it's not.) Again, it's not that we can't come up with ways of allocating responsibility for outcomes with complex new technologies like self-driving cars. More than ever we need a framework of rules to make complex circumstances manageable. The problem is that in a flat digital environment the natural candidates for rules are no longer served up by the constraints of time, place, and agency.

There's another reason that the loss of the physicality and agency of the real world upends our conventional approaches to devising rules for how we interact. We don't actually do anything in the digitized flat world. For us to interact with disembodied sequences of ones and zeros, they have to be reconstituted into the real world: displayed on a screen, played on a device, converted into an object, performed as an action. But that reconstituting can happen in a million and one different contexts.

Context matters tremendously in the design and application of rules. What is safe and acceptable behavior in one context—a display on the phone of a high school student in Shanghai, an object in the hands of an expert, an action executed on a sunny street in London—may be unsafe or unacceptable if it shows up on the phone of a young person in Yemen, falls into the hands of a novice, or happens on a muddy path in the Amazon. And as the world becomes ever more complex, the more we are called on to make judgments about what is okay and what is not okay that vary with context. This is why, for example, so many rules are written in what can often seem like frustratingly vague language: because until we know the context in which an action is taken, it can be very hard to know whether it should be allowed or not.

Tort law—the law that sets out the rules about who is responsible when someone is injured or property is damaged—is a great example of this. In most legal systems the basic rule can be stated pretty simply: people (and organizations, companies, and sometimes governments) are responsible for harm they cause if they fail to act reasonably in the circumstances. The rub, of course, is: what does it mean to act reasonably? That's what juries in America and judges in most other systems decide, based on all the facts and arguments that can be put together in the concrete context in which an injury occurred. But the core assumption in all these systems is that the people on those juries or sitting on those judges' benches are familiar enough with the contexts in which actions are taken that they can decide what is and isn't reasonable. It was pouring rain when the accident happened? Then the driver should have slowed down. The company had installed a child-proof safety cap on a dangerous household chemical? Then the company can't be blamed for what happened when it was left uncapped where a child could get it. We can judge what is reasonable or not because we understand the context. But what if the context is far removed from the experience of the judge or jury? We already struggle with this problem in getting judges and juries to make judgments in terribly complex settings, far from their personal experience. What was it

reasonable for a drug manufacturer to do when interpreting complex clinical data? What would a reasonable neurosurgeon have done in the middle
of that complex surgery when things started to go wrong? Is the architect to
blame for having constructed a building that could not withstand the more
frequent tornados brought on by climate change? The problem is orders of
magnitude more difficult when contexts don't only leap differences in experience but also differences in location, culture, and history.

Think again about the self-driving car. How are juries and judges going to
decide what is was reasonable for a programmer or manufacturer or passenger or owner or internet operator to do in the millions of different contexts
in which the cars can find themselves? In 2015, for example, it was reported
that Google self-driving cars were in twice as many accidents as cars driven
by humans.[20] The problem? The test cars were programmed to follow all traffic laws, all the time, and to be very conservative in doing things like turning right on red. Humans (well, Americans in places like Mountain View,
California, and Austin, Texas, where the Google cars were being tested)
don't expect that: it's unusual behavior. So the Google car kept getting rear-
ended—at a much higher rate than happens when the car ahead is driven by a
person. Other challenges: should the car (safely) cross over a lane marker that
means "do not cross" when there is a bicycle on the shoulder or construction,
or come to a stop, bollixing up traffic? Should the car only proceed if the
other cars at a four-way stop are motionless—even if that means the driverless car never gets its turn because human drivers keep inching up for theirs?
Researchers can say that the cars need to be more like humans, taking the
rules of the road with a grain of salt in some contexts and being sensitive to
the particular car culture in which they are driving. But that seriously ramps
up the gap between what the car is initially programmed to do and what
it ultimately learns to do based on the particular sequence of situations in
which it acquired information about local culture. And the more self-driving
cars there are on the road, the more that culture will be changing, practically
daily. Humans get stuck in their ways but computers don't.

A huge variety of possible contexts also makes it virtually impossible for
those who are generating the algorithms for digital goods and services to deal
with every possible contingency. Even ones in hindsight that look fairly predictable. In 2015, Google's facial recognition software, in addition to mistak-
ing some dogs for horses and some airplanes for cars, tagged a picture of a
black couple as "gorillas." That's an error that can prove disastrous, not just
for public relations but also for the well-being of a community. What if the
software were embedded in something other than an online diversion? What

if this were facial recognition software being used by the police or a company's security team? We are used to the misfiring between what humans intend and what they do. Digitization also misfires in some contexts—in complex ways that it will be difficult to anticipate. As digitization transitions from deterministic programming—the computer just follows the instructions in its code—to artificial intelligence—the computer updates its own code based on the ways its programmers instructed it to learn from the data received— the complexity of fashioning conventional rules to govern digitally mediated actions becomes astronomical.

The great variety of the possible contexts in which digitized information may come to life also makes it extraordinarily difficult to craft rules that don't just judge, after the fact, who is responsible but that try to give some guidance ahead of time to the digitizers. Stir into this complex mix the difficulty of predicting those different contexts and the things that can happen to digitized information on its fiber optic path from origin to context. Who might have tampered with it? How might it have been corrupted or delayed? What other data were, or were not, available at the same time?

That's why the problem of figuring out how to regulate the self-driving car is not just a philosophical question, as some popular debates suggest, of whether a car should steer into a group of schoolchildren to save the lives of its passengers or not—even if that is what would happen in the blink of an eye if a human were behind the wheel, and no one would blame the driver.[21] It is a phenomenally complex question of how the million possible different contexts in which any particular accident, on any particular day, in any particular place, with any particular history, takes place should be judged.

It's not even clear whether judgment and the allocation of responsibility for harm is the right way to go about implementing rules for self-driving cars. Maybe the best way to regulate the self-driving car is with direct technological control, exercised by a regulator with whom data is shared on a constant basis. (As I'll discuss in Chapter 10, that regulator needn't be a government; it could be private regulator, approved by government, which enters into a contract with the manufacturer or owner of the vehicle.) It's possible that our entire history of using rules and penalties for violating rules to generate the legal platform on which economic activity takes place needs to give way to accommodate some fundamentally new ways of regulating behavior to balance innovation, externalities, and fairness.

The flat world—networked, fast, constantly new—presents us with the challenge of a fundamentally more complex environment. The landscape is truly dancing, with an explosion of specialization and the division of labor far beyond anything Adam Smith could have dreamed of. Now our economic life is snipped loose in important ways from even the constraints of physicality, time, and human agency. The stable familiar world that could be organized by long-held cultural norms or the simple rules of the slow-moving economy of agriculture and craft is far behind us. And soon the world that can be managed exclusively by deliberate efforts in nation-state legislatures, regulatory agencies, and courts will be too. We need new legal tools for a flat world. Our economies have been transformed. But as we'll see in the next chapter, our existing legal infrastructure has not. Our legal approaches are strangled by cost and complexity and showing signs of a growing gap between what the flat world needs and what it gets. We need to start rethinking how we build legal infrastructure.

7

The Limits of Complexity and the Cost of Law

IN 1990 ARCHAEOLOGIST Joseph Tainter published a fascinating book called *The Collapse of Complex Societies*. In it he explored the stories of ancient societies that enjoyed great success for a period of time and then rapidly fell apart. The Western Chou dynasty in China, the Harappan Civilization of northwestern India, and the Mesopotamian empires that rose in the first and second millennia BCE and then were gone by the start of the current era. The Roman Empire that dominated the globe for almost eight hundred years until the collapse of the Western empire in AD 476. The great Mayan civilizations that flourished over almost two millennia and then swiftly disappeared by AD 900. The Chacoan populations of the San Juan Basin in northwestern New Mexico that had built thriving pueblos by AD 500 and had disappeared by the end of the first millennium.

Tainter's account of collapse contests the specific stories of ecological disaster, resource constraints, and invasion that populate most accounts. Instead he looks to an overarching theory rooted in the idea that any complex society must solve, constantly, the problems that an environment serves up. Societies become complex, he argues, because they adopt successful forms of economic and social organization that support expansion and the ever-increasing levels of the specialization that Adam Smith emphasized lie at the heart of economic growth. Societies, in short, are richly rewarded for devising systems that increase differentiation and complexity. Rome was rewarded with booty for its policy of military expansion and investments in complex administrative systems to oversee expanding territory. Individual Mayan cities were rewarded with agricultural surplus for their investments in the complex organization needed to wage warfare on neighboring regions and to build the monumental architecture that warded off reciprocal attacks. The Chacoans of New Mexico were rewarded with the benefits that come from hedging one's agricultural bets for their investments in a centrally administered network of architecturally sophisticated great houses that collected, stored, and redistributed resources from regions that had enjoyed a good harvest to ones that had not been so lucky.

Tainter's theory of collapse is essentially an application of the dismal Malthusian observation of diminishing returns. In addition to the diminishing returns to agricultural land that Malthus wrote about, however, Tainter points to the diminishing returns to any particular strategy of complexity for resolving the problems of society. Rome's strategy of military expansion to finance the complex administration needed to oversee vast lands eventually hit a limit: further expansion brought lower returns (the low-hanging fruit having already been harvested) and yet increased administrative costs as geographical and cultural distance from the center grew. As Mayan populations flourished in response to the success of their strategies of warfare and monumental architecture, per capita agricultural returns fell, spurring further investments in warfare and monuments—with the latter requiring ever-greater diversion from basic subsistence because the easier ways of building armies and the nearest materials for building massive structures had already been exhausted. Similarly, population growth supported by the ingenious system for averaging out the highs and lows of agriculture among the Chacoans eventually shrank the distance between neighboring populations. This meant neighboring regions were more alike than had been the case in the early days of the civilization and more likely to experience highs and lows at the same time. Sustaining the same level of sustenance then required ever-more complicated systems for trying to use the ups in one place to smooth the downs in others.

Tainter's point can be understood like this: initially a successful complex strategy for solving the problems facing a society makes increasing complexity worthwhile. Eventually, however, precisely because the strategy succeeds, it requires more and more complexity to support the more complex society it has fostered. To the extent that the society continues on with the *same strategy* that produced its initial success, the one that has already exhausted the easy gains, it eventually hits the limits of complexity and then swiftly unravels.

It is in this sense that we can see the problem of legal infrastructure in advanced Western countries today—the basic outlines of which emerged with the Westphalian peace of the seventeenth century and which grew into the elaborate systems of nation-state governments we now consider the very essence of what it means to have law—as having reached their complexity limits. Precisely because the legal infrastructure invented with the emergence of increasingly democratic nation-states has been wildly successful in supporting rapid growth, specialization, and global networking, it is increasingly unable to manage the level of complexity it has fostered.

How do we know this? We can see our existing systems busting at their seams through at least three different lenses trained on the most elaborate legal regime in the world: the United States. The first highlights the complexity of legal materials such as contracts and statutes. The second focuses on the cost of participating in the legal system. The third reveals the quality of the legal services available in our legal markets—or more precisely the extent to which what our legal markets offer matches up with what the new globally networked and web-based platform on which economic and social relationships are now built needs from legal infrastructure.

It's fairly well understood that both complexity and cost have been increasing rapidly in advanced legal systems over the past several decades. This is what makes what we see when we look at the quality of our legal infrastructure so surprising. As I learned from talking to the top lawyers at innovative companies that are emblematic of the transformations we are experiencing in the global economy—places like Google, Cisco, and Apple—increasing levels of complexity and cost are not producing better legal infrastructure. In fact, our legal infrastructure is growing increasingly more remote from the realities of how the globally networked economy works. This goes not only for large corporations but also for small businesses and individuals. Fundamentally, our legal infrastructure is of diminishing quality, by which I mean that it is failing to keep up with the exploding economic demand for law. The landscape is dancing like mad, but the platform on which it dances is pocked with holes and missing planks.

Complexity

In 2011 Apple Inc. came under attack for allegedly burying in its dense terms of use for the iPhone and iPad a promise by the user to allow Apple to store a year's worth of location information.[1] Apple said that the long-term storage of this information was unintentional and emphasized that people who did not want to have their location information recorded by Apple could simply turn off location services on their phone. Which is to say, allowing Apple to record the information was a quid pro quo—because you couldn't use the location features of the phone if you didn't let them record the information. The Comedy Central TV series *South Park* didn't miss a beat: In the opening episode of the show's 2011 season, the character Kyle discovers too late that by clicking "Agree" on his iPad he has agreed to a provision buried deep in the terms of service that allows a Dr. Evil version of Steve Jobs to kidnap him and force him to be joined to two other users in a HumanCentiPad: "a product," the cartoon Steve Jobs tells us excitedly, "that is part human and part centipede and part web browser and part emailing device," and which gives new meaning to the term "potty mouth." (Warning: the episode, available online, is not for those of delicate sensibilities.)

South Park creators Trey Parker and Matt Stone locked onto one of the most common experiences with the modern legal word—the densely worded and largely incomprehensible terms of use that people agree to millions of times a day across the global web as they blithely click "Agree" in order to install or update software, buy a song or shoes or detergent, open a bank account, or access a social network. Parker and Stone's hapless Kyle is not alone in not reading these things (although his cartoon friends in *South Park* feign perplexity that anyone would ever agree to something they haven't read!). NYU law and business professors Florencia Marotta-Wurgler and Yannis Bakos, together with intellectual property lawyer David Trossen, tracked (with permission . . .) almost fifty thousand households to see how often users clicked through to read the end-user license agreement (EULA) before purchasing software online—the type of contract the sorry Kyle failed to read. Result: one in a thousand. Even those careful few rarely spent more than a minute or two pondering the legal jargon, hardly enough to read something that is on average two thousand words in length and as hard to comprehend as an article in a scientific journal.[2]

Other researchers have confirmed what the *South Park* audience already knew: the vast majority of consumer contracts are hopelessly unintelligible, making a mockery of the idea that signing or clicking "I agree" means anything more legally significant than "Yeah, whatever." Berkeley information researchers Jens Grossklags and Nathan Good looked at Download.com's fifty most popular software downloads in 2006.[3] They found that the average length of the user agreement was even longer—closer to three thousand words—which is about eleven pages of double-spaced text. Adobe Reader's license agreement topped the scale at 9,313 words, or about forty pages of double-spaced text. Practically, they emphasize, these documents are even longer than this: most include links to other documents such as privacy policies and most incorporate the complex rules from other sources such as those governing a particular arbitration regime. The study also looked at the Flesch Reading Ease score, which estimates readability based on sentence length and the average number of syllables in the words used. With an average score of 35 out of 100, all of these documents would be easily readable only by those who are comfortable with college-level texts. Only one scored in the 60–70 range, achieving reading ease at the level of the average person: eighth grade. UK researchers found the same results when they studied the contracts households sign when they obtain standard services such as electricity or water and sewage.[4] No one without university-level reading ability could comfortably read his or her agreement. Another study found that health plans in the United States were written at advanced college level.[5]

Even these studies are generous. Face it, when the concept is legally complex, it doesn't matter if it appears in a short, pithy sentence using short words. "Warranty" has as many syllables as "blueberry" but that doesn't make it any more likely that ordinary readers will know what they are getting into. Even if it's good news. The website PC Pitstop proved this point by burying in its terms of use an offer of "consideration" to anyone who sent a note to a particular email address requesting it. "Consideration" is legalese meaning something of value given in exchange for something else. Four months and three thousand downloads later someone finally sent the darned email, and received a check for $1,000.[6]

Most of us quite rationally don't spend any time at all reading the thousands of words next to the "Sign/Click Here" boxes we sign and click on a daily basis. We imagine, not unreasonably, that there's nothing much in there that either matters to us or that we can do much about. And often we're right: competition among car rental companies and software providers weeds out bad terms, as does the oversight of journalists, bloggers, and Comedy Central writers. Regulation helps too—terms that are outrageous are often unenforceable because of contract or consumer protection law. But nonetheless the complexity of these ubiquitous legal terms is a distinctive feature of our legal infrastructure.

The problem goes far beyond consumer standard-form contracts.

Take a look at the Dodd-Frank law enacted in 2010 in response to the financial crisis in the United States. The statute alone is almost one thousand pages long—that's longer than *Moby Dick* and would take a college-educated reader about fifteen hours to read. The statute, however, is just the beginning. The statute calls for various federal agencies to enact regulations to implement the law. As of the summer of 2012, almost ten thousand pages of regulations had been generated—and that was only one-third of the regulations called for by the law. That's a lot of words to start with but it's still just the leading edge of the complexity problem. Where things really get hairy is with cross-referencing and overlapping rules. An analysis by preeminent New York securities law firm Davis Polk, for example, showed that there were four different regulators involved in writing forty-six rules governing one type of financial transaction—interest rate swaps.[7] Forty-six doesn't sound so bad, right? Until you find out that a complex web of thousands of references links those forty-six rules, meaning that you can't really understand what any rule says without understanding what every rule says. And that is where the real complexity kicks in. Because for every rule there will be multiple interpretations of the rule emerging from the legal departments within thousands of organizations. Some of these interpretations will spur the regulatory agencies to issue further guidance on how the rules are to be interpreted. Others might spur enforcement actions or legal challenges. Some of those enforcement actions and legal challenges will generate thousands of pages of legal argument and evidence in agency hearings and lawsuits. Those in turn will generate many, many pages of judicial decisions that will further complicate the task of figuring out what an entity can and cannot do when engaging in interest rate swaps. Moreover, on-the-ground predictions about what an entity can and cannot do will be influenced by predictions about how effective various efforts to derail enforcement or cajole regulators or lobby legislators will be; how likely it is that a violation will be detected and what evidence under complex evidentiary rules might ever make its way into a court; and so on.

This complexity is why securities lawyers make over $1,000 an hour.

It is also why it would be foolish to predict how much of what got written in the original one thousand pages of the Dodd-Frank law will ever actually operate as law in the sense of "rule of law" in financial markets.

Complexity is why the page and word counts that journalists will tell us about when new laws are passed or judicial opinions are handed down are important facts. It's true that page count would not be a very interesting number to know about the omnibus healthcare act known as Obamacare (906) if those pages could be broken into manageable chunks that were relatively easily to read and understand and if its rules were relatively predictable. And of course we should expect that anything as massive as restructuring the entire $2 trillion healthcare sector of a country of 350 million people would require some saying. US Treasury secretary Henry Paulson attempted to keep his original proposal to spend $700 billion bailing out banks and investors to confront the 2008 financial crisis short—it was only three pages long—but it was realistic to think that the ultimate legislation would be much longer (as it was—about 260 pages longer). What makes those page counts telling is what we know, systematically, about how hard legal documents today are to understand and how complex it is to predict their effects and consequences. Here I really do mean complexity in the complex adaptive systems sense of the term. The ultimate effect of all those words will be the result of millions of individuals—doctors, patients, hospitals, regulators, investors, insurance company executives, politicians, activists, judges, lawyers—making millions of decisions that will interact in millions of unpredictable ways, charting a million intersecting paths across a dancing landscape. The effect of adding words in a legal document is exponential.

So it is relevant to know that the number of words that structure the complex interactions of our legal infrastructure have been increasing steadily over the past century. The first piece of major federal legislation in the United States—the Interstate Commerce Act of 1887—contained less than six thousand words, about fifteen pages of text. Social Security was introduced in the United States in 1935 in fewer than forty pages. Moreover, each of those laws was introduced into an environment that was substantially less complex—fewer lawyers, fewer judges, less history—and so the pages of those statutes were subject to fewer crosscutting and strategic interpretations and implementations. Even in the active regulatory environment of the 1970s, Congress needed only fifty pages to say what it thought needed to be said when it passed the Clean Air Act.

It's not just statutes that litter the landscape with syllables. The number of words that lay down the foundation in our networked legal infrastructure has been growing steadily in every domain over the past century. The first issue of the US *Federal Register*, which publishes all rules and notices about rule-making emerging from federal agencies, contained 2,620 pages when it appeared in 1936; in 2012 the number was 77,249. Judicial opinions have also become longer. The median US Supreme Court opinion has quadrupled in length to over eight thousand words since the 1950s when the median was two thousand, and the longest ones have gone off the charts: the Court's opinion upholding the constitutionality of the overhaul of US health law in 2015 was 190 pages long—in excess of fifty thousand words. And because nine different Supreme Court justices battling a complex political environment produced those fifty thousand words, they are hardly easy to put together and interpret. Political scientists Ryan Owens, Justin Wedeking, and Patrick Wohlfarth have shown that opinions become more difficult to read as the ideological differences between the Court and Congress widen—dare we say suggesting that the justices are more likely to obfuscate their work to fend off close scrutiny from those who can overturn it.[8] Moreover, these same researchers show that court opinions are more complex to interpret as the number of judges signing on to a majority opinion increases, indicating that the price of judicial compromise is legal clarity. This is what makes them truly complex in the complex systems sense: the effort that must go into translating all these words into guidance and prediction for behavior is a result of the strategizing of those at the pinnacle of the legal pyramid. Layer on top of that the strategic efforts of politicians, journalists, activists, bloggers, legal departments—not to mention researchers—and a dancing landscape can turn into all-out chaos.

Judges, politicians, and regulators are not the only ones who produce the wordy planks that assemble our complex legal infrastructure. Lawyers are also major producers—crafting the words that go into contracts and disclosure statements and organizational protocols. They are the ones drafting online license agreements that average about ten pages of text. Credit agreements that top one hundred pages. Two-hundred-page partnership agreements. Supply agreements that take one hundred pages to set out general terms and then another four hundred pages to spell out details in appendices. As with the word count of statutes, the problem is not length per se (after all, some of these agreements are establishing the basis for transacting millions, sometimes billions, of dollars in complex and technical settings). It is the difficulty of interpreting the complex and interrelated terms in which contracts are written, anticipating all the possible events that might make a difference, and managing the strategic risk inherent in raising the possibility of troubles that can scuttle a deal. Moreover, few people—even the lawyers who draft these documents—really read all the details and understand them.

Contract surprises and gaps are commonplace. You can be sure that when UK-based Vodafone and the predecessors of US company Verizon Communications entered into a joint venture agreement to create Verizon Wireless in 2000, there were plenty of top-flight lawyers involved in constructing the 120-page document that sealed the deal. Still, no one paid much attention to the fact that the contractual promises made by controlling party Verizon about issuing dividends to shareholders expired after five years. The surprise came when Verizon unilaterally stopped paying dividends from 2005 to 2010, as the contract allowed, resulting in costly conflict and maneuvering in the relationship.[9] It is tempting simply to chalk this one up to botched lawyering. But it's not. Designing legal solutions is no different from designing engineering or product design solutions: sometimes what looks good on the drawing board plays out in unexpected ways when put into practice. It is routine for even the best lawyers to fall short in meeting the insuperable challenge of aligning abstract words with real-life strategic negotiations and business planning on the ground, often without the benefit of being in the room when the deals are made. As explained to me by Vodafone's general counsel Rosemary Martin, who came on board in 2010, nobody at the time the deal was being put together was thinking the joint venture would continue for more than five years in that form; all of the negotiations took for granted it would be spun off or folded into a different entity long before then. Nor is the solution the one many lawyers run to: making sure to add pages to the *next* document to avoid that problem in future deals. That just makes the documents even more complex and, sometimes, the deals harder to close. These situations are far from exceptional for even the largest, wealthiest corporations dealing with the complexity of modern contract and corporate law; they are daily fare.

The most dramatic evidence of the complexity of our current legal infrastructure comes from the 2008 financial collapse. Start with the subprime mortgage agreements that were too complex for many ordinary folks to understand what they were getting into. Stir in fancy financial instruments created by slicing up these mortgage contracts and bundling them together into complex derivatives contracts. These are the contracts that billionaire investor Warren Buffet called "financial time bombs" and "weapons of mass destruction," so complex he refused to invest in them. Referring to his partner, Harvard Law grad Charlie Munger, Buffet told shareholders of his investment company Berkshire Hathaway in 2002 that "when Charlie and I finish reading the long footnotes detailing the derivatives activities of major banks, the only thing we understand is that we *don't* understand how much risk the institution is running."[10] Combine elements 1 and 2 with what US Treasury secretary Timothy Geithner blandly referred to as a "regulatory structure that is unnecessarily complex and fragmented" and you have a perfect storm of complexity.[11] Legal scholars have a name for what happens when a regulatory system that is complex and fragmented is laid in front of a lot of very smart strategic folks: regulatory arbitrage. Or in ordinary language: making a lot of money exploiting gaps and loopholes. The strategic exploitation of a complex and fragmented regulatory environment only compounds the problem as the regulators try in vain to replace the stakes of a tent caught in a hurricane.

Cost

If you've ever had to hire a lawyer, you know they don't come cheap. Lawyers who work on personal matters—such as divorce, employment, probate, or housing—charge on average $250 an hour; finding one that charges much less than $200 is pretty difficult. Lawyers who work for businesses charge on average about $450 an hour; the average among lawyers in top corporate law firms in the United States was over $600 an hour in 2015. Finding a lawyer that charges much more—as much as $1,000-plus an hour—is not hard. In good times and bad, these hourly rates keep on increasing. Between 2000 and 2012 rates increased around 60 percent; that's twenty-five percentage points above inflation. It doesn't take many hours for bills to add up at any of these rates.[12]

Are lawyers overpaid? Some may be. The equity partners in the top one hundred law firms in the United States collectively earned about $28 billion in income in 2012—a bit more than 10 percent of the total revenues earned by all 170,000 law firms in the country and about 30 percent of the revenues earned by their own firms.[13] That averages to $1.5 million in annual take-home pay per partner. The average hides plenty of unevenness, however, with lots of equity partners making hundreds of thousands while others make multiple millions. In this, the very top end of the legal food chain is not that different from—indeed, not as highly compensated as—the top end of the corporate food chain.

These very highly paid lawyers, however, are less than 2 percent of the 1.2 million lawyers in the American legal profession. Another 5 percent of lawyers work as employees in these top one hundred firms. About a third of all lawyers are solo practitioners. In 2012 (the last year with complete census data) 40 percent of law firms had an average of about $90,000 on hand after paying an average of about $45,000 in payroll to cover an employee or two.[14] From those net revenues these mostly solo practitioners still had to pay payroll taxes and the costs of renting and operating an office—meaning they were taking home considerably less than $90,000. IRS data for sole proprietors in 2013 shows average income of $49,000.[15] Nationally, the median pay for the 600,000 lawyers who work as employees, not partners—employed as associates by law firms or in governments and corporate legal departments—was about $135,000 a year in 2014; the lowest 10 percent earned $55,000 and the top 10 percent $185,000.[16] Median lawyer income is (roughly speaking: the data, as I'll explain later, are poorly tracked) about $115,000.

Median lawyer income is thus well above median income generally, which was about $42,000 for full-time workers and $64,000 for college graduates in the United States in 2015. It is, however, only somewhat higher than the median for professional degree holders—about $100,000. We shouldn't expect lawyers to earn much less than other professionals—because those jobs represent the opportunity cost of being a lawyer. Most people who go to law school are choosing between that and some other form of graduate or professional training.

The real question is not whether lawyers earn too much but whether law costs too much. These are very different questions.

In 2013 the National Center for State Courts surveyed lawyers to develop estimates of what it would cost to litigate a typical civil lawsuit.[17] The numbers are in some sense guesses—the researchers who did this work commented on the fact that most of their survey respondents said they struggled to think about what a typical case costs; they saw each of their cases as pretty much one-off. This is an important fact about lawyers—it's one of the reasons lawyers have clung to hourly billing instead of the kind of flat-fee pricing that clients desperately want from them. Even as guesses, however, the numbers these people on the front lines throw out are revealing.

Suppose you have an employment dispute with a former employer: you want to go work for a competitor but the employer thinks that puts company secrets at risk and wants to stop you. Or suppose you believe you were fired because the new young CEO thinks older workers are a waste of money. If your case is typical and you find a law firm that charges the median hourly rates for this kind of work ($300 for the senior attorney on the case, $195 for the junior attorney, and $110 for the paralegal) and it spends the median amount of time on your case (375 hours), your legal bill will come to $82,515. On top of that you can expect to spend $5,000 on expert witnesses. That's a whopping $90,000 once you add in court filing fees, copying, and other costs. Can you afford that? If you are a professional earning median income, that's almost a full year's salary, two if you earn what the median American earns.

The numbers are pretty much the same for the other types of cases in the study: professional malpractice cases clock in with a median of about $125,000; premises liability cases (such as a slip and fall in the grocery store) at a little over $50,000; a real property dispute $65,000 and a contract dispute $90,000. These costs are not only incurred if you end up at trial; most of these costs are incurred in a process in which everyone just behaves as if the case is going to trial even though the vast majority—somewhere between 90 and 99 percent—will end in dismissal or settlement. It is numbers like these that lead most lawyers to say that it's just not worth suing about something that is worth less than $100,000.

Now think about the fact that not everyone is deciding whether it is worth it to file a lawsuit. Half of the people and businesses involved in litigation don't ask to be: they are defendants whose only choice is between showing up to play or defaulting and giving the plaintiff whatever he or she asked for. Suppose half of defendants didn't do what the plaintiff says they did and they don't owe the plaintiff anything. Doesn't matter: they too will have to pay those typical case costs to defend themselves. What does that mean? Well, if you now imagine you are the employer being sued in the typical employment case, it means that you might as well pay the plaintiff to go away if he or she is asking for anything less than $90,000.

Now step back and think about the cost not just from a plaintiff's or a defendant's point of view but from society's. To resolve an employment dispute in the legal system will cost a total of $180,000 because both sides will have to pay their litigation costs. So even if it's worth it to a plaintiff to sue over a $90,000 dispute, and worth it to a defendant to defend a $90,000 claim, it may well not be worth it for society as a whole. From a public perspective, cases worth less to society than $180,000 aren't worth the cost of resolution. Now, the value of the case to society won't necessarily be the value to the litigants. Society gets value from lawsuits from the role they play in stabilizing the rule of law, deterring people from violating legal rules, and protecting legal rights. The social value of any given lawsuit may be more or less than the amounts at stake from the litigants' point of view. But however the social value is gauged, it only makes sense from the public's point of view to go ahead with that lawsuit if the value to society is close to $180,000.

The costs of legal processes are routinely a large fraction of, and often exceed, the amounts at stake. Take bankruptcy as an example. According to a 2011 study done for the American Bankruptcy Institute and the National Conference of Bankruptcy Judges, the median total cost of filing a liquidation bankruptcy under Chapter 7—which includes court filing fees, the cost of mandatory credit counseling and education classes, and attorneys' fees— was about $1,400 between 2005 and 2009.[18] The median cost of a Chapter 13 reorganization bankruptcy was about twice that: $2,850. Considering that these are price tags that have to be paid by people who are broke—the median household income of bankruptcy filers is about $28,000—these are high price tags in absolute terms. What is especially telling, however, is a comparison between these price tags and the amounts that are being distributed to the creditors in bankruptcy. Those amounts are significantly *less* than the amounts people pay to file bankruptcy: the median payout to creditors in the period 2005–2009 was about $800 in a Chapter 7 case and $1,600 in a Chapter 13 case. That means that in more than half of personal bankruptcies, creditors would be better off just divvying up the cash the debtor would otherwise pay to the court and attorneys than waiting for a payout in bankruptcy. It also means that people who have the ability to pay creditors the amount they could receive in bankruptcy but who do not also have the cash on hand that it will cost them to file bankruptcy will be shut out of the bankruptcy system. Assuming that bankruptcy laws allowing people and failed businesses a fresh start and creditors an orderly way of getting paid generate value for society, cutting people off from bankruptcy means a loss of public value as well. Weeding out frivolous cases is one thing; weeding out meritorious cases blunts the rule of law.

Paying more for law than it's worth is not restricted to those struggling at the low end of the economy or to small cases that don't have significant public value. The American Intellectual Property Law Association estimates that in 2012 the median cost of litigating a patent suit with less than $1 million at stake was $700,000.[19] Since costs are incurred by both sides, these estimates imply that the costs of litigation exceed the value at stake. The combined costs on both sides to litigate a case valued between $1 million and $25 million is almost $6 million; $11 million for a case worth over $25 million. Taking into account the fact that litigation is a gamble—so the amounts at stake need to be a multiple of costs just to break even— these numbers imply a process that is just far too expensive for a wide range of cases. One consequence of these high numbers is the phenomenon in the technology industry known as patent trolls: companies that buy up patents and whose only business is threatening to sue other companies for infringement. If litigation were reasonably priced, this would be a good tool for enforcement of patent rights—allowing companies that come up with patentable drugs, machines, and processes to shift the risks and headaches of hunting down patent infringers to companies that specialize in finding and litigating infringement. But when litigation is so expensive, a good business tool becomes an instrument of blackmail: pay up or watch your legal bills rack up.

Everyone's favorite whipping boy for costly litigation—tort law—demonstrates the same problem. Joni Hersch and Kip Viscusi of Vanderbilt University estimate that for every dollar paid out to someone injured in an accident through the tort system, an average of seventy-five cents goes to legal fees and costs.[20] That estimate includes claims that are not litigated; those that are litigated (not necessarily going to trial) average eighty-three cents on the dollar. Mitchell Polinsky of Stanford and Steven Shavell of Harvard think even this estimate understates the cost of tort litigation, because it excludes the costs of time and judicial resources.[21] They estimate that the cost of a dollar paid out is a dollar. As they put it, that's like charging a $100 service fee to withdraw $100 from an ATM. Neither of these studies takes enough account of the fact that there are social benefits to tort litigation that go beyond the dollars transferred to injured people—these are the benefits of deterrence and the intangible benefits of knowing that we live in a world where people who cause harm are held accountable—but these benefits would have to be enormous to justify such an expensive system.

Another way of seeing that law is just too expensive is to look at how often people end up in court without any legal help at all—in cases where they really don't have a choice about being in court and we're pretty sure that some legal help would be valuable. A 2010 study of New York courts found that over 98 percent of tenants facing eviction and borrowers in consumer credit cases, a category that includes a lot of small-business owners, are unrepresented. In child support matters, 95 percent of people are unrepresented. Of those facing foreclosure, 44 percent go it alone against a well-represented bank. The numbers are comparable throughout the country. Half of landlords and 92 percent of tenants appear alone in Boston housing court. At least one person is unrepresented in 83 percent of divorce cases and 87 percent of protective order cases in Utah and in 80 percent of paternity cases and 95 percent of domestic violence petitions in Washington state.[22]

We also see evidence that law is too expensive in the rate at which people and small businesses just decide to lump their troubles. Studies show that about a third of Americans dealing with significant legal problems—facing eviction or foreclosure, engaged in custody disputes, not getting paid for work done, being denied healthcare or benefits—do nothing to resolve their legal problems. In countries with less expensive options for managing legal problems, such as England and the Netherlands, the rates are much lower, 5–10 percent.

It's easy to blame lawyers for how expensive our legal system is—and the high cost of law is their responsibility, as I'll make clear in a later chapter. But it's not as simple as the conventional rap on greedy lawyers would have it. Many lawyers—particularly those helping out ordinary people and small businesses—are not getting super rich. So why are the legal bills so high?

Roughly speaking the cost of law is the product of the complexity of law and the amount of legal process required to get to an outcome—complying with regulations, resolving a dispute, securing a bankruptcy or divorce. I've already emphasized the complexity of law as one of the key defining features of our current systems. The more complex law is, the more highly educated and experienced someone needs to be to work with it. It's true that much of legal work is not rocket science—and doesn't require four years of college and then three years of law school to get it done. I'll come back to this point in a later chapter, when we look at what the alternatives to our current system are. But a lot of our law is pretty darn complicated, even for the smart people who end up in law schools. This means that we have created a system that requires that we pay people who have high opportunity costs to manage it for us. Top securities lawyers make $1,000 an hour, for example, because they are highly intelligent and experienced practitioners who know the details of our unbelievably complex system of securities regulation. And if we didn't pay them this much, they'd put their brains to work doing something else: they have a lot of options. Reducing the complexity of law would help bring down cost by making more of it the type of work that can be done by a much larger share of people in the workforce—people who would be willing to work for a lower hourly rate.

But what is driving the legal system out of reach is not just lawyers' high hourly rates: it's also the time it takes to work through legal processes. Think back to the National Center for State Courts' estimates for hourly rates and hours to handle a typical employment case. Suppose the paralegal—who doesn't have a fancy education and who isn't protected by any kind of professional monopoly—could handle your whole employment case. The median paralegal rate in the state court study was $110 an hour, one-third of what the median senior attorney and one-half of what the median junior attorney charges. Assume the paralegal takes the same number of hours as the senior and junior attorney to get the job done: 375 hours. Your case would still cost you about $40,000—more than a year's salary for more than half of the full-time workers in the country. That's still impossibly high.

Why does that case take 375 hours of legal work to resolve? Because it is not just the content of law that is complex; the process is also tortuous. Although we might imagine that a decent way of handling a routine employment dispute is a simple process in which people exchange some documents, get testimony from a few others, and then present their facts and arguments to a neutral decision-maker who hears everything and then makes a final decision, this is not how legal processes today work. That path from complaint to decision has been sliced, diced, and julienned into a complex series of steps. There are motions to change courts, motions to exclude experts, motions to dismiss, motions to amend complaints, motions to quash subpoenas, motions to compel production of documents, motions to strike pleadings, motions for continuance: the list goes on and on. The availability of most of these motions, in the abstract, makes sense: they provide a discrete way of dealing with a real issue, such as a belief that a subpoena is not valid or that an expert is not qualified or that a legal issue is not relevant. They parse big messy cases into neat little boxes. The problem lies in the fact that at each point at which there is a box drawn neatly around an issue, there is an opportunity for argument, decision, and more argument. The opportunities for fighting—sincerely or strategically—multiply exponentially.

A RAND study in the 1990s proves the point. In response to complaints about the costs and delays of federal civil litigation, Congress passed the Civil Justice Reform Act in 1990.[23] The act created a pilot program to test different ways that judges could manage cases before trial so as to increase the speed and reduce the cost of litigation—these were efforts to curb strategic behavior and delay and to promote cooperation and resolution. The findings? Getting judges actively involved early in the process to manage cases did indeed reduce the median time to resolve a case by about 30 percent—from 495 days to 379 days. But it didn't decrease costs. In fact it *increased* costs, by about 30 percent. Both lawyers and litigants spent more time on the case: median lawyer hours went from fifty to sixty; median litigant hours went from thirty to forty. Why? Because any procedure—requiring attorneys to meet with a judge early to try to agree on a sensible way of managing the case, for example—takes time and money. And it creates something else to fight about—when it will be scheduled, how it will be conducted. New procedural obligations such as requiring attorneys to use good faith or cooperate in pretrial work create new opportunities to complain about the other side—with new motions to formally object or seek sanctions or compel compliance.

A major focus of the Civil Justice Reform Act was the problem of out-of-control discovery, the pretrial work that is done to collect documents and conduct depositions (essentially, pretrial interviews under oath) of potential witnesses. In 1990, the concerns were about bankers' boxes full of documents and the need to sift through mounds of paper to find an elusive fact that might help or hurt a case. Today discovery is dominated by e-discovery—meaning the search for electronic documents, emails, text messages, and more that might have some bearing on the issues contested in a case. American discovery procedures have always been known for their scale. The documents and testimony that can be demanded from the other side don't have to be relevant, they only have to potentially lead to the discovery of relevant evidence that could be presented at trial. Added to already expansive scope has been the massive increase in the scale of electronic communication and storage over the past two decades and legal rules and practices that conspire to make lawyers believe that they need to search every possible document. The consequence has been an enormous increase in the scale of discovery.

A study released by the Institute for the Advancement of the American Legal System (IAALS) in 2008 used an employment dispute like the one we considered earlier to illustrate the problem.[24] It suggests that the estimate of costs that the National Center for State Courts' survey came up with didn't take into account the potential for enormous discovery costs even in a medium-sized case. Suppose a small marketing company with twenty employees suffers the loss of one of its sales associates, who leaves in acrimonious circumstances to form her own company. The company contemplates suing the employee when she leaves, believing she stole company secrets and is competing unfairly, but decides not to because of the costs of litigation. Then, two years later, as the statute of limitations is about to expire, the company is surprised to find itself on the receiving end of a lawsuit the former employee has filed in which she alleges that she is owed commissions that went unpaid and that she was the victim of employment discrimination. The suit seeks discovery of all electronically stored information going back five years. That means everything stored on every desktop, laptop, PDA, smartphone, server, and backup tape used by any employee at work or at home for work purposes. The discovery demand means locating and preserving all this data, policing employees to make sure no one deletes anything, and then searching the data for documents that might be relevant to the discovery request. The technological services involved in just this part of the exercise are increasingly big business—estimated at between $3 and $5 billion annually and growing rapidly. Including the costs companies are spending on putting document management systems and litigation readiness plans into place across the board, the industry is thought to top $20 billion.

The technology bill, however, is only a fraction of the cost of complying with discovery obligations triggered by the former employee's lawsuit. All of the documents identified by the search—which the IAALS example estimates could be on the order of fifty million pages—have to be reviewed by a lawyer—usually working for an hourly fee—to decide which documents need to be handed over to the other side. In a case study of discovery costs faced by eight companies in the Fortune 200, RAND found that three-quarters of the costs of discovery were attributable to review of documents by lawyers.[25] Across forty-five cases, they saw costs for producing discovery that ranged from $17,000 in an intellectual property matter to over $27 million in a products liability case; 50 percent of those cases saw costs close to $2 million.

All told, the IAALS study estimated that conducting e-discovery in their example of a midsized employment case could cost as much as $3.5 million. Moreover, if anything was deleted after the time at which a court later decides the company should have anticipated litigation—which could be the time at which the employee left, two years before the suit was filed—the company is at risk of substantial penalties. In a dramatic, and extreme, example of this Qualcomm was ordered to pay all of opponent Broadcom's legal fees in a patent litigation case—a total of $8.5 million—because of important documents they had not found that the court decided should have been found.

This is a huge amount of process to resolve a garden-variety employment dispute. Is it worth it? There are no studies comparing the quality of outcome in this process to that of an earlier day and age, when such disputes were resolved based on the paper that happened to be on hand in the pre-electronic era of the filing cabinet. But it is not hard at all to get to the conclusion that much of this process falls in the category of things for which the game is not worth the candle. In a survey of Fortune 200 companies conducted in 2010 for a conference at Duke University, average discovery costs per case ranged from $600,000 to nearly $10 million.[26] The same survey found that the ratio of pages produced in discovery to those introduced as evidence in a trial is 1,000 to 1. Microsoft expanded on this estimate in a 2011 letter to a federal judicial committee investigating discovery costs, stating that for every page of evidence used at trial in an average case, the company had produced 1,000 pages, manually reviewed 4,500 pages, collected and processed 90,000 pages, and preserved 340,000.[27]

Anecdotal evidence of out-of-control e-discovery costs abounds. One senior litigation partner in Los Angeles told me the story of a patent case in which the estimate for e-discovery services was $20 million, five times the estimate for all lawyers' fees in the litigation. The IAALS study shares the observation from a leading law firm that the firm routinely sees cases in which e-discovery costs clock in at three to four times the low end of the amount of money at stake in the litigation and sometimes exceed the high end by a factor of two. An attorney and e-discovery consultant estimates that the bill from just the technology provider in an average case exceeds $200,000 and that bills between $2 and $4 million are not unusual. Verizon reports that it often spends up to $1 million on technology services for e-discovery. Legal bills for attorney review of all the documents produced by those expensive processes are on top of these numbers.

Evidence that increases in the amount of process—especially discovery—needed to resolve cases are significantly responsible for galloping litigation costs can be found in data from the American Intellectual Property Lawyers Association.[28] Although median billing rates among intellectual property lawyers increased between 2000 and 2012 significantly more than inflation— by about twenty percentage points—the cost of litigating most types of intellectual property cases increased much more. Hourly rates for lawyers went up nearly 60 percent, but the bill for all costs through the end of discovery for medium-sized patent cases ($1 million to $25 million at stake) went up 75 percent; for large cases with more than $25 million at stake costs increased 100 percent. The cost of litigating copyright cases worth more than $1 million increased 100 percent. Jaw-dropping numbers show up in trade secret cases— which are especially discovery-intensive: in cases worth more than $1 million we see litigation cost increases on the order of 200 percent. The fact that these total costs increase so much more than lawyers' hourly rates indicates that lawyers spent more time on the cases and, in all likelihood, that the cost of e-discovery meant big bills also paid out to technology vendors.

It's not that law should be or ever could be free. Even a simple process won't be free. It will still require legal analysis and time spent reviewing facts, crafting arguments, and hearing testimony. It will still require the services of lawyers and judges and clerks and courthouses. Nor should the only cases that have access to that process be those that are worth some minimum amount of money. It will be worth public money to cover the costs of a fair process even for very small cases—and for cases that are really not about money but are about dignity, respect, fair treatment, and ensuring the rule of law. From the public perspective, as we've seen, the great value of a reliable legal system is that it allows people to organize and interact in productive ways that promote the things we all care about. It costs resources to do that—just like it costs resources to have housing, medical care, and a political system. The problem is that the costs as they stand now are simply too high: not just for plaintiffs and defendants but also for us as a society.

Quality

Stories about the business of law rarely make it out of the business section in the newspaper. Which law firms are up, which are down, how many new graduates they are hiring: these topics just don't tend to be of interest outside of tightly drawn legal circles. But in the years after the 2008 financial meltdown, law stories captured front-page status. These were the stories, like those written by David Segal of the *New York Times*, that castigated law schools for churning out graduates who showed up in major commercial law firms without a clue about how to form a corporation and documented the explosion of law student debt. Traditional newspaper and new law-based blogs that ripped into law schools and law firms generated story after story about dramatic drop-offs in law firm hiring; they were soon followed by plunging applications to law school. The number of people bothering to sit the entrance exam for law school—the LSAT—was cut almost in half in just four years from 2009 to 2013.[29] Then there were the front-page stories of hundred-year-old law firms, like the venerable New York partnership Dewey LeBoeuf, going belly up. Firms that didn't go out of business laid off staff and lawyers for the first time in the memory of many. Disgruntled unemployed graduates sued their alma maters, claiming they had been hoodwinked by rosy and misleading statistics about graduates waltzing into $160,000-a-year jobs. The American Bar Association for the first time required law schools to disclose transparent statistics about placement and enterprising internet types created websites dedicated to making that information easily accessible to law school applicants. By 2013, as the LSAT scores of applicants began to fall, most law schools had started shrinking their class size to preserve quality, putting many of them into operating deficits. People took to speculating about how many, and which, law schools would fold. The Bureau of Labor Statistics documented continuing declines in employment among lawyers. The banks that lend money to law firms and the companies that manage electronic billing services documented the continuing drop in demand among the largest law firms, previously thought invulnerable to the vagaries of the market.

These unprecedented changes in legal markets framed a debate within legal circles: is the drop in the demand for legal work temporary or permanent? Those on the "This too shall pass" side of the debate pointed to the fact that legal markets have always known ups and downs tied to the economy. Those on the "Get used to it" side of the debate pointed to a decades-long slide in the total value of legal work as a share of GDP.

But the debate is missing the real puzzle: How can demand for legal work be dropping in a world that is exploding in complexity? A world where most individuals and small businesses are struggling through legal problems on their own and the CEOs from global companies are telling KPMG researchers that law is their biggest challenge?

Both sides of the debate get the story wrong. Demand for legal tools— legal infrastructure—to manage social and economic relationships is not dropping. It is ballooning. What's dropping is demand for what our current legal infrastructure is supplying. Law firms and law schools are finding it harder to sell what they're producing because the value of their product is declining. And that is a problem rooted in the quality of the product, not in the underlying demand for *a* product.

The quality problem is fairly easy to see if we think about the segment of the legal services market where we find small businesses and individuals looking for legal help with problems at work, home, or school or with government. Here, as we've already discovered, a big part of the story is cost: the price of legal help is just too high, meaning that the vast majority cannot afford it and have to muddle through without. But hidden inside the cost problem are two quality problems.

The first is a quality problem in the conventional sense, meaning that the legal work that people buy at those high prices is sometimes not particularly good. People won't pay high prices for low quality. There are excellent lawyers out there, but as we've seen, there are also many who are struggling to keep a solo or small firm practice afloat and in that struggle they sometimes take on cases that they're really not well equipped to handle. These generalist solo and small-firm practitioners, however, are the ones that serve individual and small business clients—large law firms, with their greater capacity for specialization, cater to big business. A lack of specialization, however, is likely to degrade quality. There are almost no data on the incidence of legal errors in the United States, but in England a study that audited completed case files involving employment, consumer debt, housing, and welfare benefits matters found that 43 percent of general practitioners performed below satisfactory levels.[30] The quality produced by specialists was better, although still not as good as we'd like: 30 percent of specialists received a score of unsatisfactory. A recent study of will drafting in England found similarly high rates of errors in the wills drafted by lawyers for secret shoppers posing as ordinary consumers: 25 percent.[31]

A more subtle quality problem is easy to overlook and of greater impact. This is a problem not of the quality of work done but of the variety of types of legal help offered in the market. If the only type of car sold at car dealerships were a $60,000 BMW, economists would say there is a problem of quality: the market is not supplying cars of lower quality that would meet the needs of those less willing or able to spend a lot of money on a car. The car market can only be said to be working well in terms of quality if buyers can also find new cars for $15,000 and if there is a secondhand market that fills out the quality spectrum even further. The legal markets in the United States and many advanced systems, however, are only offering the ordinary consumer or small business the equivalent of the $60,000 BMW: one-on-one soup-to-nuts legal representation by a highly trained professional who operates in a fairly expensive solo or small-firm practice. It is very hard to find a different quality of service, such as help from a practitioner with more narrow training who can navigate standardized procedures—collecting on straightforward amounts due to an independent contractor or small business, managing compliance challenges for local business regulations, filing for a simple patent or incorporating a business—but couldn't litigate a complicated case. Legal help with just a piece of a legal problem rather than full representation is very difficult to find. Legal help from a web-based company or nonprofit organization that uses standardized protocols and technology to deliver good-enough advice and services to people and businesses who otherwise get nothing is very difficult to find. That's a problem of quality. These are planks that are missing in the legal platform. If you can't balance on the gold-plated bar, you are looking at a gaping hole where your legal strategy might have been.

The problem of missing planks in the legal platform afflicts not just those who cannot afford the BMW. This is also a major problem for those who can afford the best of the best: our largest and most innovative companies. Here the quality problem is that what many of these companies now say they need from lawyers and legal processes simply is not available, at any price.

I discovered this fairly surprising fact somewhat by accident. In 2007 I began directing a new research center at the University of Southern California called the Southern California Innovation Project. The project was founded on the idea that there was a need to think about how well the legal environment today supports innovation. There had been a lot of work done on this topic but with a narrow perspective, focused almost entirely on the role of intellectual property laws. I wanted to know about the broader legal landscape. So I set up interviews with a handful of general counsel—GCs are the lawyers who head the legal departments inside businesses—at leading technology companies: Cisco, Google, Juniper Networks, Mozilla, and CBS Television. I started with a wide-open question: how well is the legal system working to support innovation in your company?

Not so well, it turned out. While these GCs added their voices to the growing chorus of concern about relentlessly higher billing rates and litigation costs, the real focus of their complaints was on the difficulty they had finding any lawyers, at any price, who could help them in the ways they needed help. As one GC explained, running the legal department in an innovative global enterprise these days is like trying to drink from a fire hose. All of the GCs I spoke to were desperate for help with that fire hose.

These GCs described a world in which they are moving within a constantly shifting terrain, firing on threats and grabbing brass rings that appear and disappear in the blink of an eye—bringing to mind the frenzied video games many now in the business were raised on. They were negotiating deals with local government officials in the opaque political worlds of China or India or Russia and sometimes all three simultaneously; rolling out online services in a hundred countries at once with conflicting rules on privacy, encryption, and censorship; managing a cloud-based network of engineers scattered across multiple countries with different employment laws; responding to almost instantaneous blogging by financial analysts around the globe speculating on the implications of the latest twists and turns in patent law suits; coordinating contracts with tens of thousands of advertising customers in dozens of countries; and responding to consumers, labor organizations, investors, and regulators worldwide whenever the internet broke the news of tainted products or dangerous conditions at the hundreds, sometimes thousands, of factories producing their products in a global supply chain. Not one of these GCs would challenge the conclusion of the KPMG report that law and regulation constitutes the number one source of complexity and challenge for today's global businesses. They are squarely in the middle of it.

Here's the surprise: even in the high-end law firm markets where mega-companies shop for lawyers, the supply of solutions to these challenging problems is pitifully thin. The people I spoke to identified several problems.

First and foremost, they said, most of the lawyers they work with—those outside of their own legal departments—understand little about how their businesses work. As Harvey Anderson, then the dynamic GC at Mozilla put it, "Our lawyers just don't know what we do, how a business like this works. There's a massive DNA gap." I heard the same thing in different forms from almost everyone I talked to. Mark Chandler of Cisco—we had lunch together over his company's Telepresence system while I was on the West Coast and he was on the East Coast and I later forgot we hadn't met in person—used a litigation example to say the same thing. He hires top-notch litigators for critical patent litigation—the best of the best. They can kick butt in depositions and settlement negotiations and in front of juries. But what they can't do so well is something Chandler also needs them to do: think about how their litigation strategies and tactics fit into a bigger picture. In between bites of his sandwich he told me about a particularly high-profile lawsuit, involving the allegation that a Chinese competitor had violated Cisco's patents. Early in the litigation his outside legal team proposed filing some pretrial motions. Will we win, he asked? No, came the reply. We don't think we'll win, but the motions, the lawyers argued, were nonetheless good strategy because they would set the stage for later tactics. Chandler's problem was that these expert litigators were only thinking about the impact of the strategy on competition in the courtroom—not the impact outside. As Chandler had to explain to them, if he brought those motions and lost, within minutes the news would be all over the internet, under the bleating headline "Cisco Loses First Round to Chinese Competitor!" Headlines like that can move stock prices, making investors—and CEOs—jittery. Chandler doesn't want to have to explain that this is the world he lives in to the legal experts he hires to take off his plate just one of the thousands of legal problems he has to juggle. He wants litigators who already understand that the battle is fought not only in legal papers but also in the court of public (particularly financial analysts') opinion.

Jonathan Anschell of CBS Television told me about his struggle to find lawyers who understand how businesses like his, transitioning from the era of broadcast dominance to an explosive online environment, operate. Remember those terms of use that *South Park* used to skewer Apple? Anschell's legal department is responsible for generating those for CBS content online. What he finds, he tells me, is that almost every lawyer he hands the problem to thinks that the job is to come up with one of those indecipherable online contracts that, like the terms that ensnare poor Kyle on *South Park*, basically say, "We own everything and we will hunt you down and make your life a living hell if you dare to use anything we own, even if it's something you gave us." But that's not what CBS wants. As Anschell says, "We need lawyers who understand that in the world of new media if you lock it down, you don't get the kind of user-generated content that is such an important component of the online platforms." What happens when he tells them that? The lawyers come back with the polar opposite—the contract terms that are a "user's dream but a content-provider's nightmare." What CBS needs is "something in between those two extremes," a solution that balances the need to encourage users to interact with CBS content and the need to avoid having CBS's money-making content freely distributed to all and sundry. "But we find it very hard to locate the lawyers who know how to think like that," he says.

Other evidence of the DNA gap between lawyers and clients shows up in the ways in which lawyers communicate. Kent Walker, general counsel at Google, voiced a common complaint when he told me of his frustration with lawyers who deliver their advice in lengthy analytical memos when what he needs is targeted advice keyed to the rapid time frames in which he himself has to respond. Nobody wants a disquisition on biology from a doctor when they are bleeding out on the floor. They don't want footnoted legal essays when the clock is ticking on a deal or dispute or public relations crisis either. A company president advises lawyers in a 2012 KPMG study to "make us aware of what we should be doing and tells us this in a straightforward manner, not in complex legal language." But many GCs tell me that it is rare for them to find a lawyer they would feel comfortable putting in front of their board of directors. One bemoans the fact that so many lawyers have no idea how to make a PowerPoint presentation—not because they don't know how to use the software, but because they don't understand their audience.

The evidence of frustration with how poorly even the mostly highly paid, highly trained, sophisticated lawyers understand the terrain their clients traverse is not merely anecdotal. Surveys of large corporate clients repeatedly find high levels of dissatisfaction even with premier law firms and lawyers. A 2013 survey by BTI Consulting Group, for example, found that almost 70 percent of general counsel at large companies would not recommend their primary law firms to their fellow GCs.[32] Why? Because, they say, their lawyers fail to understand and be responsive to their needs and don't do enough to help the company achieve its business goals. In an earlier 2006 survey, when asked about what law firms could do to secure their business, 25 percent of companies said "demonstrate exceptional client focus," by which they meant understand what their business lives look like and give advice that fits their particular needs. Another 50 percent identified factors that would increase the ability to work with the company in a high-value way. Law firms, they said, should "develop an understanding of our business and business strategy and stay focused on those, rather than on legal issues solely" and "have awareness of how their advice would affect the broader business."[33] A Harvard Law School study of 166 corporate counsel tells the same story: 80 percent of companies had reduced the work they had given to an outside law firm in the previous three years, and 88 percent said that the reason was a failure of quality or responsiveness to the company's needs.[34]

A second problem that large companies identify with the quality of legal help that they can buy in our current legal markets—even for top-dollar prices—is that too many lawyers don't understand how to think about risk. Jonathan Anschell's anecdote about lawyers who can't find the sweet spot between overly protective and overly generous terms of use is also a story about a problem with risk. The legal work he is describing is one that sees risk in black-and-white terms. Another anecdote Anschell told me is even more explicit about the frustration about lawyers and risk. In this story, the company was embarking on a venture in new media and met regularly with lawyers from a top Los Angeles law firm to discuss their plans. These lawyers came to every meeting, says Anschell, and fretted openly about how risky the plan was. They kept asking the executives in the room, are you sure you want to do this? But as Anschell explains, a company like his has no choice but to keep moving full speed ahead to keep pace with the rapidly evolving world of entertainment and digital media, despite the risks. What CBS needs—what most companies in a dynamic globally competitive environment need—is critical analysis and strategies for dealing with risks. What they don't need are lawyers who limit themselves just to sounding the alarm when they sniff risk.

Systematic evidence that companies need lawyers with the capacity to analyze risk in a thoughtful and business-minded way shows up in studies of how the role of GCs is rapidly changing. A 2012 KPMG study—with the telling title "Beyond the Law"—quotes leading GCs who pinpoint the capacity to deal with risk as a key driver of success. As one observes: "We are part of the business. We need to learn to run certain risks, because any business runs risks." Indeed, according to this study, the best in-house lawyers don't see their job as just reacting to risks, putting out fires when they erupt into flames. Instead, they adopt a proactive stance with respect to risk, anticipating the constant changes in the environment and helping to craft strategic responses to them. But, as the study also notes, it is still rare for GCs to recognize the problem lawyers face with risk analysis—only a third see changing their approach to risk management as a task that takes high priority. What I hear from GCs who do make business-minded risk management a priority is that they struggle to find lawyers outside of the company who can help them to execute on this approach to risk.

A third category of concerns revolves around a lack of calibration between the amount of time and effort lawyers devote to a piece of work for a client and the value of that work. Harvey Anderson of Mozilla, whose nonprofit company was a pioneer of the open-source movement online with its Firefox browser and, at the time I spoke with him, the second-most installed on computers worldwide, told me of a frustration that will ring true for many in the corporate world: "The business guys work things out and then we all have to stop for a few hours (days or months even) while the lawyers haggle over language and documents that everyone knows will be largely obsolete and unhelpful in short order." Kent Walker expressed the sentiment this way with a specific example: "Never in my time to date at Google has a dispute ever turned on the precise language of a nondisclosure agreement. Yet we still spend lots of time dickering about these things." Walker thinks many deals could get by with just a couple of simple pages to document an agreement, but he finds other lawyers just can't leave them alone. "I send them the two pages I think we need and they chuckle and send back ten or more." These may sound like small problems—but they represent a much larger one: a disconnect between what lawyers think of as a "good" job and what their clients say they need. Lawyers insist on serving up fine china when a paper cup would do. The same problem crops up in litigation, where clients who know enough to notice complain that their lawyers seem only to know one way of managing a case: full-on. But turning over every possible shovel of dirt is rarely the strategy that makes sense outside of the largest bet-the-company type of cases.

Finally, there is the problem of fragmentation. As Mitch Gaynor, then GC of Juniper Networks, explained to me, his company, which produces computer communications and networking equipment, was "global from day 1" when they opened their doors in 1996. That means that he was facing right from the start the massive challenge of managing legal environments worldwide. But, he said, "the market for legal services doesn't seem to understand" his situation. Even when the company grew to operating in more than one hundred countries, he had only a "patchwork of providers" available to give him legal help. If he had a problem that touched India, China, Brazil, and Saudi Arabia, he had to find Indian lawyers, Chinese lawyers, Brazilian lawyers, and Saudi lawyers. He needed employment experts in one place, privacy and encryption experts in another, trade law experts in a third. He could find referrals for all these experts. But what Gaynor wanted, what he would be willing to pay top dollar for, was someone to stitch them all together to advise him on a coherent strategy that addressed not a corner of the canvas but the whole picture. He couldn't buy that.

Ramsey Homsany, who was serving as an associate general counsel at Google when I started my research and later became GC at Dropbox, echoed the same frustration. When Google acquired YouTube in 2007, it also acquired a wicked compliance problem: ensuring that the service was following the laws on privacy, intellectual property, defamation, and more in over one hundred countries around the globe. Google built a solution but had to do it largely in-house. "It would have helped to build on others' experiences and frameworks for that," Homsany told me. "We would have liked to have been able to find someone who'd done more than one of these, who'd seen things we haven't seen. But that just didn't exist out there across countries and regions. So we had to do it largely from scratch."

A mechanism for integrating across borders and issues is not something our legal markets are supplying. That's a quality problem. It's not as if asking for solutions that integrate across borders and issues is like asking for the impossible—globally networked companies are not pining for a flying car or one that can sing small children to sleep. After all, Gaynor and Homsany do come up with the legal solutions their companies need to move forward. They would just like to outsource more of that to the market—and the market is not responding. That piece of the platform is missing.

The problem of fragmentation isn't limited to legal problems that straddle international borders. It pervades almost every piece of business decision-making in an environment where so much is in flux. That's because problems and opportunities in a company rarely come packaged as exclusively legal problems or opportunities. They show up as business problems. They have legal dimensions, but they also have financial, product design, government relations, engineering, and market strategy dimensions. A major complaint from corporate clients, however, is that their lawyers don't play well on teams—that is, that they don't bring the skill set that is necessary to collaborate on solutions that integrate across all the dimensions of a problem.

Collectively, these complaints paint a clear picture. Our legal infrastructure includes the styles and patterns of practice that result from how lawyers are educated and licensed and how their working lives evolve together with the expectations they have about what counts as good legal work. The traditional model of the lawyer is of an elite, highly educated professional who stands aloof from the hurly burly of the commercial world, who gives sage considered advice to the business executive and lends a helpful hand to those in need before the justice system. Good legal advice has traditionally been conceived as advice that is cautious and that reminds clients of their duties to the law and each other. Anthony Kronman, former dean of Yale Law School, writes of this image of the lawyer as the lawyer-statesman.[35] The ethics of the traditional lawyer have been rooted in concepts of noblesse oblige. The practice of law has been deliberately crafted for over a hundred years as a practice apart. But as one general counsel in the 2012 KPMG study observed, "Pure legal decisionmaking and just managing a legal process is not going to 'cut it' anymore."

Lawyers often read the litany of complaints about the system they oversee, like the litany I have recited in this chapter, and feel either defensive or despondent or both. But they should really feel some measure of pride. The system lawyers built over the last few hundred years has been enormously successful, grounding the spectacular growth the advanced world has enjoyed since 1800. And the evidence of that success is seen precisely in the fact that the baby is bursting out of its clothes. The problem is not what lawyers invented. It's what they are (not) doing to reinvent in the face of external change. Like any problem-solving system that humans have invented for managing complexity, the platform lawyers helped to create has limits. This doesn't mean we are facing collapse—as Tainter emphasizes, the difference between the collapsed ancient societies he studied and our own is that eventually complexity gave us the capacity to change strategies, largely as a result of decentralization. Kings and dictators may lead their peoples into collapse by sticking with a failed economic program, but markets are inherently structured to reward new thinking and methods, and democracy throws the bums out when things start turning south. There is constant pressure to come up with new strategies and a vibrant clashing of ideas and plans. Centuries of enough wealth to support the efforts of wonkish people like myself whose only job is to think about what works and what doesn't in markets and political organization, have produced a rich trove of ideas on which to draw in devising new strategies, slipping loose the bonds of an exhausted complex solution. The danger we face with our legal infrastructure, then, is that it has emerged from the last two hundred successful years heavily guarded against competition and change. We turn to that problem, and the way out, in the next chapters.

PART III

*Harnessing Markets
for Legal Innovation*

8

Problem-Solving through Markets

WHY HASN'T OUR legal infrastructure responded better to the changes in the global economy? While most other sectors of the economy are coming up with smarter ideas to make complex problems easier and cheaper to solve, why have our legal sectors only become more complex, more costly, and more divorced from the underlying economic demand for law? Where are the legal innovations giving us easier, cheaper, and more effective ways to meet the economic demand for a stable, reliable framework for ensuring that we have the confidence we need to invest our time and resources in our jobs, our relationships, our ventures? We have powerful computers with touchscreens in our pockets, the capacity to buy anything online with one click and next-day delivery, and access to instantaneous news about anything happening almost anywhere in the world. Why don't we have a better way to manage the legal challenges of a global supply chain, a globally networked workforce, artificially intelligent agents, or global financial risk?

Simply put, we rely too much on centralized planning and not enough on markets to build the components of our legal infrastructure—the rules, practices, and expertise we need to manage a complex global economy. We've already seen that a shift to orderly rational planning, centralized in the nation-state, generated a productive platform for the economies of the nineteenth and twentieth centuries. Comprehensive and high-quality organization—of legal rules, of court processes, of legal training and practice—promoted a great set of standards on which the emerging mass-manufacturing economy could be built. But that organization relied heavily on top-down problem-solving: rules crafted in bureaucracies, discussed in committees, and voted upon by elected or appointed officials; finely wrought analysis by highly trained judges supplied with evidence and arguments assembled by highly trained lawyers and legal scholars; educational standards and ethical rules developed in committees and adopted by state supreme courts and bar associations with exclusive power to decide who can and who cannot practice law.

Top-down problem-solving methods in theory are the pinnacle of causal abstract reasoning—the secret of our success as a species. The idea seems so obvious: collect all of the relevant information, analyze it, synthesize it, weigh it, and choose the best solution. What could go wrong? The problem is that information doesn't play nice. It hides in small places and at great heights. It reveals itself in different ways to different people, differently over time, differently across contexts. It rewards those who already have a lot and yet also misleads them. It leaks and spills and remains embedded. It falls into chasms between us. It travels for free and it demands a high price. It drives us to become different—to specialize across the division of labor—and then this very differentiation challenges our ability to come together with a shared set of ideas about how we will orchestrate all our small parts into a harmonious whole.

The stable mass-manufacturing world of mass-produced goods and processes—the economy that managed information by standardizing it—fed the growth of an economy that allowed information more room to move. The information economy is the economy that rewards the ability to play with information. To find it where it is hidden and send it across the barriers of language and culture and experience. To discover new ways to share it and pay for it. To ride the curl of what *Wired* magazine's former editor-in-chief Chris Anderson calls the long tail—the place where all of our nonstandard ideas and desires live.[1] This is the economy that makes innovation—the creation of new solutions to problems new and old—its central animating feature.

The information-saturated, innovation-central global economy is not one that is well-managed by top-down problem-solving methods alone. It requires a more liquid means of discovering, integrating, and deploying what an increasingly differentiated world knows, finding more supple ways of assembling shared ideas about how we will come back together to exchange across a division of labor—a division of information—that burrows deeper and deeper into every field of activity. That means a greater role for markets— where people solve problems locally and coordination is accomplished not by analysis and committee but, in Adam Smith's famous simile, "as if by an invisible hand." We've recognized the power of markets to generate and transmit knowledge—to innovate better solutions to more problems—in fundamentally economic settings. We just haven't—yet—seen that we need to apply those same lessons to the design of the legal infrastructure on which our economic foundations are built. But if we want our legal infrastructure to innovate in step with the innovative pace of our economy, we will have to find ways to harness the problem-solving power of markets to build more of our legal rules and practices.

The Problem of Planning

At the turn of the twentieth century, industrializing countries around the globe were facing a major complexity challenge. As urbanization and manufacturing displaced the predominance of agriculture in society—as the scale of markets swelled and the division of labor continued its relentless march toward increasing specialization and widening gaps between people in terms of how they spent their days—the question of how to coordinate economic activity loomed large. It was a question faced both by the industrialists building sprawling vertically integrated manufacturing empires and by the political groups that sought either to rein in the industrialists to serve the interests of the common man or to harness industry in the service of nationalism and military glory. It was a question many groups often answered with what appeared to be an obvious answer: centralized planning.

For the industrialists, centralized planning took the form of top-down bureaucracies, producing the managerial economy coordinated by the "visible hand" studied by Alfred Chandler. Successive layers of managers responded to targets and high-level budget decisions established by headquarters and developed the detailed rules for how money would be spent, raw materials allocated, jobs carried out. The great railway and steel cartels of the late nineteenth century in the United States used centralized planning to tell their members who could sell what goods or services where and at what price on a national scale.

For political groups, centralized planning was a means to achieve social ideals through government, and the idea that a complex economy should be expressly coordinated by a central government took on its grandest form in the Soviet Union. Planning of the minutiae of economic life cascaded down from grand targets set by the Politburo at the apex of Soviet government through successive layers of administrative entities until it reached the managers of state enterprises responsible for achieving specific production goals. Government bureaucrats decided how much steel to produce, and where to use it to make what goods; how many apartments to build and who could live in them; what clothing to manufacture when and where, and for how much it could be sold; what jobs would be made available to whom and at what wage. This was the full-on communist vision of a fair and productive society.

But the appeal of centralized planning was not limited to the far left. Far-right fascist governments in Italy, Germany, and Japan during the years between World War I and the end of World War II stopped short of state ownership but nonetheless relied on centralized organization and oversight of an ostensibly private economy to achieve their goals of nationalism and military preparedness. Centralized control was ideological for the fascists, but it was also rationalized as inexorable in the face of modern complexity. "The more complicated the forms assumed by civilization," asserted Mussolini in 1937, "the more restricted the freedom of the individual must be."[2]

Even in democratic societies, leading political groups were drawn to the idea that centralized planning was the solution to the chaos of the market economy. In 1942, the Labour Party in Britain urged that "there must be no return to the unplanned competitive world of the inter-War years. . . . A planned society must replace the old competitive system."[3] As Lionel Robbins, an economist at the London School of Economics, observed in 1937: "Planning is the grand panacea of our age."[4]

Beneath the appeal of planning across the political spectrum lay a common belief: that the complexity of the mass-manufacturing economy could not result in a stable economic system in the absence of a single centralized agency capable of putting the pieces into rational order. How to make sure that resources are being put to their best and highest use or that people are compensated fairly and protected against the vagaries of life without scientific guidance? The answer seemed as natural to the politicians, dictators, and idealists as it did to the industrialists coordinating their massive organizations and cartels. Planning, they concluded, was an inevitable stage in the evolution of more complex societies. The political fight was over who was going to do the planning and with what goals, not over whether planning was the right way to go about coordinating a complex economy.

The regulated market economy that stabilized and generated great growth throughout the Western world after the end of World War II was one structured by substantial amounts of planning, both within governments and within massive Chandlerian corporations. Planning structured in these ways—industrial activity planned by private managers in for-profit companies and regulatory and public services activity planned by politicians, bureaucrats, and judges in legislatures, regulatory agencies, and courts— worked pretty well. Indeed, even the Soviet Union's all-encompassing centralized planning model worked pretty well from a pure production point of view for a few decades. Growth in the Soviet Union was robust and may have outpaced US growth from the 1950s into the 1970s. (Of course, Soviet growth calculations don't take into account the appalling human losses in a totalitarian regime that killed millions of its own citizens and dictated the details of how and where people could live and work.)

But accelerating complexity in the latter decades of the twentieth century put increasing pressure on planning solutions, both within the corporations of the box economy and within the massive bureaucratic structures of the socialist economies. That planning was simply not up to the task of coordinating a complex technological society had been clearly understood within the later Soviet Union. As one important report published by economic reformers in the Gorbachev government of the 1980s concluded, "We have become convinced on the basis of our own experience that there is no worthy alternative to the market mechanism as the method of coordinating the activities and interests of the economic subjects."[5] In a 1990 study of the perestroika market reform efforts of Mikhail Gorbachev's government, efforts that failed to ward off the ultimate collapse of the Soviet Union, Yale University economist William Nordhaus opened with a Hungarian joke: "Question: What is communism? Answer: The longest road from capitalism to capitalism."[6]

The Soviet Union was not the only government to learn the impossibility of the centrally planned complex economy. Just before the Soviet collapse in December 1991, 25 percent of the world's population lived in self-declared socialist states with centrally planned economies. An additional 15 percent lived in highly planned (India) or administrative (Japan) states. By the time of the millennium, nearly all of these economies had shifted substantially to a market basis. Even China, which continues to identify itself as a socialist state, had begun by the 1980s to shift the balance from central planning toward markets.

Meanwhile, in the market economies of the West, essentially the same shift was appearing throughout the corporate world. In response to the hurtling complexity of a global economy with deeply networked information systems across company boundaries, the managerial model of the vertically integrated box economy was giving way to the decentralized and deverticalized global supply chain model of the network economy. Ironically, it was production methods developed in a corporation in the highly planned Japanese economy that ultimately produced the modern model of decentralized and continuous improvement dubbed the Toyota way. As we've seen, a key commitment in that model was to shift decision-making closer to where a problem lives—out of top management offices and down to the work team on the factory line or the supplier of individual parts or services. This was the model that told people to *genchi genbutsu*, or, more colloquially, "Get your boots on" and go to where the problem is if you want a better solution. While GM was giving its suppliers detailed planning blueprints for what to produce, Toyota was giving its suppliers performance targets to meet and the freedom to figure out how to build a better, cheaper, more reliable part. And while GM was using internal prices to communicate information and coordinate behavior between its different production units, Toyota was sharing information as directly and extensively as possible between suppliers and customers to improve the quality of problem-solving and the capacity for coordination up and down the supply chain.

An intense focus on opening up company boundaries so that information and ideas can flow more freely and new solutions can more quickly displace old ones is a fundamental characteristic of the global network economy. There is still lots and lots of planning within the private sector, of course, but the goal is no longer to dictate how every element in the hierarchy should be moved, like pieces on a chessboard. Instead the emphasis is on planning how to organize productive flexible relationships with suppliers, distributors, and customers with the goal of maximizing the organization's capacity to respond in faster, smarter ways to the limits and opportunities that a constantly shifting environment serves up.

The global economic shift to a reduced role for centralized planning and a greater role for markets that straddled the turn of the second millennium came with plenty of ideological overtones. Francis Fukuyama, in an influential book published in 1992 and reprinted in 2006, called it *The End of History*. He meant by this that the collapse of the Soviet Union and military-authoritarian governments around the globe was proof that the ideals of liberal democracy had prevailed over those of totalitarian dictatorship, with its centralized control of society. But, as Fukuyama also recognized, the drivers of collapse were fundamentally economic—and the fact that a parallel, albeit far less dramatic, shift from planning to markets was taking place as the box economy reconfigured itself into a global network economy demonstrates the point. The complexities of the economy by the closing decades of the twentieth simply placed far too great an information burden on anyone who tried to sit atop the pile and direct from on high. As economist F. A. Hayek wrote in the leading economics journal *American Economic Review* in 1945, the more complex an economy becomes, the less amenable it is to centralized planning.[7] The reason is nonideological and has nothing to do with liberal democracy and the proper role of government in promoting human well-being. It is supremely practical. (Hayek "was at first puzzled and even alarmed" when he found that his book *The Road to Serfdom*, still a bible for libertarians today, "written in no party spirit and not meant to support any popular philosophy had been so exclusively welcomed by one party and thoroughly excoriated by the other." In an address to the Economic Club of Detroit on his 1945 book tour he advocated for clear principles to distinguish between legitimate and illegitimate government activity: "You must cease to argue for and against government activity as such."[8]) Given the extensive division of labor and specialization that Smith taught lay at the root of economic growth, eventually economic growth produces sufficient complexity that it is simply impossible for a central agency to know enough about what is going on at ground level to implement a good and effective plan, whatever definition of good and effective—socialist, fascist, democratic—one chooses.

Hayek's deep insight that "the economic problem of society is mainly one of rapid adaptation to changes in the particular circumstances of time and place" lay largely dormant among economists for several decades—until the 1970s, when the problems of information and organization began to assume a much more central role in conventional economic analysis. Today the idea that the core problem of economic organization is figuring out how to generate information, share it, and put it to use is fundamental to mainstream economic theory.

How do markets help manage the information burden of a complex global economy? There are three parts to the answer. First, much of the information we need to produce new solutions to economic problems old and new lies deeply embedded with people scattered across the globe who are ever more specialized and differentiated one from another. Much of it will only emerge if specialization and the division of labor carves even further into problems that are more finely sliced and diced than ever before. Trying to build a car based on planning from the top is likely to result in lower-quality, higher-cost cars because much of the information about how to raise quality and lower costs is at the bottom, where the car is actually being built. So giving the folks at the bottom of the production pyramid—the people who make, ship, and assemble the parts—greater discretion to decide how to make, ship, and assemble makes it possible for that ground-level information to be put to use.

But just giving those at ground level the freedom to make production and design decisions doesn't, all by itself, generate a coordinated economic order in which cars are produced at higher quality and lower cost. The people at ground level also have to face the incentive to work hard to make the best use of what they know about how to do things better, faster, cheaper. That's the second feature of how markets manage information that helps to deal with complexity. Markets create the incentives to discover and apply information—which is costly and often requires significant investment to unearth—because they reward good ideas. Flexible market structures, like the networks in global supply chains, promote that investment by allowing those on the hunt for better ideas to sniff out where the likelihood for finding new ideas is highest, and the cost of developing them lowest. Because of one of those special economic attributes of information we considered earlier—increasing returns—the best people to look for new information and ideas to solve some problem are often those who already know a lot about the problem. Often those are people far down the value chain, not those sitting atop the heap.

The third reason that markets help manage the information burdens of a complex economy is that markets systematically transmit the information they contain. When markets do succeed in incentivizing people to come up with better ideas—when companies pay and train their workers better, price their products more affordably, treat their customers better, introduce products that serve demand better, produce higher payouts for their investors, comply with industry rules and regulation more reliably and cost-effectively—then others indirectly learn what these innovators know. It's true that there are lots of efforts made to control the flow of information, to try to make sure competitors don't learn what you invested so much in discovering. But eventually the market pretty much learns everything. Prices communicate this information, but so do a myriad other business signals. Still requiring your engineers to punch a clock and wear a suit? Well soon your HR department is going to notice that it's getting harder and harder to hire and retain the best engineers—they're all off having fun at the Googleplex, working on cutting-edge products, eating gourmet lunches, and enjoying the opportunity to spend time developing their own ideas and pitching them for development. Your hiring problem is the market is telling you what Google figured out: they can make more money staying ahead of the innovation curve by changing how they manage a workplace. Competition is taking Google's local knowledge and spreading it around.

It's not unlike how the poor blobfish "learns" via competition for lobster and crab that humans have discovered how to build deep-sea trawlers capable of scooping up the blobfish's dinner—and often the blobfish itself. Unfortunately for the blobfish, tied to problem-solving solutions written into DNA, there's nothing it can do to make use of that information to find a better way to solve its problem of finding food and not falling prey to the humans operating trawlers. But the tech company that learns that all the best engineers are getting scooped up by Google has the human advantage of storing solutions in ideas and abstract thinking. So it can make use of the information it acquires through the competitive system and put it to use winning back engineers in a post-Google world.

The information about what's happening in the ecosystem for engineers is information that planners are likely never to learn or at least not very quickly. Some local manager might have the idea to remake the workplace to motivate engineers better. But the higher-ups are not likely to hear about it and so they can't incorporate it into their grand plan for coordinating the economy. Markets incentivize the production of and specialization in information, and they provide a mechanism for the diffusion of information, systemically, throughout the economy.

Here is where the core insight that can be extracted from the late twentieth-century shift away from centralized planning and toward a greater role for markets sheds light also on the problems of our legal infrastructure. We are in great need of new ideas about how best to structure legal rules and practices to meet the new economic demands of our complex global economy. But we rely extensively on planning mechanisms, operated by governments, to produce those ideas: to write the rules, draft the statutes, design the regulatory regimes. We will figure out some of these solutions with our traditional methods—careful analysis and planning in our legislatures, agencies, and courts. But where we can create competitive markets for the production of legal infrastructure, we can harness the power of markets to drive investment and innovation in legal infrastructure design. We can build up specialization in the knowledge of how legal infrastructure works and how it can be made to work better. We can get that information transmitted widely and systemically. Our planning methods can't do that. No number of expert panels, PhD-level studies, government data analyses, or international agency reports can match the information potential of markets. If we want smart new ideas for how to deliver a stable, productive platform on which to build the more complex relationships of the global economy, we should be finding ways to get markets into the mix.

Can't We Just Fix Government?

Do we really need to figure out how to get more markets into rule-making? Couldn't we just figure out how to get governments to produce simpler, less costly, and more effective legal rules? There's certainly lots of consensus that this would be a fine objective.

Although we shouldn't give up on other strategies to reverse the trends toward more complex and expensive rules and procedures—because we are never going to be in a world without significant government-based rule-making—the prospects for broad-based transformative success are not great. People have been talking about the need for simpler, cheaper rules for a very long time. But most efforts to create simpler, lower-cost legal systems have failed, some spectacularly. As we saw in Chapter 7, when Congress in 1990 tried to reduce the complexity and reduce the cost of litigation, for example, and passed a law that mandated that litigants meet with the judge and reach a plan for a more reasonable discovery process, the effort backfired: the time spent by lawyers and litigants on the case and the cost of litigation went *up*.

There's a reason it has proven very difficult to achieve the goal of reducing the costs and complexity of legal rules and processes through our conventional rule-making methods. Complex and high-cost rules and procedures are fairly predictable outcomes of our reliance on political, bureaucratic, and judicial rule production methods in a world of increasing complexity. This is because these systems all experience the benefits of more complex rules and processes but not, in any systematic way, the costs. Political deal-making in more diverse settings is more likely to succeed with more potential deals on the table. Complex tax codes, multiple tacked-on requirements and conditions placed on access to federal funds, and byzantine exceptions, carve-outs, and special rules in regulatory regimes all can be understood at least in part as the result of getting to yes in a legislature that has to serve many interests. Taking heat and obstruction from some interest group? Add a section to the bill, as close to the one their lobbyists and advocates want. Regulatory agencies can also see complexity as a solution, a way of responding to the deluge of conflicting factors and considerations generated from studies, committees, hearings, public comments, industry negotiations, legal constraints, and political imperatives. Regulatory agencies are also staffed by increasingly specialized and highly trained people—people with PhDs in economics populate the SEC and the Federal Trade Commission; those with advanced degrees in engineering, biology, and epidemiology abound at the Environmental Protection Agency. Greater specialization in knowledge produces more complex understandings of problems—and leads to more complex solutions. This natural entropy of complex reasoning also happens in common-law systems. When people compete by presenting more elaborate views of what rules mean and how the world works—which is how lawyers compete in litigation—it's practically inevitable that the decisions that courts produce will grow more nuanced and closely reasoned over time.

In each of these settings, greater complexity solves problems for the people running a rule-making machine: it allows deals to get done, multiple interests to be met, and satisfies the intellectual search for accuracy and coherence in sophisticated reasoning. What these rule-making machines don't experience much of are the costs of the complexity they produce. Politicians and bureaucrats may come under criticism for their complex solutions, but it's easy to pass the buck and the blame. Moreover, those complaints are like far-off voices echoing in the hills. The needs of getting a deal done or a regulation published are like herds of buffalo stampeding straight at you on the valley floor. And as for the judges asked to choose between a decision that acknowledges a persuasive argument about the meaning of a legal rule by adding nuance to the body of law and one that responds by saying, "Sorry, you are right, but you still lose because explaining why you're right would make the law too complex"—well, that's just not how judges believe they are supposed to decide. They are supposed to choose the best answer to the question: what is the correct outcome in this case? Choosing less correct but less costly answers is just not a norm judges are expected to follow in our existing legal infrastructure.

From an economic point of view, this is why our existing rule production systems quite systematically produce levels of complexity that overshoot the mark: Because there are trade-offs between more subtle complex answers and the costs of complexity. At some point the marginal benefit of a better answer isn't justified by the marginal cost of the complexity it adds. That's the lesson of the RAND study that found that costs went up, not down, when perfectly reasonable-sounding rules designed to reduce costs were put in place. But when our production systems are planning-based, the product of studies and politics and deliberation, the margin between costs and benefits is abstract, intellectual. It's not a constraint. Unlike in markets, where the margin is the difference between beating the competition and being beaten.

We have discouraging experience with the effort to get government to behave more like the market. Beginning in the 1980s, governments began to use more outsourcing of public services to private contractors—to collect the garbage, build a toll road, or operate a prison, for example. Then politicians responding to perennial worries about bloated government budgets and stories of waste in government services caught the innovation and entrepreneurship bug along with the private sector. Under the banner of the 1992 best-selling book *Reinventing Government* by public management consultant

David Osborne and former city manager Ted Gaebler, governments around the globe began talking about how to build the entrepreneurial spirit in the public services sector. Picked up by President Bill Clinton in his successful 1992 election campaign, the ideas took shape on a national scale in the United States with then-vice president Al Gore's National Performance Review. Gore oversaw a massive study of ground-level operations throughout the federal government and produced an optimistic report about how to get more done better with less by freeing agencies and federal employees from red tape and empowering them to solve the problems they saw as they saw them. The aim was for a complete transformation of the culture of bureaucracy— replete with customer-service slogans printed on laminated cards and motivational consultants. The themes were not so far removed from those emerging from Gorbachev's economists just before the collapse of the Soviet Union— moving away from a command-based system and toward one based more on freeing individuals to act on what they know to move resources into better uses. Indeed, Osborne and Gaebler titled their first chapter "An American *Perestroika*." These were heady times for the idea that government could work better if it worked more like the new decentralized corporation.

The recommendations for reinventing government certainly resonated with the transformations playing out in the private sector. Osborne and Gaebler urged governments of all sizes—city, state, and federal—to become customer-focused, mission-driven, market-oriented entities, focused on results rather than rules, and relying on competition and decentralization to serve the public. In example after example, *Reinventing Government* documented success. A public works department in Phoenix that cleaned up its act and cut costs as a result of having to compete with private garbage collectors for contracts. A city manager in the San Fernando Valley who, empowered to move money around in his budget without line-item restrictions, was able to beat out other bidders on a cut-rate public swimming pool left over after the Los Angeles Summer Olympics. A school superintendent in East Harlem who was able to raise school standards in a poor urban district by letting teachers create alternative public schools, doing whatever they thought would work to get results, and letting teachers and students choose which ones they wanted to go to.

There were some enduring changes in how government worked as a result of the reinventing government movement. Governments throughout the world began to rely more on outsourcing; developed performance targets for public agencies; implemented customer-oriented websites for filing taxes, renewing licenses, or filing benefits claims; and improved patient care at veterans' hospitals. But the grand vision of government employees behaving more like agile Google employees never materialized. And with good reason. As academic critics of what they saw as the reinventing government "fad" pointed out, bureaucrats don't behave like bureaucrats just because they have the wrong culture or don't want to serve the public better. They behave like bureaucrats because they operate within a system that includes politicians, courts, the media, and interest groups. Political scientist James Q. Wilson—perhaps best known for his broken windows theory of urban crime control—was a supporter of the idea of deregulating bureaucracies and eliminating constraints on public employees so they could do their jobs better. He emphasized, however, that public employees are often heavily constrained in what they do because that's what the public, acting through elected officials and judges, wants. Those constraints are written into the laws legislators pass and the legal demands judges hearing challenges to government actions impose. Bureaucrats spend more time worrying about how to follow the rules than how to do the job better, faster, and cheaper because that's how they survive in the ecosystem defined by politics.[9] If the politics are right—if an enterprising city manager gets elected or appointed and boldly gives his or her employees the authority to respond quickly to opportunities to save the city council money without red tape—then entrepreneurialism and innovation can flourish. But if the politics are swamped by distrust, conflicting constituencies, interest groups, and a hungry press (and now blogosphere), then the entrepreneurially minded in the public service will be hemmed in on all sides by rules and requirements and face only the incentive to avoid scandal and not the incentive to think outside the box.

The insight is critical. The shift from centralized planning to decentralized market mechanisms in the business world wasn't a result of a free-floating change in the culture of business. It was a result of the imperative to compete. The Toyota way didn't spread throughout the manufacturing world and beyond because business leaders read about the ideas in a book or attended a motivational business seminar and got all starry-eyed with possibility. It spread because Toyota began eating GM's lunch. But most public services providers don't face competition from the next best thing. The politicians who run the shop may be forced to fend off challengers and critics on an almost nonstop basis, but the government agencies that administer Social Security benefits or veterans hospitals or the water treatment plant, the ones who oversee student loan and retraining programs or prisons operated by private contractors, aren't going to go out of business if they don't change the way they do business. The incentives public officials face are the incentives crafted by politics, not the incentives crafted by markets. Politics *can* seek to craft market-type incentives for public agencies if *politics* demands that. But modern democratic politics tends to demand something different. As Wilson notes, "Most red tape reflects the ability of some group—some part of the voting public—to get its interests protected in the carrying out of public policy."

The difference between political, bureaucratic, and judicial problem-solving approaches and the market is that when business people sitting around a conference table make mistakes or place the wrong bet, they get thrashed by competitors. And so they work hard to avoid such mistakes. The margin between benefits and costs is one that markets pay close attention to because you can't make profit if you continue to choose more complex solutions that are simply too expensive for most people. Markets are constantly trawling for the margin—offering a luxury automobile if there are enough people who can afford it but being sure to offer a perfectly good but not perfect automobile to the ones who cannot. Think about the smartphone in your pocket or purse. The huge success of the Blackberry in the early days of smartphones was the result of the smart idea to focus on the corporate market and email. Competitors that tried to cram too many things into that little unit suffered by comparison. There were more benefits if you could also use your phone to surf the web, listen to music, and navigate to your destination, but the complexity they created wasn't worth it. And then came the Blackberry-killer: the iPhone. It managed to pack more of those benefits into a tiny device, but only by figuring out how to make the user interface less complex, more elegant. And even then it had to give up things, like an error-free keyboard. The pressure to figure out how to hit these trade-offs right, to find the sweet spot between increased complexity costs and increased benefits, came from the market—the opportunity for Apple to steal Blackberry's profits.

That's what we're looking for: the iPhone of law. We shouldn't expect to get it without figuring out how to get more markets into the legal infrastructure business.

Markets for Data

I threw a lot of numbers at you in Chapter 7:

> $90,000 and 375 hours of legal work to resolve a simple employment dispute
>
> $250 an hour to hire a solo practitioner

$1.4 million to litigate a patent case worth $1 million

340,000 document pages preserved for every page introduced as evidence in litigation

What I didn't tell you there was just how spotty and incomplete our data are about how this critical piece of our economy works. Most of these numbers are the best we can do to report on what's going on, but they are far from the kind of hard reliable data we'd like.

To begin with, there is very little systematic collection of data on our legal infrastructure. Governments count the total number of people who say they are working as lawyers, as part of the systematic collection of data on employment that feed news reports on unemployment rates. The United States collects this data at the federal level in the Current Population Survey. But little attention is paid to factors that make law a tricky business to count. The Bureau of Labor Statistics, for example, reports numbers of employed lawyers—but half of all lawyers are either solo practitioners or partners in law firms, and they don't show up in the BLS numbers, unless the partnership has incorporated and the partners renamed shareholders. Tax authorities and census bureaus collect data on the revenues collected and wages paid by law firms. But detailed statistics are produced, in the United States at least, only every five years, and the data are not easily translated to lawyer income. In fact, no one has a good answer to the very simple question: how many people are currently working as lawyers in the United States today? The numbers from different sources—the ABA numbers on licenses held, the BLS data on employed lawyers, the IRS and census data on law firms—are hard to reconcile.

Other government offices collect data on the parts of legal infrastructure that government pays for—courts, police, prisons, and government-provided legal aid. The data on courts, however, are quite limited: expenditures on courts, numbers of judges, numbers of case filings in relatively broad case categories, numbers of trials. There are periodic surveys in some courts (but not estimates generalized to all courts) of the percentage of plaintiffs who win and how much is awarded in damages—but since these data are based on cases that go all the way to trial and produce a decision by a judge or jury and the vast majority of cases are either decided without a trial or settled, they are only a tiny slice of all litigation—about 5 percent.

What's missing from this data collection? Much that we want and need to know to assess how well our legal infrastructure is working. We don't have regular statistics, for example, on what different legal procedures cost—how much it costs to buy an hour of a lawyer's time for different kinds of help or to make your way through legal processes such as complying with regulations, filing taxes, securing financing for a start-up, or resolving an employment dispute. How long it takes to resolve legal issues with government offices and courts. How much businesses spend in the aggregate on specific legal processes or procedures—resolving discrimination disputes, challenging contract terms, settling class action claims. We don't know how much our legal systems cost or even very much about how legal resources are allocated across different kinds of people, problems, and policies.

The lack of government-generated statistics is, however, just the beginning. Most of what we know about how other economic and social institutions and systems work we know not because the government keeps records, but because researchers go out, collect, and analyze data. They spend time and money figuring out what data it makes sense to analyze, developing theories of how the institutions of modern life work. Investing in knowledge is a big part of the modern information economy. In 2012, the United States spent $400 billion on research and development, about 2.8 percent of GDP. This includes money spent by governments and charitable organizations as well as by private industry. China invested at the same average rate as the OECD countries, about 2.5 percent of GDP, or $200 billion. Korea and Israel invested over 4 percent of GDP, Russia about 1.25 percent.[10]

These are pretty big numbers. But almost none of this money is spent trying to understand more about how legal infrastructure works or how to make it work better. There is, for example, nothing in law remotely comparable to the US National Institutes of Health, which distributes $30 billion a year in federal funds to medical researchers. At $50 million, the National Institute of Justice spends less than two-tenths of 1 percent of that amount—and exclusively for research on crime and policing. The only federal research funds available for studying how our civil legal infrastructure works come from the National Science Foundation, which allocates just $6 million of its $6 billion budget—one-tenth of 1 percent—to law and social science research. The NSF spends about an average of a billion dollars each on biology, computer science, engineering, geosciences, and math and physical sciences.

There are some nonprofit foundations dedicated to research to improve our knowledge of how well law is working for us—but they are few and small. I and other law faculty have been fortunate to receive funding from the Kauffman Foundation, which has taken seriously the role of the legal environment in supporting the main object of its funding: entrepreneurship. I've already mentioned RAND, whose Institute for Civil Justice does important work on law with a focus on the public interest. But there is nothing comparable to the Robert Wood Johnson Foundation, for example, which spends over $350 million a year on grants for research on health policy. Or the Kaiser Family Foundation, which spends about $100 million a year studying healthcare systems. The largest non-profit research organization dedicated to law, the American Bar Foundation, which is funded in significant part by an endowment generated from dividends on insurance policies sold to members of the American Bar Association, spends about $5 million a year studying the legal profession.

In a sense, there's no money for research on legal infrastructure because there is no "there" there. Lawyers research what the law is. Economists and other policy-oriented researchers study what the law should be—to promote trade or investment in new technologies, improve incentives for workplace safety, or design cost-effective taxes, for example. But hardly anyone studies how law works as a system, what determines the system's costs and efficacy. There is very little systematic work on how to build law where it does not already exist or make it work more effectively. There are no fields of study in law comparable to the fields of public health or epidemiology—where we develop specialized knowledge of how our medical systems work and how disease is spread and contained. It is because those fields of study exist that we know, for example, how often knee surgeries appear to help, how hand-washing procedures in hospitals can reduce infections, and what the payoff is to preventive care. There is simply nothing comparable, publicly or privately produced, with respect to legal infrastructure.

Why do we know so little about legal infrastructure, how it's built, and how to do it better? Because we don't have enough competitive markets playing a role in the production of our legal infrastructure.

Competitive markets, as we've seen, create an incentive to invest in information—information that can help reduce costs, improve quality, or identify new products and services that people want. Of course there are all kinds of misfires on this. No doubt much of what we have in consumer culture we could do very well without, and the investment in information to "discover" these so-called needs is money badly spent as a society. Corporate profit interests can also undermine the reliability of information. We've seen this with the efforts of tobacco companies to produce research that manufactured doubt about the scientific evidence of the causal link between smoking and cancer, as Robert Proctor's work in *The Cancer Wars* has shown. (Proctor coined the term *agnotology* to denote the study of how information can be used to increase ignorance and doubt.) But, systematically, much of what we know we know because it was in someone's market-based interest to figure it out. Two-thirds of medical research, for example, is funded by pharmaceutical, medical device, and other private healthcare entities; the other third is funded by taxes and philanthropy. Even with a big adjustment for distorted priorities—do we really need research on treatments for male-pattern baldness more than we need a cure for malaria?—and even malignant priorities—ineffective weight-loss treatments or new drugs that are no better than the old drugs—that's a significant contribution from market incentives to knowledge.

Even the existence of government and philanthropic research money often owes something to markets. Government funding priorities, for example, are influenced by the costs governments incur when they participate in markets. Governments that subsidize food or housing or medical care, for example, have an interest in how well markets for food, housing, and medical services work and how expensive they are. So they collect data and sponsor research on food, housing, and medical care. Governments also respond to constituencies—which include businesses that depend on government-generated data and analysis such as consumer prices and employment projections. Philanthropists, on the other hand, are giving away money they made in markets and not infrequently—although this has been frowned upon in some philanthropic circles—for purposes connected with their profit-making careers. The Kaiser Family Foundation, for example, is giving away money for healthcare research that the Kaiser family earned in part from Henry Kaiser's development of a healthcare system for his employees to improve the profitability of his Richmond, California, shipyards during World War II. This was at a time when *Fortune* magazine reported that 90 percent of the US population could not afford fee-for-service healthcare. Kaiser, a prolific industrialist, had learned from his earlier experiences building roads and dams in remote locations about the relationship between access to healthcare and worker productivity. Not surprisingly, the Kaiser Permanente model focused on preventive care—the type of care that can reduces worker absenteeism. The Kaiser Family Foundation was established with a mission to develop the model of healthcare Kaiser had pioneered.[11] By the same token, the Robert Wood Johnson Foundation, also focused on healthcare, was funded with money earned by Johnson & Johnson, a healthcare products company. The Richard King Mellon Foundation was established to further the urban development interests of its founder; mega-banker Mellon had financed and promoted urban renewal in Pittsburgh during his lifetime.

The investments spurred by market interests not only increase the resources available for knowledge building. They can also sometimes end up generating more social benefits than public spending. This is because if it is in some company's interest to get information across to the public—about the risks of forgoing preventive healthcare screenings, for example, or what you should know about what's in the fine print of the contract with your mobile phone provider—the company is likely to devote more resources to figuring out how best to get that message across. An important set of studies carried out by Pauline Ippolito and Alan Mathios looked at how people's eating habits changed in the late 1980s after the US Food and Drug Administration relaxed its rules on advertising health claims on food products.[12] They found that people learned more effectively about what health researchers were then saying about the value of increasing fiber and reducing fat in a healthy diet from advertising by companies trying to sell people high-fiber breakfast cereals and lower-fat meat, milk, and desserts than they did from messages and advice coming from governments or medical associations. Similarly, a 2010 study done by Daniel Hosken and Brett Wendling of the US Federal Trade Commission looked at the impact of allowing drug companies to advertise their drugs directly to consumers—"Talk to your doctor about whether X is right for you."[13] They found that a 10 percent increase in the amount spent on this kind of advertising increased by 7 percent the likelihood that people with no existing diagnoses made an appointment for a regular checkup with their doctor. Such checkups allow doctors to catch conditions—such as diabetes, high cholesterol, or hypertension—that often go undetected until there are serious symptoms; early diagnosis helps ward off those worse outcomes. Other studies confirm that direct-to-consumer drug advertising increases the likelihood that people with health problems will see their doctors and obtain treatment.[14]

Of course in all these cases, there will be bad mixed in with these good results. Unless carefully regulated, food companies will no doubt also make some bogus claims about the health benefits of their wares. And they can't do better than the underlying science—the low-fat recommendations of the 1980s and 1990s may be in part responsible for the obesity epidemics of recent decades. Some doctors report giving people the drugs they ask for even if they don't need them so long as it's not harmful. And many doctors are critical of, or at least annoyed by, the impact of drug advertising on patient behavior. But nonetheless the evidence is clear and the result not surprising: markets create incentives for people to figure out how best to reach particular audiences with particular messages. Companies with profits on the line are likely to spend more money on figuring out how to get information across than governments.

Then there are the productive interactions between market interests and government investments in data collection. The breakfast cereal study, for example, analyzed data sets containing the amount spent on advertising breakfast cereals, the sales of each type of cereal, the fiber content of cereals, and the food-eating behavior of women, broken down by age, race, ethnicity, education, employment status, household size and income, geographical region, activity level, smoking and alcohol consumption, height, weight, and more. The data on advertising expenditures were collected by industry groups and paid for by industry magazines, ultimately by subscribers. The data on fiber content were collected and paid for by a consumer group. And the detailed data on food-eating behavior were collected and paid for by the US Department of Agriculture. Similarly, the drug-advertising studies used data collected by private market research companies and detailed health surveys of patients and doctors carried out by a research agency (with a $400 million budget) in the US Department of Health and Human Services.

The implication of lousy data is lousy knowledge. If we don't track, systematically and reliably, what it costs to hire a lawyer to handle an employment dispute or regulatory compliance for a small business or how long it takes to settle disputes with partners or banks or customers and how well they are settled, we can't evaluate how well our legal infrastructure is performing and what makes it perform better. Without robust market incentives to learn more about how legal infrastructure works, however, we are unlikely to find the dollars we need to collect the data and do the research. We are living in the information age, and we know next to nothing about how our legal infrastructure is working or how to make it work better.

9

Markets for Lawyers

WE DIDN'T ALWAYS have Google. It's hard to even remember this now, but in the infancy of the internet the big problem was finding stuff online. It's one thing to have figured out a shared protocol so that computers can be linked and their content shared almost anywhere anytime. But once you have all that information at your fingertips, how do you know where to go to find what? The natural experts, everyone assumed, were librarians. After all, that's what librarians do: organize the world's information—in books, magazines, periodicals, government documents—and help people find it. And all of the early efforts to solve the search problem took their cues from the library. The first search engine, Archie—developed by a graduate student at McGill University in 1990—contacted publicly available computers and created a list of the files they contained. Users could search for the files by searching this index, composed of the names of the files. That's just like looking for books in a library by searching the title index. You can find something if you happen to pose a query that includes a word in the title. More sophisticated search engines after Archie—AltaVista and Excite, for example—ramped this process up once the world wide web and powerful web browsers such as Mosaic and Netscape began to shape the internet in the mid-1990s. These search engines didn't just index titles, they indexed all the words found on web pages. Now you could find a document that included the words you put in your query even if the words weren't in the title. The problem was you got a lot of junk back.

This was the real challenge: finding the good stuff. And again the first solutions looked to the library. Yahoo! hired armies of people in the mid-1990s to do what librarians do: collect a lot of material and catalog it. Users found stuff on Yahoo! by looking through its hierarchical subject-matter lists and searching the virtual card catalog descriptions that catalogers wrote about websites. As Yahoo! cataloger Anne Callery wrote enthusiastically in a 1996 paper, Yahoo's organization of the information available on the web had a strong edge on search engines like AltaVista and Excite because its subject index allowed someone interested in information about surfing the waves to avoid having to wade through a bunch of sites about surfing the web.[1] But to produce all this value for users required huge amounts of librarian effort. In 1996, says Callery, Yahoo! was receiving "thousands of submissions" of websites each day and "Every site added to Yahoo! is examined by a human being."

The librarian solution was doomed by the explosive success of the web. In 1994 when Yahoo! was founded by Jerry Yang and David Filo as Jerry and David's Guide to the World Wide Web, there were only about 3,000 websites, many of which could be quickly ignored by a company dedicated to finding the good stuff.[2] That number, however, soon took off on an exponential growth path. In 1995 there were close to 25,000 websites, 250,000 by 1996 when Callery was proudly extolling the merits of the Yahoo! cataloging system. By the end of 1997 we were over one million. Today the number is over one billion. Moreover, with the increasing power of full-text search, the relevant number soon was no longer the number of websites—found by name—it was number of web pages—found by URL. By 1998, that number had already hit 150 million. The result was near chaos. Techies were complaining in *Wired* magazine as early as 1996 that the "obvious place to turn" for help in organizing the web—library science—was "antiquated and inadequate," and even librarians bemoaned that the impact of professional librarians on the chaos that reigned on the internet is "almost unnoticeable."[3] An article in *Library Journal* in 1998, however, still held out perfecting automated cataloging as the "Holy Grail" of the profession.[4]

The solution to search on the internet didn't come from librarians. It came from two computer science graduate students at Stanford University who were not even thinking about the problem of finding stuff on the web, much less how to catalog it. Sergey Brin and Larry Page were thinking about how to sort the diamonds from the dross, without actually going and looking at web pages like the Yahoo! catalogers were. Brin and Page didn't think of themselves in the least as librarians, but they did take their cue from something else in the librarians' bag of tricks—citation indexes. Citation indexes tell academics, with whom these graduate students did identify, how often and by whom a journal article has been cited. A journal article that has been cited by a lot of other journal articles is probably a better article than one that is never cited. An article that is cited by other highly cited articles even more so. Page and Brin figured out an algorithm for computing a number—PageRank—that ranked web pages by quality. They did this by counting the number of times the page was "cited"—that is, linked to—by other web pages and taking into account the quality of the citation—that is, how many web pages linked to the page that was linking to the original page. As they put it in their (heavily cited) 1998 paper with colleagues Rajeev Motwani and Terry Winograd, "If a web page has a link off the Yahoo home page, it may be just one link but it is a very important one. This page should be ranked higher than many pages with more links but from obscure places."[5] Their algorithm gave a way to rank the Yahoo link more highly, based on just the fact, which the computer could discover without the need for human judgment, of how many web pages linked to the Yahoo home page.

It was only after Page and Brin had been playing around with their ranking algorithm for a while that they realized they had invented a better search tool for the web. It cut the librarians out entirely. Computers could search the text of complete documents in the blink of an eye for any combination of words. And computers could, implementing the PageRank algorithm, give the user a list of the results of that search—otherwise an ungodly useless mess—neatly ordered by a pretty good indicator of how likely the page was to give users what they were looking for. Librarians couldn't touch that. Even if the Yahoo! cataloger became an expert in some minute specialty—reviewing submitted websites in the model airplanes category, for example—by the time Page and Brin were turning their academic paper into Google Inc. in the last year of the last millennium, they were handling ten thousand queries a day on a database that had indexed all the word combinations in twenty-four million web pages.

What does the history of search on the web have to do with law? The answer is that where we find ourselves today, with galloping cost and complexity and fading usefulness of legal solutions, is rather like where we found ourselves in terms of internet search in the early 1990s: a widening chasm between traditional solutions and the dramatic transformations wrought by the Web. The question is, who is going to get us across that chasm? The answer isn't: lawyers. At least, not lawyers working on their own.

Remember the basic insight of modern information economics: the economic problem of society is mainly one of rapid adaptation to change and to the detailed information that is often embedded deep within the contours of economic activity. Markets, when they are reasonably competitive, help us respond in better ways to change and increasing complexity because they create incentives to discover and apply information, they extend those incentives to the myriad who are specialized in each of the small puzzle pieces that build the picture of a new solution, and they transmit information—about what's needed, about what's possible—throughout the system, available to just about anyone who wants to look. Getting across the wide gap between what we need from law and what the legal infrastructure built up over the twentieth century is providing is a task that will require all that markets can offer, that is, all that a wide set of market participants, with diverse knowledge and expertise, can offer.

But isn't it the case that markets already are playing the major role in producing legal knowledge and expertise? The legal services that generate the strategies, norms, practices, documents, and more that make up the bulk of our legal infrastructure are indeed sold, usually by the hour, in markets. The problem is that these markets are almost completely populated by lawyers, all trained in the same way, all required to operate in the same small set of business models, all relying on the same restricted sources of capital. The reason for this suffocating environment is that lawyers over the past century made sure that these markets operated under so many lawyer-controlled restrictions that today they fail to produce what we really need from markets as a response to complexity: transformative innovations, ideas that can fundamentally change how we solve the problems the idea of law was invented to solve. Today's markets for legal goods and services are some of the most closed and constrained in the entire economy. As a result they fail to do what markets can do: harness the capacity for markets to produce transformative solutions to complex and changing circumstances.

So here's the lesson from the history of search for law. Imagine that in 1996 professional librarians had controlled library science the way the legal profession today controls law: deciding who can practice, how practitioners must be educated, what business and financing models they have to use to sell their services. In that strange universe, Page and Brin would have had to be licensed librarians with master's degrees in library science, following the rules of the librarians' professional bodies, before they could have offered to the world a transformative solution to the librarians' problem of how to organize and find information.

Believing that lawyers alone will innovate the transformative solutions we need to the problems of legal infrastructure is like believing that librarians alone would have eventually invented Google.

The Elements of Innovation

Markets, when they work well and are properly regulated, are problem-solving engines. In the highly complex world in which we now live, they are an essential tool for innovation. To understand why the markets for lawyers that we now have are not delivering on the promise of markets, let's look a little deeper into what we know about what stimulates innovation and new thinking.

Diversity

Curled deep inside the phenomenon of innovation is an information paradox. On the one hand, solving hard problems requires deep knowledge and expertise. Deep knowledge and expertise are born of concentrated and focused attention on a small set of things. As I noted earlier, this was one of Adam Smith's insights about the benefits of the division of labor. People, he said, "are much more likely to discover easier and readier methods of attaining any object, when the whole attention of their minds is directed towards that single object, than when it is dissipated among a great variety of things."

But specialization can also hobble innovation. The more a person focuses on solving the same type of problem, the more he or she comes to rely on the same type of solution. This is one way of thinking about archaeologist Joseph Tainter's observations about ancient complex societies: they tried to solve the same problems over and over again with the same—exhausted—solution. Innovation requires deep knowledge, but it also requires fresh eyes, to see a problem in a new light and to fashion a new way of resolving it. New solutions bubble up when there are diverse perspectives brought to bear, different experiences developed in a wide variety of contexts.

Open innovation, a concept championed for the new economy by Henry Chesbrough of the University of California at Berkeley, attempts to resolve the specialization paradox by drawing on a diverse mix of individuals and sources to drive new product and service development.[6] Organizations committed to open innovation have their own internal R & D departments, but they also seek to tap into the innovative thinking of outsiders. This was the system used by Goldcorp, the Canadian mining company that put all of its data up on the web and learned that collectively a global population of enthusiasts that included people with no gold-finding expertise was able to find more gold than the company's highly specialized geologists could alone. Our most successful companies today make themselves as porous as possible to the ideas that can flow in from just about anywhere. Indeed, icons of the modern economy such as Facebook and Twitter are almost entirely built on the idea that the characteristics of their products are shaped in an emergent fashion by the complex interactions of the diverse users and creators of their systems, and so they hold themselves as open as possible. Major suppliers of operating systems and programming tools like Apple, Linux, Google, and now even the formerly closed Microsoft make aspects of their software open source and freely available so that they can incorporate the input of millions of programmers and users—and then figure out how to make money from what they build on that open-source platform.

I talked in Chapter 2 about University of Michigan complex systems theorist and author of *The Difference* Scott E. Page. In work with Lu Hong of Loyola University in Chicago, Page has given us elegant mathematical proofs of the idea many know from James Surowiecki's book *The Wisdom of Crowds*: when people bring to complex problems diverse ways of perceiving and organizing information and different rules of thumb for slicing through a tangle of cross-cutting considerations, they come up with better solutions than the smartest one of them working alone.[7] Page, in other work, emphasizes the general nature of the problem Tainter identified in ancient civilizations: there are diminishing returns to type in a great many settings.[8] If the setting is stable and good solutions already known, having everyone in the room on the same page is a valuable strategy. But if you are dealing with the challenges of complexity—with its unpredictable and emergent shifts in the environment—you will do better if you have a mix of people and worldviews pitching in.

In this sense people are like potatoes. When the Irish planted only one type of potato in the 1800s and made the potato a staple of their diet, they enjoyed the benefits of standardization. But those benefits were wiped out when a new potato-destroying bug appeared on the scene. The bug exploited a vulnerability in the Irish potato, and soon vast fields of nutrition were just vast fields of foul-smelling rot. With no alternative bug-resistant potato species to turn to, with no alternative staple food to turn to, the Irish suffered terribly: nearly a million died. The lack of diversity killed them.

Feedback

Lots of solutions can look pretty good on paper. It's when you actually test them out that you discover how well they really solve your problem. Feedback from the people who need a solution and from those who have to implement a solution is essential for innovation.

This is one of the basic features of how markets work: they collect and transmit information from consumers. Suppliers who do a better job of producing a better product at a better price capture a larger market share and higher profits. Those who ignore this information struggle to retain consumers and, if not propped up by subsidies or monopoly protection, in time go out of business. Finding better ways to tap into consumer feedback has become essential for today's businesses: hence the explosion of online surveys that pop up whenever customers visit a company's website, much more intensive relationships between suppliers and customers in the supply chain, big-data analysis of buying behavior, and the creation of platforms that involve customers in generating and evaluating new product ideas, designs, and names. Wal-Mart's rise to the top of the Fortune 100 was powered in no small part by its ability to use scanning equipment to capture data at the most minute level about who wants to buy what, when, and where and sharing that data with its suppliers. Clothing innovators in the early 2000s such as Zara, Threadless, and ModCloth made customer feedback the central feature of their business models: proposing a large variety of designs to their customers, collecting feedback, and then putting the winners quickly into production. Many technology companies are dependent on their product support services to function as their ears to the ground, continually learning about problems with existing products and opportunities for new products or features. Open-source software projects thrive precisely on the ability of users to change the code so the software better meets their needs—easier, cheaper, better integrated into other systems, better able to solve their problems. Google's essential innovation in search was an algorithm that continuously responded to the feedback a web page receives from users, measured by how many links users make to that page. Google displays its proposed responses to users' search questions based on how many votes in the form of links the underlying web pages get from users, in addition to information it gathers about how often searchers click on particular search results. That makes for constant quality adjustment in response to user feedback.

The need for feedback to feed innovation is also behind a standard tool in the innovator's toolkit: the prototype. Leading design thinkers at IDEO in Palo Alto, California, emphasize the importance of rapid prototyping, not to test a final product before loosing it on the world, but to feed the innovative process. There's nothing like taking an idea out for a test drive before you plunk down lots of cash. But as some of the innovators at IDEO wrote in a

2007 article, rapid prototyping as a practice can also make people and organizations more innovative.[9] It can help to build a culture of innovation. The experience of mocking up an idea and testing it out—whether it's for a product, process, or practice—can tell you if you're misreading the road or stuck in a rut; and it can make people collectively more inclined to be on constant lookout for how they can adjust and make things better. That was the mindset Toyota created at its factories when it was remaking the manufacturing world. Everyone from the line operator to senior management was empowered to engage in continuous improvement to whittle away at the frictions and problems that raised costs and lowered quality.

Building a "what would happen if" and "how might we" orientation in organizations spurs innovation. Scott Cook, the founder of Intuit—the company that brings you QuickBooks and TurboTax—introduced the company beginning in 2009 to what Cook calls leadership by experiment.[10] The idea was to empower people throughout the organization to conduct experiments to test out ideas about how to do things better. Intuit can run five hundred experiments with TurboTax per season, getting quick real-time, real-consumer feedback on how well new features in the hugely popular tax software will serve customer needs.[11]

Intuit built its internal experimentation program on the basis of ideas developed by Eric Ries in *The Lean Startup*—who defined a "start-up" as any organization, large or small, public or private, that is trying to find ways to create new value for people under conditions of extreme uncertainty. Ries's ideas in turn find their roots in the Toyota way of continuous improvement, the strategy that Womack, Roos, and Jones dubbed lean manufacturing in *The Machine That Changed the World*. Ries emphasizes that to innovate, particularly in the "conditions of extreme uncertainty" that many organizations find themselves in the modern economy, requires recognizing that an organization's "most vital function is learning." More precisely: validated learning. Validated learning is learning based on rigorous methods of testing ideas with real potential users about what creates value and solves problems. You can learn from analyzing data, talking to experts, and surveying potential customers; you can learn better and feed innovation if you take the abstract ideas generated in those ways, treat them as hypotheses, and then exploit the power of tools like the web to test them with real customers. Intuit reports, for example, that one of their ideas was rejected by every single participant in an artificial lab experiment but adopted by 60 percent of actual consumers when the experiment was taken to the market itself. Kickstarter and Indiegogo, crowd-funding websites, made a business out of building a platform for this kind of validated learning about what works and what doesn't. Ideas for new products are put to the test of whether they can attract enough potential investors or buyers willing to commit—I'll invest/buy if enough others invest/buy—to a product that hasn't even been built yet. As Ries puts it, "This is true startup productivity: systematically figuring out the right things to build."

Risk-Taking

Harvard Business School professor Clayton Christensen puts it this way in his 1997 classic, *The Innovator's Dilemma*: failure is intrinsic to disruptive innovation, the kind of innovation that fundamentally transforms an organization or market. Disruptive innovations reach new markets, new customers, new users—and often are of little value at first to existing markets, customers, or users. The personal desktop computer was a dumb product from the point of view of the established computer industry in the 1970s—when computers were massive expensive business machines. What did an ordinary household want with a business machine? Steve Jobs and Steve Wozniak didn't really know either, but they took a flyer and built the Apple I. It flopped. So did several other early models coming out of Apple. But eventually the world turned. As Christensen sees it, the dominant companies in the microcomputer business in the late 1970s—Data General, Prime, Wang, Hewlett-Packard, Nixdorf—couldn't have built the personal computer because established companies couldn't have satisfied their (big business) customers and (big time) shareholders with the failure-filled process of developing a product no one was asking for that did less, less well, than their existing products. Companies that pride themselves on solid analysis of markets can't do disruptive innovation because "markets that do not exist can't be analyzed." They can only be discovered. Discovery involves belief, hunches, gut feelings, and leaps of faith. It involves trial and error, dead ends, and failed attempts. It means venturing into terrain that is unmapped.

Failure means risk. Serious risk. So serious innovation requires organizations that can handle serious risk. What kinds of organizations are these? These are organizations with access to risk capital—money that doesn't mind losing on ninety-nine bets out of one hundred when there's a possibility of hitting it big on one of them. Or money that is housed in a portfolio that balances risky investments on a stable base of solid returns or one that manages to hedge its bets across a spectrum of hopefully uncorrelated options. Innovators shouldn't have access to deep pockets that will just keep paying the bills when failure happens—innovators have to be intently focused on the need to figure out more better faster about what works and what doesn't as they rip through sequences of failed attempts. But they do need people with money willing to cough up the funds needed to work through failure.

Organizations that can handle risk are also those with little to lose. What was at stake for Google's Sergey Brin and Larry Page when they were roaming the halls of the computer science department at Stanford and looking for an algorithm that would rank web pages? Not much. Not even when they moved from Susan Wojcicki's garage in Menlo Park to an office above a bookstore on University Avenue in Palo Alto in 1999 and tried to turn an algorithm into a business model. And organizations that can handle risk are those that are under little pressure to show the kind of immediate and large-scale growth and returns that come from what Christensen calls sustaining innovation—the continual improvement of existing products and processes that Toyota perfected—and that large organizations that dominate existing markets expect. They need a different measuring stick—one that can squeeze out every drop of good news from the slightly-less-bad-than-the-last iteration on the possibly long road to something really great. These are organizations willing to live by the Facebook credo plastered on the walls of an office space that originally looked like an airplane hangar: move fast and break things.

Where Are the Garage Guys in Law?

So what's the problem with law? Why haven't the markets for legal services driven transformative innovations to better meet the ways in which the economic demand for law has been reshaped by the complex global economy? The short answer is that these markets aren't the kind that deliver the good stuff markets can deliver. They aren't sufficiently competitive and they aren't properly regulated. Because lawyers have designed them that way.

As we saw in Chapter 5, today's lawyers have managed to gain tight control over who can supply legal goods and services and how. Control is at its greatest in the United States, where effectively no one who has not completed a three-year graduate degree that meets requirements established by the American Bar Association and passed an exam designed and graded by lawyers in state bar associations can provide any kind of legal service. With tiny exceptions, only in-state licensed lawyers may help someone fill out legal documents or forms, advise people about legal rules or the potential legal consequences of their actions, or help people resolve their legal disputes. Only licensed lawyers can work inside governments or corporations to help these entities comply with legal rules or manage their legal relationships with others. Most lawyers work either by themselves in solo practice or in law firms that must be owned, managed, and financed by licensed lawyers. Lawyers cannot enter into business partnerships or joint business ventures with anyone who is not also a licensed lawyer. And, most strikingly, because lawyers have secured a powerful form of self-regulation, all the rules governing who can be a lawyer, what education lawyers require, and how they must practice are chosen by lawyers. This was the triumph of the ABA in the early twentieth century—and it served that century well.

The price of that triumph today, however, is a set of legal markets that fail to deliver on the key ingredients needed for innovation: diversity, feedback, and risk-taking.

The control over the practice of law exercised by the organized legal professions has produced a tremendous lack of diversity in the pool of people who are in the best position to innovate new legal solutions for a changing global economy—the people who live their lives immersed in the problems of law. Swimming in that pool of potential problem-solvers, it's lawyers, lawyers everywhere. The people serving clients are lawyers. The law professors are lawyers. The judges are lawyers. The regulators of lawyers are lawyers. The drafters of most legislation are lawyers. All these participants in the system are trained in the same way and spend most of their professional lives talking almost exclusively to other lawyers. They have all been trained to think like lawyers, to organize information like lawyers, to solve problems like lawyers, to talk and write like lawyers. Strike 1 for the organized legal profession.

I know this homogenizing process very well: it's my job. As a law professor I, like all my colleagues, have the task of taking the diverse group of people who show up in my first-year law school class, giving them the same set of reading materials that just about every other person in a first-year contracts class across the country has been given, and getting them all to give the same answer on a final exam that looks a lot like the exams every other professor is giving in every other law school class. There are even books on "how to write a law school exam," as if all law school exams were all the same. Which mostly they are.

There's an important reason for some of this uniformity. Lawyers who share a common way of taking messy human situations and saying, "Aha, the core issue we need to resolve is . . . X" can quickly coordinate with each other and reach judgments about how the law will respond. I can consult my lawyers for help understanding a contract and feel a significant degree of confidence that my contracting partner will be told similar things by his lawyers about what the two of us have agreed to. If I'm sued by someone, my lawyers can predict pretty well what the lawyers on the other side are going to try to argue at trial. And both sides can predict pretty well what the judge will be thinking as she rules on aspects of our case. Achieving this level of uniformity in legal thinking across a broader stage was a critical advance secured by the ABA in the early twentieth century. It facilitated legal planning and dispute resolution on a national scale in the Chandlerian box economy that emerged from the nineteenth century.

But a system based on this level of uniformity in thinking is an almost impossible environment for transformative change. For lawyers trained in this way, a contract just *is*, by definition, a long complex document with multiple clauses and definitions and boilerplate, all written in legalese. The proper resolution of a dispute *requires* extensive discovery of facts and intricate procedure. The proper ruling on a case *must* respond with elaborate reasoning to a creative argument that suggests a difference between this case and the ones that came before it.

Remember the librarians of the early 1990s: finding information on the internet *was*, by definition, a problem of indexing and cataloging. The reason librarians would never have invented Google is not that librarians aren't some of the smartest people around. It's that they would never have stopped exploring library solutions. They might have worked up creative ways to catalog faster or even automatically. But they would never have made the leap to mathematical algorithms to rank web pages based on the number of links to a linking page. Lawyers can be expected to come up with ideas for how to streamline procedures or write somewhat easier-to-read contracts. But they can't be expected to come up, all on their own, with entirely novel ways to coordinate economic arrangements or resolve conflicts.

Of course, even a homogeneous group can potentially learn from and respond to those who are not in the club. But here is where the second strike is called against the organized legal profession as an innovative enterprise. Legal practitioners are significantly walled off from feedback from those who use and implement the legal infrastructure they produce.

Think about the rationale for why lawyers are taught to all think, write, and talk alike. The reason is that lawyers who share a common language and framing can more easily coordinate in the management of relationships, organizations, and disputes. Lawyer A can predict pretty well what Lawyer B will think, say, write, and do. Fundamentally, lawyers are operating in a lawyer-populated ecosystem. Everything lawyers do is something to which others lawyers respond. The words they put in a statute or a contract, a policy document or a disclaimer, a subpoena or a trial brief take on a life of their own once they enter the legal ecosystem. A leading GC like Kent Walker at Google can try sending out short simple contracts, but, as we saw, the people he sends them to respond with longer, more complex ones. Litigators in my experience almost uniformly believe that while they personally would be quite happy to take a common-sense approach to the resolution of a case and avoid excessive discovery, process, and argument, the "other side" almost never is. And so what should be a straightforward case rapidly morphs into a god-awful mess. Regulators may aspire to fewer regulations, but they've learned the hard way, they will tell you, that if they don't close every possible loophole with a thousand and one pages, their efforts will be undone by some wily corporate lawyer who will find a way for a regulated entity to comply with the letter but not the spirit of the law. Or some judge in some court somewhere will agree with someone who sues over the regulations and decide that the regulators failed to think carefully enough about the implications of their plan and that they need to go back and start again.

What this means is that in a day-to-day sense, most of the feedback lawyers get is from other lawyers. Not from those who depend on legal infrastructure to get stuff done.

There are other reasons that the legal profession is insulated from feedback from those who use legal infrastructure. Escalating complexity is one of them. As legal documents and procedures become more abstruse and complicated, the harder it is for those without legal training, indeed without specialized legal training, to evaluate legal results. Or even to understand the strategies and methods their lawyers are pursuing. One of the consequences of the ABA-led control over legal education as an elite graduate endeavor in the United States has been that there is little by way of legal education for Americans who don't become lawyers. Even sophisticated CEOs who feel plenty competent to evaluate what their engineers, accountants, financial analysts, and marketing gurus are advising them to do often feel out of their depth when lawyers start talking. Many of them respond by not having the lawyers in the room in the first place. They work out the deal, the product strategy, the financing plan, and only then do they throw it over the transom for the lawyers to work out the details. (This disconnect between legal and business strategy is one way of understanding how the Vodafone–Verizon mess we heard about in Chapter 7 came about.) All of this makes for little feedback from user to lawyer.

True complexity in the law—in the complex systems sense of hard-to-predict results from the interactions of many individual agents on a dancing landscape—also insulates lawyers from feedback because even the experts can't tell if a bad result is a result of bad lawyering. Could the deal have been closed as well with fewer dollars spent on legal analysis? Would the outcome in court have been more favorable if a different litigation strategy had been followed? Could we have anticipated better the regulatory fallout from that corporate policy, identified sooner the risks of noncompliance or liability? Law is fundamentally supposed to be a reliable framework for organizing relationships—a predictable framework—and yet in our complex modern systems an oft-heard phrase off a lawyer's lips is "Well, law is always a crapshoot."

And of course the high cost of law means that there is no opportunity for those who cannot afford lawyers in the first place to register any feedback at all. Lawyers have almost no idea what ordinary people or small businesses need from law because most of those people and small businesses muddle through the legal system on their own. They're invisible to most practicing lawyers.

Many people, including many lawyers, think that lawyers are unlikely to come up with innovative new ways of doing law for another reason as well. Lawyers, they think, are inherently risk averse. They're just not built to handle the failure that is intrinsic, as Clay Christensen emphasizes, to disruptive innovation.

I'm not a fan of inherently-anything explanations. Certainly the students I meet every year in my law school classes seem like every other recent college graduate I meet. Some have risked moving alone across the country, fighting in Afghanistan, traveling through Indonesia, or teaching English in isolated Central American villages. Others have been in the finance industry before heading to law school or spent some time in tech start-ups or as programmers or in intelligence agencies. More than a few are risking a change in career or family disruption; most are risking that a hefty three-year investment in law school will pay off. So I don't think law students are inherently more risk averse than other high-performing college graduates.

What is true is that one of the homogenizing things we do to this group of pretty diverse people when they get to law school is expose them to a system that doesn't do risk well. We teach them, often not intentionally, to believe that their job is to identify any and all possible risks, to treat all risks as equivalent, and to advise their clients to avoid risk at all costs. We saw this in Chapter 7—the inability to think sensibly about and manage risk is a major complaint about lawyers. But it's not like we need everyone who ends up practicing law to be a risk-taker to generate innovative solutions to the cost, complexity, and shrinking value of legal work. Why can't even a small number of risk-happy lawyers break through?

The reason is a lack of access to what innovators in every other sector of the economy depend on—risk capital. Among the rules that the ABA put in place as it was seeking to rationalize and control the legal profession in the early twentieth century were rules that said no one other than a lawyer can invest in a legal business. Under these rules only businesses that are 100 percent owned and financed by lawyers can deliver legal products and services. These rules mean that legal innovators have no access to venture capital. They can't take money from friends and family and promise a share in the business when it gets big. Angel investors can't sprinkle any stardust on their endeavor. They can't dream of an IPO. They can't share risk with the tech wizard or business genius who wants to partner up with them. They can't access the billions of dollars in investment money floating through global capital markets.

No other industry or sector in the economy could innovate in those circumstances either. The lack of access to risk capital is strike 3 for the organized legal profession in the innovation game.

Many lawyers I talk to don't quite get the problem here. Some hear the words "risk capital" and think that that kind of money is only needed to buy capital equipment—machinery. A lack of capital is not a problem, they argue, because law is not a capital-intensive industry. Others don't see any reason why an innovative law firm can't just choose to plow partner profits back into innovative endeavors or borrow from the bank—the sources of funds that law firms everywhere rely on.

To my mind, these responses just emphasize how closed off the legal profession is from the innovative mindset. Lawyers define law as the thing that today's lawyers do in law firms and legal departments. That practice of law is indeed not in need of significant amounts of capital equipment. But that was true of the job of librarian in the pre-internet days as well. The reason Brin and Page needed capital—which they initially begged, borrowed, and stole from Stanford in the form of time on the University's mainframe computers—was to cover the cost of massive amounts of computing power to crawl the web and count links. I'd bet my second-to-last dollar that disruptive innovations in law will also—like almost every other innovation in the economy these days—involve substantial amounts of computing power and technology. The fact that existing legal practice does not is wholly beside the point. We're not looking for risk capital to support sustaining innovation on the current model. We're looking for risk capital to support game-changing innovation to develop the new models no one has even thought of yet.

Even if I'm wrong and those as-yet-undreamed-of innovations don't happen to require substantial capital assets, I'd bet my very last dollar they do require the most important ingredient for disruptive innovation that risk capital finances: failure. Partner profits are an unlikely source for financing the kind of failure-ridden process that real innovation requires. Again, this isn't because lawyers are unusually risk averse. It's because anyone is, or should be, risk averse when investments are undiversified. Law firm partners are wholly dependent on the money coming into the firm to pay their mortgages and kids' tuition bills, to cover the costs of their lifestyle. Throwing hundreds of thousands of dollars from your take-home pay at low-probability prospects doesn't make sense. That leaves bank loans. But banks don't do failure. They want business plans and solid prospects of getting paid back. As Clay Christensen emphasizes, however, the processes that lead to disruptive innovation aren't amenable to analysis and business plans. They are built on hunches and instincts, trial and error. Failure. To fund failure you need investors holding cards in a lot of different card games, only a few of which have to pay off. Those are the investors that the rules of the legal profession have put off limits for legal innovators.

So why doesn't the profession change the rules? Why does the profession persist in requiring everyone in law to have the same training, with no access to risk capital, and under strict rules about how a legal business can be conducted and with whom as a partner? This question brings us to the error that gets the organized legal profession thrown out of the innovation game: lack of competition. Lawyers acting through legal professions don't change the rules because they're not under any competitive pressure to do so.

Lawyers don't like it when I say that theirs is not a competitive business. Many lawyers feel under intense competitive pressure. The small-firm practitioner is scrambling for every client he or she can find. The big corporate law firms are forced to participate in beauty contests in a bid for big cases and transactions, and they are watching the document review and discovery work they used to staff with expensive junior associates walk out the door to legal process outsourcing firms in India and elsewhere. But that's not the type of competition I'm talking about. Even if individual lawyers may get an earful from unhappy clients, as they do, and even if large corporate clients routinely fire their law firms and take their business in-house or to legal process outsourcers whenever they can, as they do, there are few market pressures on the profession itself. If the profession is producing law that is too complex, too costly, and not of high value, if the rules the profession imposes on practice prevent innovators from bringing better ideas to market, the users of law cannot vote with their feet and move to another way of doing law. There aren't any in the current environment. The profession never gets the wakeup call: hey, we need something different from what you're giving us and we're taking our business over to the folks who'll give it to us.

This is the real damage done by the unregulated monopoly exercised by the modern legal profession. Some economist critics, like Clifford Winston, Robert Crandall, and Vikram Maheshri, authors of *The First Thing We Do, Let's Deregulate All the Lawyers*, see the problem of the legal monopoly in the United States as a problem of restricted supply.[12] That's Economics 101: monopolists limit supply and drive up prices. I'm not persuaded, however, that supply restriction is the monopoly problem we face in law. First, there is no real shortage of JDs being produced in the United States. We know this because, as we've seen, many lawyers struggle to make a decent living for someone with a professional degree: about a third are taking home what's left over from an average of $90,000 after they pay rent, insurance, and office expenses—probably on the order of about $50,000 a year on average. The lower end of the market, where this third of the profession practices, is pretty darn competitive. Second, the lawyers who are making a lot of money are making it in highly specialized fields that require enormous levels of human capital acquired from both elite education and years in the trenches. The lack of competition there is not a result of limited seats in law schools; it's a consequence of the limited supply of people with the cognitive and other skills needed to navigate enormously complex structures. This point was driven home to me when I was working as an expert consultant in antitrust litigation matters: to really understand the law in these cases required me to make serious use of my economics PhD.

The real monopoly problem is not that individual lawyers and law firms don't have competitors. It is that the system lacks competitors. As a consequence the system as a whole gets little market feedback. Even if individual lawyers lose clients, the legal profession doesn't lose customers. Anyone who comes up with a better way to train lawyers can't siphon students off from ABA-approved schools without being approved by the ABA. A professional organization that devises a set of professional qualification and practice rules that does a better job at achieving quality at lower prices than the existing legal professions can't bid customers away. So those delivering the current system don't live under the pressure to innovate to produce a better product.

The legal profession is not unlike a tribe living on a tropical island thousands of miles from other people. They might be a violent tribe, fighting each other on a daily basis for access to the fruits of their profession. But so long as they are collectively able to reproduce, whatever dysfunctions they might exhibit—strange beliefs or rules written into their biological or cultural DNA that keep them from getting healthier, smarter, and better able to harvest their crops—will persist so long as they are the only types around. This is particularly the case if upstarts among them with strange ideas are voted off the island. As a group, they won't face any pressure to adapt their ways unless and until the boats pull up and unload a horde of folks with different beliefs and rules to compete for access to the food supply.

So why aren't there any boats pulling up, challenging the modern legal profession's rulebook with different rules for doing law—rules that might diversify the education and experiences of legal practitioners, or allow lawyers to form partnerships with other types of experts, or give legal businesses access to the kind of risk capital necessary to experiment with new ways of doing law?

The first answer to this question is found in the ways the legal profession has perfected its control within the structures of the modern nation-state. Remember when the ABA was trying to figure out in the early days of the twentieth century how to defend its basic model—the law partnership—against competition from the banks, cooperatives, real estate agents, and others who had a different model for providing people with legal goods and services? The initial response was to follow the lead of the other professions—the doctors, the dentists—and seek protection from state legislatures. But that meant expensive and uncertain battles in fifty states. And so lawyers turned to the courts and took advantage of the courts' status in the American constitutional order as a separate and independent branch of government. Lawyers sitting as judges accepted the argument that they possessed the inherent authority to determine the rules governing the practice of law, displacing the authority of the legislatures. That move closed the loop, and ensured that the rules chosen by lawyers could not be challenged by outsiders. Lawyers pulled up the bridge over the moat and protected the profession's monopoly system from intruders.

The second answer to the question of why the system designed by lawyers has not come under challenge is found, as in a Sherlock Holmes's story, by listening for the dog that doesn't bark. So effective has the bar been at defining law as something that can be done only by members of the closed legal profession that few outside of the profession have much of an idea about what is going on, or what needs to change. People who are not lawyers treat law either as something to complain about—hence the tort reform and antilitigation movements that seek to limit access to law and lawyers—or as a mystery to be left to the ministrations of the initiated. Lawyers have managed to make law so mysterious—and so boring—that people are quite happy to stay off the topic. But as I mentioned in the introduction and one GC said to me during my research: law is too important to be left to lawyers. It's not that lawyers are simply too craven to give up power. It is that the lack of diversity among lawyers has led to a state in which lawyers are fairly oblivious to what is *not* working in the profession they love. Shaking up legal infrastructure will require agitation from those who, with some critical distance from outside the profession, can see what is going so awry.

Opening—and Regulating—Legal Markets

In the next chapter we'll look at a hard problem: how to develop new models for regulation that rely on competitive markets in formal legal rules and systems, populated by approved private regulators. That's a hard problem because it's a fundamentally new idea. We have little experience with designing such systems, and few models to look at. We know that there will be many issues to sort out, places where this new model could work, and places where it could not—and should not—be implemented. We don't know how hard it would be to get private entities to take up the challenge of building better regulatory regimes.

By comparison, the challenge of making our existing markets for legal work more competitive and innovative is a cakewalk. There are straightforward and obvious changes we can make, and we can make them pretty easily. There are models of how this works, and works well—many of the changes I'm going to suggest we need to make have already been made in a few places, notably the UK and Australia. Eventually we'll need to do some serious hard work to get to the next level in legal innovation, but right now there are lots of low-hanging fruit ready to be picked. The obstacles to change here are not problems of knowledge, they are problems of politics: getting lawyers on board with the change or deciding that lawyers don't get to decide how much legal innovation we'll get.

Here are fairly straightforward steps we can take to open and properly regulate our legal markets to promote the innovation we need.[13]

Give Lawyers Access to Ordinary Economic Tools

Modern economies have benefited from thousands of years of innovation in the tools of doing business. Symbolic systems for recording the quantities of things—specific numbers of goats or bushels of wheat represented by clay tokens stored inside and impressed upon hollow clay balls or envelopes, for example—emerged in what is now the Middle East ten thousand years ago, proving a boon to traders and economic bureaucrats alike. Written language emerged, also in the heart of the now-Muslim world, about four thousand years ago and was a major hit with commercial types—most of our records of early writing are clay tablets and papyrus documents spelling out business contracts and economic arrangements. Our modern numbering system, first invented by Hindus and Arabs in the eighth century BC and brought to Europe in the thirteenth century AD by Leonardo Fibonacci, played a major role in the Commercial Revolution. A numbering system that made calculations easy—which the Roman numerals did not—and verifiable—which finger-calculation and abacuses did not—boosted the development of long-distance trade and more elaborate commercial relationships by providing merchants with a better way of tracking what was bought and sold and owed. (Stanford mathematician Keith Devlin tells this story in a wonderful little book called *The Man of Numbers: Fibonacci's Arithmetic Revolution*.)

Among the tools of doing business that have spawned the growth of modern economies are the tools of economic organization. As we saw in Chapter 4, Duke political economist Timur Kuran attributes the fact that, despite being the inventors of civilization and far ahead of the Western world through to the start of the second millennium, the Muslim world slipped further and further behind in economic development because of a long delay in developing and implementing essential legal tools that flourished in the West. Chief among these were the corporate form and flexible systems of contracting.

Ironically, although these tools are elements of legal infrastructure, bar association rules that tell lawyers how they have to practice prevent them from making use of these standard tools. Most legal systems around the world insist that lawyers provide their services within business models that play only a limited role elsewhere in the economy: sole proprietorships and partnerships. Lawyers are required to provide their services only directly to clients or to other lawyers. They cannot be employed by anyone other than a client (serving as an in-house or government lawyer) or other lawyers (working in a law firm). In some parts of the world employment by anyone is prohibited—lawyers who join the bar cannot work for a corporation, and they can only serve as proprietors or partners, not associates, of a law firm. What this has produced is a profession in which substantial numbers of legal practitioners, well over half in the United States today, operate as owners rather than employees. That's pretty unusual. Across the US labor force as a whole, for example, at most 15 percent of workers are owners rather than employees.

There's a reason that most people work as employees: employment shifts much of the risk of the economy from the employee to the employer. Owners bear the ordinary risk of boom and bust, new products that soar and those that tank, business decisions and strategic choices that pan out and those that do not. Their take-home in profits from the business rises and falls with every hiccup and stumble. Employees trade the joys and woes of that variability for the stability of a regular paycheck. Employees are exposed to the risk of the business suffering major contractions or bankruptcy—producing layoffs—and to the risk of getting fired (for good reasons and bad). Those are real risks, but they don't produce the constant exposure to variability in take-home pay that ownership does. Most workers in the modern economy are employees because the companies and organizations that employ them are better equipped to handle risk than individuals are. Corporations, profit and nonprofit, can grow and benefit from economies of scale—reducing business risks by investing in new production processes and products and by reaping the benefits of job specialization within the organization. They can diversify across production processes and tasks, product lines, geography, time horizons. The owners of corporations can diversify their financial risk—investing in a wide variety of businesses exposed to different types of risks. They can draw upon the wealth of savers and those whose basic needs are amply met and who thus have money to play with.

Lawyers who are required to be owners lose out on the benefits of shifting risk to larger, more diversified, and better risk-bearing organizations. Moreover, most of our employed lawyers are also not benefiting from the potential to shift risk to those better able to bear risk. That's because most of our employed lawyers are employed by owners who are . . . lawyers. And hence hardly better situated to bear risk.

The problem goes beyond the straightforward prohibition on lawyers being employed by entities other than clients or lawyer-owned law firms. Not only are these kinds of employment arrangement prohibited. So too are the contractual arrangements that can often mimic key elements of the corporation. An individual lawyer could potentially enjoy the benefits of relatively stable income without becoming an employee by agreeing under contract to provide services for a fixed fee to an entity that collects the revenues generated from the lawyer's services. This is how contractual relationships between many hospitals or health maintenance organizations and doctor-owned medical groups are structured, for example. Or, if some risk-bearing by the lawyer would be beneficial—creating incentives for improving quality, decreasing costs, or innovating new services and procedures—then the lawyer could contract for a fixed fee plus some share of profits. Contracts like this allow a wide range of risk-sharing arrangements between the experts who provide services and others who supply financing, business support, complementary services, and so on. Other risk-shifting contracts allow people with business ideas to access venture capital to support the long haul to the development of an innovative new way of doing business. Investors are paid off by taking a percentage of the profits and, in some cases, sharing in the money raised when a new company is taken public in an IPO. That's the dream of every Silicon Valley entrepreneur and Sand Hill Road venture capital firm.

But lawyers are prohibited from using any of these risk-shifting and incentive-sharing contractual tools.

Other rules imposed on legal businesses limit the risk-sharing that supports investment in other ways. Unlike other businesses, for example, law firms cannot operate in a network arrangement under a common brand managed by a central entity and using shared protocols for delivering services to clients. This is how the Big Four accounting firms, which are actually international networks of independent firms, are structured. Law firms, unlike most other companies including accounting firms, cannot write contracts with their partners and employees to limit their ability to leave the firm and take clients and other employees with them. Both of these restrictions undermine the incentive of the firm to invest in developing new products and processes and for training employees because they limit the ability to develop a brand with a reputation that means something across a broad customer base.

Collectively, these prohibitions—the restrictions on the corporate practice of law, fee-splitting, advertising, firm names, and partnership agreements—dictate a narrow, outdated business model for law. They isolate law from the ordinary business tools used to create incentives to reduce costs, improve quality, and figure out better ways to meet economic demand.

I generally steer clear from predicting what types of solutions might emerge in a market for legal services that was not as severely constrained from using ordinary business tools as our current markets are. After all, the reason

I've emphasized the importance of markets is precisely because figuring out solutions to the problems of a complex economy is not something that can be done in abstract, top-down fashion by bureaucrats. Or academics. (The economists pushing to deregulate the airline industry in the 1970s, for example, failed to predict one of the most significant innovations that emerged post-reform, namely the development of the hub-and-spoke system.)[14] But in this case it's not hard to present a picture of at least some of what places with an overly restrictive approach to legal markets are missing. That's because a few places in the world—the UK and Australia—began dropping these restrictions over the past decade. Almost immediately, a flurry of new types of business models for legal work emerged. Private equity money began to flow in to support innovations in a bubbling market. These innovations included lawyer services delivered through grocery stores, banks, insurance companies, consumer groups, and small business trade associations. A franchise system created as a joint venture between lawyers, software engineers, and business experts selling "business in a box" software and business services to small law firms. Branded networks of law firms operating under shared customer service standards and pricing models. The licensing of accounting and consulting giant PriceWaterhouseCoopers and leading legal publisher LexisNexis to provide legal services to the public. The integration of online document services with on-call legal advice to support people and businesses who are filing required legal forms and representing themselves in court and administrative hearings. The creation of a publicly listed company operating a large network of law firms under a common brand.

All of these innovations shift the economic structure of the business of doing law, largely by relieving individual lawyers of the need to bear all of the risk of innovation, technology development, and the upheavals that face a globalizing legal market. They open the legal industry up to the critical components of innovation: diversity, feedback, and risk-taking.

There are three core elements to the opening up of legal markets to promote innovation, reduced cost, and improved quality in legal services markets. All three elements are part of the modernization of legal markets triggered in the UK (specifically England and Wales) by the adoption of a piece of legislation known as the Legal Services Act of 2007—the culmination of a reform process that began with concerns that legal professional self-regulation violated principles of competition (antitrust) law and which managed to break out of hundreds of years of professional tunnel vision by putting a banker in charge of a thorough review of the legal regulatory regime. Here are those three elements.

Licensing Entities to Be Legal Providers

The most important step in opening up legal markets is to allow legal services to be provided in a wide array of alternative business and financial models. That step was accomplished in the UK by the creation of an entity-licensing regime. (The Brits called these entities alternative business structures—ABSs. They are "alternative" to traditional law firms.) This allows grocery stores and banks, online legal advice and services companies, unions and trade associations to become licensed providers of legal services. It allows those entities to put lawyers on staff—to design legal products and to serve clients directly—and to enter into joint ventures and incentive-creating profit-sharing contracts with lawyers. It also allows those entities to obtain financing from the same kind of sources—gaining access to risk capital—as other businesses in the economy. The US company LegalZoom, for example, is now licensed to do in the United Kingdom what it cannot do in the United States: hire or enter into revenue-sharing contracts with lawyers who serve the people who come to the LegalZoom website looking for legal help.[15]

As licensed entities these legal businesses have to demonstrate to a regulator that they have in place the kinds of processes, personnel, and controls necessary to ensure that consumers of legal services are getting good-quality service. And that the lawyers working with and for these entities continue to uphold their traditional professional duties of acting in the best interest of their clients, avoiding conflicts of interest and compromises to their integrity and independence. Unlike current state-by-state attorney regulation in the United States, licensed entities are obligated to hold substantial malpractice insurance, establish compensation funds, and cooperate with a legal ombudsman who can (with client agreement) mandate compensation for or repair of faulty legal work. Licensed entities are also subject to periodic auditing and can be fined up to £500 million for legal errors.

Licensing Multiple Legal Professions

Not every legal task requires a bar-licensed lawyer with seven years of university education. But in many legal regimes, including the United States, almost all legal work must be done by one.

Compare this to the practice of medicine. Although MDs gained substantial power and control over the delivery of healthcare around the same time that lawyers through the ABA were securing their monopoly, physicians have always been only one of the healthcare professions. Osteopaths and chiropractors gained licensing and rights to practice at the same time as physicians in the early part of the twentieth century. Pharmacists emerged as a distinct profession as drug development advanced and doctors gave up compounding their own drugs. Today we have a medical system populated by a vast array of professionals and paraprofessionals who can provide some forms of medical care without MD supervision: physical therapists, registered nurse practitioners, dieticians, certified nurse anesthetists, certified nurse midwives, phlebotomists, emergency medical technicians, podiatrists; the list is long. While specific medical procedures, such as surgery or prescription of controlled drugs, must be done by an appropriately licensed provider, healthcare advice and services can be provided by those practicing alternative forms of medicine: homeopathy, massage, acupuncture. If the medical world looked like the legal world, all of our healthcare would have to be provided by or under the direct supervision of MDs. If we think medicine is expensive now, just imagine how inaccessible that healthcare system would be.

A more open approach to legal markets would license multiple legal professions. Some professional licenses could be relatively limited—the completion of documents, for example. Others could allow providers to supply significant services but only in limited specialties—family law or housing or taxation, for example. And still others could authorize professionals from competing professional perspectives to supply effectively any legal services—as our current attorney licenses do.

The UK system currently consists of nine different legal professions. Some are familiar: barristers, solicitors, and notaries. Others are more obscure or novel beyond English shores: chartered legal executives, patent attorneys, trademark attorneys, costs lawyers, conveyancers. Chartered accountants can now also be licensed to provide some legal services. These different professionals compete with one another to different degrees. Barristers, solicitors, and legal executives can engage in any legal services other than notarizing documents, which can only be done by notaries. Probate activities can be carried out by any of the professions with the exception of trademark, patent, and costs attorneys; this is the only legal service accountants can be licensed to provide. Transactions involving real and personal property, such as the sale of land, the licensing of intellectual property rights, or the creation of a lien, can be done by all with the exception of accountants and costs lawyers. This generates competition between different types of providers.

Competition also takes places between the regulators. Providers operating under these professional designations must satisfy the requirements and follow the regulations of their separate professional regulator. This creates different educational paths and styles of regulation. Barristers, for example, have to obtain a university law degree. Solicitors can follow a university or apprenticeship path to licensure. Legal executives generally follow a nonuniversity training program and engage in extended periods of apprenticeship and supervised practice before being fully licensed. This means that someone interested in being a lawyer in the UK can choose between multiple different paths and will be led to weigh the costs and benefits of different approaches to regulation.

Right Regulation

Challenges to the existing regulation of legal markets by bar associations are sometimes cast as proposals to deregulate legal markets. But the name of the game is not deregulation; it's what I call right regulation: putting in place intelligent regulations that ensure the markets for legal goods and services are functional and competitive.

Perhaps the most enduring shift that the UK has achieved in the modernization of its legal sector has been a commitment to regulate only as and where needed. They call this risk-based and outcome-based regulation. The UK doesn't require licenses at all for legal work that is low risk and where there is little evidence that outcomes are poor or that existing regulation makes things any better. In 2011, for example, the UK conducted the secret-shopper study of will-writing that I mentioned earlier. This is a legal service that anyone in the UK can provide—not just licensed lawyers—and there was pressure on the government to change that. As I noted in Chapter 7, the secret-shopper study did find that the wills being written in England and Wales had a shockingly high error rate—25 percent failed to meet the standards of an expert review board. (There's no reason to think this isn't also true in the United States and other countries—but only the UK has bothered to look.) But the evidence from this study also showed that the error rate was the same regardless of whether the person or company preparing the will was licensed or not. So the calls to allow only licensed providers to write wills were turned aside—at least pending any evidence that regulators had figured out how to regulate their licensees to do a better job.

Instead, the regulatory authorities focus on identifying where the risks really lie—which is not always where the practitioners in legal professions think they do. This has led to a de-emphasis on the traditional worries of lawyers—that shareholders of legal businesses or profit-seeking nonlawyer partners will interfere with lawyers' independence and complex business structures will hide malfeasance—and a new emphasis on the problems that are truly causing clients losses. These include risks such as failures of quality for vulnerable clients, misuse of clients' money, money laundering, cybersecurity, and pressure on lawyers from wealthy clients to engage in professional misconduct.

The UK system has achieved this shift in regulatory focus by pioneering a model of what in Chapter 10 I'll call competitive approved private regulators. The nine different professional bodies that can license and regulate individuals and the five that can license and regulate entities are only authorized to regulate if they satisfy an oversight regulator—the Legal Services Board. Maintaining their status as an approved regulator requires showing that their regulatory approach is evidence-based and achieves the outcomes required by the Legal Services Act—providing quality legal services, maintaining lawyers' professional duties such as confidentiality and independence, avoiding anticompetitive conduct. Critically, oversight requires that the professional regulators operate independently of the professional trade associations with which they are affiliated. So the Law Society—which is the English solicitors' equivalent of US bar associations—is required not to interfere with the Solicitors' Regulatory Authority, for example. And in fact throughout the UK approach, regulatory bodies are required to be chaired by and to maintain a majority of voting members who are not lawyers themselves. That change has gone a long way toward a more intelligent approach to regulation, one focused on innovation, improving quality, and reducing costs.

All of this puts the UK in a much better position to meet the challenges of building better legal infrastructure for an increasingly complex world. And provides a straightforward model for how other countries can keep up.

10

Markets for Rules

AS I WRITE THIS in 2016, we don't have self-driving cars picking us up to deliver us to meetings and dinner dates. There are still no drones dropping off our packages. Why not? Most people think that the big obstacle is building the technology. But in fact we have a lot of the core technology, and researchers can see where this is headed. The technology that's proving really challenging to develop is the technology that can navigate not just physical space but also regulatory space.

The problem, as we've seen, is not that rules are evil. Getting rid of the rules is not the solution. We need rules to manage the risks of these technologies and handle the inevitable disagreements we will have about who is responsible for the inevitable problems and complications that will crop up—the accidents that will occur at pedestrian crossings and highway on-ramps, the drones that will crash into other aircraft and onto front lawns. It's magical thinking to imagine that we don't need rules, some rules, for how this all gets sorted out. That's what we need legal infrastructure for.

The question is, how are we going to build this legal infrastructure? In the increasingly complex world we inhabit, the difficulty of building that legal infrastructure is as least as challenging as building the technology in the first place. We're still stuck, however, on the idea that regulation is something produced only by politicians, policymakers, and civil servants. Produced using only the technology of written words on paper and costly arguments about what those words mean. Implemented primarily through the threat of government-imposed sanctions for those who ignore the rules or violate them. All this in a system that is increasingly costly, complex, and failing to deliver on the most fundamental thing we need legal infrastructure to do: provide a stable and useful platform for making things and coordinating economic life.

But it's hard to take seriously the belief that we can continue to regulate phenomenally smart and agile technology and systems without legal tools that are just as smart and agile. Think ahead to the perhaps not-too-distant future in which there are millions of artificially intelligent creatures in our midst—not just AI cars, but robots caring for people in nursing homes, robots diagnosing and treating patients, robots flipping burgers, and robots building the parts and software for building robots. Robotics pays off when robots are able to process more information and use data better than humans to make judgment calls. So why is it that we think that human brains, working even in the best of circumstances (and not under the enormously heavy weight of politically charged deliberative, bureaucratic, and adversarial processes), will be able to stay one step ahead of the robots? The 2015 Volkswagen scandal involving smart cars that could detect when they were being tested by regulators for allowable emissions and rig the test results is testament to the misplaced confidence in traditional regulatory technology. Regulating AIs, almost surely, will require almost as much or more AI than the AI targets of regulation themselves.

We already have good evidence that our conventional approaches to producing regulation, exclusively through governments and public officials, are increasingly unable to cope with the levels of complexity and scale of some of our new technologies. The European data protection law creating the right to be forgotten, for example, requires online search engines such as Google to delete, when requested, links to personal data when those data are "inaccurate, inadequate, irrelevant, or excessive."[1] Judgments about when the law requires deletion involve weighing public and private interests in complex ways. Regulators have delegated those judgments in the first instance, however, to search engines. In 2016 Google was adjudicating over 500 such claims a day, relying on a team of Google lawyers, paralegals, and other employees. But this is a purely private process. Unless they appeal to a court, claimants don't get hearings to explain their case. Although Google provides outline reasons to the claimants for the decisions made, the public—including the publisher of the information that's being deleted—can't get access to records, as they can with public regulators, to see what's going on in practice. Individual claimants who are unhappy with the result can appeal to state regulators—that happens in less than 1 percent of cases. So why are European regulators, having granted expansive data-protection rights, not adjudicating more of these cases themselves instead of leaving the bulk of the task to search engines? According to a 2016 *New York Times* report, it's because public regulatory agencies lack "the financial, technical and human resources" to do the job.[2]

Are these our only two choices: relying on public agencies with limited financial, technical, and human resources to regulate complex systems or relying on companies to regulate themselves?

In this chapter I argue that there is a third option: rules and regulation supplied by competitive private regulators that are overseen as necessary by public regulators. This approach harnesses the benefits of private regulators but without turning to self-regulation. Instead of Google adjudicating its right-to-be-forgotten claims, companies and other private organizations specializing in providing this service would compete to adjudicate them. Google would be required to choose a regulator from among these competing providers. Google's private regulator, however, would have to meet targets and follow rules set by government. That's why this is not self-regulation: the regulator is a third party. It's just not a government third party; it's a government-accountable third party.

This approach shifts the role of government from primary regulator to superregulator—a regulator of regulators—and it tracks the shift from central planning to markets that we've already seen underlies the basic transformation in the global economy over the past several decades. This isn't an approach that's right for all types of regulation, but it is an approach that we can add to the options available to confront the challenges of complexity.

Getting to smarter regulation will require markets. Markets that can suss out information and alternatives using multiple lenses and perspectives. Markets that can underwrite the risk of innovation and rope in the investment needed to fund costly experiments with regulatory schemes, systems, and technology by dangling the prospect of profit and, for the philanthropically minded, social impact. Markets that are responsive to the feedback from both the targets and the beneficiaries of regulation about how well things are working. Without a greater role for markets in the production of legal infrastructure, we are fairly doomed to see the gap widen between what our complex economy is up to and where we want to be. That's not just a problem for the potential victims of technology and systems gone awry. It's a problem for everyone who wants to build the technology and systems of the future. Unless some of the money, energy, and intensity of focus that powers the Silicon Valleys of the world is also directed to building better legal infrastructure, the prospects for spectacular innovations like the self-driving car—not to mention transformative goals in energy, biotechnology, finance, logistics, communications, and more—recede further into the future.

Markets for Legal Rules: The Easy Case

Think back to the thought experiment we conducted in Chapter 4. You are an entrepreneur working to build a new web-based company. We saw there that, maybe surprisingly to you, you will need a lot of law to get your project off the ground and into profitable skies. Most basically you and your partners need some rules to govern the deal you have worked out between you about how you will share the costs of starting up your new business, decision-making authority about how the business is run, and how you will divvy up profit, in the hopeful scenario in which you make a profit. You will want those rules, and expect that everyone expects that everyone expects (etc.) that they will be enforced, so that each of you can make fairly reliable predictions about how each of you will behave in the venture. If you agree that you'll share profits equally, that the partner who came up with the original business idea does not have to put any money into the venture, that any business decisions will require a majority vote, and that none of you will participate in a competing venture, then you want comfort that this is how profits, decision-making, capital contributions, and competition will in fact play out in the future.

The way things work now, you and your partners can all expect that if any of you reneges on the deal, the others can, if they're so inclined, file a lawsuit and sue for breach of contract. And if the court agrees that there has been a breach of the contract, after applying the rules that determine whether your agreement is legally binding and whether it was breached, the court will order some kind of remedy. What the remedy will be will depend on other legal rules. The court might order the person who breached to pay damages or it might order the person who breached to do something—stop competing with the venture, for example.

The rules that will operate in this case, and the courts that can decide the case and provide a remedy, will be the rules and courts that other legal rules deem to be the relevant jurisdiction. If all the partners are in California, for example, and the business is in California, then the default is that the rules and courts will be the ones developed and run by the State of California. That's because there are fairly clear legal rules that say that the relevant jurisdiction is the one with the closest connection to the deal. If one of you tried to get the rules of, say, New York applied to the case, neither California nor New York courts would go along with that.

But those same rules also give you and your partners an option at the outset. If you don't like California's contract rules, then you can all agree up front that you want your deal governed by the rules that New York's legislature and courts have developed. You can agree to go into California courts and ask the California court to apply New York law—which it will do if it agrees that you have a binding agreement to apply New York law. Or you can agree to go into New York courts and ask them to apply New York law, even if none of you otherwise has anything to do with New York. And here's the beauty of this scheme: even if you ask the New York court to decide your case using New York law, you can still go to California and ask those courts to enforce the judgment of the New York court. In fact, this is what you'll want to do if the partner you're suing has no contact with New York: he or she has no assets or wages there to seize. That means one government—California—is allowing its power to seize assets or wages to be used to enforce rules it didn't write and doesn't control. California doesn't get to weigh in on whether it thinks New York used the right rules or good rules. Under the US Constitution, each state's courts are obligated to give "full faith and credit" to the judgments reached by other states' courts.

The government of each state thus allows you to pick some other state's contract rules and courts to operate its enforcement machinery. In a sense, New York is competing with California for the business of providing legal rules governing contracts and operating California's enforcement machinery. New York might even make some money from this, in the form of filing fees if it attracts business. And lawyers in New York might make more money because their expertise in the set of rules chosen by the market is more valuable as demand for those rules goes up—which makes their professional monopoly over New York legal work more valuable. The benefits of winning the competition for the business of providing rules might explain why New York's legislature, for example, passed a law in 1984 authorizing people with big deals (over $250,000) to choose New York law to govern their contract even if their deal has no relationship to New York whatsoever—meaning the New York judgment is practically unenforceable by New York's own enforcement machinery. New York lawyers and courts, apparently, wanted the business.

So the next question is obvious: is there any reason private companies shouldn't be able to compete for the business as well?[3] Suppose I see a demand for simpler, less expensive contract law, a demand not being met by either New York or California. I set up a company—let's call it unimaginatively Simple Contracts Inc.—and charge people to use my rules. Because I know enough about how courts can take a simple set of rules and make them complex, I also provide adjudication services—using judges I train and procedures my company determines. And because I know that lawyers trained in conventional contract law might behave in ways that make even my simple rules complex and expensive to use, I also train and provide lawyers who are experts in my system and who agree to charge for their services in a way that controls the cost. In fact, let's suppose I come up with a workable business model where all of these services—the production and maintenance of the set of rules, the provision of a judge and procedures, and the supply of legal assistance—are included in the package price or subscription fee paid by the people who choose my system to govern their contracts. (That's also a business model to help protect my investment in the intellectual property of developing the system, since my rules will be hard to keep secret.)

In order to be truly competitive with the states that are offering their contract rules and courts to venturers such as yourself, I'm going to need to be able to guarantee that the decisions my system makes in contracting disputes can be enforced with the full power of the state. If all the assets that could be used to make your partners pay up if they breach their agreement with you are in California, you're not going to use the law I'm offering to govern your agreement unless decisions in my system are as effective at reaching those assets as the ones coming out of New York or California state courts. So the question is: should my company, Simple Contracts, be recognized as a provider of contract law for your business venture, competing with New York and California for business, and authorized to operate the enforcement machinery of the California government?

A first possible worry here is that if Simple Contracts competes in a market for contract law, the rules might be bad for the people who choose them. I'll admit it. There might be lots that I get wrong in my design and management of Simple Contracts. The rules I choose might be too simple—missing too many of the nuanced details of what the contracting parties really expected would happen. Or I might advertise my rules as simpler and cheaper to use, but they might turn out to be much more complex and expensive than I promised. Maybe my judges will develop a bias in favor of the wealthier party, or the little guy. So you and your partners may find that when it comes to a dispute about managerial authority or profit-sharing or what counts as "competing" with the business, the result under the Simple Contracts system isn't what you wanted. (Of course, it is in the nature of disputes ruled on by a third party that the final result in any system will not be what at least one person wanted—but the question is, was the result what all of you would have said you wanted at the outset and did you think the process by which even a result you don't like was reached was fair and unbiased?) And maybe I'll be too successful and gain too much market share and manage to extract an outrageous fee for my company's services from you.

Of course, that makes the legal rules and services you buy from Simple Contracts no different from what you buy from anyone else in a market economy. The food may be bad, the car of faulty design, the accountant dishonest or wrong, the internet service overpriced. What protects you in those markets is competition and regulation.

If a market is competitive, companies are working hard to capture business by delivering products that are in fact a better match with the features and quality people want, at a better price. If a market is competitive, then a business that sells goods of a lower quality than promised or that charges too high a price gets a bad reputation and loses customers. The internet, in fact, has made this basic protective mechanism a much more protective one—by amplifying the capacity for people who have had good and bad experiences with a product to broadcast that to just about anyone. That's the power of Yelp, Amazon reviews, rankings, ratings, and hashtags. The capacity of customers to protect themselves by choosing a different provider is a major source of protection against bad deals. (It's a mode of protection that people living in centrally planned economies with low-quality goods would dearly love to have.) That's a primary way in which you and your partners will be able to protect yourselves against buying a bad product from Simple Contracts.

Markets can only protect against bad deals, however, if they are in fact reasonably competitive. We want the driving force of markets but, like a wild horse, without a harness that force doesn't necessarily take us where we want to go. And that's where a good legal framework—the superrules—comes in. A competitive market is one where you know what you're buying and you get what you thought you were buying when you decided to plop down your money. So we have basic laws that combat fraud and misleading advertising and require companies to pay compensation if they sell faulty products or products different from what was promised. Those laws will apply to Simple Contracts too. A competitive market is one in which there are enough buyers and sellers to ensure that good information flows and that when signals of bad outcomes emerge—such as poor quality, inadequate features, or excessive prices—a competing seller can jump on the opportunity to provide a better product at a better price. Getting to this result requires a slew of laws—antitrust laws that control the creation and behavior of monopolies, financial regulation that ensures access to capital for start-ups, maybe even internet rules that ensure small businesses have as much access to critical communications infrastructure as established ones. Those laws will apply to Simple Contracts' market as well—making sure that if I supply a poor product, competitors with better rules and better ways of delivering them will be there ready to steal my customers away. It's possible that special features of the kind of legal product I'm offering will require special rules to ensure competition can work reasonably well. Maybe providing a legal system requires durability over a long period of time, much like providing, say, insurance does. So maybe Simple Contracts will be subject to special rules, like insurance companies are. These rules allow regulators to make sure that the company will have the resources it needs in a distant future to live up to its promises, a reasonable plan for transferring obligations to another provider in the event it goes belly-up, or a mechanism that minimizes the likelihood that the company simply won't be around to deliver when needed—such as requiring contracts to expire after a short time.

The point is that if what we're worried about is making sure that you and your partners are getting a decent product from a competitive legal rules provider like Simple Contracts, that challenge is really no different from the one we face in making sure that you get a decent product from all the other businesses that compete to provide you with what you need to run a profitable business of your own. And remember: the alternative to what Simple Contracts offers is not perfect affordable law. It's what you can get from entities that rely on planning, political mechanisms, and state-to-state competition—state legislatures and courts—to protect your interest in good legal rules. If New York and California are today competing for your business, what is your protection against bad quality and high cost? If you choose California law and courts, and you are a California voter, you might be able to get the politicians and judges (who, in this state, run for election) to respond better to your needs. But that's a blunt instrument at best. And if you choose New York law, you have no recourse as a voter at all if you live in California. You may be able to lobby legislators or contribute money to their campaigns. But by and large your main source of protection against bad law out of New York or California is the same as it would be if Simple Contracts were on the scene: if you don't like it, don't choose it. Indeed, you have more recourse against Simple Contracts if it doesn't live up to its promises than you do against New York and California. You can't sue New York or California if they fail to fund their courts adequately and it takes a year to get a court date or if the simple procedural rules on the books get so bollixed up in practice that it costs you millions in e-discovery costs to litigate your case. You can sue Simple Contracts if it promises something different and it doesn't deliver.

The case for competitively provided commercial contract law is probably the easiest case for market-based legal rules that we can identify. For one thing, you and your business partners are probably not the type of people we worry about not being able to protect themselves in ordinary market settings—people with poor education or who are marginalized or vulnerable. And for another, we're not talking life and death here. No one's going to jail if the rules are badly written or wrongly enforced; people are not at risk of being degraded or abused. The interests are pretty much limited to money and job satisfaction: are you going to make as much money and get as much personal fulfillment out of this venture as you would have if the rules were done right? The cost of bad law here is in the same category as what you're risking when you buy a house, invest in a retirement fund, agree to work for a new employer, or choose a college. These are risks that we all routinely manage through markets operated within a good legal framework.

What about risks to people other than you and your contracting partners? Here's another reason that the commercial contracting case is an easy one. Even if the business venture you are putting together with your partners might pose a risk that it will harm people—generating pollution, producing defective products, failing to protect customer data, treating employees in discriminatory ways—the rules governing your deal with your partners have no impact on those risks. No contract rules do. Your business has to comply with the regulations governing pollution, defective products, data privacy, and employment discrimination—the rules protecting other people's interests—regardless of how you decide among yourselves to share profits, decision-making authority, and capital contributions. So this is an easy case because the only people affected by the choice to use Simple Contracts' rules are the people making the choice. In economist lingo, there are no direct externalities from your choice of a system of commercial contract law.

There could, however, be indirect externalities. It's possible for a state to have an opinion—that is to say, policy—about how even the private arrangements you reach with your partners are structured. The state may have an interest in protecting your interests—such as by requiring that any deal you reach must be in writing to make sure you really know what you're getting into or that you can cancel without penalty within a few days if you have a change of heart. Or the state may have an interest in how the ecosystem of business deals works. California, for example, unlike many other states, has a strong public policy that refuses to enforce private agreements, known as noncompete agreements, that prevent an employee or entrepreneur from going to work for a competitor once the job or partnership is over. There are lots of reasons for the California legislature to have decided to put this policy in place: people may do a poor job of protecting their own interest in continuing to work in their field when they change jobs. Noncompete agreements might limit the quality of the pool of workers available to other businesses. And they may restrict the free-flowing mobility of the labor force, mobility that can promote innovation and faster, smarter adaptations to market changes. Some believe, for example, that California's policy on noncompetes is part of the explanation for the success of Silicon Valley: engineers and entrepreneurs have been free to move around from company to company, start-up to start-up, and this has created a vibrant community for innovation, as engineers and entrepreneurs cross-fertilize expertise and experience from place to place. California believes that legitimate trade secrets can be adequately protected through legal means other than preventing employees and entrepreneurs from switching employers or partners.

Now, California may be wrong about this. But that's what the political system is for: to make those kinds of policy decisions. Suppose you and your partners are all located in California, you opt for Simple Contracts, and my legal system treats your noncompete agreement as fully enforceable. Then your choice of my system could undermine the power of the California legislature to implement the policy chosen by the elected officials of the state.

This is a legitimate concern. It's also one that is already addressed in the legal framework for our existing system of state-to-state competition in contract law. Right now, people can choose the contract law of any state to govern their contracts, even a state they have no other relationship with. If you and your partners choose New York law and New York courts, you may be able to run a business in California that doesn't follow the California rule against noncompetes—because New York thinks enforceable noncompetes are dandy. If enough California businesses did this, it would make it hard for California to achieve its policy goals. That's why the legal framework governing choice of law already puts a limit on choice: courts deciding whether to honor a choice of law take into account whether doing so would compromise important policies in the state that, but for the choice, would have its rules in play.

Introducing Simple Contracts into this framework does change the shape of this problem. The way things work now, if you and your partners choose New York law and you go to New York courts to enforce your not-valid-in-California noncompete, it will be up to the New York court to decide which law to apply. You will be arguing New York law applies—respect the choice-of-law clause!—and the partner who is trying to work for a competitor will be arguing California law applies—respect California policy! As you might imagine, New York courts might be a little biased toward their own law. But even so, New York judges will by and large work hard to live up to their professional obligation to respect the law of other states—their peers in the constitutional system—and to decide in a good faith way how much weight to put on California's interest in achieving its policy goals.

The tone of this solution changes if we just substitute my for-profit corporation and my judges for New York's publicly accountable courts. It may work in a constitutional system to leave protection of California's policies somewhat in the hands of New York courts. To some extent, that's part of what giving full faith and credit to the courts of other states in a constitutional democracy means. But California's citizens can't have the importance of their policies judged by a private corporation like mine. I'm in the business of producing a good product and making money, not upholding constitutional relations. California doesn't owe me and my business full faith and credit. Simple Contracts may develop great market legitimacy, but it will never have political legitimacy. And that seems important here.

The solution? Leave the decision about the extent to which California parties can depart from California contract law when they choose a private provider of contract rules up to California. This could happen in the same way it can happen now: the party trying to get the California rules applied can go into a California court and ask for a court order prohibiting the parties from proceeding in the system the parties chose by contract—whether New York or Simple Contracts. Sometimes these cases end up with dueling efforts to get one state's courts to order that the parties stay out of the other state's courts. Of course, that could eat up all the benefits of my system—if people using my system still have to deal with a really slow and expensive public courts regime to resolve their contracting disputes. But if I'm really smart in running Simple Contracts I'll figure out a better solution than this. I could make arrangements with the California courts to get quick rulings on which law applies—and pay the courts for that fast-track service. I could lobby the California legislature or put an initiative on the ballot for clear guidelines on when my system's rules will be allowed to rule and when they won't in cases like this. I could modify my rules so that these cases don't arise much—by conforming my rules to California policy, for example, or by offering killer mediation services that get these issues reliably settled without anyone getting the California courts involved. And better entrepreneurs than me, no doubt, could come up with even better solutions.

The point is: this is a problem with a solution. This is the kind of solution we need to develop all the time—creating the right legal framework to ensure that markets work to produce the kinds of outcomes we want.

There's one last objection that seems pretty powerful, but isn't. On first take, it sounds rather shocking to think that private parties could order government enforcement agencies around—telling courts when they have to use their public authority to order the sheriff to seize assets or to order a former employee to stop working for a competitor, for example. But in fact this is how our entire civil (that is, not criminal) justice system works. It sits there sleepily, not doing anything, unless and until some private party gins it up by starting a lawsuit. This is true in just about every civil legal system in the world. Courts don't act in noncriminal matters unless private individuals or organizations ask them to act. (For purposes of civil litigation, governments are like any other private party with a right to sue or be sued.) In systems like we have in the United States, England, Canada, and the rest of what's known as the Anglo-American legal world, the role of private parties in operating the levers of the government's enforcement machinery goes even further. The parties to a lawsuit determine what issues will be decided, what evidence will be presented, and what remedies sought. They do this by playing a type of tennis: one side serves up the issues it believes should be decided by the court; the other side returns the serve and either agrees those are the issues or proposes to throw some out or add some on. The court then decides who wins the point, based on the rules, and proceeds to structure the litigation to decide the winning issues. The same volley is exchanged on what evidence to hear and what remedies to consider. The court does very little on its own say-so. In some systems around the world—in what are confusingly known as civil law systems or, misleadingly, inquisitorial systems such as those in Germany or France—judges play a more active role; they can decide for themselves what issues they think should be explored or what evidence collected. But even so, the whole process doesn't get underway unless a private party calls "Game on."

The extent to which private parties are empowered to call the plays for a government enforcement authority is pretty much at its maximum in our easy case of private contracting between business partners. The defining feature of contract law in advanced market economies is that the parties are free to put into their contract just about anything they want. They decide, by agreement, what legal obligations will be created for each of them. Because they are in a world where courts enforce (most of) those obligations, they are effectively telling the government enforcers what to do: make him pay damages if he doesn't deliver the goods on time; make her cough up the money she promised to contribute to our venture. Failing to live up to those privately crafted legal obligations is a wrong against the contracting party. Before the contract is written, the state doesn't care when goods are delivered or who contributes money to your venture. It just puts its enforcement powers at the disposal of private parties: if private parties care about these things and they put them in a valid contract, the state will show up, adjudicate, and enforce.

Even this connection to the state's power to enforce against assets is shrinking, at least for private contracting. This is the potential of blockchain technology, which underlies the development of digital currencies like Bitcoin. Blockchain technology operates like a huge publicly accessible peer-to-peer web-based spreadsheet or ledger, a massive list of who owns what. The things on the list are assets only identified by a string of characters; the owners are identified only by a private ID, also a string of characters. The ability to change the name attached to an asset is controlled by the owner through the use of a private encryption key, another string of characters. Bitcoin works by enabling someone who owns coins—has her private ID associated with entries on the ledger—to transfer those coins to someone else's private ID. That's just the way money works: inherently worthless pieces of paper change hands, and because everyone is willing to agree that paper with a particular set of marks on it is worth a fixed amount ($10 for a ten-dollar bill), we can use those pieces of paper to exchange value: work for wages, for example. Bitcoin works so long as people are willing to accept uniquely owned strings of characters in exchange for things of value like goods and services.

Using blockchain technology for contracts involves layering a contract enforcement mechanism on top of this basic system of asset ownership. And that's where Simple Contracts gets interesting. California's public legal system is now offering two separate services: adjudication of contract claims together with the capacity to send out a sheriff to make people hand over stuff like physical assets, bank accounts, and wages. We've been looking so far at how Simple Contracts might compete with California for adjudication services, relying on California for enforcement of Simple Contracts' decisions about who owes what to whom when the assets that can be used to pay up are located in California. But with blockchain technology, Simple Contracts could potentially enforce its own decisions, without the need to ask California to go in and seize assets located in California. To do this Simple Contracts would just need to get the parties who want to use its contracting system to store enough assets to keep everyone feeling secure in blockchain—entries on the great spreadsheet in the cloud—and then give Simple Contracts the ability to switch assets from one party's ID to another if needed to satisfy a ruling in a contract dispute. California sheriffs might still need to get involved—to evict someone from a home that is no longer listed with his or her private ID in the blockchain or to arrest a bank officer who draws on an account to pay the bills of someone who no longer owns the account—but now we've shifted from the role of the state in contract enforcement to the role of the state in enforcing basic property rights. The buck stops there, but there are a lot of bucks on the way down.

Markets for Legal Rules: The Harder Cases

The easy case of commercial contracting can help us think through the harder cases of how to build markets for legal rules by pointing to the dimensions we need to pay attention to. A key part of the easy case, for example, is the extent to which the people affected by the rules can protect themselves by opting out if rules are inadequate, too costly, or unfair—that is, the nature and extent of externalities. As we've seen, we need to think both about direct externalities on third parties and indirect externalities on policy and systemic goals that are, quite properly, under the control of politically accountable people and institutions. The other dimension we need to consider is the potential for creating a regulatory framework that ensures that markets for the production of legal rules and procedures are reasonably competitive and that market outcomes do a reasonable job, relative to law produced through legislatures and public courts, at achieving our social goals. Let's think through some examples.

Business Organizations

Could private companies offer corporate law on a market? This is the law that allows you and your partners to create a distinct legal entity that can sue and be sued, own assets, settle debts, and be regulated in its own name. The rules of corporate law determine what it takes to bring this legal entity into existence and govern the relationships among different participants in the organization. Corporate law rules determine how the corporation is to be managed, what role shareholders have, what duties corporate officers owe to the corporation and its shareholders, and so on. These rules also govern the relationships between shareholders, protecting minority shareholders from being taken advantage of by majority shareholders, for example.

As with commercial contracting, people setting up corporations already are allowed in many cases to choose between state providers of corporate law. In the United States, companies can decide to incorporate under the law of any state they like, regardless of where they are doing business. Most choose either their home state or Delaware, a small state that has captured a large market share. A corporation established under Delaware law enjoys status as a distinct legal entity in the courts of any state: it can sue and be sued in those courts, it is entitled to limited liability, its ownership of assets that are not available to the personal creditors of its owners is respected, and it is taxed and regulated as a corporation and not as a bunch of individuals. Most countries now also recognize a corporation formed under the laws of another country as a distinct entity, allowing them to sue or be sued in their courts.

Many of the rules of corporate law are ones that the people affected can avoid if they don't like them. The original owner-founders make the initial choice of which corporate law to use. People who come to the corporation after it is formed—new shareholders, directors, officers—can stay away if they don't like the legal rules the founders chose to govern protections for minority shareholders, establish the duties of directors and officers, or determine how and when shareholders can act.

But once an entity is formed, decisions about how the corporation is operated, including what rules it is operated under, can be made without agreement from everyone who is affected. Majority shareholders can, for example, vote to merge the corporation into a new corporation that leaves out some of the original participants, in what is known as a squeezeout. (A squeezeout is what happened to one of the founders of Facebook, the story told in the movie *The Social Network*, which pulled off the fairly amazing feat of making a corporate lawsuit that doesn't involve murder or toxic chemicals compelling.) People who are owed money by the corporation can be harmed if the corporation chooses a body of corporate law that lets the corporation pay out dividends to its shareholders that leave it without enough assets to pay its debts. Personal creditors might be harmed if a borrower can easily form a corporation and put his or her assets in the corporation to keep them out of creditors' hands. Employees, even entire communities, can be affected by decisions to sell or merge the corporation. People at risk of being harmed by the rules under which the corporation operates can take some steps to protect themselves—requiring collateral for debts, for example, or refusing to buy from or work for a corporation that can too easily be stripped of the assets it needs to pay its bills. But this market mechanism will not do everything that every state would want it to. Many consumers, employees, and investors will have little knowledge of the minutiae of corporate governance and how they might affect their interests. And there will be people affected by the actions of the corporate entity that have no choice they can make to protect themselves—motorists or pedestrians injured by an automobile that loses control due to defective steering, for example.

The question is whether a market for private corporate law systems can be placed within a regulatory framework that allows states to continue to exercise control over policy. The answer is that in many cases, it can. States with the power to regulate and control access to their public courts can retain the power to set the rules governing what can, and what cannot, be chosen through a choice of corporate law. If there are concerns about adequate capitalization to protect consumers or creditors, for example, states can require adequate capitalization—essentially moving rules about capitalization out of the body of corporate law and into a body of public regulation. This is, for example, what happened over the course of the twentieth century with respect to some aspects of corporate disclosures to shareholders. Originally only corporate law and the private stock exchanges on which companies wanted to list their stock imposed disclosure rules. After the stock market crash that triggered the Great Depression of the 1930s, however, securities statutes passed by legislatures imposed new disclosure obligations to protect investors and support efficient and liquid capital markets at a national level.

What would be the benefit of introducing private rule providers into the market for corporate law? The benefit would be market incentives to develop systems that work better for shareholders, directors, and officers—within whatever regulatory framework the state decides it needs to put in place to protect the interests of those who don't participate in that market directly. That may mean simpler rules and procedures. It may mean new mechanisms of disclosure, ones that take advantage of the potential to bundle legal rules with other mechanisms such as data-sharing systems that don't rely on reams of small print that few can parse. (Corporations may not want to give the state authority to directly access corporate information, but they may be willing to participate in private systems, including blockchain systems, for voluntary data-sharing with investors. We see this phenomenon today in the different reactions people have to knowing that Google's computers are combing through emails and search engine results and knowing that government security agencies are doing the same thing.) And it may mean the development of business entities that are better tailored to different circumstances, rather than one-size-fits-all. My coauthor Eric Talley of Columbia University and I have shown as a matter of economic theory why we should expect competition between private profit-motivated corporate law providers to do a better job than competition between state legislatures to produce a range of options suited to different kinds of companies.[4] The reason is that profit-oriented companies will keep innovating until they have reached the point where the marginal benefit of a new system is equal to the marginal cost. State legislatures are just not likely to keep at the innovation in the same way: all they want to do is a good-enough job to stay in office. There's no big insight here: it's just the basic fact that competitive markets, regulated properly, can harness information and ingenuity in ways that politically based centrally planned systems—even when they are competing with other planned systems—cannot.

Employment and Consumer Law

We only want to put our faith in market mechanisms when they are in fact competitive, when the people affected by the rules have a meaningful capacity to opt in to good law and opt out of bad law. Meaningful choice requires that people have a good understanding about what they are choosing and that there are fairly good alternatives to choose from. One of the reasons the commercial contracting case is fairly easy is that we imagined a scenario in which the people doing the choosing—you and your partners—are likely to be relatively sophisticated, to have only business interests at stake, and to probably face a lot of other reasonable options: other potential partners and investors, and a decent job if the prospects for the business don't pan out.

But these conditions are less likely to be met when the contracting takes place between a large organization and an individual with little market clout acting alone. These are the conditions under which many employment and consumer contracts are struck. In fact, in those settings we tend to see organizations that offer employees and consumers a standard-form contract on a take-it-or-leave-it basis. You know these types of contracts: we met them already in the form of "Click Here" online agreements that everybody clicks and nobody reads. They are also the way in which a whole slew of the contracts that we enter into every day are structured. We take a job and sign on to the rules in the organization's standard employee handbook. We rent a car and sign a dense agreement that determines the terms of the rental. We lease an apartment and initial page after page of small print.

The failure of the assumptions of competition here are twofold. First, we doubt that many people "agreeing" to these contracts really know what they are agreeing to. It's just too complicated, particularly for ordinary individuals without legal advice. A recent study found that fewer than nine percent of people shown a standard agreement to arbitrate in a cellphone contract—with the arbitration language in bold, italics, and capital letters—knew that the provision was an "arbitration" agreement and that if they signed it they would have no right to take a dispute with the credit-card company to court.[5] I find confusion between mediation and arbitration is widespread but the difference is fundamental: mediation can't result in any outcome you disagree with; arbitration means you've given up your right to disagree with the result.

Second, in most cases where people are being asked to agree to standard consumer or employment contracts there just aren't good alternatives to saying yes. Apple is not going to negotiate the terms of the contract with you. If you want one of Apple's products, then you have to agree to its terms. These are called contracts of adhesion: because you're stuck with them. Of course, you do have a choice. You can choose not to take the job, rent the apartment or car, buy the iPhone. But, in most cases, that's a big, lumpy choice—the differences between this job, this apartment, this phone, and the alternatives are significant to you. It's not the kind of close substitute that the economist's perfect world of perfect markets assumes. Moreover, even if there are reasonably close substitutes—not much difference to you whether you rent a car from Hertz or Avis, for example—because almost nobody reads or understands the standard terms anyway, neither Hertz nor Avis is likely to bother competing by offering the same car with a better contract. So you don't see an option in the market to get essentially the same product or service but with different contract terms.

Our legal infrastructure appears to be of two minds about contracts like these. On the one hand, we have some regulation that wraps around these contracts, much more so than in the commercial contract setting, limiting the extent to which the terms written by the large organization end up being the law of the relationship. Consumer law often gives people a few days to change their mind about a deal and in some cases prevents a company from getting consumers to agree that they will never sue the company or that the company is not obliged to follow laws requiring products to be safe, for example. Employment law and industrial regulation can limit the power of the employer to require employees to agree to work in unhealthy or harassing environments or to allow the employer to use discriminatory criteria when giving out raises and promotions.

But although we have some, we don't have very much regulation that wraps around these contracts. By and large, they are enforced as the organization writes them and the hapless employee or consumer clicks, initials,

or otherwise accepts them. What that means is that we have a large swath
of relationships in modern economies where the law of the relationship is
chosen by a large organization and imposed on everyone who deals with the
organization as an employee or consumer, with little oversight or interference from governments. Clearly this situation would only be made worse
if the organization were free to select a private provider to supply the rules
governing these contracts as well—as opposed to being required to at least
subject them to the rules established by politically accountable legislatures,
regulators, and courts. That market would not work well at all: the private
provider would only be interested in selling a product that appealed to the
only entity making the choice—the large organization. So the only legal rules
we'd expect to emerge in this market would be those that favored the organization at the expense of consumers and employees.

This seems like a setting where we want *less* privately provided rules and
not more. And yet: what we also see is that this is a setting that our state-based
regulatory systems have not managed to address very effectively. Consumer
protection law is often cumbersome and expensive. Lengthy warnings don't
help consumers who are poorly equipped and situated to read and understand what they're getting and often don't have much of a choice in the first
place. California can pass a law saying that online companies cannot offer a
subscription service that automatically renews and charges a credit card on
file unless this is prominently disclosed and the consumer has to affirmatively
consent at renewal, but how many of us read and understand the disclosure?
How many of us could litigate to get back the $40 or $140 dollars involved
if the law were violated? And for companies trying to comply with consumer
protection law, the sheer volume and fragmented nature of the rules and the
frequency with which they are poorly designed to achieve their objectives at
reasonable cost makes the prospect that the law will be effective slim indeed.
Law on the books does not necessarily mean law on the ground.

Is it possible to take advantage of markets to find better ways to regulate?
We turn to that question next.

Superregulation: Creating Accountable Competitive Markets for Regulation

The problem of overly complex, expensive, and poorly crafted state-based
legal rules, of course, is precisely where we started. And while it would be a
great move forward to introduce more markets into the production of commercial contracting and corporate organization rules, the real Holy Grail is

regulation. This is the law that is growing in leaps and bounds in terms of complexity. It's the law that is holding up things like self-driving cars and slowing down progress on goals like climate change and global financial stability.

We can have a larger role for competitively produced regulatory regimes. Not all regulation can be produced like this. And markets for private regulation would require substantial public oversight—superregulation—directed toward making sure that the markets for regulatory rules are both competitive in fact and overseen in such a way that they produce the results that the politically accountable state sets out for them. But there are settings in which developing the kind of superregulatory infrastructure needed to make reasonably competitive markets for regulatory regimes could reap the benefits of markets over planning: the capacity for greater innovation, lower costs, higher quality, and better responsiveness to multiple conflicting interests.

Here's how this might work. Think about the problem of workplace health and safety. This is something that, as we've seen, states have been regulating with detailed rules since at least the nineteenth century and the dawn of large-scale factories. We regulate workplaces because we expect that worker choice about whom to work for—competition between employers for workers—won't, by itself, be adequately protective of workers. Workers may lack reasonable alternatives if jobs are hard to come by, for example, and they have to take whatever they can. They may lack reasonable information about the risks of a particular workplace—the risks of exposure to chemicals or carcinogens, for example—because it's hard to assess the risks from the outside, or because the risks are many and complex, or because the risks are ones that don't make themselves known until long in the future. And some people may worry that even with information about risks, some workers will make poor choices, exposing themselves to risks that a reasonable person would avoid. People with these motives for regulation prefer not to live in a world where people are left to make bad choices and suffer the consequences. People of different political persuasions will come down differently in terms of when and how much regulation is called for to address these different concerns. Differences will also exist in terms of beliefs about how much we as a society should be willing to pay to protect workers from risks. Democratic politics sorts through these differences and produces a set of goals for workplace safety and its costs.

There are three basic ways that our current systems create laws to achieve those democratically set goals. The first, and oldest, is for governments to write explicit rules about how a workplace is to be organized and run. These types of regulations delve into the minute details: what size mesh must be used to enclose the cage on a personnel hoist; what size and type of rock bolts must be used to secure a mining tunnel; what mathematical formula is to be used to calculate permissible noise exposure in construction jobs. This is the way the vast majority of regulation is still done.

A second approach to regulation, called performance- or principles-based regulation, avoids setting detailed rules about how a workplace is to be built and operated. Instead, regulatory agencies write down performance criteria or principles that businesses are obligated by law to meet. Performance criteria in the workplace, for example, might establish acceptable levels for workplace injuries or factory air quality. More abstract principles might establish the objective of achieving reasonable risk reduction that balances the costs and benefits of preventive measures. Regulated businesses then have to figure out how to design and operate their workplace—what kind of safety equipment or ventilation to implement, for example—to make sure they meet these performance measures.

A third approach, called management-based regulation, creates legal rules requiring businesses to engage in a process for identifying the risks in their workplace—the risks of chemical exposure for workers, for example—and then to design and implement a plan for how to manage those risks.

In each of these approaches either civil servants or company managers are responsible for designing the details of how to achieve workplace health and safety. Their decisions determine the cost, complexity, and efficacy of regulation.

Here's how a market-based fourth alternative could be added to this mix. Instead of civil servants or the managers of a regulated company designing the details of how to achieve politically set goals for workplace health and safety, private for-profit and nonprofit companies could offer this as a service in the market, for a fee. In order to participate in this market, these companies would have to be approved as private regulators by the government. Approval would be based on meeting the policy objectives established by the government for regulation—developing a system that ensures that regulated businesses meet targets for maximum injury rates or exposure to harmful chemicals, for example. Regulated businesses would be required to choose a regulator from among the approved private regulators. The private regulators would regulate businesses, and the government would regulate the private regulators. Government would establish the regulatory objectives and targets for the scheme, set some rules for how private regulators operate, conduct reviews of the regulators' systems and audits of the the regulator's performance: the extent to which the regulator's rules are followed by regulated companies and the regulator's system achieves government objectives and targets.

This is what some call metaregulation and what I'm calling *superregulation*.[6] It shifts the boundary between central planning and the market up a level.

The model of competing private regulators is not entirely unheard of in the modern world. As I noted in Chapter 9, since changes made in 2007 lawyers in England and Wales have been regulated in an explicitly superregulatory system. A Legal Services Board appointed by the government has authority to approve regulators of legal services. As of 2015, there were nine approved regulators, all of which were private nonprofit organizations. With the exception of notaries, none of the approved regulators oversees professionals with a monopoly. (This is a change from the historical practice under which only barristers, for example, could appear in higher courts and only solicitors could submit the paperwork required to conduct litigation.) In order to provide certain legal services, such as appearing in court or signing legal papers, a legal professional in England and Wales is required to choose from among the set of approved private regulators.

Approval as a private regulator is contingent on demonstrating to the Legal Services Board that the private regulator oversees a regulatory regime that meets the objectives of the governing law, the Legal Services Act. These objectives are set out in the form of principles, such as protecting the rule of law and the interests of consumers, promoting competition in the provision of legal services, and ensuring competence, duties toward courts, and confidentiality. The Board monitors the performance of the private regulators as well as the legal system as a whole, tracking the impact of regulation on prices and quality, for example. The Board also is authorized to create rules that the approved regulators must follow—such as rules setting the maximum penalties they can impose and requiring that they, like the Legal Services Board itself, must have a majority of members and a chairperson who are not members of the profession regulated by that regulator—solicitors must be in the minority and cannot chair the Solicitors Regulatory Authority, for example.

The English model of competitive private regulation for legal services, however, is a relative rarity. There are many examples of settings in which governments delegate regulatory authority to private organizations. As I noted earlier, reliance on voluntary compliance and self-regulation is widespread, often because the technological challenges make any other solution seem impossible. Governments also often incorporate standards set by private standard-setting organizations into their regulations. For example, the US Occupational Safety and Health Administration (OSHA) has a regulation requiring that tractors used in agriculture have seatbelts that meet the standards set by the Society of Automotive Engineers, a private membership organization. Governments also routinely authorize some nonprofit organizations to regulate their members in a more arm's-length form of self-governance. The Financial Industry Regulatory Authority—FINRA—is a nonprofit corporation authorized by Congress to license and regulate broker-dealers who buy and sell securities on behalf of investors.

But all of these solutions have critical weaknesses. Self-regulation's primary weakness is that it is *self*-regulation, not third-party regulation. That puts a conflict of interest at the heart of the regulatory approach, even while it recruits the superior ability of the private entity to navigate complex technologies and systems. And third-party standard-setting or industry self-governance systems are not competitive systems. Governments generally select only one organization, often a nonprofit membership organization composed of those with industry expertise, to supply standards or industry rules and licensing. With a monopoly and as membership organizations, private standard-setting and self-enforcement organizations tend to operate on the central planning model, with studies and committees and votes on what standards to adopt.

The superregulatory alternative I'm suggesting differs from the existing use of private regulators because private regulators under superregulation would operate in a market in the sense that they would compete to provide regulated businesses with a system for achieving regulatory goals. To succeed in this competition, a private regulator would have to offer a system that *simultaneously* meets government criteria for approval *and* is attractive, relative to the market alternatives, to regulated businesses. Private standard-setting organizations and self-governing bodies with a monopoly role in regulation aren't subject to that market discipline. They can bring more expertise to bear on a problem than government can—because they are comprised of professionals such as engineers or members of the securities industry. But expertise alone is not enough to get us to lower-cost, less complex, and more effective systems in a complex world.

We can also find current examples of competition between approved regulators but the competition is thus far limited to government regulators. These are cases of Government A selectively approving the regulatory regimes of Governments B, C, and D and allowing those subject to regulation by Government A to choose the regulatory regime of one of those other governments. We see this within federalist systems such as the United States, where, as I mentioned earlier in this chapter, each state allows companies in its borders to choose to be governed by the corporate law of any other state. We also see some examples of this in the international setting. Many countries recognize the system for issuing drivers' licenses in other countries: you don't need to pass a French driving test to drive a rental car on vacation in the south of France. More elaborate systems for what is sometimes called mutual recognition are beginning to emerge. Just before the global financial crisis upset the apple cart in 2008, the securities regulators in the United States and Australia had agreed to recognize each other's regulatory regimes for stock exchanges, brokers, and dealers, meaning that these financial services providers only had to worry about complying with one set of rules even if they operated in both countries. The plan was put on hold in the aftermath of the crisis, but the idea is back on the table—laying the groundwork for potential competition between states for more effective ways of delivering regulations that states recognize as achieving comparable results to their own.[7] Still these countries are not yet talking about allowing nonstate providers to enter the competition.

The key to a market-based approach to regulation is to create the potential for innovation and incentives to invest in smarter, more effective, and less expensive systems for meeting regulatory objectives. Private regulators that secure a larger market share and higher profits (or better returns on nonprofit goals—the motive animating many nonprofit organizations such as private universities and hospitals) by offering a better regulatory service have powerful incentives to figure out how to achieve regulatory objectives more effectively at lower costs.

Some private regulators might design systems that follow one of the three existing approaches we see in government regulation—explicit technology and process rules, performance criteria, and management-based oversight. But in the competition for market share, we can also expect private regulators to invest in developing alternative methods as well. Some regulators might specialize in particular industries or even particular regulatory objectives (such as limiting chemical exposure, ensuring data security, or achieving greater safety in self-driving cars). Others might implement experimental protocols to identify risks and lower-cost means of managing them. Systems could emerge that integrate employee selection, compensation, and promotion with health and safety performance. Almost certainly we could expect to see regulatory approaches that are rooted in data systems and blockchain technology, and integrated across multiple locations, participants, and facets of the business—there are likely to be economies of scope in achieving compliance not only with regulatory requirements but also with corporate strategy and contracts. Private regulators would not focus exclusively, or even, perhaps, very much at all, on writing complex rules and then hunting down and adjudicating violations—which is the only technology available to government (whether it writes the rules or requires the regulated business to write its own). Private regulators can employ the full range of alternatives for coaxing outcomes closer to the targets set by policy.

The greatest promise of market-induced innovation in regulatory design is much-improved understanding of the relationship between the complexity of a regulatory setting and the complexity of regulation. Our current regulatory technology, largely limited to writing rules and enforcing compliance with them, increasingly operates on the basis of the idea that the more complex the regulatory problem, the more complex regulation has to be. This is the justification we hear for thousand-page statutes and volumes upon volumes of regulations. But there is good reason to think that this reasoning is faulty in important ways. For one thing, as the complexity of regulation increases, there comes a point at which compliance must begin to fall off, simply because of the high cost of figuring out what you're supposed to do. There's also the increased likelihood that specific instructions in one place conflict with those in another.

The designers of checklists understand this. If the checklists that airline pilots or surgeons are supposed to work through before they respond to an emergency or start surgery are too long and complicated or if they are filled with ambiguous terms, they become less effective because they are less likely to be implemented correctly or at all. Moreover, sometimes the best way to intervene in a complex setting is with simplicity. Some management strategies recognize this: a simple but powerful principle—support the decisions of your flight attendants (Southwest) or eschew periodic sales in favor of everyday low pricing (Walmart)—can outperform efforts to control and fine-tune responses to a complex environment. As management experts Donald Sull of the London Business School and Kathleen Eisenhardt of Stanford's School of Engineering show in their work on simple rules for a complex world, picking a small (but very carefully chosen) set of objectives can lead to better overall results than trying to manage every detail.[8]

The hope that regulated businesses can figure out better ways to achieve regulatory objectives is of course the idea behind two of the three standard regulatory approaches we already see in governments now: performance- or principles-based regulation and management-based regulation. And clearly regulated businesses have an incentive to find better, less-costly ways to implement regulation. There are two additional benefits, however, that come from getting this incentive through the use of private regulators rather than relying on the regulated business itself, both of which come from the fact that private regulators operate within a market. First, private regulators who can sell their system to multiple companies in a market have an incentive to invest in innovation at a higher rate than an individual company does. They can spread the cost of innovation across larger scale. Second, private regulators operating in a market may have better incentives to ensure that the system they design achieves compliance with regulatory objectives than the regulated business itself. The reason is that the private regulator, if properly regulated itself by government, will have an interest in maintaining its reputation for compliance. Failures of compliance won't just bring the risk of fines; they will bring the risk of losing status as an approved regulator. We could expect that regulated businesses would have an interest in choosing only those private regulators that are expected to reliably achieve compliance and maintain their status as an approved regulator: regulated businesses will incur costs if they have to switch regulators, costs they would like to avoid. For the private regulator, that means the risk of going out of business.

Of course we're assuming here that the superregulator—the government—puts its teeth into actually regulating private regulators and does so without bias or corruption. Private regulators have to fear losing their approval status if this market is to work. An assumption like this may seem ambitious, which it is. (The failure to effectively regulate private contractors such as those operating prisons in the United States is a case in point.) But this is the same expectation we have now of how government regulates under any model—an expectation that is, and would continue to be, only as good as our systems of political accountability. Superregulation doesn't solve that problem—although it may shrink it by making it easier to understand and see what the government is failing to do. It is pretty demanding to expect voters to be well informed and active in evaluating how well the government's occupational safety and health agency is choosing thousands if not millions of specific workplace standards, like what kinds of seatbelts need to be used in the luggage trucks airport workers use to load and unload airplanes. It may be less demanding to expect voters to be well informed and active in evaluating how well the agency is policing the obligation on a private regulator to meet targets for workplace injury.

There's another important benefit that comes from creating a market for private regulators. It's the core benefit of specialization and the division of labor. Regulated businesses are not primarily in the business of regulation. They are in the business of manufacturing cars and chemicals, operating restaurants and mines, transporting packages and people, selling securities and soap. Under performance- or management-based regulation, these businesses also have to figure out how to design systems to achieve regulatory objectives. This requires these businesses to be somewhat vertically integrated when it comes to regulation services. But as we've seen, the increased complexity of the modern economy has made vertical integration more and more costly. Creating a market for private regulators would allow businesses to do with regulation services what they are doing throughout their value chain—coordinating across a global network rather than producing everything in-house.

We can already see evidence of the incentive for businesses to find ways to get out of the business of designing their own compliance systems. Over the past decade or so, the market for compliance services has grown substantially. These services consist of various combinations of systems design consulting and data- and transaction- tracking software. Banks that are obligated by law to avoid participation in money-laundering schemes, for example, have a demand for software and services that help them to identify and report suspicious transactions. US companies doing business in foreign countries have a demand for software and services that help them to detect whether their employees are violating the Foreign Corrupt Practices Act, which makes it a violation of US law to bribe a foreign official. These compliance services operate within the framework established by government regulations. And one of the key services they offer is expertise in the regulations, both where they are and where they may be going.

A competitive market for private regulators would take compliance services to the next level: drawing on a combination of technological and regulatory expertise not only to design systems and software, including blockchain technology, to manage compliance but also to develop the criteria for judging compliance. These criteria might take the same form as government regulations—detailed written rules. But, perhaps more likely, they could also be embedded directly in the software and systems these private regulators develop to achieve their own regulatory goal of maintaining their status as an approved regulator.

Regulating private regulators would almost certainly be a new and substantial challenge for governments. Private regulators will, if the market works well, gain substantial expertise in their fields, potentially outstripping the expertise available in government bureaucracies, making oversight difficult. But there are two reasons to think that this challenge is nonetheless one worth taking on.

First, our current regulatory approaches already face this challenge. Banking and financial services regulators, for example, are already faced with trying to understand the complex systems developed by thousands of individual banks and financial services firms. The difficulties they face in doing so, because of the gap in expertise, were undoubtedly a factor in the failures of regulation to ward off the global financial crisis of 2008. At a minimum, a shift to overseeing private regulators reduces the number of entities that need to be overseen.

Second, a focus on regulating private regulators shifts the regulatory expertise burden from unpacking the complex details of how a business operates—the ins and outs of financial transactions, for example—to evaluating outcome criteria. Regulation of private regulators can, for example, rely on audits and indicators to evaluate systemic achievements and failures within a private regulator's client base. That allows government regulators to take a broader view that requires less knowledge of the details. It also exploits the benefits of a larger database: private regulators can be evaluated on the basis of the results achieved across a set of regulated businesses, rather than the results achieved in a single business. Regulating private regulators is a different task for government than direct regulation of business but it is not necessarily a more complex or expensive one. Indeed, there are good reasons to think that in several settings it will place lower demands—in terms of expertise and money—on governments.

The deeper challenge may lie in identifying those cases in which a market for private regulation can be structured so as to be reasonably competitive. Although this is a hard problem, it is a completely familiar one. For any good or service that we want, we need to determine whether markets can operate reasonably competitively or whether we need the state to step in. Economists are weaned on this problem, one of analyzing the risk of market failures and the relative performance of markets and governments in light of those failures.

A first question is whether the market can support enough private regulators to ensure there is competition between them. This is largely a matter of the scale of the market—how many users of the service there will be—relative to the fixed costs of providing services—that is, costs that are the same regardless of how many users there are. The fixed costs of providing regulation services will likely be substantial. The design of systems to achieve the outcomes that our political process seeks—lower workplace injury rates, greater financial stability, fewer data breaches—will require significant upfront and ongoing investment in understanding the complex relationships between those outcomes, the way businesses operate, and the opportunities for effective regulation and change. Indeed, inducing those system-design investments in a complex setting is precisely why we are interested in finding ways to get private market-based providers into the act. These relatively high fixed costs will need to be spread across enough users, relative to how much each is willing and able to pay, to make the business of a private regulator sufficiently profitable that people want to get into the business. (This is true even for private regulators that organize as nonprofit companies: short of substantial and ongoing philanthropic contributions, they still need to be able to cover the costs of providing their services.) Unlike standard markets, where buying a good or service is completely voluntary, approved private regulators would be able to count on the fact that regulated businesses are required by the government to buy regulation services from one of them. But still the total number of users would have to be high enough that these users can be shared across multiple private regulators, with enough for a given regulator to cover its fixed costs. That doesn't mean a guarantee of enough users to cover fixed costs: the point of competition is that a private regulator that fails to produce an attractive cost-effective service while still meeting the standards necessary to maintain status as an approved regulator will not stay in business for long. It's the risk of not generating a return on that investment that secures the incentive for developing better, lower-cost, more effective regulatory systems. That's the incentive we want to harness to address the problems of overly costly, overly complex regulatory regimes. But if private regulators succeed in that, there have to be enough users to go around. That means we can't look to this regulatory approach for overly narrow or specialized areas that are relevant to only a few regulated businesses.

In some markets, the relationship between fixed costs, scale, and competition can, perversely, undermine competition. This happens when there are great returns to getting bigger and bigger. The modern information economy sees a lot of this, in the form of network externalities and increasing returns to scale. These are the effects that make everyone want to use a widely installed operating system, a widely subscribed social network, and a widely used website for restaurant reviews. They are what gave us free broadcast TV and now Facebook. They are why Jeff Bezos started Amazon selling books online—and why he named his business after the biggest river in the world. In all of these cases, the more people who are using the system, the more valuable it is to be a member of (or an advertiser on or an app developer for or a retailer distributing through) the system. Bigger is better. But if bigger is better, then there will be powerful forces driving the number of providers in a market down to just a few, or maybe even one. That undermines competition.

There might be powerful drivers toward a small number of megaproviders in private regulation. Almost without a doubt, a system that gets more users will become smarter faster and hence have an accumulating edge over competitors that lag behind. Regulated businesses may also discover that they prefer to be on the same system as their own competitors, partners, and collaborators to reduce the costs of compliance. To the extent that private regulation systems require complementary services—such as software or consulting—that are supplied by third parties, those services may be more widely available and lower cost for a widely adopted regulatory system than they are for a new entrant that is still working to gain market share. All of these effects can make markets for private regulation less competitive.

But these are not new problems. Indeed, they are pervasive, as we've noted, in the modern economy. Network externalities and powerfully increasing returns to scale abound. Clearly, however, we don't want every good and service that is subject to these pressures produced with central planning by governments. The fact that Microsoft operating systems are installed on three-quarters of all desktop computers doesn't mean we want a government-produced—or government-designated—operating system for our computers. What we do want is regulation—antitrust law, for example—that tries to make sure Microsoft cannot exploit that market dominance and that new competitors can find every chance to get a foothold. We would need the same, where possible, for private regulators. It may not be possible in all cases—and in those cases we do need to turn to government. But that is the same question we face (and may not yet be answering very well) in many other markets. There's nothing special, in this sense, about regulatory services as compared to other economic goods and services.

Regulatory services will also be much like many other economic goods and services in that they may need some level of intellectual property protection. Indeed, the hope is that a market for regulatory services will induce innovation and substantial investments in knowledge about how regulation can be designed to work better. In some cases those types of investment require some form of protection in order to give innovators a chance to recoup their investment. As in other markets, protection might be secured formally by embedding the innovation in a patentable piece of software or business process or through copyright of written materials or by keeping new ideas secret, protected by confidentiality agreements and trade secret law. As in other markets, protection might be secured through business models that embed the benefits of innovation in services—smart consultants and arbitrators, for example—that are difficult to appropriate without purchasing the service. Again, these are challenges faced in many markets, and regulatory services are not all that different.

It will also be important to design the superregulation of private regulators to protect the capacity of regulated businesses to switch providers. Competition requires this kind of user mobility. This may require ensuring that private regulatory systems do not require users to bear all the costs of switching to a new provider. User data stored with one system, for example, may need to be easily transferable to another. Pricing models may have to be regulated so that systems do not rely too heavily on nonrefundable upfront fees and low maintenance fees. Other features of regulation might similarly make it difficult to switch. One challenge encountered by the regulatory system in the UK's new regime for legal services is that although lawyers can ostensibly choose their regulator from an approved list, they must make highly specialized investments in becoming a member of a particular regulatory regime. Switching professional membership—which means switching between approved regulators—is a very costly proposition. Avoiding lock-in to a particular regulatory regime will be important to support competition in fact between multiple private regulators.

Ultimately, relying on market-based private regulators will be only as effective and attractive as the quality of the government oversight of the system. If corporations are making the choice, for example, between alternative providers of regulatory systems for protecting the consumer's interest in safe products or the security of private financial information, they will be looking for a regulator that helps them maximize profits, not protect consumers. Consumers will be depending on the government to ensure that private regulators are only offering systems that serve the regulatory goal of protecting consumers—and so limiting the capacity of regulators to cater to business and not consumer interests. This is a very real threat. In the areas of consumer and employment arbitration, for example, companies offering arbitration services have an incentive to design systems that serve the interests of the corporation over consumers and employees. This is because the corporation chooses which company's system to put into the arbitration clauses of the standard-form contracts that consumers and employees sign—without much awareness of what they're signing and often without much alternative. Consumer and employee interests aren't well protected in this regime because the arbitration systems on offer are not regulated to ensure that they protect those interests. That's a flaw, and it's a flaw that any regime of market-based private regulation would have to be able to correct for this to be a reasonable alternative to our other methods of government-based regulation. Weak government oversight of private regulators—like weak government oversight of the operators of private prisons or highways—could quickly gobble up the potential benefits of harnessing market incentives to develop better, simpler, less costly, and more effective regulatory systems. But that is a challenge we should be taking up.

PART IV

Global Legal Innovation

II

Life in the BoP

THE CHALLENGES OF bringing the legal infrastructure of the advanced world into line with the demands of the globally networked economy are significant, as we've seen. But they are nothing compared to the challenges, and the urgency, of building legal infrastructure in what C. K. Prahalad and Stuart Hart, in an important 2002 paper, called the BoP—the bottom or base of the pyramid.[1] The BoP consists of the four billion people who survive on the equivalent in purchasing power of less than about US$8 a day. These are the same four billion people whom the UN Commission for the Legal Empowerment of the Poor described in 2008 as living outside of the rule of law—with little access to basic legal tools such as reliable rules of property, contract, and labor.[2]

The challenges we've explored for advanced economies in this book thus far and the challenges facing the BoP are deeply related. The transformation of advanced economies over the last few decades is in significant part a result of the fact that the poor countries of the world, where those four billion live, are beginning to participate in the global economy. Tom Friedman's original story of the flattening of the world begins with the fall of the Berlin Wall and the move of nearly 40 percent of the world's population—from the former Soviet states, China, and India—out from under central planning and into the global market economy. These are the people who exploded the box economy into the globally networked economy. These are the people whom advanced economies are trying to reach, both as suppliers and consumers, in global supply and distribution chains.

But even though the percentage of people living in extreme poverty—less than a dollar and a quarter a day—has been cut to less than half of what it was when the Berlin Wall fell, more than half of the global population still lives on incomes of less than the equivalent of $3,000 a year. Practically everyone in Bangladesh, for example, lives in the base of the pyramid at this standard. Indeed, almost three-quarters live on less than $1,000. Yet Bangladesh is second only to China in exports of clothing to the rest of the world and was identified in 2011 by McKinsey consultants as the next "hot spot" for global buyers of ready-made garments as wage rates rose and capacity limits were tested in China.[3] That was just before two major disasters in Bangladeshi garment factories—the 2012 Tazreen Fashions fire and the 2013 collapse of the Rana Plaza factory complex—together killed over twelve hundred workers and spurred international efforts to improve workplace safety in the country. Improving the well-being of Bangladeshi garment workers, not to mention helping the country to raise its population out of the base of the pyramid, depends critically on the quality of legal infrastructure. In a globalized world, this is not just a matter of domestic economic well-being. The legal infrastructure in the poorest places on the planet is also the legal platform on which our global economy balances.

It is widely understood that building law and legal institutions is a critical element of the goal of reducing poverty around the world, yet our existing approaches focus entirely on delivering legal infrastructure through legislatures, state courts, government officials, police, and lawyers. But impoverished, weak, or corruption-riddled governments—the types of governments that we find throughout poor and developing countries—are hardly in a position to deliver on all the complex structures needed to manage their participation in the globally networked economy. After all, we've seen that delivering the legal infrastructure needed to support the complexity of the modern global economy is a task that has begun to outstrip the capacity of even the stable, wealthy, and (largely) noncorrupt governments of advanced nations. Moreover, whereas the West enjoyed a somewhat blank slate on which to innovate new legal structures to manage increasing, and increasingly complex, trade in medieval Europe, today's developing world is attempting to build its legal infrastructure under the heavy weight of laws and procedures transplanted from advanced economies and the taken-for-granted role of the nation-state as the exclusive site for legal development. Nowhere is innovation in how we think about law more urgent than in the poor and developing countries that are home to over half of the people on the planet.

Four Billion Excluded from the Rule of Law

The idea of the rule of law gets thrown around a lot in talk about globalization and development. After billions of dollars in foreign aid have failed to make a significant dent in the problems of poor countries, almost everyone, left and right, agrees: what the poor need are better legal systems. Political economists Daron Acemoglu and James Robinson give the following answer to the question in the title of their book *Why Nations Fail*: "Institutions, institutions, institutions." What they mean by institutions is: law. New York University professor William Easterly, author of *The White Man's Burden: Why Capitalism Thrives in the West and Fails in the Rest*, advocates encouraging the adoption of common-law systems in beleaguered nations so that they can evolve legal solutions adapted to local settings. Jeffrey Sachs diagnosed the failures of growth in former Soviet States after 1990 as failures of law. Hernando de Soto in *The Mystery of Capital* places heavy emphasis on the need to develop stable property rights systems to allow the poor to leverage what little they have into loans to grow businesses. Paul Collier, author of *The Bottom Billion: Why the Poorest Countries Are Failing and What Can Be Done about It*, ultimately attributes the worst poverty to failures of governance. By governance he means basic legal rules and institutions that limit things like corruption, vote-buying, homicide, and attacks on independent speech and the press. Nobel laureate Joseph Stiglitz argues in his book *Making Globalization Work* that accomplishing that objective for the poor means developing effective global legal institutions and establishing the political conditions that generate demand for the rule of law. Abhijit Banerjee and Esther Duflo, MIT economists and authors of *Poor Economics: A Radical Rethinking of the Way to Fight Global Poverty*, criticizing the difficulty of extracting concrete policy prescriptions from the political economists who emphasize the importance of institutions, urge a focus on the ground-level rules of the road—law—for economic activity.

Global institutions dedicated to eradicating poverty and promoting global development have taken all these lessons to heart. The World Bank and the International Monetary Fund now make rule of law a central plank of the development agenda, and a central requirement of access to their funds. The Sustainable Development Goals established by the United Nations in 2015 added access to justice to the list—a goal overlooked in the UN's Millennium Development Goals in 2000. The World Trade Organization requires developing countries to reform their legal systems to achieve rule of law in order to participate. Cambodia, for example, was required as a condition of membership in the WTO to enact a new civil code, civil procedure code, criminal code, and criminal procedure code and create new commercial courts—in addition to adopting new laws regarding arbitration, intellectual property, customs, land rights, fisheries, highways, merchant shipping, commercial leasing, competition, securities trading. And more. China amended its constitution in 1999 to include a commitment to the rule of law, just prior to its gaining membership in the WTO in 2000; it has made rule of law a major focus of policy.

The first problem with all this talk about the rule of law is that it's a rubber band of a term—stretched around to mean lots of different things.[4] To some it means law and order and the absence of crime—even if crime is controlled by the threat of official violence from an authoritarian state. To others it means eliminating the use of government violence to terrorize citizens and political opponents. To some it means enforcement of the financial deals that foreign investors make with local governments—guarantees that foreign-owned investments won't be appropriated by those same governments. To others it means that the government won't let domestic companies get away with appropriating foreign intellectual property. To the World Bank the rule of law refers to a multitude of treasured ideals: Government itself is bound by the law. Every person in society is treated equally under the law. The human dignity of each individual is recognized and protected by law. Justice is accessible to all.

With such elasticity, rule of law can mean just about anything. As a practical matter it usually ends up meaning the constellation of laws and legal institutions found in advanced market democracies. Which brings us to the second problem with all the talk of rule of law in global development: everyone is talking not about law, but about governments. Rule of law almost always means, in these conversations, rules about how governments behave: what protections they offer their citizens, what limits they observe on their power. Rule-of-law development work then focuses on what laws the governments in poor and developing countries should pass, how their state courts should be designed and managed and made accessible. Almost all rule-of-law development work is done by lawyers and judges from advanced market democracies. Well-meaning souls from the bar associations and courts of countries like the United States, Canada, Germany, Japan, Sweden, the Netherlands, France, and the United Kingdom regularly travel to places like Cambodia and Kenya to hand these governments their civil and criminal codes and procedures as templates, together with their legislation on topics from A to Z. They run training sessions for judges to teach them how to use these imported laws and procedures. They work to secure money from global legal development funds to help poor governments equip state-run courts with up-to-date case management systems and computers.

But as long as the rule-of-law agenda is focused exclusively on shaping governments and state institutions in the countries where the four billion excluded from the rule of law live, it is bound to fail. Governments in poor countries are poor. That's why they need better legal infrastructure: so they can grow their economies. The legal infrastructure of the advanced nation-state is expensive and complex. It is paid for out of the extraordinary wealth that this legal platform helped Western nations achieve over the past two hundred years. How can it make sense to tell poor governments that in order to lift their populations out of poverty they need to implement legal systems that require great wealth to sustain?

This may be the greatest damage done by the taken-for-granted assumption that, by definition, what it means to have law is to have the set of legal institutions of the modern nation-state. The assumption leads us to prescribe to ailing countries a remedy they can't afford—and won't be able to afford until they are healthy. We should not expect that the governments in poor countries are capable, even with the subsidized technical assistance of foreign governments, of building and delivering all of the legal infrastructure their desperate citizens and failing economies require.

The problem of figuring out what the people living in poor countries really need from law is probably one of the most complex the world has ever seen. And yet we invest almost nothing in trying to solve this problem, assuming that all it takes is the paraphernalia of modern law: legislation, courts, judges, police, lawyers. But if the advanced modern state needs the iPhone of law to manage the complexities of the globally networked economy, the poor country attempting to participate in that economy needs the as-yet-uninvented personal jet pack and flying car that Silicon Valley entrepreneurs still only dream about. The poor and developing world needs innovative legal infrastructure even more than the affluent West.

Kukiya-kiya: *The Informal Economy*

When the UN Commission for the Legal Empowerment of the Poor issued its report in 2008 and made the startling claim that four billion people around the world are excluded from the rule of law, it wasn't talking about the grand goals of equality, dignity, and access to justice for all that the World Bank's definition includes—goals that are aspirational even in many advanced democracies. It was focusing on the more concrete on-the-ground legal rules and systems, ones taken for granted in well-established legal environments. In this more grounded sense, being excluded from the rule of law means not having a legal identity that allows you to enter into binding agreements to pay for supplies or labor on credit or to hold others responsible for shoddy goods or dangerous working conditions. It means not being able to prove that you own the building, be it ever so humble, where you live and work and so being unable to use that property as collateral for a loan. It means lacking official authorization to operate a business—a market stall, a small workshop—and so being at risk of getting shut down on the whim of a local politician or person more powerful than you. It means having no recourse when a private company or a member of the local elite grabs all or part of the land your family has harvested for decades. It means having no choice but to pay whatever a customs official asks when you cross the border with your goods. It means having no protection against having the cash you earned from selling your goods in the market in town stolen on the way back to your village, and no way to send the money you earn as a migrant laborer safely to your family back home. It means having nowhere to turn when those wages go unpaid, the promised job is given to someone else, or the factory collapses.

This world without the basic ground rules for managing economic life is what many call the informal economy—not to be confused with the illicit economy consisting of illegal activity such as trafficking in human beings, drugs, or counterfeit goods and currency. The informal economy is the world of the street vendor in India or Zambia or Bogotá selling fruit, shoes, T-shirts, tools, spare auto parts, shampoo, or mobile phones. It is the world of the home-based worker in Mexico or Pakistan or Morocco, paid by the piece for weaving rugs, repairing televisions, assembling electronics, rolling cigarettes, packaging pharmaceuticals, doing laundry, styling hair. It is the world of the migrant worker, the day laborer, and the casual domestic worker in Egypt or Malaysia or Bolivia. It is the world of the cross-border trader in Zimbabwe who travels into Mozambique, South Africa, and Botswana to sell crocheted doilies, reed baskets, and baked goods and brings back appliances, utensils, flour, and shoes—and the cross-border courier who transports the trader and her goods, navigating the checkpoints and border officials. It is the world of the small unlicensed and unregulated sweatshop in the Philippines or Bangladesh or Ghana, painting toys, sewing garments, or recycling electronic waste. And sometimes it is the world of the large factory in China, Vietnam, or Brazil, assembling cell phones and computers, producing sports shoes and handbags, under contract with the global companies that deliver goods to consumers in advanced economies.

The people of Zimbabwe have a word for this: *kukiya-kiya*. The *kukiya-kiya* economy is the economy in which you do whatever you have to do to get by.[5]

What defines an economy as "informal"? To most researchers, policy-makers, and development experts, being outside the rule of law means being untouched by the formal legal framework provided by the nation-state. This can mean many things. A worker might be deemed to be outside a formal legal framework because there is no formal legal structure available to that person. In much of the poor and developing world, for example, many people lack legal identity—their birth was never registered and they have no fixed address—and so they cannot enforce their rights or participate in government programs or policy. But a worker might also be deemed to be in the informal economy because formal legal rules, requiring employers to provide safe working conditions or governments to provide public services, for example, are unenforced. Or unenforceable—because there are no functioning courts or lawyers or legal information. Or because the price of access to these legal institutions is far beyond what most can afford. Or because those who are supposed to enforce rights, grant permits, or distribute benefits have to be bribed to do their jobs.

Given the multiple ways in which work can fall outside of a formal legal framework, the methods of counting those working in the informal economy vary. Official statistics such as those collected by governments for the UN's International Labour Organization focus on identifying people who are self-employed—working alone on their own account—or who serve as employers, employees, or unpaid family workers in small unregistered businesses, as well as casual or day laborers, domestic workers, unregistered or undeclared part-time workers, and some homeworkers who provide goods and services to formally registered companies. Often these counts are based only on urban populations. Others emphasize the importance of including rural agricultural workers, since most if not all agricultural work in poor and developing countries is done on an informal basis. When agricultural work is included, the proportion of the working population employed in the informal economy is estimated to exceed, sometimes swamp, the formal economy across much of the globe: 99 percent in Tanzania, 92 percent in India, 86 percent in Pakistan, 83 percent in Bolivia, Vietnam, and Zimbabwe, 80 percent in the Philippines and Liberia, 65 percent in Egypt and Thailand, 57 percent in China, 51 percent in Brazil.[6]

The informal economy is *the* economy for the billions living in the great base of the global economic pyramid.

There are debates about what to do about the informal economy. When the idea of the informal economy first entered the lexicon in the mid-1970s, many economists expected that the building of factories by multinational corporations to produce cheaper goods for the rest of the world would pull poor countries along a natural path toward industrialization and development. As countries industrialized, it was expected, the informal economy of street vendors, day laborers, and homeworkers weaving in their shacks would gradually give way to the formal economy described in economics textbooks, where firms pay workers regular wages to produce goods and services for sale to consumers and other firms. The textbook economy is an economy organized by a stable government that can set taxes; regulate firms to promote safe workplaces and products, competitive pricing, and environmentally responsible practices; and provide public goods like education, highways, and police protection. In this view, there was nothing to be done about the informal economy because it was a natural stage in the process of growth. After all, the advanced countries of the West had all gone through this stage on the path to achieving the enormous gains of wealth and stability that followed industrialization.

But over the past few decades, it has become clear that the informal economy is not withering away. It is growing. The worldwide economic shift from the nation-based box economy to the globally networked economy, and the absorption of billions of people from centrally planned economies into global markets, has fueled this growth. Instead of pulling people inside the box of the textbook firm, the transformation of the global economy is pushing them out into complex contractual networks. Whether this is seen as good or bad depends on one's politics and predictions. Seen from an optimistic angle, the transportation- and technology-fueled capacity for flexible and extensive global supply chains means that many more people can participate and share in the production of economic wealth. In this optimistic vision, the people who are self-employed or operating microenterprises in Africa or Latin America or Asia are entrepreneurs who can build their businesses with access to microfinance, the internet, and global distribution networks. A shift of the lens shows a bleaker picture: like most people in the developed world, most poor people would greatly prefer a stable job, where the risks of ups and downs in prices, politics, and markets are born by a large, diversified employer instead of by them and their families. These people are not "entrepreneurs." They are people trapped in an economy where they have to do whatever they can—*kukiya-kiya*—in order to scrape together the few dollars a day on which they subsist. They are the last link in the value chain, with no bargaining power and no choice but to take what they can get for their efforts—any price, any risk, any humiliation. If they won't do it, there are millions of others, some half a world away, who will. Their connection to the value chain can be severed with the click of a mouse.

But although there is heated debate about whether the informal economy is the seedbed for entrepreneurial growth or simply the new normal for the world's vulnerable poor, there seems to be widespread agreement about what needs to be done about the informal economy. The four billion excluded from the rule of law, it is thought, need to be brought within the formal legal framework of the nation-state. The optimists who see entrepreneurs in the informal economy want to give those entrepreneurs access to formal property and contract rights created and enforced by the state. The critics who see exploited workers in the informal economy want to give those workers access to government-enforced legal rights: to minimum wages, safe workplaces, healthcare, pension benefits, freedom from violence and degradation.

Both views recognize that the legal ordering of economic relationships in the informal economy is a critical step on the path to real economic development. But they both also make the shared mistake of assuming that this means coaxing, cajoling, and threatening the governments of these poor countries into enacting formal laws and building formal legal institutions. There certainly are things that the governments in poor countries can and should do to help build the legal infrastructure their citizens need. And advanced nations should demand that the governments in poor countries observe limits on their power to use violence against their people and punish those governments that use their position to extract massive bribes and divert aid from the needy and into their pockets. But the failure to think innovatively about how legal infrastructure can be built for the mundane operation of ground-level economic activity in these enormously complex settings—the exclusive focus on governments as the source of all legal infrastructure—is making this problem worse, not better.

Law, Law Everywhere, and No Legal Order in Sight

It's not that there are no formal legal rules and systems in poor and developing countries. Indeed, there are often so many rules and systems that no one could possibly comply with them all. Hernando de Soto, the Peruvian economist who was among the first to shine a light on the problem of the exclusion of the poor from the basic legal tools needed to climb up the income ladder, has shown this in dramatic form. A few decades ago, he and his research team tried to legally register a small business in Lima, Peru. It took them 289 days, working six hours each day, to complete all the required procedures. They tried to build a house legally in the Philippines and estimated it would have taken thirteen to twenty-five *years* to complete the 168 steps required by some fifty-three government offices. In Egypt, they were looking at seventy-seven procedures required by thirty-one government agencies and five to fourteen years to buy and legally register a lot on state-owned desert land.

De Soto's argument, in a widely read and much-debated book published in 2000 called *The Mystery of Capital*, was that billions of poor people effectively had no choice but to operate in the informal economy. The absurd demands of legally registering a business or land or building project make the price of access to the formal system simply too high. With simpler systems for registering property or businesses, he argued, poor people would gladly come into the formal sphere—paying taxes in exchange for the formal right to resist arbitrary shutdown of their business by the government or granting creditors the security interest they need to lend the poor the money they need to build their businesses.

De Soto's message was taken up with gusto in the World Bank. In 2004, the Bank launched the Doing Business project, which began annual surveys of lawyers and experts in the major city in (now) 189 countries to determine the formal government requirements to complete basic steps in the life cycle of a business—starting the business, dealing with construction permits, enforcing a basic contract, and so on. The resulting rankings—Singapore, New Zealand, Denmark, Korea, and Hong Kong making up the top five for 2015; Eritrea, Libya, South Sudan, Venezuela, and Central African Republic making up the bottom—have been used over the past decade to spur poorly performing governments to improve their ranking by streamlining procedures. And indeed, over the past decade, the worst-performing countries have steadily decreased the number of steps and days required to satisfy the formal requirements for doing business. The World Bank now estimates that it takes twenty-six days and six steps to register a business in Lima, Peru, for example, a tenth of the time de Soto and his colleagues estimated in the 1980s.

The Doing Business project has no shortage of critics. The rankings only give the formal answer obtained from local lawyers, not the real experience of businesses in practice; the measures have only recently begun to evaluate some aspects of the quality of regulations; and there is no robust empirical evidence that shows that reducing formal steps causes significant gains in country wealth. But few take on what I think is the major conundrum of improving the legal infrastructure in poor countries. The regulations Doing Business is looking at are those created by governments; the advice Doing Business is giving (and the changes the World Bank and other lenders are requiring) is for governments to change their regulations and procedures. But this ignores the fact that complexity in regulation is caused by, among other things, poverty. How did poor countries end up at the bottom of the list, with absurd formal requirements, in the first place? Haiti, holding the eighth-to-last spot on the list, is one of the poorest places on the planet, with average income in 2014 of less than $1,750 per capita. But registering a business in Haiti requires twelve formal procedures estimated to take ninety-seven days to complete, at a cost of almost two-and-a-half times the annual per capita income—over $4,000. How did that happen?

The answer is that, as many a writer (and reader!) of a college essay or business report can attest, it is harder to be succinct than to be loquacious. It is harder to produce a coherent and consistent process than it is to produce a jumble of steps and requirements. Simple, intelligent, and yet effective regulation is an expensive undertaking. Identifying and resolving conflicts in sets of overlapping rules that evolve over time and are produced by different agencies and ground-level officials demands high-level and often complex analysis. Governments that are reactive and poor—not to mention often in upheaval (the bottom of the Doing Business rank could also be a list of countries drowning in war, violence, and revolt—Libya, Afghanistan, South Sudan)— can with relative ease issue decrees, pass laws, amend laws, repeal laws, grant exceptions, change procedures, create agencies, and abolish offices. They have no resources—financial, intellectual, or political—to do the much harder work of systematic reviews, evaluations, and design to promote coherence, consistency, simplicity, and efficiency in their legal frameworks.

Making matters worse is the effort of the global community to overcome the lack of lawmaking resources in poor countries. When well-intentioned countries and international organizations—like the World Bank—send armies of lawyers and judges and administrative experts to poor countries, they arrive with sophisticated law codes and regulatory procedures in hand. This is how Cambodia (127 on the Doing Business ranking, with a per capita income of about $3,000) ends up with a modified version of Japan's civil code (itself originally based on the sophisticated German civil code), Australia's property law, and Canada's commercial court system. As we've already seen, these are complex modern bodies of law that grow only more complex over time—and are expensive to operate. Add to their complex foreign origins the fact that once the foreign legal consultants go home, the complex codes they left behind are subject to misunderstanding, amendment, indifference, obsolescence, and inevitable conflicts with later-made law, and you have the makings of an incoherent and expensive mess. Not the rule of law.

It should be small wonder that poor countries are riddled with formal legal rules, complex statutes, executive orders, and regulatory policies. It's as if you took a fleet of BMWs with all the latest technology—rear-view cameras, self-driving capabilities, GPS navigation systems—and plopped them down in a land with muddy, rutted roads, only a few gas stations that are usually out of gas, a handful of mechanics with the expertise to repair complex computer-based systems, and no spare parts. Don't be surprised to come back in a few years and find most of the cars abandoned, used to store fertilizer, or unrecognizably rebuilt with parts scavenged from thirty-year old tractors, lawn mowers, and city buses. And most people still walking or riding on a donkey.

"No One at the Border Is Honorable"

The cost of complex and incoherent collections of rules, regulations, procedures, and policies is not just that they are not very helpful for people trying to work their way up out of the BoP. Complex and incoherent collections of rules also exacerbate one of the biggest challenges to rule of law in poor countries: corruption.

Corruption is a big, bad word, but the practice is pretty mundane and it's related to ordinary and acceptable behavior known the world over. Slipping the maître d' a twenty for a better table or giving a handsome tip to the baggage handler at the curbside check-in to take extra care to get your bags on the plane—it's a natural thing to do. You're offering people something to use their discretion in your favor. And it becomes a natural thing for people who have this discretion to expect a little something. The problem arises when the natural thing undermines the integrity of rules. It's one thing to realize that the announced rule for getting the table you want at your favorite restaurant—make a free reservation on the phone or online—is not really the way it works. It's another to realize that the published fees for registering a business, securing required permits, or getting electricity connected are not really the prices you'll pay. That you can't get a court clerk to put your case on the calendar to hear your case, much less persuade the judge to decide in your favor, unless you offer a bigger bribe than the other side. That the formal rules saying that you have a right to continue farming the land your family has farmed for generations mean nothing if a local official is enticed by an important foreign company to look the other way when the company engages in a land grab.

Corruption is the bane of rule-of-law development efforts because it snips the stitches that knit together formal rules and actual behavior—enough snipping and the fabric of a formal legal framework eventually unravels. Advanced nations experience public corruption as well—both grand and petty. The United States, for example, is home to state governors who attempt to sell their right to appoint people to Congress to the highest bidder and politicians who take gifts and campaign contributions in exchange for influencing the outcome of regulatory processes.[7] The United States is also home to police officers in some rural areas who seize money and cars from ordinary people without proving that the money or cars are the proceeds of crime, and city prosecutors who collaborate with local judges to extract fines and fees from poor, often minority, people who have the misfortune to be unable to pay a traffic ticket on demand.[8] Or judges and city attorneys who ignore the constitutional obligations of due process to rig a municipal court system that makes court appearances essential for resolving municipal code and traffic violations—like failing to use a turn signal or letting your four-year-old pee in the bushes—and then makes it next to impossible for people to figure out when their court dates are. Which is how Ferguson, Missouri, in 2014 ended up with sixteen thousand outstanding arrest warrants for a population, two-thirds black, of twenty-one thousand people.[9] What sets poor countries apart is not the fact of corruption. It is the extent of corruption—extending into routine interactions with officials for large shares of the population countrywide. The fabric of the formal legal framework doesn't just have holes in it; it has unraveled to such an extent that it is no longer recognizable.

The problem of widespread corruption is not just that there is a bribe to pay in addition to the published fee at the office that issues the construction permits you need. If everyone knows the amount of the bribe and to whom it is to be paid, how, and when; if permit officials accept the bribe, paid in the same way and the same amount from everyone who is entitled to obtain a permit; if permit officials can't change the bribe amount overnight on a whim—then the bribe is just another tax. Mathematically, the following are the same thing. A: the government sets a tax at $50 while paying the official who collects the tax $20 in wages. And B: the government sets the tax at $40, pays the official $10 in wages, and the official collects a $10 "bribe" from the permit seeker. In both cases the government collects $30, the official earns $20, and the permit seeker pays $50. The total tax may be too high—or too low (it has to be high enough to net the official an acceptable wage and government the funds needed for public services)—but businesses and entrepreneurs can make their plans with some confidence about how much a project is going to cost them. And governments can have some confidence that their tax policies are translating through to business decisions—when the government cuts taxes to promote trade, businesses pay lower fees in fact.

But endemic corruption doesn't work this way. It's hidden, unpredictable, and uneven. A friend of mine who grew up in India as a member of an ethnic minority tells of an unexpected consequence when his father (who had been a local government official) passed away. The father had always negotiated the regulatory apparatus—and his status in the government had made most negotiations go relatively smoothly. Once he was gone, the remaining family members had no idea how to get things done since now, absent the father and his status, they were expected to pay bribes—and they didn't know the basics of how much to pay, when to pay, whom to pay, and so on. What distinguishes a formal tax from an informal bribe is that you can call the office and ask whoever answers the phone how much the tax is. It's probably not advisable, or much use, to use the same technique to find out who and how much to bribe.

When corruption is widespread, nobody knows what the real rules are.

The complexity of the formal rules that poor governments inevitably produce—made worse by demands from advanced countries and international organizations for the enactment of sophisticated legal codes and procedures borrowed from wealthy governments—can make the problem of corruption in poor countries even worse. The more complex the formal law, the more entry points there are for the dynamics of bribery to sneak in.

A postdoctoral researcher from Zimbabwe whom I met at a conference at Harvard Law School in 2013, Pamhidzai Bamu, taught me a lot about what ordinary and endemic corruption looks like at the base of the pyramid in a low-income country. Bamu, who specializes in labor law and the informal economy and its regulation in Africa, had done a study of cross-border trade in the informal economy in Zimbabwe.[10] She first described the complex set of laws and regulations governing cross-border trade. There is the Control of Goods Act, which authorizes the president to issue regulations to control the manufacturing, pricing, distribution, sale, export, or import of goods. These regulations can include an obligation for traders to give officials access to premises, books, or other documents. One of these regulations requires anyone importing or exporting agricultural products to obtain permits from the Ministry of Agriculture. Another regulation requires exporters of wooden goods to present proof to border officials on both sides of the Zimbabwean border that the goods have been fumigated. Under the Exchange Control Act, the president has issued regulations requiring commercial exporters to complete a customs declaration, indicating when funds from export will be repatriated to Zimbabwe. The form is not required if the value of goods is below a minimum threshold, which the minister of finance can adjust from time to time. Ordinary travelers bringing goods into the country must pay duty (55 percent for audiovisual equipment, 40 percent for anything else) for goods valued above US$300 and may not bring more than six of any particular item. Duty is based on the weight of goods. Commercial importers have to submit several forms—a bill-of-entry form, suppliers' invoices, an income tax form, consignment notes, freight statements, cargo manifests, and any required permits. They must also be registered for tax purposes and have a business partner number activated for customs purposes. Rates of duty for commercial importers are determined by the Harmonized Tariff System, which is published as a manual that is 2,025 pages long. And then there are the regional trade agreements, among southern African countries and between southern and eastern African countries, which exempt some goods from duty, provided the trader can produce certificates of origin. One of the regional agreements includes simplified procedures that relieve a trader of the obligation to produce certificates of origin if the trader is instead able to produce the list of those common goods agreed upon by member countries. The exemption applies only up to a specified value of goods.

Got all that? Most Zimbabwean traders didn't either. When Bamu interviewed them, they knew some key things. They knew ordinary travelers were allowed to bring back goods up to $300 a month and that they had to have permits to import or export agricultural products or wood. But some (incorrectly) thought they could only bring back four of any one item. They knew the flat tariff rates charged on goods in excess of $300, but were unsure if the higher rate of 55 percent applied to all electronic goods or just audiovisual goods. They knew the duty for goods they took into neighboring countries such as South Africa, Zambia, and Botswana was calculated on the basis of weight. But they didn't know the formulas used for computing duty. Almost none knew of the requirements for commercial traders to register with the tax authorities or to have a business partner number for customs. Almost none of them knew about the exemptions from duty available for some goods as a result of regional trade agreements.

Here's what they all knew: it is pretty impossible to comply with all the requirements. None of them were eligible for the ordinary traveler rules for imports because they weren't bringing goods in for personal use. This obligated them to follow the rules for commercial traders. But they traveled on public buses and minivans, which border officials, under standardized protocols intended to reduce border delays, are required to clear on a vehicle-by-vehicle basis using the procedures for ordinary travelers. So the traders rarely if ever followed commercial procedures. They just tried to get around the ordinary traveler rules—asking suppliers to falsify invoices and receipts, not declaring all their goods, switching goods with other traders to satisfy the "no more than six of one item" rule—I'll take four of the ten pairs of socks you're bringing back if you'll carry six of the dozen kitchen utensils I've got.

And of course the border officials surely know all of this. (Bamu didn't interview them.) So there is a natural economy of paying officials off to clear customs. All they have to do is identify some potential violation—some threat of enforcing a rule, real or made up—and they have a basis for extracting payment. Given how many rules there are, how complicated and therefore poorly understood they are, and how hard it is to comply with all of them, that threat is omnipresent and credible. In fact, the cross-border couriers, who drive the buses and minivans transporting traders in and out of Zimbabwe, are known for their contacts at the border and their ability to manage the bribe payments needed to ensure a load of passengers are quickly processed with little inspection and little duty charged. Some buses collect $5 from all the passengers and pay off the border official before inspection; others just build it into the bus fare. Some couriers offer to take the goods across the border themselves, meeting the traders on the other side, and using their contacts and repeat interactions with the officials they pay off to lower duty payments still further. As one *malayisha*—as the couriers are called—told Bamu: "To speak of *malayisha* is to speak of someone who has connections at the border. He is someone who knows the [border] officials and the police. No one at the border is honorable."

Buses keep to their schedules. Border officials avoid pressure from their bosses (who are in turn no doubt pressured by politicians) to cut border delays. Couriers and traders hang onto enough money, maybe, to ring up a few dollars a day in earnings. The government collects a small fraction of the duties and taxes set out in its formal regime—and has even less money in its budget to pay the border officials. Follow the rules? What rules?

The standard response, worldwide, to the corrosive power of corruption is: more law. The Zimbabwean government, realizing how much money was leaking out of taxes owed by informal traders at the border, responded in 2010 by introducing a postclearance audit system. The system placed officials from the tax authority at several places along major roads leading away from the border and authorized them to stop and search buses and minivans to determine if the proper procedures had been followed and duties paid at the border. But of course these officials have the same incentives, and operate within the same murky world of what is right and what is expected, as the border officials. So they too can collect bribes in exchange for looking the other way. The police get in on the action as well, setting up their own, sometimes unauthorized, roadblocks—threatening to confiscate goods or impose fines for violations of a set of formal rules that almost no one really understands or can verify. The consequence of the effort to squelch corruption at the border may be to increase the amount paid out in bribes and force informal traders to give up and find some other way to survive in the *kukiyakiya* economy. As one *malayisha* told Bamu, "*Isilayisha* [cross-border courier services] used to take care of our families. Now, it's like gambling. Sometimes you are lucky, but most days you go home with nothing." The net effect for the government: even smaller amounts collected under its formal rules. And that means even less government revenue available to pay the border officials, tax collectors, and police a decent-enough wage to make keeping their jobs more valuable than taking advantage of the bribe opportunities that a complex system presents.

Beefing up enforcement and enacting more laws might work to fight corruption in well-established and stable legal systems—where almost everyone is operating within the formal legal framework. It might work to curb corruption at the highest levels—where top government officials in poor countries get multi-million-dollar payoffs from companies and individuals who live within the stable legal infrastructure of advanced wealthy countries. That's the aim of laws like the Foreign Corrupt Practices Act in the United States, which makes it illegal for US companies and individuals to make payments to foreign officials to secure business. But enacting more laws in Zimbabwe can't do much to repair the economic fabric of daily life when, as is the case throughout most of the poor and developing world, 80 percent or more of the population is excluded from that framework. Endemic corruption is not a disease that formal legal frameworks catch. Endemic corruption is just another way of saying: the formal legal framework is missing in action. More law requiring more resources for enforcement can't solve the problem of law that doesn't work and is too expensive to enforce. You can't stop yourself from being dragged under the waves by rocks in your pocket out at sea by asking someone to throw you more rocks.

The goal of building politically accountable, stable, and competent governments is one that poor countries and the international community should keep center stage. But it is critical that the project of developing legal infra-structure to support economic development in these countries pivot, and soon, from the idea that the way to build legal infrastructure is to rely exclu-sively on poor governments to write and enforce all the rules that the four billion excluded from the rule of law need. It is critical that the agenda for legal reform expand, quickly, to explore innovative ways of delivering stable legal order. That means adding nongovernmental and market-based solutions to the mix.

The proposal shouldn't be shocking. As we've seen, it's the same path the advanced West took. And the developing world today faces a far more com-plex challenge that the West did when it was poor.

12

Building Law for the BoP

ENGLAND IN 1300 was as poor as Sierra Leone is today. The Netherlands and Italy—the wealthiest places on earth at the beginning of the sixteenth century—were as poor then as Zimbabwe, Kenya, and Uganda are now. The California gold miners in 1848 (assuming some average between the GDP per capita in the United States and Mexico) were also probably as poor as the people living in Zimbabwe, Kenya, and Uganda today.[1]

When the West was poor, the economy was simple, and legal infrastructure was simple too. It was also, as we've seen in earlier chapters, built up through a diverse set of institutions and groups. Much was built before the presence of an all-encompassing state with a monopoly over making and enforcing rules. Guilds, churches, religious communities, popes, towns, monarchs, wealthy nobles, and ad hoc groups developed rules and enforced them largely through social sanction and exclusion of rule-breakers. People who wanted to be governed by a different set of rules could sometimes just set up their own set of rules—even if that required moving to a new camp or community. Or continent. That's what the Vikings who settled medieval Iceland and the colonists who set sail for America did. That was easier when every corner of the globe was not already divvied up between nation-states.

What lessons might we take from the development of legal infrastructure when the West was poor for today's poor countries? Not that we should revert to the world of the Wild West and terra incognita, where breakaway groups can set up camp and thumb their noses at established governments. Foreign entrepreneurs may dream of setting up shop on a converted ocean liner in international waters twelve miles off the coast of Silicon Valley to avoid US immigration laws, or take over an abandoned antiaircraft platform in the North Sea and declare themselves sovereign (both ideas have been floated, so to speak), but we don't have to get as outlandish as that.[2] The essence of legal innovation before all-encompassing nation-state governments was not the escaping of government; it was the coexistence of multiple sources of rules, some as narrowly targeted as the ones governing "those men of Ypres and Douai who go to England"—the Flemish cloth merchants who wrote a set of rules and enforced them through boycott and expulsion of transgressors in the thirteenth century. It was the potential for competition among different rule systems that generated new ideas about how to deal with the problems of organizing economic life as it grew more complex and differentiated. What the poor world needs today is some space for entrepreneurship in the fundamental building blocks of legal infrastructure.

Catch-22 and Surprising Lessons from Ancient Athens

One of the biggest obstacles to the development of adequate legal infrastructure to support economic growth in poor countries is the idea that the poor governments in those countries have to produce and enforce it all themselves. That's a catch-22 because adequate legal infrastructure for an exponentially complex global network economy is costly and demanding. In fact, as we've seen, it's even too costly and demanding for wealthy, stable, and advanced market democracies to build entirely on their own anymore. So expecting poor governments to construct and supervise the entire legal infrastructure they need to integrate into the global economy is like telling them their countries can grow wealthy, just as soon as they get wealthy.

Nor is it any good to tell governments in poor countries just to copy the laws and legal institutions of the affluent West. That's painfully naive about what building effective legal infrastructure is all about. Some of those laws and institutions can be useful. But as an exclusive approach, it's doomed to fail. We've tried it, lots and lots, and it has failed.

And then there's the problem of weak governments. If the rule of law means rules enforced exclusively by state officials, then we know that corruption will chew away at the rules until they are meaningless. The platform of legal infrastructure will be so riddled with holes and missing planks that smart, wary citizens will stay away, building nothing there. You can't patch the holes in the platform with more law because, well, the materials for that patch are as rotten as the planks you're trying to fix.

It's at this point that many in the development world have started to say uncle. Or, rather, they have started to say "culture." We need rule of law in poor countries, they say, but until the people there develop rule-of-law culture—until they respect and want the rule of law, and so resist paying and taking those bribes and evading those regulations—there's nothing we, the international community, can do to help.[3] Other than to keep lecturing them about the need to be more like us and respect the law.

That's not only insulting (although some bribery is born of craven greed, the endemic variety is born of poverty and desperation), it's wrong. And it's not how the now stable legal infrastructure of the West was built. Modern Europeans and Anglo-Americans didn't build legal infrastructure on an innate respect for the rule of law. They built better institutions, from the ground up, using the same tools, and facing many of the same challenges, that the BoP faces today. Rule-of-law culture—the widespread confidence that most people most of the time treat official legal rules as relevant and binding even without a credible threat of penalty—emerged because some smart steps were taken to build institutions to cultivate that confidence in early European societies.

Together with my coauthors, Stanford political scientist Barry Weingast and University of Indiana political scientist and classicist Federica Carugati, I recently looked at how ancient Athens built legal order.[4] We'll admit straight out that figuring out what legal life was like in ancient Athens—some four or five hundred years BCE—is a tricky business. Our records of the ancient legal world consist of caches of written contracts, some preserved legal speeches from famous Greek orators, a few legally minded plays written down by famous Greek playwrights, some laws carved into stone, and some archaeological rubble. These records provide bits and pieces of evidence, evidence that we can only interpret. But our interpretation of the evidence has led us to see in ancient Athens important new strategies to help crack the modern puzzle of how to build legal order in places where now there is little.

What we see in ancient Athens is this. Like most societies built up over the thousands of years that spanned the time between the end of nomadic hunter-gatherer life through the invention of agriculture and the emergence of large-scale cities and the birth of civilization (mostly in the part of the world that we now call the Middle East and southern Europe), ancient Athens was originally a city ruled by oligarchs and despots. There were some written laws—but they were written by elites and could be changed on a whim. There were judges—but they could be bought. Mostly there was violence—elites battling elites for power over a population that could do little more than try to survive.

And then came the invention of institutions the world had never seen before. Popular assemblies, where ordinary citizens met to decide on written laws. Popular courts, where ordinary citizens sat with hundreds and some-times thousands of their fellow citizens as jurors to decide cases. There were no professional judges—just other citizens who served in yearlong volunteer stints as magistrates, responsible for scheduling trials. There were no lawyers—plaintiffs and defendants had to find the laws and argue their cases on their own (although they could hire some pretty fine speechwriters—which is how we know some of what they said.) There were no police, sheriffs, or bailiffs—if you as plaintiff wanted the defendant or witnesses to show up at the trial, you had to go get them. And, most importantly, there were no officials who carried out the punishments ordered by the jurors when they found someone guilty as charged—usually a monetary penalty. If you won your case, it was up to you to find friends and fellow citizens to help you get what you were owed. If the loser didn't pay up voluntarily, you had to go back to the court to ask the jurors to authorize you to use force. Probably most people paid up.

This system worked remarkably well. At least, the Athenians appear to have loved their courts, using them all the time. By the time this system was in full swing in the fourth century BCE, the Athenians were litigating between two thousand and eight thousand cases a year. That suggests regular legal involvement for a population of 250,000, only 30,000 of whom were citizens allowed to participate in Athenian courts and institutions. The courts were mostly located in the agora—the central marketplace—public and open for all to see and viewed as a form of entertainment.

The best evidence the courts worked well is that, with these exceptional institutions, ancient Athens was exceptionally prosperous in the ancient world. Ian Morris, a historian and archaeologist at Stanford University, has argued from the archeological record that the Greek city-states of the fifth and fourth centuries BCE enjoyed a level of economic growth that rivaled Holland of the sixteenth century—the richest place in late medieval and early modern Europe. Unlike the rest of the ancient world, large portions of the Greek population could spend their time doing something other than producing just enough food to live on. About half of the citizen population worked outside of agriculture, producing goods and services for trade. As many as three-quarters of Greek citizen families could afford to buy a house, and over the two centuries of what Stanford classicist and political scientist Josiah Ober in his book *The Rise and Fall of Classical Greece* calls Greek efflorescence, the median size of a home grew over 350 percent. Moreover, although Greek city-states like Athens were in no sense fully egalitarian (women, slaves, and non-native males lacked citizen status), wealth was remarkably evenly distributed for a premodern society. Inequality between citizens in Athens around 320 BCE was roughly comparable to inequality in the United States in the 1950s.

Ober argues that the remarkable economic success of the Greek city-states, and especially Athens, was a consequence of their broadly democratic political system, which implemented fair rules of trade, treatment, distribution, and competition. These rules encouraged individual Greek citizens to innovate and invest and were especially highly developed in classical Athens. We agree that the rules made a difference. But we emphasize that it wasn't just that Greek city-states like Athens had fair rules on paper (more accurately, on clay and stone). What produced the kind of widespread confidence that rules of procedure and governance would be followed, bills and wages paid, property respected, and profits shared was the fact that Athenian legal institutions were remarkably well designed to build the confidence and support of ordinary citizens.

To appreciate what the Athenians accomplished, it helps to think about a hypothetical ancient Athenian looking for a little justice. Carugati, Weingast, and I posit the story (based on a real case from around 330 BCE) of Nomios, a citizen who has purchased a slave from a foreigner living in Athens. Much to Nomios's chagrin, he discovers only after the sale is completed that the slave owes a significant debt. In the fine print of the contract (yes, there really was such stuff, even back then) it says that the slave's owner is responsible for paying any debts contracted by the slave. Nomios wants his money back, and he wants to make his foreign neighbor pay the debt. How can he do that?

Imagine first that Nomios is living in the world of Athens before the invention of open democratic institutions—the world of despotism, elite rivalry, and corrupt magistrates. In that world, Nomios has to rely on family, friends, and favors to get his money from the foreigner. He can try asking a magistrate to adjudicate his case, but the magistrate might be paid off by the foreigner or his elite cronies to look the other way. He can try to take the foreigner's property himself, but for that he might need a group of friends willing to risk being beaten up by the foreigner and his friends. Indeed, if Nomios and his friends try to take what Nomios thinks he is owed, they might all find themselves in court accused of theft and facing severe and unpredictable punishment from a corrupt magistrate. If the foreigner or his friends are powerful enough, Nomios may not feel safe making a fuss about the hidden debt.

Of course, maybe Nomios is the one with the better friends and connections—after all, he is a citizen and the foreigner is, well, a foreigner. Maybe Nomios can take what he wants, with impunity. In fact, maybe he can do this even if there is no legitimate contract dispute between them—he just wants the foreigner's stuff. Of course if that's the Athens Nomios and the foreigner are living in, one in which the foreigner has little defense against being robbed and beaten by the locals, then there's a good chance the foreigner doesn't bother coming to town to do business with Nomios or anyone else in the first place.

Now imagine Nomios is living in the Athens of popular assemblies, courts, and a well-ordered, citizen-run system for resolving disputes. Nomios can find the written laws in the public archives that say it is illegal to lie to a buyer in the marketplace. He can find a magistrate, a fellow citizen serving a volunteer one-year tour of duty in the job, who will schedule the case to be heard some day not too far in the future when the jury—some four hundred ordinary citizens—is assembled. Nomios has to notify the foreigner himself, and perhaps will need help from some friends getting the foreigner to show up on the day of the trial. Then Nomios and the foreigner will each have to get up and argue their case. They can get witnesses to testify, who are obligated to appear—but both Nomios and his opponent may have to again call on their friends to help get the witnesses to show up. The jurors listen to the speeches and evidence, and then, without any discussion allowed among them, vote secretly by dropping one of two disks they were given at the start of the trial into a bronze urn. (The other is dropped into a wooden urn, so nobody can tell how anyone else has voted.) The votes are counted and the result announced.

Suppose Nomios wins and the law says that the foreigner owes Nomios quite a lot of drachmas as damages for his deceit. Now what? To get his money, Nomios can try asking nicely. And that might work. But suppose the foreigner refuses to pay. Nomios in response to this refusal could do what he could have done all along—just get some friends and try to take what he wants. But in the orderly world of Athenian law he's not likely to do this—he's already shown he's willing to follow the rules instead of using brute force in the first place. So he goes back to the court, and brings a second suit, saying that the foreigner has refused to pay up. Now he gets the verdict he needs: the judgment that he is entitled to use force to collect the damages he was awarded in the first lawsuit. He and his friends can return to the foreigner with right on their side to take what Nomios is owed.

Here's the question to ask yourself. Suppose you are Nomios's friend. Do you help him collect the money the court says he is owed?

Remember that there is no sheriff to come collect on Nomios's behalf. And Nomios probably needs some help to physically take on the foreigner. So if you don't help out, Nomios is probably out of luck. All of those court procedures, all the time Nomios spent preparing for the trial, arguing his case, trying to collect peacefully, going back for authorization to use force— all of that will have been a just a lot of hoopla if at the end of it all Nomios can't count on his fellow citizens to help him collect his damages.

As Nomios's compatriot, the question of whether to help him out is ultimately a matter of, what's in it for you? After all, even if you are a good friend, there is risk to you: you might get injured, the foreigner and his friends might retaliate, powerful people might take the foreigner's side and refuse to do business with you in the future, you might be accused of theft or assault and hauled into court yourself. Suppose that the fear of these outcomes is in fact what kept you sitting on your hands in the old Athens—the one without democratic institutions and courts—and left Nomios without recourse for the wrong done him in the marketplace. What's different now? Well, now there is this popular court. Hundreds of your fellow citizens sitting as jurors, and perhaps many more spectators enjoying the show, have heard and seen the case and its outcome. And they all know that everyone else knows (that everyone else knows etc.) that they heard and saw the case and its outcome. There is common knowledge that if you go to help Nomios, you are acting consistently with the jury verdict. There is common knowledge that the foreigner and any citizens who want to help him resist enforcement are acting at odds with the jury verdict. If nothing else, once these institutions are in place, and you see that hundreds of people are showing up to judge a case and following all the procedures for doing so, you are likely to predict that helping Nomios is less risky to you than it was in the bad old days.

Your willingness to help Nomios enforce the verdict might even extend to the case in which Nomios in the past was your sworn enemy. First, there is the argument eloquently made by Demosthenes, one of the greatest of the Athenian orators. In his own case, Demosthenes urged the citizens in the jury to see the connection between what they, personally, did as participants in the legal process and the benefits they, personally, enjoyed from peaceful legal order based on procedures and rules known and available to all. "What is the power of the laws?" he asked them. "Is it that, if any of you is attacked and gives a shout they'll come running to your aid?" Of course not, because "they are just inscribed letters and have no ability to do that." The only thing that makes the law effective is "you, the jury," for "the laws are powerful through you and you through the laws." To make the laws powerful, you as a juror, as a citizen, must "secure them and make them authoritative whenever anyone asks for aid." If Nomios needs your help collecting compensation for what those mere scribbles on stone say is a wrong against him in the marketplace, then you should look to those scribbles—"make them authoritative"—in deciding how you respond. Even if Nomios is a stranger to you; even if he is aligned with your enemies; even if you would rather not get involved. For if you decide not to act when the law says Nomios is entitled, then the laws are powerless. And poor Athens is back to the bad old days of despotism, elites, and violence.

The jurors' oath said it all. A juror solemnly and publicly promised his fellow citizens to decide "in accordance with the laws and decrees of the Athenian people" and not on the basis of "enmity or favor." Relying on enmity (acting against your enemies) and favor (helping out your friends) without regard to law—that was the way of the past. The Athens without legal order in which laws were really nothing much more than something someone more powerful than you wrote down at some point.

So here's what's in it for you if you help Nomios: you let your fellow citizens know, and see, that you are on board with these new institutions—not (only) by jawboning at the local watering hole about the verdict, but by stepping up if needed to help carry out it out. And, even if the individual impact is small, you have done your part to help maintain the stability of a system that makes your own life more orderly, less risky, and more productive.

It is this close attention to creating a system that encouraged ordinary individuals to help enforce the laws that suggests important lessons for poor countries today struggling to shift from a world organized on the basis of "enmity and favor," elite power struggles, and corrupt officials, to one operated as, in the definition from Harvard law professor Lon Fuller that we saw in Chapter 1, "an enterprise of subjecting human conduct to the governance of rules." What are those lessons?

The Participation of Ordinary People

As we've seen, our advanced Western legal systems had their roots, too, in regimes that depended on the participation of ordinary people in helping to enforce the laws. Official enforcers—professional police, public prosecutors, full-time judges, and specialist lawyers: these become routine only after the consolidation of the nation-state. Most advice to poor countries today on building rule of law, however, assumes that these countries should go directly to this state of public and official enforcement, exclusively. They pay little attention to the role of ordinary citizens. Much less do they strive to make ordinary people the backbone of the enforcement system. But what the Athenian case suggests is that involving ordinary people—in creating rules, in managing adjudication, in declaring what counts as a violation, in enforcing the penalties for rule violation, in watching all this as a shared public spectacle—may be critical for building an institution that is solidly rooted in day-to-day exchanges and relationships. Those development experts who argue that poor countries can't get rule of law until they develop rule-of-law culture aren't wrong—it's just that you can't build rule-of-law culture by lecturing the populace or encouraging them to all of a sudden start trusting a bunch of elite officials who have a long history of exploiting them. What Athens teaches us is that rule-of-law culture can be built by regular, widespread, and authoritative participation of ordinary people in the day-to-day operation of legal institutions. That's more than periodic attendance at village meetings or sporadic jury service.

Common Knowledge of the Rules

The genius of Athenian democracy was its almost fanatical attention to achieving common knowledge. Josiah Ober, the Stanford classics and political science professor, paints a compelling case for the importance of common knowledge in ancient Athens in his book *Democracy and Knowledge: Innovation and Learning in Classical Athens*. Building in part on an argument advanced by University of California at Los Angeles political scientist Michael Chwe, Ober demonstrates the extensive way in which Athenian life was organized so that just about everyone knew what just about everyone else knew.[5] The Athenians were huge fans of public festivals and ceremonies, with events happening as many as 170 days a year. They conducted public business and events in massive inward-facing circles, where most people could see what everyone else saw and know that they saw it—a setting not found in ancient architecture before or after democratic Athens. They cultivated what sociologist Mark Granovetter in 1973 famously called "the strength of weak ties."[6] They did this by allocating participation in public offices using a device that ensured random selection of citizens equally across ten artificially created tribes composed of populations in noncontiguous and diverse parts of the Athenian territory. They thereby created a social network that ensured that (everyone knew that) everyone was likely to know someone who was there when an argument was made or a decision taken. To this they added the important ingredient of simplicity in rules and procedures—again ensuring that all could be reasonably confident that rules and procedures were known to all.

Together these deliberate elements of Athenian democratic design helped to create a governance environment that was both highly dispersed, with almost no persistent role for elites or permanent officials, and highly transparent. Ordinary people knew—and knew that almost everyone else knew—what the rules were, who had faithfully executed their official duties, who had been accused of what violation, how the crowd had reacted to this prosecution or that public proposal. Common knowledge prevailed. That's not achieved when rules are made in some far-off city, known only to the elite.

Universal Benefits

Playing one's part in the hugely dispersed Athenian system—serving in office and on juries, attending public festivals, helping to enforce the rules—clearly must have required substantial time and effort. These are two things that are often in heavy demand in a society that lives above, but not far above, subsistence. Why not just stay home and tend the crops?

Although over time various formal incentives to participate did emerge (small payments to jurors, public honors for those serving well in office, fines and dishonor for those failing in their duties) perhaps the most important spur to participation for ordinary Athenian citizens was the universality of the Athenian rules. All citizens—rich or poor, urban or rural, sophisticated or not—played an equal role in decisions about what the rules should be and how they should be enforced. Repeat players and professionals simply did not have special status—what influence they wielded had to be indirect. Such palpably distributed power over rule-making and enforcement helped ensure that ordinary citizens could look at the rules defining the Athenian platform and conclude that their own interests were taken into account—at least, far more assuredly than under the alternative, which was a return to elite domination of politics. Athenians who helped support the system could have some confidence that when their ox was getting gored, they too would be able to count on the courts and their fellow citizens to behave according to the rules. That's the essence of reliable infrastructure.

It is important to emphasize that what I'm calling universality was of a highly qualified and limited form. It didn't apply to everyone, just the adult males native to Athens who were designated as citizens. I think, as most people now do, that it's awful that the Athenian system excluded women from citizenship and treated some human beings as objects of property to be traded, exploited, and killed at will by other human beings. No modern country should take this as license to oppress in the name of creating law. But it is the qualified nature of Athenian universality that tells us that universality emerged for *practical*, not moral reasons. The Athenians didn't design their system for abstract ethical reasons. They weren't trying to satisfy anyone's definition of human rights. They did it to secure the stability of what the people who overthrew the tyrants—the native male citizens of the broadly defined Athenian territory—wanted to create: a system that was responsive to them and not run by tyrants. They extended universality to those who were in a position to help enforce the rules—those who had the resources, freedom, and physical ability necessary to seize, punish, or exclude those who violated the rules. These potential enforcers needed encouragement to play their part. Women and slaves had little choice in the matter.

The fact that the adult male citizens native to Athens didn't need to look beyond their own kind to sustain their system doesn't mean that they couldn't have done so had the moral case appealed to them. And had Athenian women and the enslaved been important to carrying out enforcement of the rules, the Athenian men would have had to include them. Like it or not. In poor countries today, looking to be a part of the global community, excluding whole segments of the population from the benefits of law is simply unacceptable. Enslaving people and subjugating them to the tyranny of others is unacceptable. Moreover, it is unwise. Many of the development efforts of the past decades have discovered, for example, that women play a critical role in the economic life of poor and developing countries. The microfinance movement, which I discuss later in this chapter, has focused almost entirely on channeling money to women's business efforts because of this. So failing to ensure that women benefit from new rules is not just wrong; it's stupid. If women don't support new rules, they're bound to fail. On the other hand, focusing *only* on benefits to women is also wrongheaded. Men in poor and developing countries who do not yet share the equality goals of the advanced world also need a reason to support the success of a new legal order if the global conditions of equality are ever to change.

Continuity with Preexisting Norms

To many classical scholars, the law courts of ancient Athens did not look very lawlike. Not only did they lack formal legal personnel—professional judges, lawyers, police—the nature of legal argument seemed highly undisciplined. Although hauling someone before a court required alleging violation of a written law, once in front of the jurors and spectators, the litigants could bring up whatever arguments they liked. In our hypothetical, Nomios could attack the foreigner who sold him a slave with an undisclosed debt by trying to stir up the jurors' antipathy toward foreigners and accusing the stranger in their midst of being a pathological liar. The foreigner in return could accuse Nomios of having been a former prostitute who treats his parents badly, drinks too much, and fails to contribute his share to public festivals. Although modern lawyers may work hard to get such irrelevant arguments before a jury, an eagle-eyed opposing attorney and alert judge will squelch the effort. The evidence and argument is supposed to be strictly tied to the law allegedly violated.

To modern legal minds, such a free-for-all is the antithesis of the orderly rule of law. But my colleagues Weingast and Carugati and I think that the Athenians were on to something in their willingness to let litigants argue the kitchen sink. We think that the openness of the Athenian courts reassured citizens that the rules they cared about—long-standing norms about families, virtue, honor, public obligation, and so on—were not displaced by the written laws that otherwise governed access to the courts. This reassurance furthered the goal of encouraging voluntary participation in the Athenian legal institutions—and voluntary compliance with its judgments.

The lesson here brings to the fore a major mistake, easily made, in the effort to build legal infrastructure in environments still organized by long-standing traditional norms and informal social order. The great value of legal infrastructure for poor countries lies in the capacity to *change* old rules that stand in the way of economic development. But the *capacity* to change the rules depends first on the establishment of an institution that, as a matter of common knowledge among all the necessary participants, reliably implements the rules it announces. So the thinking has to go like this: let me see how well this newfangled, sounds-great-on-paper thing works out first with the rules we already have. I'm a skeptic—show me it works, because in my experience it's all promises and no delivery. Then maybe—after I've seen enough evidence that most people are playing along—we can talk change.

This may be one of the most important reasons the Athenians enjoyed the success they did. They were patient. They built the institutions first and then reaped the benefits of their investment only when the new institutions were secure enough to be taken for granted. Only then did they enjoy the real value of legal infrastructure: the capacity to change the rules.

Of course the modern world is a dangerous place, even more lethal than was the old Athens of tyrants and rival elites. Today the thugs have automatic weapons, car bombs, and viral videos of beheadings. The idea of involving ordinary people in the routine enforcement of legal judgments no doubt stirs fears of mob violence. And this is certainly a grave consideration in any modern effort to follow the Athenian model. But it is critical to recognize that we're not talking about building an extensive, all-encompassing, citizen-run legal regime on day 1. Especially in the context of unpredictable violence, the best place to start—as just about any Silicon Valley entrepreneur looking to build a platform will tell you—is small. Here that means with things the elites and thugs don't care much about. Legal order can be built up in parts of daily life—the enforcement of simple contracts, for example, or the management of property boundaries in a neighborhood. Make that the beta version. Put to work the lessons of experimentation and iteration that are now powering the growth of companies like Intuit running hundreds of experiments with TurboTax each tax season to figure out what works and what doesn't. And maybe the practice can build the confidence of ordinary poor people in a set of novel institutions that can shift their world from chaos to productive order.

Maxing Out on Microfinance

An ideal place to start thinking about what might be possible if we applied the lessons of ancient Athens to the poor and developing world is in the realm of microfinance—an industry worth $80 billion globally as of 2012. One type of microfinance is microcredit, which is already well established in many poor countries as a system that relies on enforcement of simple contracts—the promise to repay a small loan—by ordinary people. Think about the model 2006 Nobel Peace Prize winner Muhammad Yunus and his Grameen Bank established, for example.[7] Groups of five women self-organize as a borrowing group, often spurred on by a Grameen officer who has identified an enterprising and persuasive woman in a village to serve as a chairwoman. Groups are organized into clusters, with six to ten groups in what is called a Center. All of the members of the group undergo training in the way Grameen handles loans and the principles of Grameen. ("Discipline. Unity. Hard work. Courage.") The members of a group must be of similar age and socioeconomic and educational background. Together they must pass an oral examination before the group can be certified by the bank as eligible for loans. Groups must be approved by the members of the Center in their area before joining. The process starts small. Loans to two women in the group are made first, often of a standardized amount. The borrowers have to have their loan and their plans for how they will use the money first approved by their group, then unanimously by the members of their Center, and then by the bank. All groups belonging to a Center meet weekly in a dedicated Center house, built and maintained by the Center members. Repayment of the loans in small installments, conducted in front of all members of the Center, begins almost immediately. The first two borrowers in the group have to meet their payments for several weeks before the others in the group can take out their first loans. Later, the maximum loan amounts available to a member of the group depend not only on her history of repayments and meeting attendance but also on the repayment status of all the other members of the group and the center. There is no collateral. The borrowers sign no legal documents. And yet Grameen claims a repayment rate of about 98 percent and the bank is a profit-making organization, with no reliance on donor funds. How does it work?

The secret to the system lies with the groups: the small five-person borrowing groups and the larger groups they constitute as members of a Center. Even when microcredit lenders drop a formal linkage between one member's payments and the other members' loan eligibility, researchers still find that repayment rates are highest when the lenders retain the group organization and meetings. Group members help to enforce repayment by bringing pressure to bear on each other to do what is necessary to keep up with their payments (including using the loans only for the income-generating purposes for which they were approved). The pressure they use consists of the ordinary social sanctions that govern everyday life everywhere: gossip, criticism, moral suasion, reputation, ostracism.

Individual women who help out with these social sanctions do so because they have an interest in maintaining a good reputation for supporting the Grameen way. Doing so is a way of demonstrating that they support the family-improvement goals of the "Sixteen Decisions" that Grameen calls a cornerstone of their program and which they learn about in training. These sixteen decisions include promises to uphold the four principles of the Grameen Bank and to do things like repair their houses, use pit toilets, grow vegetables, drink only clean water, undertake bigger investments to increase income, help each other, and help to enforce discipline if it breaks down in any Center. Helping to achieve discipline in meeting attendance, loan utilization, and repayments increases their own access to loans, both formally and informally. Formally, Grameen's criteria for increasing loan ceilings for an individual are dependent on the repayment status of the groups and Center to which a borrower belongs, and access to housing loans is dependent on a Center's repayment record and implementation of the Sixteen Decisions. Informally, demonstrating support for enforcing Grameen rules increases a woman's access to loans through the willingness of others who belong to their Center to participate with her in a borrowing group, approve her loans and business proposals, or help her out with repayments or restructuring of the loan in hard times. The idea of collective responsibility is repeatedly invoked, in weekly affirmation of the verbal contract each Grameen member undertakes, along the lines of this one suggested in guidelines for credit programs seeking to replicate the Grameen model: *We pledge to attend regularly the weekly Center meetings, to utilize our loans for the purposes approved, to save and pay our installments weekly, to use our increased incomes for the benefit of our families, to ensure that other members of our group and Center do likewise, and to take collective responsibility if they do not.*

As Muhammad Yunus recounts in his book *Banker to the Poor*, Grameen's system was developed as a workaround for a dysfunctional state legal system, one with too many documents and requirements for poor people and courts that are either inaccessible or corrupt. It secures its stability with small scale and high degrees of standardization in loan and repayment amounts. It also requires a large investment of time on the part of borrowers and the bank in getting to know and keeping tabs on group members: meetings are every week at the same time and every group member must attend. A group's chairwoman and the Center chief (elected from among chairwomen) are required to check that a borrower has invested her funds for the approved purpose within a week of receiving her loan. Several Center members are required to visit together the home of anyone who has missed a payment.

Economists Abhijit Banerjee and Esther Duflo and other researchers have shown that access to microcredit has helped borrowers start microbusinesses and make more purchases of durable goods like bicycles and refrigerators.[8] That's a plus. But these same researchers have also shown that microcredit has by no means solved the problem of poverty. There is no evidence of a substantial impact on economic growth or standards of living. Few people take up the opportunity for microcredit, and few grow their businesses much beyond adding a few goats or a new sewing machine. Banerjee and Duflo, in *Poor Economics*, argue that this may be because of the rigidity of the microcredit model and a basic economic fact: microenterprises are inevitably low-income prospects. What is needed to lift the poor is not for everyone to grow tiny businesses to be a little less tiny, but for some of them to grow sustainable businesses capable of paying decent wages to others. As they remind us, the vast majority of people in wealthy economies are employees, not entrepreneurs—and that's probably what the global poor want and need also. To grow larger businesses, however, the microcredit rules need to be more flexible and scalable to larger loans.

The challenge, then, is to take the basic model of socially enforced loan agreements that do not depend on a dysfunctional state system and increase flexibility and scale. How can we do that? The key is to see in the group-based lending that is at the heart of Grameen and most other microcredit systems a microcosm of ancient Athens: ordinary individuals with a shared interest in enforcing a set of rules. The rules need to be simple and familiar—not a huge leap from existing norms. They need to generate benefits for all those who play an important role in enforcement. And, most importantly, the rules, the way they are applied in practice, and everyone's continued willingness to enforce them using the procedures and methods of a novel institution need to be matters of common knowledge. The Grameen system achieves common knowledge with standardized loans and repayments and weekly meetings where payments are made in view of all group members. To expand this system and make it capable of greater flexibility in loans and larger scale requires finding more scalable ways of generating common interest and common knowledge among a set of borrowers.

Grameen achieves common knowledge and shared incentives to enforce its rules by building at the village level, where communication is personal and attendance at weekly meetings is physical. That's effective but costly: interest rates for Grameen loans are on the order of 20 percent annually—not so that the Bank can earn fantastic profits, but because each loan is such a costly administrative proposition. The "interest" Grameen is earning is paying off costs, not generating high profits. Grameen also explicitly limits its microcredit program to the poorest of the poor, those with no land or assets, excluding those who have achieved any significant growth into microenterprise. They do this, they say, because they have found that the nonpoor tend to drive the poor away from the program and that discipline—following all the Grameen rules and ultimately repayment—breaks down if the slightly better off participate. The poor need to follow the Grameen rules because there is nowhere else to turn for their $100 loans. The microenterprise seeking larger loans has other options, and so is less interested, Grameen has come to believe, in helping to enforce the rules. Grameen has also chosen to target women participants, having found that men are less motivated to support the Grameen system and more likely to default.

These are significant constraints on what microcredit could ever accomplish. So is it possible to break out of the costly physical constraints? Build groups with more diverse borrowers or composed of members who are growing larger businesses and with more options than the abject poor? Is there something, other than conventional bank loans, to which women, and men, who succeed in building their businesses, can graduate?

Now, I'm an outsider to the on-the-ground realities of microcredit and the lifeworlds of the poor. My goal is to identify experiments we should be running, not to try to predict how a sortie will fare on the dancing land-scape. Grameen's multidecade experiment and conclusion that only weekly in-person meetings consisting only of women who are just a step above desti-tute may be all there is here to see. But if we see in Grameen's experience the fundamental elements that the Athenians implemented successfully, across wide domains of daily life, across a large and diverse population, there are clues as to how microcredit might evolve. Or at least to the experiments we should be running.

The challenge is to build virtual networks of more diverse borrowers. Could such virtual groups have shared reputations for repayment and the capacity to monitor group members' repayments without attending a meet-ing in person? Could a shared interest in helping to enforce repayment be rooted in a base broader than shared poverty and life experiences?

There are two reasons to think that the answer is yes. First is the success with which virtual communities are now built over web-based social net-works in the advanced world. It is now commonplace for social relationships to be made or sustained electronically—using email or text or video-chats or on web-based platforms such as Facebook or Twitter. We interact over websites and mobile apps to find romantic partners, job connections, fel-low gamers, teachers, likeminded activists, and more. We share experiences with restaurants, doctors, moving companies, and online retailers to build web-based reputations for sellers and providers. With the development of cheap and available high-quality video, we have the capacity for a face-to-face with anyone, at any time, anywhere there is internet access. People still get on planes, still need to confirm some relationships in person, still can't tell everything about someone from the bits that fly over fiber optic cable. But there's no question that real relationships can take place in a virtual space. Particularly if they are limited to just a few characteristics such as speed of delivery or reliability in game play or educational expertise.

The second reason to think that virtual microcredit networks are a possi-bility for poor countries is the fact that the electronic tools we associate with the advanced world are already on their way to becoming widely available in poor countries. Kenya and Honduras and the Philippines are not pass-ing through the full sequence of communications technology experienced by the West in the twentieth century—telegraph poles, phone lines, broad-cast television, fax machines—on their way to modern technology. They are going straight into the twenty-first century. Mobile phones, for example, are already ubiquitous in many poor countries. According to research from the Pew Research Center, in 2013, 95 percent of the people in China and

Jordan owned a mobile phone. It was 85–90 percent in Chile, South Africa, Malaysia, Egypt, Tunisia, Turkey, Lebanon, Venezuela, and Argentina. It was around 80 percent in Kenya, Bolivia, Senegal, Brazil, El Salvador, Ghana, Nigeria, and Indonesia, 60–70 percent in the Philippines, Mexico, and Uganda, 53 percent in Pakistan.[9] Granted, many of these phones are not (yet) the smartphones advanced Westerners carry in their pockets and purses. The highest penetration of smartphone technology in the above countries occurs in Lebanon, China, and Jordan, at around 40–45 percent, and access to the internet via smartphone or otherwise ranges between 25 percent and 65 percent across the countries listed above. (Pakistan and Uganda are outliers with about 10 percent access to the internet.) Moreover, many poor users have to buy phone time minute by minute from kiosks in their local villages. Still, even under these constraints, innovative companies and non-profits are building out phone-based systems using text and voice messaging for banking, shopping, healthcare, education, and other services. Around two-thirds of Kenyans, for example, were already using phone-based systems to make or receive payments by 2013. This phenomenal achievement is thanks to the aggressive development of phone-based banking system m-Pesa (*pesa* is Swahili for money), launched in 2006 by Kenyan-based Safaricom—40 percent owned by the British communications giant Vodafone. Similar phone-based banking systems are rapidly developing in other poor countries.

Access to the web technology that supports virtual communities is also accomplished using innovative ways of sharing computer connections. Indian conglomerate ITC has established what it calls e-Choupal networks among Indian farmers.[10] (*Choupal* means village meeting-place in Hindi.) ITC identifies a well-respected and literate farmer in a village and installs an internet-access kiosk in his home. This farmer's home then serves as a hub for farmers in the region to access information about crop prices and trading volumes. Today, there are over sixty-five hundred kiosks across India, reaching about forty thousand villages and four million farmers.

Once connected to the internet, people in poor countries are just as likely to use it to connect in virtual communities as anyone else on the planet. Many farmers in the e-Choupal network use their access broadly—not only getting information about prices and weather that helps them with their decisions about crops but also accessing entertainment, news, sports, and email. Throughout the developing world, over three-quarters of those with some kind of internet access say that they use it for social networking.

Clearly, then, it is technologically feasible to extend the borrowing groups at the heart of the Grameen model of microcredit into virtual networks.

Indeed, there are already models of how these networks might be constituted. M-pesa, for example, was originally developed as a pilot project to facilitate microcredit payments for a Kenyan microfinance institution, Faulu Kenya.[11] Although the pilot demonstrated the appetite for phone-based payment systems, it failed as a microcredit tool because Faulu Kenya dispensed entirely with group meetings. Those meetings, however, are critical to the Grameen model's success in generating the common knowledge necessary to support group enforcement of repayments. Other microfinance institutions, recognizing this, have adopted mobile payments but retained the weekly meetings. Instead of showing up to pay in cash, group members pay ahead of time on their phones, and payment status is verified collectively at the meeting. This recovers the common-knowledge component, but only by significantly reducing the gains available from technology—the capacity to reduce the costs and rigidity of the microcredit system. Clearly the next frontier for experimentation is common-knowledge electronic notification of payment status for group members and figuring out how to facilitate social sanctioning within the group in way that reduces the need for a rigid in-person meeting schedule.

This last step, facilitating social sanctioning in a more diffuse network, is critical to expanding the potential scale and diversity of borrowing groups. The leverage group members currently have over each other is a combination of social face-to-face pressure and the threat of being excluded from access to future loans. The latter is a more scalable tool—but it depends on the future value of access to group membership. Given the low take-up rate for microcredit (in one cross-country review of studies, Bannerjee and co-authors Dean Karlan, and Jonathan Zinman find take-up rates of less than 30 percent of the target population),[12] there's some risk that, especially for an expanded group, the marginal borrower may not place a large weight on the ability to borrow again in the future. That marginal borrower might thus not be much deterred from reneging on payments, and not much encouraged to expend effort pressuring others to pay up, by the threat of getting booted out of the group or having loans capped at a relatively low level.

A solution to this problem is suggested by the story of ancient Athens. Recall that a key attribute of the stability of that citizen-based enforcement system was universality—the idea that everyone who played a role in sanctioning those who violated the laws benefited personally from the system. That suggests that expanding the activity of the group to include other benefits that members care about accessing could help the group enforce its rules. Some microfinance institutions, for example, are accepting villagers' deposits for savings purposes as well as making loans. If the ability to make deposits with a particular system is valuable to a wider range of people, then including depositors who have real-life local interactions with borrowers could expand enforcement—remember the ingenious network of loose ties that the Athenians created by combining people with strong ties in local communities into larger, more diffuse (and artificial) "tribes." Depositors could be given incentives to help enforce the rules for borrowing by making access to the deposit system contingent on the repayment status of the group as a whole, and making repayments a matter of common knowledge to all.

The model for group-based savings mixed with credit is already evident throughout poor countries.[13] Under the enormous pressure of poverty to spend any income as soon as you have it in hand, there is high demand for a means of disciplining both your own immediate spending needs and urges and those of your family in order to achieve longer-term goals like buying a bicycle or building a better home or sending your kid to school. In response to this demand, people in poor countries the world over create small savings clubs. These clubs are known as *tontines* in francophone Africa, *esusu* in West Africa, *tanda* in Mexico, *hui* in China, *bishi* in India, *gameya* in Egypt. Development experts call these ROSCAs: rotating savings and credit associations. Although the specifics can vary, all follow a basic pattern. Members of these clubs contribute either a fixed amount or what they can to a common pot on a regular basis, such as weekly. Members of the group then take turns as the recipient of the pot. The money is used to finance further progress on the new room someone is building in the place where they live and work, a new tire for the bicycle they use for deliveries, fertilizer for their crops, repairs to the small refrigerator that keeps the food cool in their market stall. The ubiquity of these clubs in the developing world is evidence of widespread demand for access to ways to save, as well as to lend.

Other bundles of benefits are also imaginable. Perhaps e-Choupal-type groups could pool together interests in access to credit with an interest in access to the internet. Or access to a network of potential trading partners. The key is to tie the benefits I get from maintaining my access to and the stability of a group and its rules to your compliance with the rules, and vice versa. And to make all of this a matter of common knowledge.

The Problem, and Promise, of Ambiguity

Expanding the scope of activities in a virtual group, tied together by its members' collective efforts to uphold a set of rules, does come at a price: it sacrifices some of the simplicity that makes common knowledge easier to sustain. The original simple Grameen system of small loans of standardized amounts, with standardized weekly repayments, is easy to keep track of, particularly for those who are also borrowers. ROSCAs tend to be composed of people with similar incomes and interests, and often require fixed contributions. Sometimes they allow funds to be used only for a specific purpose. Expanding the diversity of interests within a group, then, generates a bit of a problem: what counts as a violation of the rules of the group? The same problem arises when groups attempt to be more ambitious and flexible—crafting solutions for individuals that meet their specific needs rather than shoehorning everyone into the same model. (Remember, one of the key things that happens with economic development is that specialization and differentiation increase.) How can close calls in ambiguous cases reliably be made matters of common knowledge—so that everyone knows that everyone knows when the rules have been violated?

Delivering a common-knowledge way of resolving ambiguity about rule violations across a diversifying population is exactly what the Athenian jury was up to. Contending parties got up and argued their cases, the jury voted, and the result was announced in a very public setting where everyone knew that everyone knew who was in the right—even if the facts were complex and the considerations multiple and cross-cutting. Moreover, the people deciding what was right were the people who stood to benefit from a stable regime. That's what an expanded virtual microcredit system would need to do—develop a user-led, common-knowledge system for resolving inevitable ambiguity about what the rules allow and what they don't.

The idea that we would need to layer on a system to resolve ambiguity sounds like it counts against any effort to develop expanded virtual microfinance networks out of the seedbed of existing microcredit and savings groups. But actually it's where the real promise of this effort lies. That's because the real goal is not to build microfinance institutions per se. The real goal is to create a foothold for new institutions capable of administering shared and stable common-knowledge rules to govern behavior. That's what the Athenians understood well. The initial focus was not on devising new rules but on reassuring everyone that the institution operated in a reliable, neutral, and open way to decide when the rules had been broken. Once that framework has been built, it becomes a powerful tool—because once it is stable and trusted, it is capable not only of enforcing the rules it starts with but also expanding its reach. What might start out as a reliable way of administering a more flexible rule for repayment of small loans—one that allows larger amounts or more leeway in repayment or gives people a break when unexpected circumstances come up, for example—eventually can turn into a vehicle for resolving uncertainty about when insurance payouts are owed or refunds due for faulty products or compensation for workplace hazards payable.

And that is what the legal infrastructure of poor countries really needs—what every country needs from legal infrastructure: a trusted mechanism for deciding what the rules of transactions and organizations and relationships are and when they are transgressed. Ambiguity and disagreement about rules and their violation is a major obstacle to economic development.

Bannerjee and Duflo in Poor Economics offer a critical example of this. Why, they ask, do the poor—who live lives of extraordinary uncertainty—not buy more insurance? Insurance is a basic mechanism for smoothing risk and improving planning—essential for generating the good incentives for investment and efficient allocation of resources that underpin economic growth. But even when weather insurance is available for farmers and health-care insurance is available for all, few poor people take up the offer. Bannerjee and Duflo suggest that a significant reason is that the insurance available to poor people is severely limited to deal with the problem of moral hazard—the challenge facing insurance markets the world over. Moral hazard is the risk that people with insurance will stop taking reasonable steps to avoid bad outcomes when they know someone else will pay if things go wrong or, worse, that they will simply lie when they make an insurance claim. There is also the converse risk: that the insurance company will refuse to pay out, even when a payout is legitimately called for.

Banerjee and Duflo recount the example of a poor Indian woman (let's call her Ameena) who was required to purchase health insurance from her microfinance provider as a condition of her access to loans. She decided to abandon her microfinance loans after the company refused to reimburse her for a trip to hospital for a stomach infection. Problem? Ameena's policy only covered catastrophic events, and a stomach infection didn't count. Now, I haven't seen this policy. But I'm betting it was fairly incomprehensible to this poor woman and that the insurer's legal obligation was determined by formal opinions formed by remote legal experts based on baroque Indian law. And I'm quite sure she had nowhere to turn to argue her case: the Indian courts are positively Dickensian in their delays—one senior Indian judge estimated in 2010 that it would take 320 years to clear the backlog of thirty million cases in the country, and some estimate that the average case takes ten years to resolve.[14] But even these delays are irrelevant to Ameena: she can't afford to hire the lawyer she needs to file her case anyway.

Ah, to be in ancient Athens. Remember Nomios? Nomios also had an argument with someone about the terms of a deal: was the seller obligated to pay for the slave's debt or not? Our Indian insurance-holder wants to know if her premiums cover stomach infections that require a hospital stay. There's ambiguity about the answer (even if the insurance company is very sure there is none.) But Nomios has a robust system—populated by people just like him—to decide the answer and make it common knowledge. Ameena has no option but to take the insurance company's answer. If she doesn't like it, she can stay out of the insurance market. Which she did. Just like the group of women Bannerjee and Duflo also heard about who stopped buying insurance (and taking out loans) en masse when one of the women's husband died of an infection and their insurer refused to cover the cost of medicine and treatment—because he never went to hospital. As Bannerjee and Duflo put it, "What could be more catastrophic?"

The problem is not limited to health insurance or ambiguous terms capable of meaning different things to different people. Bannerjee and Duflo also discuss the problem of weather insurance for farmers—where payouts are based on rainfall measured at a specified rainfall station. That's a crisp, unambiguous term. But in a region with many microclimates, the measurement at the station may bear little relationship to the rainfall experienced by an individual farmer. The farmer who pays out for weather insurance but isn't covered even when his crops have all dried up isn't going to keep buying weather insurance. Nor is anyone who hears his story.

Bannerjee and Duflo take the usual economist's turn on this problem: they suggest that the solution to this market failure is for government to subsidize insurance premiums. That may be a good policy response (if the government is not incompetent, corrupt, poor), but it doesn't really get to the heart of the problem—solving the ambiguity obstacle.

Imagine instead that some enterprising organization comes along and offers to both the insurance company and people like Ameena and the farmer another way of managing the problem of deciding when the insurance company can say no and when it can't. Let's suppose this organization takes the Athenian lessons to heart: it creates a system in which ordinary people—the purchasers of insurance along with the providers—participate equally and in a common-knowledge setting to establish and adjudicate the rules about when insurance pays out. The rules probably have to be fashioned—by these ordinary participants—to ensure that they are perceived to be universal, generating benefits for both those who buy and those who sell insurance. This means that the microfinance organizations need to see a way to at least cover their costs and possibly (if social entrepreneurs or donor organizations don't show up) earn a reasonable profit. So too must the terms be adjudicated to keep the insurance viable as a financial proposition—that appeal must be made directly to the ordinary people who are deciding about payouts in particular cases. And, if this enterprising solution is going to work, the story of Athens suggests, it will be very important to maintain as much continuity as possible with any preexisting or informal norms in the determination of when a payout is deserving and when it is not. Such openness, as we saw in Athens, is critical to underwrite the willingness of ordinary people to support the enforcement of the rules and the ways of this novel organization. Importing the "correct" or "legal" interpretation of a contract drafted on an advanced Western model and managed by distant experts is just not likely to fly.

We get away with legal rules and processes far removed from ordinary people in advanced Western legal systems only because they are advanced and stable—and most people (poor and minority people in even these countries, particularly in interactions with the criminal law, are probably an exception) perceive the legal system as a whole to be beneficial for them—giving them meaningful rights to collect their wages or money owed or use public resources, for example. But if we're trying to help build stable legal infrastructure in places where there is now little to none, we can't start at the finishing line.

13

Global Markets for BoP Legal Infrastructure

IT WAS NO accident in the last chapter that the solution I proposed to solve the problem in insurance markets for the poor was for a third party to step in with a new type of mechanism for resolving ambiguity in insurance contracts. That's a critical point. Today, almost all innovation in rules and procedures is second-party: coming from the providers of goods and services to the poor—the microfinance, mobile phone, and consumer products companies that are trying to do business in the BoP. That's like Google being handed the task of creating a workable system for implementing the right to be forgotten on the internet in European law. It's encouraging to see these organizations and businesses working creatively to fill the vacuum in legal infrastructure. But for real change and sustainability, we should be looking for the emergence of competitive markets populated by dedicated legal providers who can develop scalable third-party systems.

There are two reasons to look toward third-party provision of legal infrastructure. First, there's an inevitable conflict of interest in the rules that a business or organization develops to control its own behavior. True enough, there are market incentives for these providers to tie their hands to some extent—no one buys insurance from a company that says, "We can do anything we want when you make a claim," for example. And socially minded businesses like the Grameen Bank and the new breed of social impact investor in the developing world are sincerely driven to make choices that are good for poor people and not just their companies. But even the well intentioned, not to mention the merely market constrained, are unlikely to explore solutions that complicate their business models or challenge deeply held presumptions about what works and what doesn't in the developing world. Moreover, poor people—like all of us—are likely to be suspicious of an organization that chooses its own rules. Building trust in the neutrality of a set of rules and procedures, however, is absolutely essential. Third parties can make it their business to develop that reputation for neutrality.

Second, the challenge of building legal infrastructure for poor countries is a staggeringly complex one. Real solutions that make sense on the ground and fulfill the promise of flexibility and scalability will require serious investment and the same kind of experimentation and iterative development that our most creative companies deploy elsewhere throughout the economy. We need a dedicated market for legal infrastructure to make those investments, to conduct those experiments, to be the global innovators in the legal space that the world now lacks. There's expertise to be developed here, and the way to do that is for legal innovation to be a specialized enterprise of its own. We now have social impact stock exchanges in the developing world to match investment funds with a social entrepreneurship agenda. We have private equity funds devoted to environmental or health innovation. Next stop, investment funds for legal innovation.

Our goal should be to build effective, competitive, and well-regulated global markets for legal tools and providers from which poor countries can source increasingly generalized legal infrastructure—rules that go beyond specific or local domains such as microcredit or insurance schemes for a particular village. Practically speaking, we want to create a global marketplace in which Zimbabwe or Cambodia or Honduras can buy legal regulatory services supplied by stable, competent providers in the same way that poor people now access mobile phone service from global companies—tailored to the realities of life in the BoP. Nobody thinks, anymore, that the way to get Kenyan traders access to mobile phones and phone-based banking is to have the Kenyan government, all by itself, invent the technology and business models that adapt phone-based banking systems to the Kenyan environment, build cell towers and mobile phone manufacturing plants, and operate a phone company and a bank. That shouldn't be what they have to do to get access to stable legal infrastructure either. It may take a mix of profit and nonprofit organizations, and it almost certainly will take smart research, dedicated philanthropy, and international support, to get from where we are today—zero options for sourcing legal infrastructure from outside domestic nation-state governments—to where we want to be—flourishing, innovative, and sustainable markets for the basic components of effective legal infrastructure. But we can get there.

Imagining the Future of Global Legal Infrastructure

I don't believe for a minute that there are off-the-shelf models to build the legal infrastructure poor countries need that an armchair economist, development expert, or legal scholar can blueprint from thousands of miles away. That's why I emphasize the need for research, dedicated investors, entrepreneurs, and competitive markets for global legal infrastructure. I do believe, however, that it is important to snap the boundaries of our currently conceived approaches to solving rule-of-law problems, and for this purpose it is important to fire the imagination of what might be possible. I've spent several years thinking about innovative solutions for legal infrastructure, participating in workshops to rethink the delivery of legal services, working with global legal innovators at places such as HiiL Innovating Justice in the Netherlands and the World Economic Forum and encouraging law students at the University of Southern California, the University of Toronto, and Harvard to think differently in my legal innovation courses. We're still quite far from real on-the-ground solutions for the developing world, but the place to pick up this work is with the imagination. So here are some ideas.

Simple Contracts, BoP Edition

Remember Simple Contracts? That was a thought experiment we carried out in Chapter 10 to explore what private for-profit companies supplying businesses with better contract law and dispute resolution might look like. We saw there that this was a relatively short step from the world we already live in—where businesses can choose a government provider of contract law and dispute resolution by stating in their contract that they want their deal governed by the law of New York, for example. And it was a case in which we could feel reasonably confident that Simple Contracts would not be able to exploit its users because users were free to choose another provider if it did, and because users could narrowly tailor their choice to submit to Simple Contracts' system to just one transaction—they didn't have to decide to put their entire lives under the regulatory regime of New York.

Now imagine Simple Contracts, Kenyan edition. Step 1 in this thought experiment is to think about what the potential user in Kenya needs from an innovative contracting provider—and to avoid the threshold error of thinking that what the Kenyan user needs is exactly the same as what the businesses in advanced market settings need. If Simple Contracts is going to invent a contracting product that's valuable to Kenya, it will have to target the 80–90 percent of people in Kenya who are now operating in the informal economy, with little to no contract regime at all. What could work for them?

This first thing to know is that Kenya already has sophisticated contract law on the books. In fact, it has the English law of contracts on the books—literally: "The common law of England relating to contract, as modified by the doctrines of equity [and] by the Acts of Parliament of the United Kingdom . . . shall extend and apply to Kenya," says the basic Kenyan contract statute. But that law is almost certainly unnecessarily complex for the vast majority of Kenyan traders in the informal economy. It requires, like American law, expensive lawyers to interpret and implement it. That level of complexity may be worth it in some settings—but not when you're just trying to get a basic system off the ground and in the context of simple transactions.

The second thing to know is that Kenya ranks 145 out of 175 on Transparency International's Corruption Perceptions Index. Corruption in the judiciary is widespread—the Kenyan Anti-Corruption Commission of 2010 reported that 50 percent of judges were implicated in corrupt practices. Even for those at the top of the food chain in the formal economy in Kenya—sophisticated businesses with greater wealth to spend on sophisticated lawyers—the value of formal law enforced by state courts is limited.

These two facts suggest that Simple Contracts should probably be focusing on developing appropriately simple rules (together with a way to keep them simple) that don't require going to Kenyan courts for enforcement—a system that relies, for example, on reputation, repeat business incentives, and ordinary social sanctions. And, following the model of most start-ups trying to introduce something truly novel to the world, it should probably start small and targeted to narrow domains.

How about a phone-based system for voice- or text-recording simple agreements—to pay back a small loan, make a delivery, do a job, share revenues—with a simple and limited set of terms from which to choose? The simpler the rules for these simpler contracts, the more likely it is that the rules can be understood—and become a matter of common knowledge about what's expected, what's allowed, what's excused in the Simple Contracts system. How about a kiosk in the market or someone's home (like ITC's e-Choupal system) where a person—or a person on a video screen or a voice on the phone—can make a determination of whether simple and verifiable things were done? Was money transferred to a phone-based bank account? Was a picture of the delivered goods or the complete job uploaded? Was a verification of time of delivery or adequacy of quality entered on the phone of a third-party witness to the transaction? Maybe informal traders need a way to check the reputation of participants in the system—a way to check with Simple Contracts whether a prospective trading partner has failed to perform his or her contract or compensate for breach in the past. Maybe they need a system that operates like a club—where those who fail to live up to the rules they pledge to respect are excluded from opportunities to trade within the club. And maybe they need easy access to people who can help them to understand how to use the system and model its use.

How about a smart, simple contract mechanism built on top of a block-chain technology platform? Blockchain technology holds enormous potential for the poor world, struggling to develop reliable contract systems in the face of rampant judicial corruption and inaccessible, far too costly courts. Small traders could register assets—just small amounts of money to begin—on the block-chain and authorize Simple Contracts to transfer funds automatically when performance of contractual obligations has been verified and when compensation is due for a failure to live up to a contract. To a large extent, as we saw in Chapter 10, what the state of California is offering—as a monopoly provider—is the capacity to seize assets and wages to satisfy the court orders presented to it. Even if those court orders are issued by New York judges or private arbitrators or a private contracting system like Simple Contracts. Blockchain technology could free Simple Contracts from any need to go to a nation-state's courts at all.

In addition to enterprising founders and funders, Simple Contracts may also need partnerships with NGOs or foreign governments that offer to audit and certify the quality and fidelity of the legal product being offered. Is the phone- or blockchain-based agreement being accurately transcribed and safely stored? Is the kiosk declaring whether performance has occurred or not accurately and honestly implementing the announced rules? Is the reputation system operating without corruption? Are decisions about club membership being made exclusively on the basis of announced criteria, in a nondiscriminatory fashion? Does Simple Contracts charge and collect fees according to its contract? If it manages escrow accounts or bonds, does it follow appropriate accounting and safeguard client funds? If so, Simple Contracts maintains its global status as an approved provider in this market. Which it should care about: because so long as it does, and so long as it keeps producing value for poor people and their contracting partners, it can beat its competitors to the punch in taking the product beyond Kenya to billions of poor traders around the world.

Such a system might help more small and medium-sized companies to follow in the footsteps of Magatte Wade, a successful Senegalese entrepreneur who is committed to helping build African businesses.[1] Wade, educated in France and now living in the United States, started a beverage company called Adina For Life (together with Odwalla founder Greg Steltenpohl) with the vision of producing a soft drink based on the native hibiscus drinks she remembered from her childhood. Wade was, and in her continuing ventures such as Tiossan skin care products still is, passionate about integrating African producers into global supply chains and international markets. Along the way, however, she has struggled with the difficulty of doing business in Africa—beginning with the problem of quality control and reliability in supply and heading on up into problems of local transportation, permitting, customs, and shipping, not to mention the obstacles to her real dream: building African manufacturing capacity. She tells the story of how in just the second shipment from the four hundred suppliers she had recruited, the US processing plants she had contracted with discovered all kinds of detritus in the bags of hibiscus they had sent: dust, hair, stones, even a dead bird. A particularly large rock that made its way into the product had damaged expensive machinery in an Oregon plant. Wade flew to Senegal and met under a tree with forty representatives of the women who had picked and packed that shipment, showing them (to their disgust) what their relaxed approach to hairnets, protocols (don't pick up any flowers that fall to the ground), and sealing bags (the dead bird having flown into an open bag) had produced. And why practices like that would stand in the way of ever selling their product to the world market. Wade relied on her local connections and standing (she wasn't the white man or NGO worker coming to tell the women what to do) to build a system that was able to enforce the terms of the deal she needed—wearing hairnets, following quality protocols, keeping to delivery promises, meeting the requirements for organic and fair trade certification necessary to market to wealthy Western consumers. Soon the four hundred women supplying hibiscus numbered more than forty thousand, and Adina had grown to a multi-million-dollar company. Simple Contracts tools, supplied by a dedicated contract provider with the capacity to coordinate local enforcement of contract terms, may allow more entrepreneurs—local and global—to achieve similar success at lower cost.

Simple Registration and Permitting

We saw in Chapter 11 that a major problem in many poor countries is the rococo complexity of the steps required to create and operate a legitimate business or transfer property rights. The World Bank's Doing Business project hopes to advise poor governments about how to streamline these processes. But maybe more of these governments need to be buying registration and permitting services from companies that specialize in the developing country setting. This doesn't just mean outsourcing to a local private company management of the now-government-operated offices that shuffle the heaps of paper needed to gain official approval to operate or recognize a property claim. It could mean getting third-party specialized businesses to both develop and execute registration and permitting rules and procedures. If those businesses operate on a global scale, with global reputation to protect, they might be able to sidestep the seeming inevitability of corruption in these procedures.

LegalZoom, for example, is the leading provider of online document services in the United States. In 2015, it incorporated almost a quarter of all LLCs in California and prepared more trademark filings for the US Patent and Trademark Office than any other single entity. At present, it just executes on rules set up by government authorities. But it is well placed to help figure out how to streamline those rules—even to help, using data and technology where it makes sense, to figure out what the substantive rules should be to achieve a government's objectives. Is there a cheaper—and just as reliable—way of making sure a company is adequately capitalized than requiring submission of many years of tax forms, for example? Documenting that a security interest has been registered by a lender than publication in local newspapers? Better ways than expensive upfront requirements and inspections to reassure the regulators who worry about environmental risks or labor standards that the proposed company doesn't fall outside of the norm for potential compliance? Mechanisms for integrating local business registration with global blockchain platforms? Companies like LegalZoom, if they developed expertise in developing countries and competed for the business on a global stage (with a global reputation to worry about), could substantially diminish the roadblocks to business formation and transactions.

Of course, some poor governments maintain all those registration and permitting requirements because at each step there is an opportunity for some government official to extract a bribe. Bureaucratic incentives don't always align with the effort to make things easier and less costly. This isn't just a problem in poor countries: LegalZoom and other enterprising companies such as online mediation company Modria with great ideas for streamlining legal processes have run into surprising resistance from US government officials when they have offered, usually free of charge, to re-engineer some aspects of state registration or dispute-handling operations. Some government department heads, it turns out, just aren't interested in reducing their expenses because that can diminish future claims on budgets and threaten job security. So there's no sense in which this is a simple path to better processes. But international pressure on poor governments to adopt approved providers of these kinds of services is probably a better use of international pressure than the current pressure exerted for them to streamline procedures themselves.

Competitive Regulation

Poor countries would also be well served by the emergence of approved competitive private regulators, an idea that I introduced in Chapter 10. As we've seen, poor countries already adopt, often wholesale, the legal and regulatory apparatus of other countries. Kenya's contract law is whatever English lawyers, judges, civil servants, and parliamentarians produce. Cambodia's commercial courts copy the models of Canadian court administrators. Both global and local markets for approved private regulators could dramatically expand their options, and increase the likelihood that models emerge that do more than simply replicate the over-the-top complexity and expense of legal infrastructure that, as we've seen, is now too complex and expensive even for wealthy developed environments.

The approved private regulators could be local—and surprising. What about the cross-border traders in Zimbabwe, who now face a ridiculously complex legal regime with which no one—border officials, couriers, traders, police—can or do consistently comply? Could the *malayishas* who now navigate the border procedures for cross-border traders compete as licensed border clubs—establishing their own rules and fees, paying the government (electronically, or via phone-based systems?) a share of what they collect, maintaining their license only if they meet collection targets and pass periodic audits? Currently the *malayishas* compete over the comfort and timeliness of their vehicles and the speed with which they can navigate the bribes at the border. Expanding the scope of their competition to include the methods and costs of their authorized screening and collection of customs duties could produce innovative solutions for cross-border traders—ideally eliminating the uncertainty that make life as a cross-border trader a daily gamble. No system will completely escape the risk of corruption (although, again, a blockchain platform with which traders and *malayishas* have registered some assets dangles as a tantalizing possibility), but it's easier to maintain the integrity of a system that supervises a small number of operators than the entire population of cross-border traders. Moreover, auditing could also be outsourced to global organizations, which can be under greater international scrutiny and competitive pressure (for auditing contracts) than individual police on the road from the border.

Indeed, there is a substantial role for global organizations in a world of approved private regulators. We already have thousands of global entities involved in supplying standards and overseeing compliance for governments and businesses worldwide—just as there are numerous domestic standard-setting groups that are relied on to produce the detailed rules that domestic regulators enforce. Many of these are in the category of voluntary standards and certifications. Magatte Wade, for example, sought to boost Adina's potential sales in wealthy countries by choosing to comply with the standards set and monitored by private (nonprofit) organic and fair-trade certifiers. The International Organization for Standardization (ISO) supplies a portfolio of widely adopted voluntary standards for practices such as those affecting quality (ISO 9001) and environmental impacts (ISO 14000). Social Accountability International supplies voluntary standards for workplace practices based on the UN Declaration of Human Rights, international labor conventions, and national labor laws (SA 8000). Users of these standards pay for access to the standards and auditing by privately operated and accredited certifying bodies.

A global market for approved private regulators could simply take these models to the next level. That next level involves (1) approval by domestic governments based on an assessment of whether the private regulator meets governmental criteria in some area of regulation (such as rates of workplace injury or production of environmental toxins), (2) a requirement that the people and entities to be regulated must select an approved regulator, and (3) a mechanism for ensuring that the market for approved private regulators is in fact competitive and noncorrupt. This latter requirement might entail, for example, fraud and competition/antitrust oversight at a global level, much as we see in other industries, such as limits on mergers of major players. In the world of global standards, this requires a mental shift from a prioritizing of the simplicity of a uniform global standard to an emphasis on the benefits reaped when regulators compete on a global stage.

Third-Party Governance for Global Supply Chains

Innovative ways to provide the local legal infrastructure that supports contractual relationships and domestic regulation is fundamental to expanding the participation of poor countries in the globally networked economy. Almost as important, however, is building the legal infrastructure to support the global supply chains and global regulatory relationships that stitch rich and poor countries together in the global economy. That means not only developing the sets of rules and enforcement systems that can regulate the behavior of the people living in poor countries—the Senegalese farmers who supply Magatte Wade's businesses—but also the rules and enforcement systems that can regulate the behavior of the sometimes massive global corporations and organizations that link the poor with international markets and the wealth of developed economies.

Global supply chains are already active sites for privately provided regulation. Nike, Walmart, GE, Apple: these megacompanies use their contracts with suppliers in poor countries not only to set the mundane commercial terms of a deal—price, quality, delivery—but also to establish standards for workplace health and safety, child labor, environmental practices, and more. These companies undertake to inspect local suppliers—sometimes through third-party auditors—and wield the power of terminating a contract if violations of their privately developed codes of conduct are found. They are motivated both by the sincere humanitarian goals of their owners, investors, and employees, and by the profit incentives generated by the distaste of affluent consumers for products produced under appalling or unsustainable conditions. For both reasons, Apple worries about suicides in response to overwork at its Chinese supplier plants, Nike worries about child laborers sewing its soccer balls in Pakistan, and Walmart, L'Oréal, and Hershey worry about links between deforestation in Indonesia and Malaysia and the products they sell.

Global corporations are responding to global demand for higher standards of workplace health and safety and environmental stewardship in poor countries by creating and policing their own standards. There is much to credit in that system. But we could do even better with third-party-provided regulatory systems. Rather than crafting their own standards, global corporations could submit to the regulatory systems of private regulators, choosing among a competitive set of participants approved by global organizations.

A shift to third-party regulation can help to ensure that not only poor-country suppliers but also the global corporations that buy from them are bound to rules about how they manage their global supply chain relationships. In the global supply chain contract, the corporate buyer not only chooses the standards, it also retains ultimate authority to judge when standards have been met, or violated. There are few provisions establishing enforceable commitments on the part of the corporations themselves. A regime based on expectations or requirements that global corporations will submit themselves to the regulation of approved private regulators also reduces the extent to which the regulatory regime rests on the fickle tastes of affluent consumers. And creating a global market of dedicated private regulators, not merely NGOs supplying standards, generates market incentives for investment in developing more effective regulatory systems.

The need for third-party global regulators to bind not only poor suppliers but also wealthy corporations to appropriate legal standards was evident, for example, in the wake of the 2013 Rana Plaza factory collapse in Bangladesh that killed 1,127 workers. In response to international public outcry prompted by the disaster (coming soon on the heels of the 2012 Tazreen Fashions factory fire that killed 117 Bangladeshi garment workers), global clothing retailers adopted two strategies for improved workplace safety in Bangladesh's garment industry.

In one approach, American giants Gap and Walmart recruited other North American clothing companies to form the Alliance for Bangladesh Worker Safety.[2] Members of the Alliance fund the organization and elect a board of directors. The board develops strategies to achieve commitments such as to "work with factories that ensure a safe working environment," "empower workers to take an active role in their own safety," and "provide safety inspection and safety and empowerment training for 100 percent of factories in the Members respective supply chains." The Alliance effectively operates as an NGO with a set of goals but no external legal enforcement: Members can resign from the organization whenever they want and the only reason a Member can be sued is for failing to pay dues. The Alliance members' agreement expressly states that the agreement is not intended to give any third parties (workers, for example) a right to sue members for failures to carry through on the goals of the organization.

In a contrasting approach, European clothing companies, led by Swedish clothing giant H&M, entered into a formal contract, dubbed the Bangladesh Accord on Fire and Building Safety, with international labor unions.[3] Like the Alliance, the Accord commits the companies that signed to require their Bangladeshi suppliers to accept safety inspections, remediation plans, and fire safety training. These inspections, plans, and training are to be conducted under the oversight of an independent safety inspector who is appointed by the Accord's steering committee—a committee composed of three company representatives, three union representatives, and a neutral chair appointed by the UN's International Labour Organization.

Companies also commit to make it financially feasible for the factories to maintain safe workplaces, for two years not to change suppliers just to avoid the requirements of the Accord, to make reasonable efforts to find safe jobs for workers who lose their jobs when a noncompliant supplier has its contracts terminated, and to make inspection and remediation reports public. (These public reports, available online, show the enormous rate at which Bangladeshi factories continued to fall short of safety standards well after these solutions were put in place. Most of the almost thirteen hundred factories inspected in the two years after the Rana Plaza collapse were still not constructed in accordance with structural design drawings; almost all factories lacked fire separation between floors and lacked adequate fire doors.) As a formal contract, the Accord is enforceable through international arbitration. That means that a union, for example, could obtain an order ultimately enforceable in the courts where a company is headquartered requiring a company to live up to its obligations in the Accord and/or provide compensation to those harmed when it didn't.

Clearly there are more teeth in the European approach. American companies balked, however, at a process that put power into the hands of international unions and created what they perceived as a risk of class-action lawsuits and possible antitrust challenges in the United States. An established third-party regulator could provide a third way, designing and enforcing standards to achieve workplace safety goals. Such a private regulator would operate under the dual pressure of maintaining its global approval status by implementing standards that meet internationally sanctioned goals and of delivering a system that adequately balances workplace safety with commercial realities. An international system that recognized reputable global private regulators could also help to mitigate the risk of domestic lawsuits—if the results achieved by the regulators warrant it, domestic governments could put in place protections against private litigation for companies that choose to submit to third-party regulators. And a global regulator may be more effective at enforcement because its interests are linked across multiple countries and domains. Enforcement and follow-through is clearly a shortcoming of solutions like the Gap/Walmart Alliance. It's also a practical reality that even when third-party enforcement is theoretically available, as with the H&M-led Accord, whether enforcement actually takes place depends on the in-the-moment relationship of the parties directly involved. Unions may not find it in their interest to enforce, for example. A truly global marketplace for private regulators can link the incentives to enforce standards to broader market incentives—the global regulator that speaks a good game but doesn't enforce won't maintain good standing as an approved regulator. Not just in Bangladesh and the garment industry, but throughout the world.

Competitive Law Zones

The key to innovative legal infrastructure solutions for the poor and developing world is, as always, to foster specialization and competition—rather than relying entirely on either governments or self-regulation. As one final jolt to the possible, let me close out this chapter with two tales—one encouraging, one cautionary—about experiments underway to compete for business in global markets by building entire enclaves, even cities, with innovative legal infrastructure.

Legal Entrepreneurs in the Desert

In October 2014 I traveled to Dubai as a new member of the Global Agenda Council on Justice for the World Economic Forum. This was my first trip to the Middle East, and I was excited to see this part of the world. Many travelers come to Dubai to see what this formerly very poor fishing village flanked by desert has become in just a few short decades: the home of the tallest building in the world, an indoor ski hill, a hotel with underwater suites on a man-made island shaped like a palm tree, expansive beachside resorts, the world's largest indoor mall. But, law-nerd that I am, I was especially excited that on the second day of the Global Agenda Summit, the Dubai government was hosting a gala to celebrate the tenth anniversary of the Dubai International Financial Centre.

The DIFC is one of the world's first modern competitive law zones.[4] The Centre was created by the Dubai government to attract international financial services to Dubai. The attraction includes exemption for businesses registered in the Centre from taxes and customs duties and the absence of any ownership restrictions or limits on repatriation of funds earned in the zone to one's home country. In this sense, the DIFC is like the thousands of economic zones created by many governments around the world to attract business investment. Dubai itself has well over a dozen free zones dedicated to healthcare, technology, higher education, media, manufacturing and distribution, and more. But what makes the DIFC so interesting as an example of legal innovation is that financial services companies registered in the Centre, and businesses operating within the Centre (such as hotels, apartment and office buildings, and restaurants) are subject only to the laws created by the Centre—and not the laws of Dubai or the United Arab Emirates. The DIFC has its own regulatory system for financial services, its own civil and commercial laws, and its own court system—with jurisdiction over any dealings taking place within the Centre, between companies registered with the Centre or, in the furthest-reaching provisions, between contracting parties anywhere in the world that choose to be governed by the DIFC's law. Even government agencies of Dubai can, if they choose, submit themselves to governance—exclusive governance—by the DIFC legal regime. (The only limit on the DIFC's legal reach is that it cannot displace the criminal or family law of Dubai.) The language of the court is English, and it applies common-law principles to the interpretation and application of the Centre's laws—which are drafted by the administration of the Centre and issued by the ruler of Dubai. The Centre has written codes, based on Anglo-American legal principles, on subjects ranging from contract, real and personal property, corporate and securities law to torts, employment, and data security. If a case comes up and there is no DIFC law on the matter, and the parties haven't contracted for some other law to apply, English law applies. The court's procedures are modeled on the London commercial courts. And the DIFC courts can, and do, use English caselaw to help decide cases. The judges who serve on the court are former high-ranking judges from England, Singapore, Malaysia, New Zealand, Australia, and Dubai—all appointed by the ruler of Dubai. Judgments in DIFC courts are enforceable in Dubai and in other countries to the same extent as judgments of a Dubai court. (Notably, this gives DIFC judgments the ability to reach assets in a number of Arab states.) The DIFC has reached special agreement on guidelines for enforcement of its judgments in England, Australia, Kenya, Singapore, and the Southern District of New York.

Of course the proof of the pudding is in the eating—and what does this Dubai law-pie taste like? Well, eight years in (the court went into full operation in 2008), the flavor is of a very well-run and efficient English legal system. The laws are straightforward and familiar to any Anglo-American lawyer. The contract law, for example, looks very much like the basic principles I have taught to first-year American and Canadian law students for twenty-five years. The procedures are easy to understand and also familiar. The written judgments—all available online—are clearly written and to the point, and quite reasonable to this lawyer's eye. In fact, much of the system looks (as anyone can see, if he or she doesn't nod off, by watching videos of full hearings available online) very much like the Western legal systems revered the world over.

With one striking exception. When you read, as I did, a sample of the published cases, it is clear that this court operates much faster, and seems much more accessible, than courts in the United States or throughout much of the Western world. In American courts, for example, it is rare to come across an employment case, as I did in the DIFC records, in which an employee who is fired from a job on April 2—who claims he was shorted two days' salary and did not receive thousands of dollars in promised severance, vacation, and gratuity payments—to get a hearing on the matter on June 9 and a judgment ordering the former employer to pay up on June 22. A result that should not be remarkable but is, it is a product of the DIFC's small-claims tribunal—a court with much greater ability to deliver accessible resolution of mundane disputes than any American court I know. The DIFC small-claims court hears any matter worth less than about US$125,000. So long as both parties agree, the amount can go up to as much as $500,000 and there's no cap at all if the matter involves employment and both employer and employee want to use the small-claims court. The average claim in 2015 was for $25,000. These amounts far exceed the limits in American small-claims courts. In California, for example, the most an individual can sue for is an annual maximum of $7,500, and the most a corporation can sue for is $5,000. The DIFC's procedures for filing are relatively simple, and the first step in the procedure is for the parties to meet, without lawyers, for a consultation with a judge to attempt to resolve the dispute. If they can't resolve it, the matter is set for hearing, before a different judge. The judgment is given with written reasons. A written judgment is very rare in American small-claims courts, where small-claims judges—many of whom are lawyers doing volunteer work as judges a few days a year—often hear as many as fifty cases a day, able to devote only a few minutes to each one. Judgments are published online, for anyone to read, but without identifying the parties. According to the DIFC courts' administrator, over 90 percent of small claims in 2015 were resolved within four weeks. Cases in the regular (not small claims) DIFC court, with an average value in 2015 of $25 million, take longer, but decisions are fast: in 2014, half of all judgments issued within a month; the average took two and a half months.

Make no mistake about it. The DIFC is in the business of selling a product: efficient and fair laws and courts that will be attractive to businesses and employees who might set up shop in the DIFC. It is competing with Singapore, London, and New York. The courts' annual review is a glossy sales brochure, highlighting the growth in the use of the court systems, the rapid resolution of cases, the impressive bios of its judges and management personnel, and its accomplishments and accolades (taking home in 2014 the Law Society of England and Wales' "Excellence in International Legal Services" award and short-listed for their "Excellence in Pro Bono" award—plus earning the first five-star rating for efficiency in government services from the Dubai government, no small matter in a country that ranks first worldwide, according to the Swiss International Institute for Management Development, in government efficiency).

But it's not just marketing materials. The DIFC courts' rules establish as "The Overriding Objective" the goal of "enabling the courts to deal with cases justly." That is of course what any court promises. What stands out in the DIFC rules of court is the attention paid to cost and financial factors in the express statement that "justice" includes not only "ensuring the parties are on an equal footing" and "ensuring that [the case] is dealt with expeditiously and fairly" but also "saving expense," "dealing with the case in ways which are proportionate (a) to the amount of money involved; (b) to the importance of the case; (c) to the complexity of the issues and (d) to the financial position of each party" and "allotting to it an appropriate share of the Courts' resources, while taking into account the need to allot resources to other cases." Many courts, of course, aim to operate efficiently. But by putting this in the formal rules of court, as an *overriding* objective no less, the DIFC courts authorize their courts to operate in a way that few Western courts can hope to. This commitment to efficiency and fairness as a selling point for the DIFC helps explain the level of resources available to the court—ten judges (albeit not all resident and full-time) and a substantial professional management team for a caseload that in 2015 stood at about three hundred cases. American judges can only dream of such levels of funding.

Some, Western lawyers in particular, may find the idea of an organization, not to mention a hereditary monarchy, "selling" justice a bit unseemly, if not a logical impossibility. Indeed, the Singaporean chief justice and the English administrator of the Dubai court (and the recently landed Australian admin-istrator for a new upstart, a comparable court available in the Abu Dhabi Global Market) all demurred when I asked them about whether they saw themselves as competing for judicial business. But as we've seen, we could do with more efforts to sell high-quality justice, if the sellers have an incentive and the capacity to design legal infrastructure that better meets the needs of users. As in most markets, the question is: do you value the quality the seller is offering? Do you trust the seller to continue to support the product? Is this a scam or a solution?

At least in these early days, the Dubai government appears to be trying to commit to a product of enduring value. It has struck its own balance between making the law of the DIFC the law of the rulers of Dubai (whose own laws, they have perhaps concluded, are not a product global businesses want to buy), and giving the power to design and implement the law to largely imported judges and legal administrators from advanced Western-style legal systems. In addition to the chief justice from Singapore, a former judge and vice chairman of the International Chamber of Commerce, the current bench consists of two former appellate judges from England and Australia, three former judges from the commercial court in London, the former chief justice of Malaysia, and three judges from Dubai. Having met the chief justice and the principal administrator in Dubai, it appears to me that these people are as committed to upholding the integrity of advanced legal systems as any of the judges and administrators you will find in the highly respected home courts of the UK and the Commonwealth world from which they hail. With their own international reputations and professional values on the line, I expect these judges and administrators can be trusted to carry out their duties as much as if they were operating in a court in London, Singapore, or Sydney.

In effect, Dubai has done what some former British colonies did when they made the Judicial Committee of the Privy Council in London, composed of the same judges who serve on the UK's Supreme Court, their final court of appeal: borrowed the integrity and expertise of judges from an advanced and stable legal system. (This may be part of the success Malaysia and Hong Kong have enjoyed as financial centers, although it hasn't worked as well for, say, Jamaica.) But Dubai has done so without subjecting itself constitutionally to another country, and by empowering its outside legal experts not only to judge cases, but also to design rules and court systems that work best for its customers.

Does that mean there are no risks? No. Judges in advanced systems are not infallible or completely incorruptible. And clearly there is nothing formally stopping the rulers of Dubai from reneging on any of the promises that underlie the legal infrastructure of the DIFC. The rulers can oust all the judges, fire the administrators, rewrite the laws whenever they want. It could happen, but it would be short-sighted. Among other things, if the product begins to stink, other reputable court systems around the world will run from it like a festering wound. And since the value of DIFC judgments will often depend on the willingness of those other court systems to recognize those judgments and seize assets in their jurisdiction (England or New York, for example) to satisfy them, maintaining a sterling reputation among leading world legal systems is an important part of what the Dubai government's investment in the whole exercise is based on. Dubai's rulers can destroy the value of the legal system they are selling in the DIFC, but it's hard to figure out why they would do that, so long as it is powering the enormous success of their effort to shift the basis of their economy away from a dependence on oil and fishing and toward financial services and global business. Moreover, the risks of being cheated by the DIFC are limited to the amount those who elect into the DIFC put at risk. Nobody who is using the DIFC has to be there: they can take their business elsewhere. That limited scope and mobility is a critical piece of this story. And why it's a mistake to think—as the next story about Honduras tells us—that you can fix a legal regime just by outsourcing judicial authority.

Selling a City in Honduras: A Cautionary Tale

The idea of sidestepping all the problems of legal infrastructure in developing countries by starting afresh with a new set of smart rules and clean institutions is terrifically appealing. In the abstract, it sounds like a silver bullet. But there are clear traps to be wary of, as the story of Honduras and the charter city reveals.

The idea of the charter city was launched by Paul Romer, a leading economist who earned his reputation with theories about how investments in knowledge impact economic growth and who became Chief Economist for the World Bank in 2016.[5] In Romer's vision, developing countries could break out of the catch-22 of legal development by reaching an agreement—a charter—with another, advanced and reliable, country to oversee the development and implementation of the legal rules governing a new, undeveloped, and currently unoccupied territory—a new city. Why currently unoccupied? A critical premise of Romer's model is that the businesses that operate and the people who live and work in the charter city have complete freedom to join, or abandon, the charter city. To attract and keep businesses and people, then, the city has to have good rules. Ideally that mobility, together with the integrity of the outsiders (foreign judges) who ensure that the charter for the city is being honored, is what keeps the system in check. So far, this sounds like the Dubai recipe.

When I first met Romer at a conference at the National Academy of Sciences in December 2010 he was at the height of his excitement about the concept of charter cities. He was making great strides convincing Honduras to amend its constitution to allow the creation of a charter city in this country with a devastating level of violence and per capita income of the equivalent of a little over US$4,000 a year. He was hard at work trying to identify a guarantor nation that would take on the role of overseeing the faithful implementation of a charter that would aim to secure an intelligent and fair system for businesses, workers, and residents alike. (The natural candidate—the Privy Council of the United Kingdom—declined.)

We spoke of the challenges for the concept. I wondered why he felt it was important to develop an alternative legal regime in a manner tied to territory. Why not create virtual legal regimes, allowing businesses and individuals to choose an alternative set of rules without moving home or headquarters? And why start at the scale of a city, composed of so many different types of legal relationships: work, commerce, family, security, health, environment, education? That was a lot to get right, right out of the gates. And last, I worried that Romer's plan reflected the common naiveté among economists about how legal rules evolve and are implemented over time. It's not simply a matter of choosing the "right" or "best" rules and then just making sure those rules are enforced. Rules almost always have to be sensitive to context—including the entirely novel context of something called a charter city. And they require ongoing, on-the-ground cultivation and adaptation. A judge thousands of miles away, even if he or she came for periodic field trips, would inevitably in my view be drawing on the experience of the developed context of advanced countries to make the inevitable hard calls. I wondered whether the building of local enforcement institutions wasn't a necessary ingredient for success and sustainability.

Romer's plan never will come to the test in Honduras. His version of the charter city was squelched by the type of political chaos that is a daily reality in many poor countries. By the time the statute authorizing the creation of what Honduras called Special Development Regions (REDs in Spanish) was passed by the Honduran legislation, Romer's plan for a guarantor nation had disappeared, although the regions were authorized to delegate judicial functions to other jurisdictions on a temporary basis. Instead, governance of the regions would be overseen by a nine-person Transparency Commission, initially chaired by Romer. Then the politics heated up. As Romer told me, he had expected the Honduran government to appoint to the Transparency Commission an internationally reputable group of which he approved. But then those appointments failed to materialize. Fights also broke out as the government pushed back on a key component of his plan: a path by which a charter city would eventually come under local democratic control, once basic institutions had been stabilized. Romer ultimately resigned from the project in protest of what he saw as official dishonesty.

Then in October 2012 a five-judge panel of the Honduran Supreme Court found in a four-to-one decision that the creation of a charter city that was not subject to the ultimate legal authority of Honduran courts was unconstitutional, subverting Honduran sovereignty. The decision was confirmed by the full fifteen-member court by a vote of thirteen to two. Within the space of few months, however, the four judges who voted on the original panel against the REDs had been removed from their positions. The Honduran government passed a new statute, renaming REDS as ZEDES (*Zonas de Empleo y Desarrollo Económico*—Areas of Employment and Economic Development). The ZEDEs statute is comparable to the REDS statute struck down by the

Supreme Court, but it replaces the Transparency Commission with a twenty-one-member Committee for the Adoption of Best Practices, appointed by the Honduran president. All rules and policies adopted by the ZEDE are subject to approval by this committee, and any judges are first nominated by the committee and approved by the Honduran legislature. Unlike the original statute, the new one provides for the possibility of establishing a ZEDE in a populated area (requiring a majority vote of the residents if the area is higher density, but otherwise not). The committee appoints the (Honduran) administrator for each ZEDE and holds the power to remove that person; in a high-density region the administrator is proposed by the residents, and in a low-density region the administrator is proposed by the "promoters or organizers" of the ZEDE. There is no provision for ultimate transition to local democratic control at the level of the ZEDE. (There is ostensibly democratic control over the entire ZEDE in the sense that the Honduran government and its elected Congress can change the law constituting the ZEDE.) The ZEDE law was upheld by a reconstituted Supreme Court in 2014, and the process of establishing these new zones is underway.

Critics are worried that the new plan effectively sells the right to control the legal regime in the ZEDE to investors and the businesses that set up shop. It's hard to tell from the ZEDE statute how laws will be made in practice. The Committee for the Adoption of Best Practices appears to hold ultimate authority to approve or disapprove proposed laws, but the committee is clearly an oversight body that will have to rely substantially on others for the nitty gritty. That of course can, perhaps likely will, mean rules, judges, and administrators proposed by the investors the country is seeking to sign up to build factories, call centers, and offices in the ZEDE—not to mention the houses, schools, prisons, utility systems, and administrative offices contemplated by the plan. That is how legislation in the United States is often written: lobbyists draft bills that they then present to legislators to get passed. The difference here is that those with the authority to make those proposals law are not elected. All told, this arrangement seems to run the risk that the ZEDE devolves into a company town, with very little in the way of democratic appeal.

None of these plans are off the ground yet, so we can't know how the ZEDEs will evolve in practice. But we can see some of the same problems that I raised with Paul Romer in early conversations about charter cities. Tying the project to territory, instead of virtual communities, creates the risk of locking people in—namely those who originally live or ultimately move to the region. Even if there is freedom of movement on paper, sunk costs in living arrangements can sink quickly. This problem is exacerbated by the aim to take on the project of building an entire city of relationships—that means not just a targeted set of rules for a targeted set of transactions or business activities, but the whole nine yards: schools, prisons, healthcare, social security, and so on. Then there's the added risk, not so apparent in Romer's initial vision, of a major role for the businesses a ZEDE is trying to attract in writing the rules, and maybe even choosing the judges and the administrators. (Indeed, in low-density regions, the promoters and organizers of a ZEDE are authorized by the statute to propose administrators.)

Although the boosters for the Honduran project consistently point to Dubai as a beacon of hope for what can be accomplished with a fresh start on a legal zone, Dubai's International Financial Centre is a very different beast, one that minimizes these three critical problems. The DIFC's domain is organized primarily around the development of a set of rules for a specific set of industries: global financial transactions. Its reach extends to things like housing, food safety, and employment only insofar as people choose to take jobs, rent apartments, or eat at restaurants in the few city blocks where the Centre is located. People can choose to limit their exposure to the DIFC courts and regulatory system: workers don't have to live there. And the DIFC base of customers extends to a virtual community—any contracting parties, or even government agencies, that choose to be governed by the DIFC's laws. That means that the DIFC is competing to create a regime that is attractive to people who really are, and largely maintain, their freedom to leave if the system goes awry. The DIFC has an interest in growing its market beyond its current users. And, although this may or may not be a comfort, the jurisdiction of the DIFC courts does not extend into family and criminal matters. Finally, there is the critical fact that Dubai is a very wealthy country. Even more specifically, most of the people involved in the DIFC system are relatively, if not exceedingly, well off—brokers, traders, investors, and white-collar employees. They are much less at risk of exploitation than poor people living in the informal economy on a few dollars a day. Even the lower-income workers at the Centre—the custodians and hotel maids and restaurant workers—are operating in the formal economy.

These differences make the project of building legal infrastructure for the DIFC a very different one from the challenge in Honduras. As we've seen, what poor countries with a high proportion of people living in the informal economy need from law is quite different from what large, international companies need. The vision for Honduras is that foreign investors will come in as employers, but the ZEDEs are also envisioned as places where people live, eat, and go to school. That implies either that everyone in the town works for the foreign company or there will continue to be people eking out a living in the informal economy, selling goods and services to the people who live there. Neither sounds like a recipe for well-balanced and effectively run legal infrastructure: in either case, the foreign investor will dominate the buy side of the legal infrastructure market that the ZEDE is offering. I would expect, for standard economic reasons, that the legal infrastructure will focus on what that buyer wants and needs. The development of basic tools for people living and working in the informal economy may be a low priority.

In contrast, by targeting a defined and limited type of commercial activity and broadening the base of potential "customers," the DIFC courts and the legal administrators who write the laws reduce the risks that the rule-making and adjudication process will be captured by individual investors. Indeed, the fact that the Dubai government—and not the businesses that would be subject to the DIFC's rules—made the investment in building and financing the infrastructure for the Centre is a major bulwark against capture. The DIFC courts can really focus on doing the job of creating a transparent and effective set of legal rules and processes that they market to the world because they don't have to pay back the investors who built their offices and pay their salaries—or the international overseers who wield fairly opaque authority. True enough, as I noted before, the Dubai government could renege on its promises of noninterference and strike crony deals. But that would likely kill the goose that right now is laying a lot of golden eggs for the country. Dubai has a stable and wealthy government. Such short-sighted strategies are the recourse of the desperate. Honduras might be desperate.

I'd be more optimistic about Honduras if the DIFC judges and administrators—or people like them—decided to set up shop as a global business, selling their expertise in establishing and running targeted legal regimes for narrowly defined projects, with lots of potential for exit and with as much done on a virtual, rather than territorial, basis as possible. A global base of competition is critical because it helps to ensure that the legal provider sees a global return—and a global cost—to how it delivers on its reputation for the things that are attractive about a refresh in legal infrastructure: fidelity, efficiency, neutrality, cost-sensitivity, goal achievement. Such a venture would be driven by a mission to improve the delivery of legal infrastructure, a mission lived by people who are passionate (as the judges and administrators of the Dubai courts evidently are) about a well-run, fair, and squeaky-clean legal process. One worries that the mission of the ZEDE project is the ideological mission of some its foreign patrons. Many of those appointed to the Committee on Best Practices are staunchly libertarian free-marketeers. (The committee includes Grover Norquist of American tax-revolt fame; American conservative political activist Morton Blackwell; Texas oil magnate Alex Cranberg; and Alejandro Chafuen, president of the libertarian Atlas Network.) Many see the experiment as a way of facilitating an escape from regulation and government control, rather than (just) the creation of more effective, useful, and accessible legal infrastructure. Grover Norquist is after all best known to an American audience as the person who famously said in 2001: "I don't want to abolish government. I simply want to reduce it to the size where I can drag it into the bathroom and drown it in the bathtub." That's a goal rooted in politics, and not the effort to invent more effective and sustainable legal infrastructure to support economic growth in the global economy.

I'd like to be wrong about the prospects for Honduras and its ZEDEs or whatever is the next iteration of the charter cities idea. Honduras, like the rest of the BoP, desperately needs innovative approaches to building essential legal infrastructure to support economic development. But like much of the thinking about law and legal infrastructure, even this model is too focused on the idea that the problem is how to change government, rather than how to harness the benefits of specialization, innovation, and competition in the design of legal rules and processes. Benevolent dictators—like the committees and commissions envisioned as ultimate authorities in the charter city model—may be able to dig some places out of the mud, but the likelihoods to me seem small. A better bet is to recognize the complexity of the task of building legal infrastructure, particularly for the BoP in the globally networked economy, and figure out how to get more creative investment and innovation into the process with arms-length and dedicated legal providers. For that, I think the more promising road lies in forging what's needed for competitive global markets in legal infrastructure, starting small, and iterating toward more robust and large-scale solutions.

Conclusion

OUTSIDE OF THE somewhat boring common rooms where economists meet, most people talk as if they either love or hate markets. Libertarians love them—because they think markets mean less government and government is bad. Progressives hate them—because they think markets mean no government and government is good. Economists, on the other hand, don't really love or hate markets: they mostly just recognize that, love 'em or hate 'em, you can't make a complex economy work without 'em. There's no such thing as an unregulated market: markets don't exist without basic legal infrastructure defining rules about who owns what, what deals people can strike and how, what happens when plans go awry or participants behave badly or people get caught in the crossfire or fumes given off by someone else's deal. All markets exist within a framework of what a community decides, collectively, is acceptable and a set of institutions that intervene when some feel cheated or poorly treated by others.

The more competitive markets I'm urging us to build in order to innovate and deploy the legal infrastructure required by a complex global economy are no different. They have to be regulated markets, and they have to be politically accountable markets. So it's important not to come away from this book with the idea that getting more markets into the production of legal infrastructure is just a sneaky way of undercutting government attempts to promote shared goals such as reducing income inequality, protecting workers, promoting justice, or balancing the effort to spur technology with the effort to protect privacy, security, and the planet. The role for government in the world I'm envisioning is still central. It is focused on the politically accountable determination of *what* we want from our legal infrastructure and oversight of *whether* we are getting it.

I have been writing and talking about the ideas in this book for several years. And in those discussions I hear worries about all this talk of markets for law and lawyers from two very different groups of people. The first group consists of those in the international community who are passionate about building justice for the poor and the victims of violence in developing countries. These committed souls are laser-focused on holding governments in such countries accountable to the rule of law. They mean by this the idea that those governments are obligated to deliver fair, neutral, equal treatment of citizens, and to govern within the limits of law (not abusing government power, for example, to victimize vulnerable groups or political opponents). These human rights warriors worry that shifting to a conversation about how not all law is produced by governments could reduce international pressure on weak, corrupt, and abusive governments.

There can be no debate about the urgency of that mission. And if I thought that promoting consideration of markets to help generate law for struggling countries would only plunge them further into poverty and violence, I would stop the train. Keen attention to that risk has to be part of any research agenda devoted to legal infrastructure. But I think this worry belies a misunderstanding about the fundamental role that legal infrastructure plays in supporting social and economic order. Law is not just a set of constraints on how governments behave. Modern countries, rich or poor, need healthy governments to provide services and security, protect human dignity and equality, and set a sustainable path for development. And that means they need law to ensure governments behave as they are supposed to. But the ordinary citizens who live in these countries also need very mundane legal tools to support daily economic life: the ability to protect their property, get compensated for their work and investments, hold sellers of the goods and services they buy to the standards of quality they paid for, gain reasonable access to credit and insurance, and so on. Providing that critical legal infrastructure isn't something that can be kicked down the road, something to figure out once a strong and responsible government is in place. Indeed, without that legal infrastructure in place, there is no way to generate the wealth needed within a country to sustain a strong and responsible government.

The history of legal infrastructure in the West has to be part of the story here. Throughout that history, building legal infrastructure for mundane economic life took place within the context of upheaval and insecurity. Where we need to be smarter is in figuring out how to pick a safe set of stepping-stones across a fast-moving and ever-changing river. Governments must be held to account. And any markets that emerge to supply legal infrastructure need to be subject to politically accountable oversight. If a government is still too weak and illegitimate to do that, then the international community can help to certify the integrity of market options. But where we can carve out a calmer place for others to supply useful and reliable legal tools to help the citizens of poor countries make a living or build a business, we should do so. The challenge has to be seen as one of figuring out where the footholds for a more robust form of legal infrastructure might be found, amid the chaos of unstable and poor governments.

The other group of people who get very worried when I start talking about markets for law and lawyers is lawyers. Some of these people are expressing pure and poorly informed protectionism—like the president of the New York State Bar Association who sat next to me on a panel at an ABA meeting in 2016 to discuss a proposal to establish regulatory goals for law that would promote cost reduction and access to justice. He roused the crowd with the assertion that the proposal was really just a plot to "open the doors to entrepreneurs trying to make money off the backs of lawyers who are starving for work."[1] That's pretty shameful coming from one of the officers of a self-regulated profession that has asserted exclusive rights to decide, on behalf of the public, who can provide what kind of legal services to whom and how. Lawyers overseeing the public's access to justice simply cannot complain that making law more accessible and affordable is a bad idea because it might be bad for lawyers. (Actually, it wouldn't be. Making law more accessible and useful would create more work for lawyers, provided they are willing to adapt like everyone else in the economy does when things change.)

But it's not really that crass protectionist complaint that merits a response. The lawyers' worry that merits a response is the worry that if we dismantle our existing closed systems of professional regulation then we are facing the Wild West of an unregulated market in which con artists will swindle people in legal troubles out of money and well-meaning but incompetent legal helpers will fail their clients, the courts, and our ideals of justice.

Changing the way we regulate the markets for lawyers to make those markets more competitive and thereby more innovative, however, does not mean not regulating them. As I remind lawyers who raise this concern, the world we live in is a world in which *all* markets are regulated. Critical markets, like those providing legal services, are ones we need to regulate carefully. Indeed, we need to develop regulatory methods for legal markets that work differently, and better, than our current approaches. Today the only protections clients in most countries have against shoddy legal work are the upfront protections provided by requiring that lawyers earn a law degree, pass an exam set by a bar association, and follow some basic rules, only some of which might actually help ensure lawyers provide good quality service. In the United States it's extremely difficult to sue a lawyer for malpractice—much harder, because of legal rules lawyers and courts have put in place, than suing other professionals like doctors or engineers or architects. Complaints to the disciplinary committees of bar associations produce little in the way of redress. And American lawyers assert that consumer protection rules, including antitrust rules, don't apply to them. The regulation of lawyers is carried out almost entirely by lawyers themselves in volunteer capacities and with very little funding. There are few policy experts on bar association and court staffs to guide policymaking. Rules are chosen by votes among lawyers elected by other lawyers to represent their interests. That's not how a serious regulatory agency operates. That's not how the more competitive markets for lawyers that I'm advocating would be regulated.

So where do we go from here? Here are five steps we can take to get started.

Number 1: Change the Conversation

Innovating legal infrastructure for a complex global economy needs to be on the global agenda. That means that in our lists of the great challenges of the twenty-first century—income inequality, climate change, the future of work, robotics and AI, poverty reduction, disease eradication, sustainability, cybersecurity—we need to start including the challenge of building the legal infrastructure required to support innovative solutions to those challenges. The challenges here are both challenges of knowledge—figuring out what to build—and politics—figuring out how to build coalitions for change, particularly in light of the resistance that is to be anticipated from those who now enjoy a monopoly over legal rules and processes. How we will implement the rules, policies, and political choices that we need to manage those challenges cannot be an afterthought. It has to be front and center.

Number 2: Don't Leave It to Lawyers

How do we change the conversation? I'd like to think that the policymakers and people who are supposed to be worrying about this stuff—lawyers and judges—will get the message. But I've also been talking about these issues with such folks for too long to be entirely sanguine about the prospect. I recognize that the message often falls into the great chasm between the legal experts, who have trouble seeing how the legal world could be different from the one they already inhabit and who have little interest in upending their own professional lives, and everyone else, who think law is something that the lawyers take care of. "Everyone else," however, is who is paying the price of inadequate, complex, and costly legal infrastructure. These are the people, businesses, and organizations that need to start asking hard questions and demanding better answers. These are the people who experience the economic demand for better legal infrastructure.

In economic theory, demand that exists is demand that is heard. But that is not the way the world always works in practice. The suppliers of legal infrastructure today are not feeling the pressure of that demand. They are not hearing it. We need to hear the voices of the small businesses and ordinary people trying to navigate the legal world without guidance. The four billion people living outside of workable legal frameworks around the globe and trying to make sure their land is not stolen, their businesses allowed to operate, and their savings safe. The sophisticated global corporations that find themselves facing a world in which economic logic is being rewritten by digitization and global supply chains, and regulatory logic is collapsing. The citizen groups that worry about the future of work, the climate, privacy, security, income inequality. The demand for legal infrastructure needs to speak up.

Getting people other than lawyers into the conversation, telling lawyers what they want, won't be enough, however. Innovation of better legal infrastructure also needs to be a challenge taken on by a broad and diverse group of people and organizations. It cannot be left to lawyers. Not because lawyers aren't smart and capable of being creative. But because discussions among lawyers take place in an echo chamber. Lawyers need to be prodded and poked by ideas they have never even thought of as a way of meeting the need for law. The solutions up for development need to include ones that lawyers can't, especially working alone, deliver: solutions that require new technology, new business models, new forms of organization.

Finally, lots of people other than lawyers—engineers, managers, social entrepreneurs, activists, development economists, and more—need to gain basic legal IQ: an understanding of what legal infrastructure is, what it needs to accomplish, how it has been done in the past, and how it might be done in the future.

Number 3: Change the Rules

It's critical that we get a lot of people other than lawyers working on the problem of innovating better legal infrastructure, and that means changing the rules about who is allowed to do, and invest in doing, law. Opening legal markets to competition and investment, in the ways I discuss in Chapters 9 and 10, should be top of the to-do list for anyone who wants to spur the vitality of any economy, global or local. It's essential that we recognize that *legal policy is economic policy*. If our markets for legal infrastructure are monopolized and stymied, then that's as much a drag on our economic success as if we required everyone who wanted to invent an app to be licensed by the current frontrunners in Silicon Valley.

Number 4: Catalyze and Fund Research

There's really only one word for the state of our knowledge about legal infrastructure: abysmal. I recounted in Chapter 8 the terrible lack of data about even the most basic facts about how our legal systems work: how much they cost, how effective they are, who has access for what purposes. Governments need to be spending much more on data collection about the legal environment than they currently do and releasing much more data about the operation of legal institutions to the research community.

The bigger research problem, however, is that there is next to no research on the fundamental questions of how most effectively to provide legal infrastructure in different environments. The dearth of public research dollars devoted to law is just the starting point. More troubling is the fact that legal infrastructure is simply not on the research agenda in our universities. Most fields of research, even those that reach out into the private and government sectors, depend on the presence of a vibrant body of university-based research—to generate a scholarly agenda, develop methodologies, conduct peer review, and supply young researchers to universities, industry, government, and nonprofit research institutes alike. Within universities, however, law schools have been almost exclusively oriented to professional education, and the research done within law faculties is largely organized around the internal issues generated by our existing bodies of law: how to interpret the decisions coming out of our courts, what rules we should have to achieve justice or policy goals, how effective those rules are in practice, and so on. Research on how to build legal infrastructure in the face of mounting costs, with the dramatic upheavals of the complex global economy, or in places where legal order is absent or broken—that is barely on the radar. But it needs to be.

Serious research on legal infrastructure, aimed at understanding needs in both advanced and developing countries, will require the kind of field and experimental research that is standard fare in healthcare and, increasingly, the social sciences. Alongside our clinical studies to determine whether a new drug or innovative public health strategy improves health outcomes, we should also be running studies to determine whether innovative legal tools improve legal outcomes—supporting higher rates of small-business success, for example, or more effective achievement of workplace safety goals. Conducting in-depth local research and policy experiments in poor and developing countries is critical to any agenda that hopes to improve legal infrastructure in the BoP (including countries where Western militaries are often thrust into the role of trying to help establish basic governance in the aftermath of civil war or violent upheaval). I would like to see the emergence of innovative research centers doing for legal innovation what entities like J-PAL—the Abdul Latif Jameel Poverty Action Lab run out of MIT but with close to 150 affiliated professors from across the globe—are doing for innovation in social programs.

To get there, we need visionaries in university leadership and among donors who are willing to pour substantial resources into jump-starting a serious and cross-disciplinary, university-based research community. There are pockets of research activity in our departments of economics, sociology, international relations, psychology, computer science, political science, biology, anthropology, and more that are working on questions of how norms and rules are developed, evolved, sustained, and changed. But they are disconnected from each other and from expertise about law and legal theory. These researchers need to be connected, and their collaboration directed to the fundamental global challenge of building the legal infrastructure we need for the twenty-first century.

Number 5: Invest in Legal Innovation

Research funded by philanthropists and universities can help us build basic knowledge. But serious innovation of new legal tools and regulatory systems is, as I've argued throughout this book, likely to only emerge with the investment in potentially profitable innovations that market incentives can unleash. That's why we need steps 1, 2, 3, and 4: to enable investment from a diverse group with access to the kind of risk and human capital needed for truly new directions in legal infrastructure to emerge.

We need investment targeted in at least three domains. First, we need investment in the technology that supports legal processes—even as they exist today. We need phone apps that can take a picture of a legal document and for a couple of bucks or a low subscription fee, send to the user key information about what the document means. We need online ways to get answers to basic legal questions and legal support for preparing basic documents needed to form a company or file for a patent or establish a partnership. We need phone- and tablet-based support from legal experts for the millions of people who are showing up in court on their own to manage their family or employment disputes, their traffic and municipal fines, their evictions, and their consumer and small-business debt matters. We need better ways for people and small and medium-sized businesses to resolve their disputes—online mediation and arbitration, crowd-sourced resolution platforms, electronic courts. We need more sophisticated AI systems to manage contracts, risks, litigation, and compliance in large companies, globally. We have an emerging community of legal tech entrepreneurs, coordinating through groups such as ReInvent Law and Stanford University's Codex, and they need greater access to capital. They need investor support to develop the capacity to move beyond their current focus on figuring out how to tweak the delivery of legal services to high-end law firms.

Second, we need investment in new types of regulatory systems, ones that could be provided by third-party private regulators. Our current compliance industry, which develops software to track and manage compliance with complex regulations, for example, could be encouraged to move up the chain with innovations in the rules and methods used to achieve publicly set goals. Entrepreneurs could be figuring out how to deliver more effective privately supplied contracting regimes and voluntary legal environments. Investors could help to seed the development of such regimes to serve potential users both in advanced markets and in global emerging markets. Innovators could be figuring out how to deploy software and technology more effectively— as with blockchain contracts—to meet the economic demand for legal infrastructure.

Third, the companies now investing in the technology of the flat world—self-driving cars, drones, private space travel, digital currency, global peer-to-peer platforms, artificially intelligent agents—need also to invest in developing the legal infrastructure that these technologies demand. This means moving beyond setting up government strategy offices to lobby for legislation and funding research that focuses on the moral implications of new technologies (such as the question of whether a self-driving car should take an action that kills its driver in order to save children on the sidewalk). While these will continue to be important issues, they hardly exhaust the terrain of figuring out how to create a legal environment that supports the integration of complex novel technologies into a well-ordered society. The regulatory solutions for these advanced technologies are almost certainly going to involve technology. We need engineers dedicated not only to the project of developing the autonomous vehicles or the robots that will populate our highways, hospitals, schools, homes, and workplaces but also dedicated to the project of developing the regulatory AI that ensures that these artificial agents continue to perform and evolve in ways consistent with the human goals of a complex, dynamic, and ever-faster global economy.

I end with a call to philanthropists and social impact investors. Build into your goals for reducing poverty, developing sustainable energy, advancing education for women and girls, or eradicating disease the budget and attention that legal infrastructure demands. There are no sustainable solutions to these critical challenges without the legal platform on which they can be built. Disrupting our taken-for-granted approaches to delivering the legal tools a robust and fair economy needs may be the most important contribution to innovation that anyone can make. The long history of failed top-down efforts to accomplish change in communities that struggle, both in advanced countries and around the globe, tells us this important fact: finding solutions to the challenges generated by the evolving complexity of economies requires problem-solving that taps into what those closest to the problem know and that is guided by incentives to deliver value on the ground. Legal infrastructure is the critical platform on which that kind of problem-solving happens. Without sufficient legal innovation to build that platform, we can't hope to leap, as we must, into a better future.

Notes

CHAPTER 1

1. Lon L. Fuller, *The Morality of Law* (New Haven: Yale University Press, 1964).
2. For the story of the California Gold Rush see J. S. Holliday, *The World Rushed In: The California Gold Rush Experience* (New York: Simon and Schuster, 1981); John A. Sutter, *The Discovery of Gold in California* (1848), http://www.sfmuseum.org/hist2/gold.html, accessed April 8, 2016; Charles Howard Shinn, *Mining Camps: A Study in American Frontier Government* (New York: Charles Scribner's Sons, 1885); and Melissa O'Meara, "1848–1850: A Timeline," http://www.calgoldrush.com/resources/gr_timeline.html, accessed April 8, 2016. Other discussion of the California Gold Rush in this chapter draws on Gillian K. Hadfield and Barry R. Weingast, "Law without the State: Legal Attributes and the Coordination of Decentralized Collective Punishment," *Journal of Law and Courts* 1 (2013): 3–34 and sources cited there.
3. For the story of Goldcorp see Don Tapscott and Anthony D. Williams, *Wikinomics: How Mass Collaboration Changes Everything* (New York: Penguin, 2006); U.S.$575,000 Goldcorp Challenge Awards world's first 6 million ounce internet gold rush yields high grade results! http://www.infomine.com/index/pr/Pa065434.PDF.

CHAPTER 2

1. Joan B. Silk, "Empathy, Sympathy, and Prosocial Preferences in Primates," in *Oxford Handbook of Evolutionary Psychology*, ed. R. I. M. Dunbar and Louise Barrett (Oxford: Oxford University Press, 2007), 115–126; Joan B. Silk et al., "Chimpanzees Are Indifferent to the Welfare of Unrelated Group Members," *Nature* 437 (2005): 1357–1359; Victoria Horner, J. Devyn Carter, Malini Suchak, and Frans B. M. de Waal, "Spontaneous Prosocial Choice by Chimpanzees,"

Proceedings of the National Academy of Sciences 108 (2011): 13847–13851. See generally Peter M. Kappeler and Joan B. Silk, eds., *Mind the Gap: Tracing the Origins of Human Universals* (Berlin: Springer-Verlag, 2010); and Peter M. Kappeler and Carel P. van Schaik, eds., *Cooperation in Primates and Humans: Mechanisms and Evolution* (Berlin: Springer-Verlag 2006).

2. Jessica C. Flack and Frans B. M. de Waal, "'Any Animal Whatever': Darwinian Building Blocks of Morality in Monkeys and Apes," *Journal of Consciousness Studies* 7 (2000): 1–29.

3. Michael Tomasello and Amrisha Vaish, "Origins of Human Cooperation and Morality," *Annual Review of Psychology* 64 (2013): 231–255.

4. Katrin Riedl, Keith Jensen, Josep Call, and Michael Tomasello, "Restorative Justice in Children," *Current Biology* 25 (2015): 1731–1735.

5. Josep Call and Michael Tomasello, "Does the Chimpanzee Have a Theory of Mind? 30 Years Later," *Trends in Cognitive Science* 12 (2008): 187–192.

6. Jessica C. Flack and Frans B. M. de Waal, "Context Modulates Signal Meaning in Primate Communication," *Proceedings of the National Academy of Sciences* 104 (2007): 1581–1586.

7. Jessica C. Flack and David C. Krakauer, "Encoding Power in Communication Networks," *American Naturalist* 168 (2006): E87–E102; Jessica C. Flack, Frans B. M. de Waal, and David Krakauer, "Social Structure, Robustness, and Policing Cost in a Cognitively Sophisticated Species," *American Naturalist* 165 (2005): 126–139.

8. Polly Wiessner, "Norm Enforcement among the Ju/'hoansi Bushmen: A Case of Strong Reciprocity?" *Human Nature* 16 (2005): 115–145.

9. Robert C. Ellickson, *Order without Law: How Neighbors Settle Disputes* (Cambridge, MA: Harvard University Press, 1994).

10. Nili Shupak, "A New Source for the Study of the Judiciary and Law of Ancient Egypt: 'The Tale of the Eloquent Peasant,'" *Journal of Near Eastern Studies* 51 (1992): 1–18. For law in the ancient world see generally Raymond Westbrook, ed., *A History of Ancient Near Eastern Law* (Boston: Brill, 2003); J. N. Postgate, *Early Mesopotamia: Society and Economy at the Dawn of History* (London: Routledge, 1992); and Martha Tobi Roth, Harry A. Hoffner, and Piotr Michalowski, *Law Collections from Mesopotamia and Asia Minor*, 2nd ed. (Atlanta, GA: Scholars Press, 1997).

11. For a discussion of Hammurabi's code see Martha T. Roth, "Mesopotamian Legal Traditions and the Laws of Hammurabi," *Chicago-Kent Law Review* 71 (1995–1996): 13–39.

12. For the text of Hammurabi's code see M. E. J. Richardson, *Hammurabi's Law: Text, Translation and Glossary* (London: Sheffield Academic Press, 2004). My estimate of the proportion of the code that deals with commercial matters is based on the assumption that missing text contains commercial provisions similar to those immediately before and after the missing text.

13. William Miller, *Bloodtaking and Peacemaking: Feud, Law, and Society in Saga Iceland* (Chicago: University of Chicago Press, 1997), 191–192.

14. Miller, *Bloodtaking and Peacemaking*, 223.

15. The following discussion draws on Gillian K. Hadfield and Barry R. Weingast, "Law without the State: Legal Attributes and the Coordination of Decentralized Collective Punishment," *Journal of Law and Courts* 1 (2013): 3–34 and sources cited there.

16. The discussion in this section draws on Hadfield and Weingast, "Law without the State," *Journal of Law and Courts* 1 (2013): 3–34 and sources cited there.

17. In addition to other sources cited in this section, see Robert-Henri Bautier, *The Economic Development of Medieval Europe* (New York: Harcourt Brace Jovanovich, 1971); Francis B. Bickley, ed., *The Little Red Book of Bristol* (Bristol: W. Crofton Hemmons, 1900); and Adolphus Ballard, *British Borough Charters, 1216–1307*, (Cambridge: Cambridge University Press, 1923).

18. See William Mitchell, *An Essay on the Early History of the Law Merchant, being the Yorke Prize Essay for the year 1903* (Cambridge: University Press, 1904), esp. Chapter 3; Edgcumbe Staley, *The Guilds of Florence* (London: Methuen, 1906), esp. Chapter 2.

19. For the text of the *Carta Mercatoria* see A. E. Bland, P. A. Brown, and R. H. Tawney, *English Economic History: Select Documents* (London: G. Bell and Sons, 1914).

20. Avner Greif, *Institutions and the Path to the Modern Economy: Lessons from Medieval Trade* (Cambridge: Cambridge University Press, 2006); Paul R. Milgrom, Douglass C. North, and Barry R. Weingast, "The Role of Institutions in the Revival of Trade: The Law Merchant, Private Judges, and the Champagne Fairs," *Economics and Politics* 2 (1990): 1–23; Avner Greif, Paul R. Milgrom, and Barry R. Weingast, "Coordination, Commitment, and Enforcement: The Case of the Merchant Guild," *Journal of Political Economy* 102 (1994): 745–776. For additional perspectives and historical detail see Emily Kadens, "Order within Law, Variety within Custom: The Character of the Medieval Merchant Law," *Chicago Journal of International Law* 5 (2004): 39–65; Emily Kadens, "The Myth of the Customary Law Merchant," *Texas Law Review* 90 (2012): 1153–1206; and Sheilagh Ogilvie, *Institutions and European Trade: Merchant Guilds, 1000–1800* (Cambridge: Cambridge University Press, 2011). There is a debate in this broad literature about whether merchant guilds arose to solve efficiency problems in trade or to serve distributional interests. My take on the debate is that both are right and that the critiques have helpfully served to counter some early and excessively simple accounts of how the medieval guilds operated in relation to other institutions such as municipalities and the extent to which they produced "uniform" commercial law.

21. Robert D. Putnam, *Making Democracy Work: Civic Traditions in Modern Italy* (Princeton, NJ: Princeton University Press, 1993).

22. The ordinance is included as an appendix in Ellen Wedemeyer Moore, *The Fairs of Medieval England: An Introductory Study* (Toronto: Pontifical Institute of Medieval Studies, 1985).

23. Quoted in Greif, *Institutions*, 95.

24. Phillipe Dollinger, *The German Hansa* (Stanford, CA: Stanford University Press, 1970).

25. Moore, *Fairs of Medieval England*.

26. Daniel Klerman, "The Emergence of English Commercial Law: Analysis Inspired by the Ottoman Experience," *Journal of Economic Behavior and Organization* 71 (2009): 638–646.

27. Timur Kuran, *The Long Divergence: How Islamic Law Held Back the Middle East* (Princeton, NJ: Princeton University Press, 2012).

CHAPTER 3

1. KPMG International, *Confronting Complexity: Research Findings and Insights*, https://www.kpmg.com/Global/en/IssuesAndInsights/ArticlesPublications/Documents/complexity-research-report.pdf.

2. Daniel W. McShea and Robert N. Brandon, *Biology's First Law: The Tendency for Diversity and Complexity to Increase in Evolutionary Systems* (Chicago: University of Chicago Press, 2010).

3. Scott E. Page, "Uncertainty, Difficulty, and Complexity," *Journal of Theoretical Politics* 20 (2008): 115–149.

4. Stuart A. Kauffman, *The Origins of Order: Self-Organization and Selection in Evolution* (New York: Oxford University Press, 1993).

5. John Tooby and Irven deVore, "The Reconstruction of Hominid Behavioral Evolution through Strategic Modeling," in *The Evolution of Human Behavior: Primate Models*, ed. Warren G. Kinzey (Albany: SUNY Press, 1987).

6. Robert Boyd, Peter J. Richerson, and Joseph Henrich, "The Cultural Niche: Why Social Learning Is Essential for Human Adaptation," *Proceedings of the National Academy of Sciences* 108 (2011): 10913–10925.

7. David W. Buchanan and David M. Sobel, "Mechanism-Based Causal Reasoning in Young Children," *Child Development* 82 (2011): 2053–2066.

8. For a discussion see Steven Pinker, "Language as an Adaptation to the Cognitive Niche," in *Language Evolution: States of the Art*, ed. S. Kirby and M. Christiansen (Oxford: Oxford University Press, 2003), 16–37.

9. E. Adamson Hoebel, *The Law of Primitive Man: A Study in Comparative Legal Dynamics* (Cambridge, MA: Harvard University Press, 1954), 73.

10. Joshua Gans, *Information Wants to Be Shared* (Boston: Harvard Business School Publishing, 2012).

11. Adam Smith, *The Wealth of Nations* (New York: P. F. Collier, 1902), 44–50.

12. Alison Gopnik and David M. Sobel, "Detecting Blickets: How Young Children Use Information about Novel Causal Powers in Categorization and Induction," *Child Development* 71 (2000): 1205–1222.

13. Smith, *Wealth of Nations*, 55.

14. Smith, *Wealth of Nations*, 57.

15. Sarah Mathew, Robert Boyd, and Matthijs Van Veelen, "Human Cooperation among Kin and Close Associates May Require Enforcement of Norms by Third Parties," in *Cultural Evolution: Society, Technology, Language, and Religion*, ed. Peter J. Richerson and Morten H. Christiansen (Cambridge, MA: MIT Press, 2013), 45–60.

16. Scott E. Page, *The Difference: How the Power of Diversity Creates Better Groups, Firms, Schools, and Societies* (Princeton, NJ: Princeton University Press, 2007).

17. Fuller, *Morality of Law* 130.

18. H. L. A. Hart, *The Concept of Law* (Oxford: Oxford University Press, 2012), 89–90.

19. Gillian K. Hadfield and Barry R. Weingast, "What Is Law? A Coordination Model of the Characteristics of Legal Order," *Journal of Legal Analysis* 4 (2012): 471–514.

CHAPTER 4

1. The earliest reference on the web that I can find to the idea of a frieNDA (trusting your friends not to tell anyone your ideas rather than relying on an NDA) is http://yaron-galai.com/2006/08/frienda.html. Somebody drafted a template: http://friendda.org/.

2. The discussion that follows draws on Joseph P. Strayer, *On the Medieval Origins of the Modern State* (Princeton NJ: Princeton University Press, 2005); Walter C. Opello Jr. and Stephen J. Rosow, *The Nation-State and Global Order: A Historical Introduction to Contemporary Politics* (Boulder, CO: Lynne Rienner, 2004) and sources cited there; Nathan Rosenberg and L. E. Birdzell Jr., *How the West Grew Rich: The Economic Transformation of the Industrial World* (New York: Basic Books, 1986); Steven E. Ozment, *Reformation in the Cities: The Appeal of Protestantism to Sixteenth-Century Germany and Switzerland* (New Haven: Yale University Press, 1980); and Marvin B. Becker, "Church and State in Florence on the Eve of the Renaissance (1343–1382)," *Speculum* 37 (1962): 509–527.

3. For discussions of the rise of professional policing and bureaucratized punishment see David Garrioch, "The People of Paris and Their Police in the Eighteenth Century: Reflections on the Introduction of a 'Modern' Police Force," *European History Quarterly* 24 (1994): 511–535; and Norval Morris and David J. Rothman, eds., *The Oxford History of the Prison: The Practice of Punishment in Western Society* (New York: Oxford University Press, 1998).

CHAPTER 5

1. For data in this and the following paragraph see Angus Maddison, *The World Economy: A Millennial Perspective* (Paris: Organization for Economic

Cooperation and Development, 2001) and data available at the Maddison Project, http://www.ggdc.net/maddison/maddison-project/home.htm, 2013 version.

2. This discussion draws on Alfred D. Chandler Jr., *The Visible Hand: The Managerial Revolution in American Business* (Cambridge, MA: Harvard University Press, 1977), Part I.

3. Max Weber, "Science as a Vocation," in *From Max Weber: Essays in Sociology*, trans. and ed. H. H. Gerth and C. Wright Mills (New York: Oxford University Press, 1946), 129–156.

4. For sources for this section see Lawrence M. Friedman, *A History of American Law*, 3rd ed. (New York: Simon and Schuster, 2005); Lawrence M. Friedman, *American Law in the Twentieth Century* (New Haven: Yale University Press, 2002); Anton-Hermann Chroust, *The Rise of the Legal Profession in America* (Norman: University of Oklahoma Press, 1965), Bruce H. Mann, *Neighbors and Strangers: Law and Community in Early Connecticut* (Chapel Hill: University of North Carolina Press, 2001); William E. Nelson, *Americanization of the Common Law: The Impact of Legal Change on Massachusetts, 1760–1830* (Athens: University of Georgia Press, 1994); and Michael Moran, "Understanding the Regulatory State," *British Journal of Political Science* 32 (2002): 391–413.

5. *Lochner v. New York*, 198 U.S. 45 (1905). The law at issue was the New York Bakeshop Act of 1895, available at http://regulationonline.com/ny-bakeshop/.

6. For the story of airline deregulation see Steven Morrison and Clifford Winston, *The Economic Effects of Airline Deregulation* (Washington, DC: Brookings Institute, 1986).

7. This section draws on Edson R. Sunderland, *History of the American Bar Association and its Work* (Ann Arbor, MI: R. H. Smith, 1953); American Bar Association, *Annual Reports, 1878–1881*; biography of Simeon Eben Baldwin (Connecticut State Library); and George Harris Smith, "History of the Activity of the American Bar Association in Relation to Legal Education and Admission to the Bar," *American Law School Law Review* 7 (1930): 1–7.

8. American Bar Association, "Address of E. J. Phelps," in *Annual Report 1878*, 188.

9. American Bar Association, *Annual Report 1879*, 19.

10. American Bar Association, *Annual Report 1880*, 49.

11. "Vermont Ready to Vote," *New York Times*, September 6, 1880. Available at http://query.nytimes.com/gst/abstract.html?res=9B0CE3D9143FEE3ABC4E53 DFBF66838B699FDE.

12. Jerold S. Auerbach, *Unequal Justice: Social Change in Modern America* (New York: Oxford University Press, 1977).

13. E. Lee Shepard, "Lawyers Look at Themselves: Professional Consciousness and the Virginia Bar 1770–1850" *American Journal of Legal History* 25 (1981): 16.

14. Lincoln's Advice to Lawyers, http://www.abrahamlincolnonline.org/lincoln/speeches/law.htm.

15. Laurel Rigertas, "Lobbying and Litigating Against 'Legal Bootleggers': The Role of the Organized Bar in the Expansion of the Courts' Inherent Powers in the Early Twentieth Century," *California Western Law Review* 46 (2009): 65–136.

16. Roscoe Pound, "The Causes of Popular Dissatisfaction with the Administration of Justice," *American Law Review* 40 (1906): 729–749; Roscoe Pound, "The Rule-Making Power of the Courts," *American Bar Association Journal* (1926): 599–603; Edson R. Sunderland, "The Grant of Rule-Making Power to the Supreme Court of the United States," *Michigan Law Review* 32 (1934): 1116–1129; and Russell R. Wheeler, "Roscoe Pound and the Evolution of Judicial Administration," *South Texas Law Review* 48 (2007): 943–967.

17. Sunderland, *History*, 163.

18. American Bar Association, Canons of Professional Ethics, http://www.american-bar.org/content/dam/aba/migrated/cpr/mrpc/Canons_Ethics.authcheckdam.pdf.

19. Lawyer counts in this and following paragraphs are from the American Bar Association, http://www.americanbar.org/content/dam/aba/administrative/market_research/total_national_lawyer_counts_1878_2013.authcheckdam.pdf.

20. Canada has about 90,000 lawyers for a population of thirty-five million (http://docs.flsc.ca/STATS2013ReportFINAL.pdf). England and Wales have approximately 175,000 barristers and solicitors for a population of fifty-six million (https://www.barstandardsboard.org.uk/media-centre/research-and-statistics/statistics/practising-barrister-statistics/, http://www.sra.org.uk/sra/how-we-work/reports/data/population_solicitors.page). Australia has approximately 66,000 lawyers for a population of twenty-three million (http://www.lawcouncil.asn.au/lawcouncil/index.php/12-resources/231-how-many-lawyers-are-there-in-australia).

21. Data on law schools, enrollment, and degrees awarded available at http://www.americanbar.org/content/dam/aba/administrative/legal_education_and_admissions_to_the_bar/statistics/enrollment_degrees_awarded.authcheckdam.pdf.

22. Data in this paragraph are from Robert L. Nelson, *Partners with Power: The Social Transformation of the Large Law Firm* (Berkeley: University of California Press, 1988); American Bar Association, *Lawyer Demographics*, http://www.americanbar.org/content/dam/aba/administrative/market_research/lawyer-demographics-tables-2015.authcheckdam.pdf; and "The 2015 AmLaw 200," *American Lawyer*, May 28, 2015.

23. John P. Heinz and Edward O. Laumann, *Chicago Lawyers: The Social Structure of the Bar* (New York: Russell Sage Foundation, and Chicago: American Bar Foundation, 1982); John P. Heinz, Edward O. Laumann, Robert L. Nelson, and Ethan Michelson, "The Changing Character of Lawyers' Work: Chicago in 1975 and 1995," *Law and Society Review* 32 (1998): 751–775.

24. Calculations based on US Census data, GDP by Industry, Legal Services.

CHAPTER 6

1. Christopher S. Tang and Joshua D. Zimmerman, "Managing New Product Development and Supply Chain Risks: The Boeing 787 Case," *Supply Chain Forum* 10 (2009): 74–86.

2. Richard Baldwin and Javier Lopez-Gonzalez, "Supply-Chain Trade: A Portrait of Global Patterns and Several Testable Hypotheses," *World Economy* (2015): 1682–1721.

3. Oliver E. Williamson, *Markets and Hierarchies: Analysis and Antitrust Implications* (New York: Free Press, 1983).

4. The story of Toyota and lean production is told in James P. Womack, Daniel T. Jones, and Daniel Roos, *The Machine That Changed the World* (New York: Free Press, 1990).

5. Tang and Zimmerman, "Managing New Product Development"; Suresh Kotha and Kannan Srikanth, "Managing a Global Partnership Model: Lessons from the Boeing 787 'Dreamliner' Program," *Global Strategy Journal* 3 (2013): 41–66.

6. Stewart Macaulay, "Non-contractual Relations in Business: A Preliminary Study," *American Sociological Review* 28 (1963): 55–67.

7. Richard Baldwin, "Global Supply Chains: Why They Emerged, Why They Matter, and Where They Are Going," Centre for Economic Policy Research Discussion Paper No. 9103 (2012).

8. Oliver E. Williamson, *The Economic Institutions of Capitalism: Firms, Markets, Relational Contracting* (New York: Free Press, 1985), 11.

9. This discussion is based on Toshihiro Nishiguchi, *Strategic Industrial Sourcing: The Japanese Advantage* (New York: Oxford University Press, 1994).

10. Nishiguchi, *Strategic Industrial Sourcing,* 47.

11. Gillian K. Hadfield and Iva Bozovic, "Scaffolding: Using Formal Contracts to Build Informal Relations in Support of Innovation," *Wisconsin Law Review* 5 (in press).

12. Deloitte, *Corporate Development 2012: Leveraging the Power of Relationships in M&A* (2012), http://deloitte.wsj.com/cfo/files/2012/08/Corporate_Development_Survey_2012.pdf.

13. http://www.berkshirehathaway.com/letters/2002pdf.pdf.

14. Baldwin and Lopez-Gonzalez, "Supply-Chain Trade," 1682–1683.

15. Richard Metters and Rohit Verma, "History of Offshoring Knowledge Services," *Journal of Operations Management* 26 (2008): 141–147.

16. Susan Athey and Scott Stern, "The Nature and Incidence of Software Piracy: Evidence from Windows," in *Economic Analysis of the Digital Economy*, ed. Avi Goldfarb, Shane M. Greenstein, and Catherine E. Tucker (Chicago: University of Chicago Press, 2015).

17. For discussions of the Microsoft case see Carl Shapiro, "Microsoft: A Remedial Failure," *Antitrust Law Journal* 75 (2009): 739–772; and David A. Heiner, "Microsoft: A Remedial Success?" *Antitrust Law Journal* 78 (2012): 329–362.

18. See Mark Scott, "European Firms Team Up to Target Google in Civil Lawsuits," *New York Times*, September 1, 2015.

19. Katharina Pistor and Chenggang Xu, "Incomplete Law," *International Law and Politics* 35 (2003): 931–1013.

20. Brandon Schoettle and Michael Sivak, "A Preliminary Analysis of Real World Crashes Involving Self-Driving Vehicles" (2015), available at http://www.umich.edu/~umtriswt/PDF/UMTRI-2015-34_Abstract_English.pdf. Discussed in http://www.govtech.com/fs/First-Driverless-Car-Crash-Study-Autonomous-Vehicles-Crash-More-Injuries-Are-Less-Serious.html.

21. See, for example, Patrick Lin, "The Ethics of Autonomous Cars," *Atlantic*, October 8, 2013.

CHAPTER 7

1. "iPhone Keeps Record of Everywhere You Go," *Guardian*, April 20, 2011. Apple's press release is at http://www.apple.com/pr/library/2011/04/27Apple-Q-A-on-Location-Data.html.

2. Yannis Bakos, Florencia Marotta-Wurgler, and David Trossen, "Does Anyone Read the Fine Print? Consumer Attention to Standard-Form Contracts," *Journal of Legal Studies* 43 (2014): 1–35.

3. Jens Grossklags and Nathan Good, "Empirical Studies on Software Notices to Inform Policy Makers and Usability Designers," in *Financial Cryptography and Data Security*, ed. Sven Dietrich and Rachna Dhamjia (Berlin: Springer-Verlag, 2007), 341–355.

4. Ewa Luger, Stuart Moran, and Tom Rodden, "Consent for All: Revealing the Hidden Complexity of Terms and Conditions," *ACM CHI 2013* (Paris): 2687–2696.

5. John Aloysius Cogan Jr., "Readability, Contracts of Recurring Use, and the Problem of Ex Post Judicial Governance of Health Insurance Policies," *Roger Williams University Law Review* 15 (2010): 93–126.

6. Larry Magid, "It Pays to Read License Agreements," http://www.pcpitstop.com/spycheck/eula.asp.

7. Eleazar David Meléndez, "Dodd-Frank Rules Nearly 9,000 Pages, But It's Less Than One-Third Finished," ibTimes.com, July 19, 2013, http://www.ibtimes.com/dodd-frank-rules-nearly-9000-pages-its-less-one-third-finished-726774.

8. Ryan J. Owens and Justin P. Wedeking, "Justices and Legal Clarity: Analyzing the Complexity of U.S. Supreme Court Opinions," *Law and Society Review* 45 (2011): 1027–1061.

9. Andrew Parker, "Vodafone Confident of Upper Hand in Verizon fight," FT.com, March 28, 2010.

10. http://www.berkshirehathaway.com/letters/2002pdf.pdf.

11. https://www.treasury.gov/press-center/press-releases/Pages/tg71.aspx.

12. There are no systematic and reliable national surveys of lawyer billing rates. I am drawing in this section on surveys done by the *National Law Journal*, Altman-Weil, Major, Lindsey & Africa Legal Search Consultants, and TyMetrix.

13. "The 2015 AmLaw 200," *American Lawyer Magazine*, May 28, 2015.

14. These calculations are based on data from the 2012 Economic Census, EC1254SSSZ4: Professional, Scientific, and Technical Services: Subject Series— Establishment and Firm Size: Receipts/Revenue Size of Establishments for the United States: 2012.

15. These data are from the US Internal Revenue Service Nonfarm Sole Proprietorship statistics for legal services including part-time and negative net income filers and excludes solos who file as a corporation.

16. US Bureau of Labor Statistics, Occupational Employment and Wages, May 2014 (23–1011, Lawyers).

17. Paula Hannaford-Agor and Nicole Waters, "Estimating the Cost of Civil Litigation," *Court Statistics Project: Caseload Highlights* (National Center for State Courts, January 2013).

18. Lois R. Lupica, *The Consumer Bankruptcy Fee Study: Final Report* (December 2011).

19. American Intellectual Property Lawyers Association, *Report of the Economic Survey 2012*.

20. Joni Hersch and W. Kip Viscusi, "Tort Liability Litigation Costs for Commercial Claims," *American Law and Economics Review* 9 (2007): 330–369.

21. A. Mitchell Polinsky and Steven Shavell, "The Uneasy Case for Product Liability," *Harvard Law Review* 123 (2010): 1437–1492.

22. For sources for this and the following paragraph, see Gillian K. Hadfield and Jamie Heine, "Life in the Law-Thick World: The Legal Resource Landscape for Ordinary Americans," in *Beyond Elite Law: Access to Civil Justice in America*, ed. Samuel Estreicher and Joy Radice (Cambridge: Cambridge University Press, 2016).

23. James S. Kakalik et al., *An Evaluation of Judicial Case Management under the Civil Justice Reform Act* (Santa Monica, CA: Rand Institute for Civil Justice).

24. Institute for the Advancement of the American Legal System, *Electronic Discovery: A View from the Front Lines* (2008).

25. Nicholas M. Pace and Laura Zakaras, *Where the Money Goes: Understanding Litigant Expenditures for Producing Electronic Discovery* (Santa Monica, CA: Rand Institute for Civil Justice, 2012).

26. "Litigation Cost Survey of Major Companies," Statement Submitted by Lawyers for Civil Justice, Civil Justice Reform Group, and US Chamber Institute for Legal Reform to the Committee on Rules of Practice and Procedure, Judicial Conference of the United States at 2010 Conference on Civil Litigation, Duke Law School, May 10–11, 2010.

27. Available at http://www.bricker.com/documents/attachments/microsoft.pdf.

28. American Intellectual Property Lawyers Association, *Report of the Economic Survey* (various years).

29. http://www.lsac.org/lsacresources/data/lsats-administered.

30. Richard Moorhead, "Lawyer Specialization: Managing the Professional Paradox," *Law and Policy* 32 (2010): 226–259.

31. Legal Services Consumer Panel, *Regulating Will-Writing* (July 2011). Available at http://www.legalservicesconsumerpanel.org.uk/publications/research_and_reports/documents/consumerpanel_willwritingreport_final.pdf.

32. http://www.bticonsulting.com/themadclientist/2013/6/25/after-5-year-upward-march-client-satisfaction-plummets.html

33. BTI Consulting, *How Clients Hire, Fire and Spend* (2007).

34. John C. Coates, Michele M. deStefano, Ashish Nanda, and David B. Wilkins, "Hiring Teams, Firms, and Lawyers: Evidence of the Evolving Relationships in the Corporate Legal Market," *Law and Social Inquiry* 36 (2011): 999–1031.

35. Anthony T. Kronman, *The Lost Lawyer: Failing Ideals of the Legal Profession* (Cambridge, MA: Harvard University Press, 1993).

CHAPTER 8

1. Chris Anderson, *The Long Tail: Why the Future of Business Is Selling Less of More* (New York: Hyperion, 2006).

2. Benito Mussolini, *Grand Fascist Report* (1929), quoted in E. B. Ashton, *The Fascist: His State and His Mind* (New York: William Morrow, 1972), 63.

3. National Executive Committee of the Labour Party, *The Old World and the New Society: A Report on the Problems of War and Peace Reconstruction* (London: Transport House, 1942).

4. Lionel B. Robbins, *Economic Planning and International Order* (London: Macmillan, 1937), 3.

5. http://articles.philly.com/1989-11-30/news/26137118_1_leonid-abalkin-gorbachev-economic-woes.

6. William D. Nordhaus, "Soviet Economic Reform: The Longest Road," *Brookings Papers on Economic Activity* 1 (1990): 287–318.

7. F. A. Hayek, "The Use of Knowledge in Society," *American Economic Review* 35 (1945): 519–530.

8. F. A. Hayek, "Planning and 'The Road to Serfdom': Friedrich Hayek Comments on Uses to Which His Book Has Been Put," *Chicago Sun Book Week*, May 6, 1945; F. A. Hayek, "The Road to Serfdom, an Address before the Economic Club of Detroit," April 23, 1945, p. 6. Both sources quoted in Bruce Caldwell, (ed.) *The Collected Works of F. A. Hayek: Volume II: The Road to Serfdom, Text and Documents, The Definitive Edition* (New York: Routledge, 2014), pp. 19–20.

9. James Q. Wilson, "Reinventing Public Administration," *PS: Political Science and Politics* 27 (1994): 667–673.

10. Organization of Economic Cooperation and Development, *OECD Factbook: Economic, Environmental and Social Statistics* (2014).

11. This history of Kaiser's health system is based on Rickey Lynn Hendricks, *A Model for National Health Care: The History of Kaiser Permanente* (New Brunswick, NJ: Rutgers University Press, 1993).

12. Pauline M. Ippolito and Alan D. Mathios, "Information, Advertising and Health Choices: A Study of the Cereal Market," *Rand Journal of Economics* 21 (1990): 459–480.

13. Daniel Hosken and Brett Wendling, "Informing the Uninformed: How Drug Advertising Affects Check-Up Visits," *International Journal of Industrial Organization* 32 (2013): 181–194.

14. Qiang Liu and Sachin Gupta, "Direct-to-Consumer Advertising of Pharmaceuticals: An Integrative Review," in *Innovation and Marketing in the Pharmaceutical Industry*, ed. M. Ding et al. (New York: Springer, 2014).

CHAPTER 9

1. Anne Callery, *Yahoo! Cataloging the Web* (1996). Available at http://misc.library. ucsb.edu/untangle/callery.html.

2. http://www.internetlivestats.com/total-number-of-websites/.

3. Steve G. Steinberg, "Seek and Ye Shall Find (Maybe)," *Wired*, May 1, 1996.

4. Roy Tennant, "Interoperability: The Holy Grail," *Library Journal*, July 1, 1998.

5. Lawrence Page, Sergey Brin, Rajeev Motwani, and Terry Winograd, "The PageRank Citation Ranking: Bringing Order to the Web," *Stanford InfoLab Technical Report* (1998).

6. Henry W. Chesbrough, *Open Innovation: The New Imperative for Creating and Profiting from Technology* (Boston: Harvard Business School Press, 2003).

7. Lu Hong and Scott E. Page, "Problem Solving by Heterogeneous Agents," *Journal of Economic Theory* 97 (2001): 123–163.

8. Scott E. Page, *Diversity and Complexity* (Princeton, NJ: Princeton University Press, 2011).

9. Peter Coughlan, Jane Fulton Suri, and Katherine Canales, "Prototypes as (Design) Tools for Behavioral and Organizational Change: A Design-Based Approach to Help Organizations Change Work Behaviors," *Journal of Applied Behavioral Science* 43 (2007): 1–13.

10. http://ecorner.stanford.edu/videos/3598/Innovation-Fueled-by-Experimentation.

11. Eric Ries, *The Lean Startup: How Today's Entrepreneurs Use Continuous Innovation to Create Radically Successful Businesses* (New York: Crown Business, 2011).

12. Clifford Winston, Robert W. Crandall, and Vikram Maheshri, *First Thing We Do, Let's Deregulate All the Lawyers* (Washington, DC: Brookings Institution, 2011).

13. The following discussion draws on Gillian K. Hadfield, "Legal Barriers to Innovation: The Growing Economic Cost of Professional Control over Corporate Legal Markets." *Stanford Law Review* 60 (2008): 1689–1732; Gillian K. Hadfield, "Producing Law for Innovation," in *Rules for Growth: Promoting Innovation and*

Growth Through Legal Reform, ed. R. Litan et al. (Kansas City: Ewing Marion Kauffman Foundation, 2011); Gillian K. Hadfield, "The Cost of Law: Promoting Access to Justice through the (Un)Corporate Practice of Law." *International Review of Law and Economics* 38 (2014): 43–63; Gillian K. Hadfield, "Innovating to Improve Access: Changing the Way Courts Regulate Legal Markets," *Daedalus* 143 (2014): 83–95; and Gillian K. Hadfield and Deborah L. Rhode, "How to Regulate Legal Services to Promote Access, Innovation, and the Quality of Lawyering," *Hastings Law Journal* 67 (2016): 1191–1223.

14. Elizabeth E. Bailey, "Air-Transportation Deregulation," in *Better Living through Economics*, ed. John J. Siegfried (Cambridge, MA: Harvard University Press, 2010), 196.

15. I am on LegalZoom's Legal Advisory Council but I do not have a financial interest in the company—only a shared sense of mission to make better legal help available at lower cost to more people.

CHAPTER 10

1. http://ec.europa.eu/justice/data-protection/files/factsheets/factsheet_data_protection_en.pdf.

2. Mark Scott, "Europe Tried to Rein In Google. It Backfired," *New York Times*, April 18, 2016.

3. The following discussion draws on Gillian K. Hadfield, "Delivering Legality on the Internet: Developing Principles for the Private Provision of Commercial Law," *American Law and Economics Review* 6 (2004): 154–184; and Gillian K. Hadfield, "Privatizing Commercial Law," *Regulation* 24 (2001): 40–45.

4. Gillian K. Hadfield and Eric Talley, "On Public versus Private Provision of Corporate Law," *Journal of Law, Economics and Organization* 22 (2006): 414–441.

5. Paul F. Kirgis, Jeff Sovern, Elayne E. Greenberg, and Yuxaing liu, "'Whimsy Little Contracts' with Unexpected Consequences: An Empirical Analysis of Consumer Understanding of Arbitration Agreements," *Maryland Law Review* 75 (2015).

6. For a discussion of metaregulation, see Cary Coglianese and Evan Mendelson, "Meta Regulation and Self-Regulation," in *The Oxford Handbook of Regulation*, ed. Martin Cave, Robert Baldwin, and Martin Lodge (New York: Oxford University Press, 2010), 173–195.

7. https://www.sec.gov/News/Speech/Detail/Speech/1365171515006.

8. Donald Sull and Kathleen M. Eisenhardt, *Simple Rules: How to Thrive in a Complex World* (Boston: Houghton Mifflin Harcourt, 2015).

CHAPTER 11

1. C. K. Prahalad and Stuart Hart, "The Fortune at the Bottom of the Pyramid," *Strategy + Business* 26 (2002): 1–14.

2. United Nations Commission on Legal Empowerment of the Poor, *Making the Law Work for Everyone* (2008).

3. McKinsey and Company, *Bangladesh's Ready-Made Garments Landscape: The Challenge of Growth* (2011).

4. The following draws on Gillian K. Hadfield and Barry R. Weingast, "Microfoundations of the Rule of Law," *Annual Review of Political Science* 17 (2014): 21–42.

5. Jeremy L. Jones, "Nothing Is Straight in Zimbabwe: The Rise of the Kukiya-kiya Economy 2000–2008," *Journal of South African Studies* 36 (2010): 285–299.

6. Calculations based on data from the International Labour Organization, *Women and Men in the Informal Economy: A Statistical Picture* (Geneva: ILO, 2013); and World Bank Employment in Agriculture, http://data.worldbank.org/indicator/SL.AGR.EMPL.ZS.

7. Monica Davey, "Blagojevich Sentenced to 14 Years in Prison," *New York Times*, December 7, 2011.

8. Sarah Stillman, "Taken," *New Yorker*, August 12–19, 2013.

9. US Department of Justice, Civil Rights Division, *Investigation of the Ferguson Police Department* (March 4, 2015).

10. The following discussion is based on an unpublished paper by Pamhidzai Bamu entitled "'I Take Goods across the Border for a Living': An Analysis of Zimbabwe's Informal International Trade and Its Regulation," presented at the Harvard Stanford International Junior Faculty Forum, for which I served as a judge and commentator, October 3–5, 2013 at Harvard Law School. I am grateful to Pamhidzai for permission to discuss her work.

CHAPTER 12

1. Stephen Broadberry and Leigh Gardner, "Africa's Growth Prospects in a European Mirror: A Historical Perspective," *CAGE-Chatham House Series* 5 (February 2013).

2. For the fascinating story of Sealand, an attempt to establish a sovereign nation on an abandoned antiaircraft platform in the North Sea outside the legal reach of any established government—and the view that the effort collapsed because of a lack of law—see James Grimmelmann, "Sealand, Havenco, and the Rule of Law," *University of Illinois Law Review* (2012): 405–484. For efforts to establish a start-up community on a ship in international waters see http://blueseed.com/.

3. See, e.g., Rosa Ehrenreich Brooks, "The New Imperialism: Violence, Norms, and the Rule of Law," *Michigan Law Review* 101 (2003): 2275–2340; Lan Cao, "Culture Change," *Virginia Journal of International Law* 47 (2007): 357–412.

4. The following discussion draws on Federica Carugati, Gillian K. Hadfield, and Barry R. Weingast, "Building Legal Order in Ancient Athens," *Journal of Legal Analysis* 7 (2015): 291–324 and sources there.

5. Michael Suk-Young Chwe, *Rational Ritual: Culture, Coordination and Common Knowledge* (Princeton, NJ: Princeton University Press, 2001).

6. Mark S. Granovetter, "The Strength of Weak Ties," *American Journal of Sociology* 78 (1973): 1360–1380.

7. The following discussion draws on Muhammad Yunus, *Banker to the Poor: Microlending and the Battle against World Poverty* (New York: Public Affairs, 1999); and M. Nural Alam and Mike Getubig, *Guidelines for Establishing and Operating Grameen-Style Microcredit Programs* (Grameen Foundation, 2010).

8. Abhijit Bannerjee, Esther Duflo, Rachel Glennerster, and Cynthia Kinnan, "The Miracle of Microfinance? Evidence from a Randomized Evaluation," *American Economic Journal: Applied Economics* 7 (2015): 22–53; Britta Augsburg, Ralph De Haas, Heike Harmgart, and Costas Meghir, "The Impacts of Microcredit: Evidence from Bosnia and Herzegovina," *American Economic Journal: Applied Economics* 7 (2015): 183–203; Orazio Attanasio et al., "The Impacts of Microfinance: Evidence from Joint-Liability Lending in Mongolia," *American Economics Journal: Applied Economics* 7 (2015): 90–122.

9. Pew Research Center, *Survey Report: Emerging Nations Embrace Internet, Mobile Technology* (February 13, 2014).

10. http://www.itcportal.com/businesses/agri-business/e-choupal.aspx.

11. Kabir Kumar, Claudia McKay, and Sarah Rotman, "Microfinance and Mobile Banking: The Story So Far," Consultative Group to Assist the Poor Focus Note (July 2010).

12. Abhijit Bannerjee, Dean Karlan, and Jonathan Zinman, "Six Randomized Evaluations of Microcredit: Introduction and Further Steps," *American Economic Journal: Applied Economics* 7 (2015): 1–21.

13. The following discussion draws on F. J. A. Bouman, "Rotating and Accumulating Savings and Credit Associations: A Development Perspective," *World Development* 23 (1995): 371–384.

14. "Courts Will Take 320 Years to Clear Backlog Cases: Justice Rao," *Times of India*, March 6, 2010.

CHAPTER 13

1. The following draws on an interview with Magatte Wade conducted by the Center for Ethics and Entrepreneurship and published on March 25, 2013, available at http://www.ethicsandentrepreneurship.org/20130325/interview-with-magatte-wade/.

2. http://www.bangladeshworkersafety.org/.

3. http://bangladeshaccord.org/.

4. https://www.difc.ae.

5. The following draws on conversations with Paul Romer; materials from the Honduras experiment shared with me; "Honduran Judges Rule against Privately

Run 'Model Cities' Project," *Guardian*, October 4, 2012; Alberto Arce, "Honduran Supreme Court Rejects 'Model Cities' Idea," Yahoo News, October 18, 2012; Maya Kroth, "Under New Management," *Foreign Policy*, September 1, 2014; and materials available at http://zede.gob.hn.

CONCLUSION

1. Susan Beck, "Divided ABA Adopts Resolution on Nonlawyer Legal Services," *American Lawyer*, February 8, 2016.

Index

among medieval Icelanders, 46–48, 52
among Shasta county ranchers, 39–41
in ancient Athens, 305–306
challenges to achieving in medieval
    Europe, 96–99
citizen-based enforcement, 317
effect of nation-state on, 99–100,
    103–104
exchange relationships and, 67–71
Grameen Bank, 311–315
importance to human
    adaptability, 63–64
importance to human
    societies, 76–77
in medieval Germany, 53
in medieval merchant guilds, 50–52
participation of ordinary people,
    306–307
potential for corruption in, 75–76
relationship to retaliation, 40
in virtual networks, 317
Collier, Paul, 283
commercial law
    efforts of ABA toward developing, 115
    in medieval Europe, 48–54
Commercial Revolution of the Middle
    Ages, 7, 48, 79, 91–96, 106,
    129, 238
commitment, securing in
    business, 92–93
Committee for the Adoption of Best
    Practices (Honduras), 342, 345
common-knowledge rules
    among nonhuman primates, 34
    in ancient Athens, 305, 307–308, 321
    benefits of larger groups for, 97–98
    challenges to achieving in medieval
        Europe, 96–97
    coordinating decentralized
        enforcement through, 102
    corruption and, 293–294
    defined, 25

development of laws and, 71–79
effect of Peace of Westphalia
    agreement on, 99
fictitious example of Simple
    Contracting, Inc., 326
in group-based lending, 314
Hammurabi's code as, 77
importance of, 25–26
in medieval merchant guilds, 49–50
in microfinance, 317–319
origins of systems characterized
    by, 31–32
process of changing, 310
undermined by complexity, 70–71
common-law systems, 283
communications technology, 1, 128. *See
    also* digitization
community responsibility system, 51
competition law. *See* antitrust law
competitive law zones, 335–345
competitive markets
    digitization and, 155–156
    innovation through, 205–207,
        211–212, 346
    lack of in legal system, 7–8,
        234–237
    protection provided by, 252–254
    regulation of, 4, 346
competitive regulation, 330–331
complexity
    advanced by human adaptability, 64
    brought about by globalization, 78–79
    caused by innovation, 150
    caused by legal regulations, 148
    centralized planning and, 204–205
    definition of, 58–59
    developed during Industrial
        Revolution, 110
    effect on legal profession, 122–124
    emergence of law and, 90
    faced by general counsel, 188–191
    finding innovative solutions, 223–237